Innovating European Labour Markets

Innovating European Labour Markets

Dynamics and Perspectives

Edited by

Peter Ester

General Director, OSA, Institute for Labour Studies and Professor of Sociology, Tilburg University, the Netherlands

Ruud Muffels

Professor of Socio-Economics (Labour Market and Social Security), Tilburg University, the Netherlands

Joop Schippers

Professor of Labour and Gender Economics, Utrecht University and Research Director, OSA, Institute for Labour Studies, Tilburg University, the Netherlands

Ton Wilthagen

Professor of Institutional and Legal Aspects of the Labour Market, Tilburg University, the Netherlands

Edward Elgar

Cheltenham, UK • Northampton, MA, USA

Published by
Edward Elgar Publishing Limited
The Lypiatts
15 Lansdown Road
Cheltenham
Glos GL50 2JA
UK

Edward Elgar Publishing, Inc.
William Pratt House
9 Dewey Court
Northampton
Massachusetts 01060
USA

A catalogue record for this book
is available from the British Library

Library of Congress Control Number: 2008937109

ISBN 978 1 84844 007 4

Printed and bound in Great Britain by MPG Books Ltd, Bodmin, Cornwall

Contents

PART III LIFE COURSE TRANSITIONS AND CAREERS

Contributors

Christian Brzinsky-Fay graduated in Political Science at the Free University Berlin. He is currently working on his dissertation on the role of policies and institutions in the school-to-work transition in European countries within the LabourNet Graduate School on Labour and Welfare Studies at the Social Science Research Center Berlin (WZB) and the University of Tampere, Finland. His main fields of interest are quantitative research methods, comparative political science, labour market and education policies and policy analysis. Recently, he was engaged in two European projects, 'Qualification Needs in OECD Countries – Identification, Analysis and Implementation' and 'Managing Social Risks through Transitional Labour Markets (TLM.NET)'.

Sandrine Cazes is Senior Economist in the Economic and Labour Market Analysis Department of the International Labour Office in Geneva since December 2005. Prior to that she was the Employment Specialist of the ILO Subregional Office for Central and Eastern Europe, in Budapest. Her main topics of interest are labour market policy and social reforms, the role of labour market institutions and flexicurity in both OECD countries and Central and Eastern Europe. She is author and co-author of numerous publications – books, research papers, policy advisory reports and articles in referenced economic journals.

Heejung Chung is a PhD candidate in the Flexicurity Research Programme at Tilburg University. She has graduated from Yonsei University in Korea (BA, MSW) and University of Edinburgh in Scotland (MSc Research in Social Policy). She also held research positions in the Korean Labor Institute (KLI) and the Institute for Labour Studies (OSA) in the Netherlands. She was a visiting researcher at the Social Science Research Centre Berlin (WZB) and is currently affiliated to the Amsterdam Institute for Labour Studies (AIAS). Her main research interests are cross-national comparison of European labour markets, especially regarding labour market flexibility, flexicurity, working time and work–life balance issues. Her dissertation is on working time flexibility behaviours of European companies.

Peter Ester is General Director of OSA, Institute for Labour Studies and Professor of Sociology at Tilburg University, the Netherlands. He is chairman of CentERdata, an Internet-based panel survey research institute at Tilburg University, member of the Advisory Board of Statistics Netherlands (CBS), and member of the advisory board of IAB (Institut für Arbeitsmarkt- und Berufschforschung), visiting professor at Gesis-ZUMA, Centre for Survey Research and Methodology in Mannheim. Peter Ester is former Director of GLOBUS, Institute for Globalization and of IVA, Institute for Social Research. He was visiting professor at several international universities, including the University of Michigan, Virginia Tech, University of California. He is a former Fulbright scholar at Claremont College, California. Peter Ester has published extensively on cross-national labour market trends, flexibility, youth and the labour market, work orientations, work and mobility. One of his main interests is the impact of the cultural factor in the domain of work.

Didier Fouarge studied Economics at the Facultés Universitaires Notre-Dame de la Paix (FUNDP) in Namur, Belgium. He holds a PhD from Tilburg University on the topic of poverty dynamics and social policy in Europe. From 1999 to 2007 he was researcher at the Institute for Labour Studies (OSA) and post-doc at Tilburg University. Since November 2007, he has been a researcher at the Research Centre for Education and the Labour Market (ROA), Maastricht University. His main research interests lie in scientific and applied research on labour market and income dynamics, working times, retirement, income distribution and poverty, and the welfare state. He has published in national and international journals as well as in books with distinguished publishers. For a full CV, see: www.roa.unimaas.nl /cv/fouarge/fouarge.htm.

Leen Heylen studied Sociology at the University of Louvain, Belgium. Since 2004, she has worked as a researcher for CELLO, Centre for Longitudinal and Life Course Research, Faculty of Political and Social Sciences, University of Antwerp, Belgium. Her research interests are, among others, life course and careers. Currently she is involved in a project from CoViVE concerned with the loneliness and social isolation of the elderly, in a university consortium researching the socio-economic impact of ageing in Flanders and Europe.

Eckart Hildebrandt is Professor and Senior Researcher at the Social Science Research Center Berlin (WZB). He is a member of the 'Education, Work, and Life Chances' department. Research areas are the design of work and working-time policy, industrial relations, employment policy and environment and sustainability. In recent years, he has carried out various national and international projects on the 'future of work and sustainability', 'flexible working times' and 'day-to-day conduct of life'. Currently, he is coordinator of a project on lifetime working accounts at the Social Science Research Center Berlin (WZB), funded by the Hans Böckler Foundation. The project investigates the effects of lifetime working accounts with regard to firms' human resource management and employees' working time transitions over the life course.

Marcel Kerkhofs is Labour Economist at the OSA Institute for Labour Studies. He graduated from the Erasmus University in Rotterdam and has since worked at Tilburg University and Leiden University. He obtained his PhD in Economics at the University of Groningen. His research interests are in the field of empirical labour economics, particularly related to mobility, health and retirement.

David Marsden is Professor of Industrial Relations at the London School of Economics and Political Science (London, England UK). His expertise lies in employment relations in western Europe and the link between pay systems and performance. He is currently working on the effects of pay inequalities and HR management practices on economic performance in the EU and on the effectiveness of performance related pay in the British public services, notably in schools.

Ruud Muffels is Professor of Socio-Economics (Labour Market and Social Security) at the Department of Sociology and Research Professor at the Institute for Labour Studies (OSA) at Tilburg University. His main research interests deal with labour market dynamics, income distribution and social exclusion, comparative analyses of the welfare state and the socio-economics of ageing. He has published in a wide range of sociological, economic and interdisciplinary journals and (co)-edited a number of international academic volumes. His most recent book is entitled: Flexibility and Employment Security in Europe: Labour Markets in Transition (2008, with Edward Elgar).

Alena Nesporova is Deputy Director of the Regional Office for Europe and Central Asia of the International Labour Office in Geneva since March 2005. Prior to that she was Chief of the Employment Policies Unit in the Employment Strategy Department of the ILO. Ms Nesporova holds a PhD in economics. Her main topics of interest are comparative research and policy advisory work in the field of employment policy, labour market institutions and policies and flexicurity, in particular in the countries of Central and Eastern Europe and Central Asia but she has also worked on China, Vietnam and Egypt. She is author and co-author of numerous publications – books, research papers, policy advisory reports and articles in referenced economic journals.

Amelia Román studied Sociology at Tilburg University and received a PhD from Utrecht University Department of Economics. Since 2001 she has worked for OSA (Institute for Labour Studies), Tilburg, the Netherlands as a senior researcher. Her research interests are the changing dynamics of life course patterns and how they affect careers, life course labour participation, early career choices and path dependency, effects of part-time work, non-participation and periods of unemployment, as well as the influence of human capital investment for labour participation continuity. More recently she has also begun researching motivations and barriers for work-related mobility across regions and countries.

Joop Schippers is Research Director of OSA, Institute for Labour Studies. He combines this task with a professorship in labour economics and gender economics at Utrecht University and coordinates the EU-research project ASPA (Activating Senior Potential in Ageing Europe). He has been on different advisory bodies of the Dutch government on issues like equal opportunity policies, gender mainstreaming and life course policies.

Günther Schmid is Professor Emeritus for Economic Theory of Politics at the Free University of Berlin and director of the research unit 'Labour Market Policy and Employment' at the Social Science Research Center Berlin (WZB). He has been Visiting Professor at the University of Wisconsin in Madison (USA), Paris Sorbonne (France), Stockholm and Växjö (Sweden), the Institute for Advanced Studies in Vienna (Austria), Aalborg (Denmark) and the Netherlands Institute for Advanced Studies (NIAS). His main research interests are labour market policy and unemployment insurance, comparison of employment and welfare systems, evaluation and implementation of labour market policies, political economics and philosophy. He has also served as consultant for the OECD in Paris and the European Commission in Brussels, and was appointed to the Commission on Modern Services for the Labour Market (so-called Hartz Commission) in 2002 and to the European Employment Task Force (so-called Kok Commission) in 2003.

Frank Vandenbroucke is Vice-Minister-President of the Flemish Government and Flemish Minister for Employment, Education and Training (since July 22, 2004). Before that he was Minister for Social Affairs and Pensions (1999–2003) and Minister for Employment and Pensions (2003–2004). He studied Economics at the University of Leuven (1978) and received an MPhil

Economics from Cambridge, UK (1981–1982) and a DPhil from the Faculty of Social Studies of the Oxford University, UK (1996–1999).

Greet Vermeylen is Research Manager in the Monitoring and Survey Unit of the European Foundation for the Improvement of Living and Working Conditions in Dublin. She is involved in the European Establishment Survey as well as in the European Working Conditions Survey. She is also working on the European Working Conditions Observatory. She has been involved in numerous other research projects of the European Foundation, such as projects on working poor, on flexicurity and on case study guidelines.

Ton Wilthagen is Professor of Institutional and Legal Aspects of the Labour Market at the Faculty of Law of Tilburg University, the Netherlands, and director of the Tilburg Flexicurity Research Programme. He is a member of the European Flexicurity Research Network, the TRANSWELL, and the RecWoWe (Reconciling Work and Welfare in Europe) research networks. He was affiliated with the Institute for Labour Studies (OSA) in Tilburg and with the Hugo Sinzheimer Institute and the Amsterdam Institute for Advanced Labour Studies at Amsterdam University. He has been a visiting researcher at the Social Science Centre Berlin (WZB). His research interest is in labour market and employment regulation, labour law, industrial relations and a variety of labour market issues. His main focus lies on the themes of flexicurity, transitional labour markets and life-course approaches.

Philip Wotschack is researcher in the 'Education, Work, and Life Chances' department at the Social Science Research Center Berlin (WZB). Research areas are flexible working hours, life-course policies, and working time arrangements over the life course. His main interest lies in the impact and interaction of firm policies and household arrangements. From 2000 to 2005, he was researcher at the University of Groningen in the Netherlands and worked in the integrated research programme 'Time Competition. Disturbed Balances and New Options in Work and Care', financed by the Netherlands Organisation for Scientific Research. Currently, he is working on a project on lifetime working accounts at the Social Science Research Center Berlin (WZB), funded by the Hans Böckler Foundation. The project investigates the effects of lifetime working accounts with regard to firms' human resource management and employees' working time transitions over the life course.

Preface and Acknowledgements

Innovating European Labour Markets: Dynamics and Perspectives highlights and traces the consequences of the increasing turmoil on the labour market resulting in more volatility and creating a rather diverse landscape of employment forms that will shape people's life courses. The book particularly aims at discussing innovative labour market policy practices and perspectives with a view to changing working careers and life courses. The 'best practices' on life course policies presented in the book can be considered potential answers to the challenges and requirements labour market and employment systems are confronted with now and in the near future. This way the book's focus on 'innovation' is understood as an adequate and effective, possibly even a proactive, response to these challenges and requirements. The carefully selected contributions in the volume deal with various dimensions and different levels of the flexibility–security nexus within the life course perspective. This not only concerns labour market policy at the national and the EU level but especially also at the firm and sector level. Innovating firms' policies with respect to the creation of flexible working time options and to the elaboration of life-course-oriented human resource policies seem critical to respond successfully to the ongoing fundamental changes. The book hopefully contributes to raising our understanding of the driving factors that determine the performance of the dissimilar pathways in Europe with a view to their impact on the flexibility–security nexus over the life course.

The authors address issues as to how innovative policies are designed, how they are put to the test and why they became more or less successful in the various European contexts in improving the work–life balance, that is the balance of flexibility and security over the life course. These issues have become key now in the current European policy debate. The EU member states already since 2003 have endorsed the need to progress on policies aiming at improving the work–life balance and also accepted at the end of 2007 common principles of 'flexicurity' policies on which future policies in the member states should be vested.

The book is the outcome of the Institute's of Labour Studies (OSA) four year research programme during the period 2003–2006, entitled: 'The Transitional Labour Market: Towards a New Social and Economic Dynamic'.

OSA is a research institute that operates on the border of science and policy, conducting research dealing with issues considered of structural importance for policymaking as well as pure academic research. This volume also represents one of the results of the three year research programme 'Flexicurity: A New Paradigm for Labour Market and Employment Regulation?', funded by the The Netherlands Organisation for Scientific Research (NWO). The book contains a selection of the papers that were presented in a first draft form at the closing conference of both research programmes, held in November 2006 at the Royal Netherlands Academy of Arts and Sciences (KNAW) building in Amsterdam.

Acknowledgements

The editors are primarily indebted to the authors of the chapters for their invaluable contributions to the substance of the book. The book focuses on life course issues but within the framework of two major socio-economic approaches: 'Transitional Labour Markets (TLM)' and 'Flexicurity', of which the founding fathers were contributors to this volume. The editors are therefore indebted to Professor Dr Günther Schmid for his work on the TLM approach that inspired so many researchers collaborating in the four year research programme at the OSA institute of Tilburg University, and also to Professor Dr Ton Wilthagen for his contributions on the topic of 'flexicurity' that now has become one of the leading concepts on which future European social policy is likely to be elaborated and progressed.

Further we want to express our gratitude to a number of people from the policy and scientific field who contributed directly or indirectly by acting as invited speaker, commentator or discussants at the various occasions that preceded the book. We are much indebted to: Professor David Marsden (London School of Economics), Mr Maarten Camps (Dutch Ministry of Employment and Social Affairs), Dr Frank Vandenbroucke (Flemish Minister of Employment and Education) and Mr Egbert Holthuis (European Commission).

The editors also owe much to Kees Boos for his punctilious organisation of the editing process and for his diligent compiling of the typescript. A special word of gratitude goes to Edward Elgar for the trust they have shown in the endeavour and for the careful way they have guided the publishing process.

Peter Ester, Ruud Muffels, Joop Schippers and Ton Wilthagen

1. Innovating European Labour Markets: An Introduction

Ton Wilthagen, Ruud Muffels, Peter Ester and Joop Schippers

1.1 INTRODUCTION

It is not a big secret that when politicians and policymakers are speaking of 'challenges' they are actually referring to severe problems that are very difficult to handle. The labour market is such an area of challenges or, phrased differently, large problems. It represents a societal domain where, in the words of the Portuguese social theorist De Sousa Santos (1995), we are facing modern problems but are lacking modern solutions. Moreover, there is an awareness, fed by a classical sociologist such as Durkheim (1960) and a modern economist such as Sen (1985), to mention just two of them, that the labour market as a domain is a major vehicle for social integration, cohesion, wealth and well-being creation, and the distribution thereof. This implies that when labour markets are not operating properly this not only creates problems of 'function', that is problems in the labour market itself, but also problems of 'performance', that is negative effects on the society at large.[1]

The aims of this book are to portray and examine the ongoing changes in employment forms and people's life courses and particularly to present, put to the test and further develop innovative labour market policies and perspectives. The policies and perspectives can be considered potential answers to the challenges and requirements labour market and employment systems confront. It is in this manner that we can define the key concept of 'innovation', namely as adequate and effective, possibly even proactive, responses to these challenges and requirements.

We will now further elaborate on the typical paradoxes and challenges in modern societies and labour markets in particular (Section 1.2), present the policy and scientific perspectives (Section 1.3) and from there on elucidate the themes and the structure of this book (Section 1.4).

1.2 PARADOXES AND CHALLENGES

The mammoth tasks at hand for European, national and local labour markets and employment systems can further be conceptualised and summarised by using Talcott Parsons' well-known analytic AGIL model (Adaptation, Goal Attainment, Integration and Latency) which he designed for analysing all types of collectivities (Parsons and Smelser, 1956). This model shows the four basic functions that all social systems should perform in order to survive.

The first function is *adaptation* which pertains to the necessity of obtaining sufficient resources and advantages, in particular in economic production and competition. Companies – employers, workers, other stakeholders and shareholders – are key actors here. Both external and internal labour markets are crucial in providing the mechanisms for optimally allocating, using and developing resources – human and nonhuman – to guarantee flexibility and timely adjustment to changing market circumstances and to warrant high levels of productivity and performance.

The second function is called *goal attainment* and it deals with the problem of setting goals and effectively implementing policies and strategies – in our case concerning labour market and employment goals and policies. Governments, social partners, collective bargaining parties, inspectorates and European agencies are the main players here, responsible for designing and mapping out innovative and effective strategies that facilitate and support individuals and companies in their development and risk management, keeping a specific eye on weaker groups in the labour market.

Thirdly, there is the function of *integration*, referring to the problem of preserving security, cohesion, solidarity and coordination within the system, preventing segmentation and exclusion in the labour market. The 'integrative' agencies required from this perspective are the same actors as under goal attainment with the addition of courts and social security and social policy organisations.

The fourth and final function is called *latency* and points at the issue of creating, preserving and transmitting the distinctive culture and values within the system. Training and education organisations and institutions play a prominent role here and the school to work transition represents an example of a crucial period. People's preferences in working lives, such as working time and retirement preferences, are another major aspect of latency in the realm of the labour market. The latency issue is rather pressing from a European point of view, as it touches upon the current debate whether the European Union can provide and preserve a distinctive European Social Model, based on a set of European values.

The current challenges to labour market and employment systems are a neat illustration of the more general paradoxical tension that we can observe in European societies. Part of these challenges originate from tendencies that we can label 'converging pressures', or, in the words of Pierson (1998), 'irresistable forces', that is the development of new interdependencies that increasingly expose workers, companies, sectors and national governments to 'global' or common conditions. Globalisation, the integration of markets – with the EU internal market as a prominent example – increased international competition, labour migration and, though varying across countries and continents, demographic developments such as ageing and decreasing workforces are all aspects of this tendency (Giddens, 2007). Other challenges, on the contrary, result from tendencies that can be characterised as forms of diversification or divergence. Major manifestations here are the increasing diversity in work-related preferences and choices, in labour market transitions, in patterns of working, working time and caring, in educational trajectories, including risks of mismatches between education, skills and labour demand, in career paths and, finally, in overall life courses (Van den Heuvel et al., 2004). These work-related diversities are also related to the larger variation in consumer behaviour and consumption patterns.

The paradoxical nature of this twin set of challenges evidently influences the way that they can be addressed. 'Global' tendencies generally require forms and efforts of coordination, whereas divergent tendencies generally call for diverse policies, decentralisation and a tailor-made approach. The current state of the European Union illustrates that both coordination and decentralisation are indispensable – causing a kind of acrobatic 'split' – and that striving for a 'unity in diversity' seems to be the best way forward (Silva Peneda and Albino De Rossa, 2006). We can label this interdependence the coordination–decentralisation nexus, which represents, in essence, a governance issue.

On the national and European level policy responses towards this nexus have been developed, with the European Commission's 2001 White Paper on European Governance as a very good case in point.[2] These policy responses are inspired by the academic debates and scientific theory formation on multi-level regulation (Léonard, 2001; Sisson and Marginson, 2002), coordinated or controlled decentralisation (Traxler, 1994, 2003), actor-centered institutionalism (Mayntz and Scharpf, 1995; Scharpf, 1997; Van Lieshout, 2008) and reflexive law and governance (Teubner, 1993; Rogowski and Wilthagen, 1994; Rogowski, 2007).

In a practical way, some of the current and urgent major labour market challenges and problems Europe faces can be summarised as follows, reflecting issues of adaptability, goal achievement, integration and latency:[3]

- A major challenge for the European Union is how to combine inclusive with highly productive labour markets. Although employment rates have recently increased in the EU, coupled with a drop in unemployment over the last three years, unemployment is still too high in most Member States and unevenly distributed. Particular categories of the population, that is the young, women, older workers, minorities and third country nationals, continue to suffer much higher unemployment risks and unfavourable working and living circumstances, such as discrimination and limited access to social security and other arrangements.
- At the same time over a million unfilled job vacancies exist, reflecting a severe mismatch between labour supply and labour demand. Labour mobility, migration and the posting of workers across the borders of EU Member States has accelerated in recent years, providing on the one hand possible resources for resolving labour market shortages, but at the same time producing a new economic, social and cultural issue in both the host and donor or home countries of these workers.
- There is underinvestment in lifelong learning by all actors concerned. Compared to the EU's main competitors (depending on which EU countries are taken into account), there is also a considerable productivity gap both in terms of productivity per worker and productivity per hour worked.
- Moreover the adaptability of European companies needs to be further enhanced to successfully deal with global competition, while at the same time providing new and more dynamic securities to workers. It is crucial that not merely current risks but also future risks are addressed, as the needs for flexibility and security can and do vary across the life course and the business cycle.
- The trust of European citizens in future employment opportunities, in the development of human capital, in decent work and labour market developments urgently needs to be strengthened, while companies require a supportive business climate and a transparent and predictable legal framework in order to increase business potential and create employment.
- More effort is needed to hit the EU target agreed in 2006 for every young person who has left school or university and becomes unemployed to be offered a job, apprenticeship, training or other employability measures within 100 days.
- Early school leaving is a particularly severe problem among immigrants and minorities.
- Gender gaps remain wide, both in terms of wages and career opportunities. Availability of affordable child care is a problem in a

number of Member States, which makes it more difficult to reconcile work and private life.

- Member States have put some effort into increasing the labour market participation of older workers, but more is needed to create real job opportunities for them. The sustainability of pension schemes is at stake and at risk in many of the EU Member States.

We now turn to policy views and academic perspectives that have been developed in response to these challenges and issues.

1.3 POLICY VIEWS AND ACADEMIC PERSPECTIVES

In this section we briefly introduce the innovative policies and perspectives that have inspired many of the contributions in this book. It will become clear that the demarcations between the policy responses and the scientific responses are, although visible, not always very strong. In the field of labour markets and employment issues, policymaking and academic approaches, although bound by their own rationalities and goals, are often characterised by a strong mutual influence. Much of the relevant academic work in the field has been picked up rather rapidly by policymakers, evidently applying the concepts and evidence in their particular fashion and geared towards their own needs and interests.

1.3.1 The Transitional Labour Markets and the Life Course Approach

The theory of transitional labour markets (TLM), as developed by Günther Schmid (Schmid, 2000; Schmid and Gazier, 2002) from the mid 1990s onwards, responds, in Schmid's words, to the 'requisite variety' that results from trends in modern labour markets and individuals' life courses. The basic assumption of the theory reads that 'the borders between the labour market and other social systems have to become more open for transitory states between paid work and gainful non-market activitities, which preserve and enhance future employability'. This is expected to result in a new form of full employment, as 'the institutionalisation of transitional labour markets would encourage mobility ("transitions") across the border of social systems without inducing downward spirals of social exclusion by optimising people's lifetime social participation' (Schmid, 2000, pp. 223–4). As such the TLM approach forms a life-course-oriented view on the interactive relationship between (external and internal) labour markets and other socially productive domains, including private households, education, non-work activities and retirement. The transitions included in the model are best seen as status transitions. They do not necessarily require full-blown 'sequential' transitions, but can also be analysed in term of people's combinations of activities within the various domains. A core distinction is between 'good transitions', which contribute to people's empowerment in the labour market and 'bad transitions' (or 'dead end street transitions', which limit opportunities). The main policy implication of the TLM approach is formulated as 'make transitions pay', that is reduce the institutional, organisational and cultural barriers and social and financial disadvantages for people to move (to and from) between the different social spheres and the labour market by offering them transition opportunities and facilities. A life course perspective is being advocated by Schmid when he argues that working hours could vary across the individual's life course, depending on the stage of life, resulting for example in an average of 30 hours per working week on a lifetime basis. During the transitional periods it would offer employment opportunities to others.

In general the life course literature is multidisciplinary, including disciplines such as sociology, economics, psychology, demography and biology. Notwithstanding the differences, these research lines share the fact that they all add an explicit temporal dimension to human behaviour and development.[4] Early conceptualisations of the life cycle were influenced by the Darwinian theory of evolution and concentrated on the process of social reproduction, and in psychology also on socialisation and the psychological development. In the 1960s and 1970s, neoclassical economists designed dynamic models to account for individuals' inter-temporal choices, for example between work and leisure time, bringing different tastes and preferences into the focus. More recently, the rational choice framework was related to aspects as the inherited social capital as well as social and individual welfare. Norms, traditions and institutions are core elements in understanding individual behaviour over the life course, as it is a person's 'habitus', as Bourdieu and Giddens have argued (see Adams, 2006). Neoclassical economists have come up with different assumptions about how the future affects current decisions through the way agents discount the future. However, the question how the past influences current decisions was often ignored. It was not until the 1990s that social scientists (for example Mayer, 2000; Elder et al., 2003) started considering the life course as a whole, acknowledging the importance and consequences of early transitions for later decisions and events.

In our view, theoretically speaking, life course arrangements and policies acknowledge that, from the individual workers' perspective, his or her different activities in a certain life phase have to be reconciled; in particular paid work has to be combined with other social activities at a given moment. This can be called a first level of synchronisation. The workers' wishes and potentials can differ according to his/her sex, age, education, family context, interests and so on. At the same time a life course policy has to deal with the diachronisation (that is synchronisation through time) and the follow-up of different life-phases throughout the life course of individuals, since the individual worker's situation is not stable, but can change over the life course.

Explicit life course policies have been absent until recently. Today the life course perspective is clearly visible in European labour market and social policy (; Klammer et al., 2006; Muffels et al., 2008; Klammer, forthcoming). The increasing interest in education and training propelled by the concepts of 'lifelong learning' and of an 'investive social policy' are clear signs of this new perspective. The emphasis on the development of a 'knowledge-based society' demands long-term strategies. The goals of the Lisbon strategy to increase the labour market participation of older workers and the actual retirement age (Barcelona and Stockholm targets, see European Commission, 2003) have also contributed to the need to focus on work biographies, on long-term employability of workers and on sustainability in labour market participation. Accordingly the European Directives for the national action plans explicitly state: 'this requires developing comprehensive national strategies based on a life course approach' (Council of the European Union, 2003, Paragraph 15).

Integrated Guideline no. 18 of the European Employment Strategy[5] asks the Member States of the EU to promote a life-cycle approach to work through:

- a renewed endeavour to build employment pathways for young people and reduce youth unemployment, as called for in the European Youth Pact,
- resolute action to increase female participation and reduce gender gaps in employment, unemployment and pay,
- better reconciliation of work and private life and the provision of accessible and affordable childcare facilities and care for other dependants,
- support for active ageing, including appropriate working conditions, improved (occupational) health status and adequate incentives to work and discouragement of early retirement,
- modern social protection systems, including pensions and healthcare, ensuring their social adequacy, financial sustainability and responsiveness to changing needs, so as to support participation and better retention in employment and longer working lives.

In the current proposal by the European Commission for the 2008–2010 Guidelines the text of Guideline 18 is similar to the 2005 version. However, references to the life-cycle approach are now being made under more Guidelines.

Moreover, in some countries specific life course arrangements have emerged in recent years. Between 2001 and 2002 in the Netherlands a number of reports and articles were published, mainly initiated by the Ministry of Social Affairs and Employment, resulting in an 'Exploring the life course' (*Verkenning levensloop*) report in 2002 and a comprehensive annex containing examples of and barriers to a life course approach. These studies ultimately resulted in the introduction of the Life Course Saving Arrangement (*levensloopregeling*) by law in 2006.

Another example of a life-course-oriented scheme is the Belgian career break/time credit system, that came into force in 1985 and that was extended by the Flemish government in 1994. This scheme entails a fiscal measure that allows people to flexibly reduce their working hours or exit their job without any restriction as to the underlying motive (see Román et al., 2006 and also Chapter 12 of this book). Finally, working time accounts can be considered to be yet another type of life course arrangement, which can be observed in various countries.

1.3.2 The Flexicurity Approach

Traditionally, policies aimed at enhancing security are of a reactive nature, that is they follow, usually with a significant delay, the political recognition and assessment that a lack of security exists or that developments in or outside the labour market are harmful to the security of certain groups. In turn, flexibilisation policies are usually launched, also after some delay, to adjust labour market or social security arrangements and institutions that are considered too 'tight', protective or static and presumed to hamper economic development, dynamism and competitiveness.

In many Western welfare states job and social security systems (employment protection, social protection, unemployment and disability insurance, welfare schemes) developed after the Second World War, generally reaching their 'completion' in the late 1960s and 1970s. The 1980s, however, following economic and budget crises, can be typified as an era where deregulation and privatisation appeared as the dominant political concepts. In the course of the 1990s policy scientists started to notice that the 'deregulation versus regulation' or 'flexibility versus security' debate might be positioned and conceptualised too narrowly. Institutional and regulatory settings in the labour market are no longer seen as mere economic barriers. Rather, certain settings and forms of (re)regulation are considered conducive to economic performance (Streeck, 1992). Social policy is increasingly being typified as as a 'production factor' and social institutions are either perceived as 'harmless' with regard to economic growth, or are thought to matter in a positive sense (see Auer, 2001). As Esping-Andersen and Regini (2000, p. 340) put it in their book with the meaningful title *Why Deregulate Labour Markets?*: 'Managing unemployment is greatly facilitated when, and if, the social partners are capable of strong coordination and consensus-building.'

This scientific debate has led to the observation of European labour markets as displaying yet another nexus, which has been referred to as the flexibility–security nexus (Wilthagen and Rogowski, 2002; Wilthagen and Tros, 2004). The quest for a new (dynamic) equilibrium, facilitating and enhancing the adaptability and capacity to deal with the change of both individuals and companies has come to be labelled 'flexicurity' (Wilthagen, 1998). Flexicurity is defined as a policy strategy to enhance, at the same time and in a deliberate way, the flexibility of labour markets, work organisations and employment relations on the one hand, and security – employment security and social security – on the other (Wilthagen and Tros, 2004). From a theoretical point of view flexicurity policies can be characterised as a form of coalescence and synchronisation of economic and social policy (Wynn, 2000, p. 501) or as a post-deregulation strategy (Keller and Seifert, 2000, p. 293).

The flexicurity concept has met with much acclaim *and* criticism after becoming a key policy concept within the European Employment Strategy, as documented, in particular, by the adaptation of Common Principles on flexicurity by the European Council on 5 December 2007,[6] the report and resolutions on flexicurity from the European Parliament on 29 November 2007,[7] the joint labour market and flexicurity analysis presented by the European social partners on 18 October 2007,[8] the Communication on flexicurity by the European Commission dated 27 June 2007[9] and the much debated Green Paper on the Modernisation of Labour Law issued 22 November 2006.[10]

All in all, a European policy framework has now been established, more or less, and it is now up to the Member States of the EU to make flexicurity work in a decent and constructive way. According to the European Commission and the European Expert Group on Flexicurity (2007) the current socio-economic challenges require a more flexible labour market combined with satisfactory levels of security to respond simultaneously to the new needs of employers and employees. New forms of flexibility and security are needed, for individuals and companies, to be provided by the Member States and the Union as a whole. Individuals increasingly need employment security, to complement job security, as fewer workers have a job for life.

Flexicurity, as an integrated policy strategy, should address many of these issues at the same time. Its objective is thus to combine employment and income security with flexible labour markets, work organisation and labour relations. This approach transcends the simple trade-off between flexibility and security, where the former is seen to be in the exclusive interest of the employer and the latter in the interest of the employee. The key principle that underpins a flexicurity strategy is that flexibility and security should not be seen as opposites, but can be made mutually supportive. Flexicurity strategies should set off from a win–win perspective, based on trust and highly-developed industrial relations.

Flexicurity could best be seen as a system of joint and mutual risk management for workers and employers (Evers and Wilthagen, 2007). Employers face the risk of a weakening market position due to increased competition, but also the risk of a quantitative and qualitative mismatch of labour supply as a result of technical progress, demographic change and varying preferences and competences among workers. For workers, job or employment security and the possibility of reconciling work and private life may be at risk due to business responses to globalisation and intensified competition. Therefore joint and mutual risk management is needed. Contributing to the risk management of the other party contributes to managing one's own risks.

A flexicurity approach should also take account of the long-term, dynamic relationship between flexibility and security needs and preferences. From the flexicurity approach it is important to stress that a longitudinal view does not only concern individuals. Perspectives of different social and institutional actors have to be considered, notably those of companies, addressing the coordination between companies' business cycles and their employees' life cycles. Business cycles have become shorter and less predictable. They are not necessarily congruent with the workers' time horizons. Companies have to adjust to fluctuations in market demands and with the overall need to warrant and enhance competitiveness. Thus, a second arena of synchronisation – business needs versus individual needs – can be identified, adding to the synchronisation necessity that was perceived already within the transitional labour market and life course perspectives. Moreover, the business process itself can also be seen as a synchronisation process, that is as an endeavour to fine-tune market demands and production means and capacities. Finally, as not only individuals but also businesses have a need for diachronisation processes (across the respective business cycle and life cycle) there exists an ultimate need for synchronising these diachronisation processes.

Regimes and pathways

Considering the wide differences in country practices and challenges, the EU rightfully does not believe in a one-size-fits-all approach. Rightful, because the existing evidence derived from the welfare regime (Esping-Andersen, 2002; Muffels, 2007) and Varieties of Capitalism literature (for example Hall and Soskice, 2001) convincingly suggest that countries' policies seem to follow their own national routes. There is also little or no evidence from empirical research that due to internationalisation and globalisation pressures these policy regimes signal a strong trend of convergence over time across the various policy routes. These routes are based on historical social, political economic and cultural roots and heritage making them strongly path-dependent without suggesting that there are no common features or that transferability of policies are inconceivable and that regimes are unable to learn from each other. On the contrary, regimes might learn from 'best practices' in other countries but it does not need to imply that they depart strongly from their original roots rather than staying largely on their original tracks. Various contributions in the book use or refer to the regime type approach providing evidence about the performance of the various regimes in Europe to balance flexibility and security goals in their respective societies. The idea of pathways as brought forward recently very much hinges on the view that there are different roads with similar levels of success or unsuccess in attaining high or low levels of flexibility and security (for example Muffels, 2008). The concept of flexicurity pathways also suggests different roads countries can take to improve their labour markets, based on different challenges, priorities and possibilities. Another reason is related to the 'subsidiarity principle' of the EU, implying that the Commission also has to respect the autonomy that each Member State has regarding their national labour market and social policies. For these reasons the EU has recently proposed (in its Communication on flexicurity) a set of flexicurity pathways, based on the work of the European Expert Group on Flexicurity (2007), addressing different challenges and possible solutions in Member States.

Flexicurity pathways can be designed and implemented across four policy components, as defined by the European Commission, which in her view need to be taken into account as a whole:

1. flexible and reliable contractual arrangements;
2. efficient active labour market policies (ALMP) to strengthen transition security;
3. systematic and responsive lifelong learning (LLL);
4. modern social security provisions that also contribute to good mobility in the labour market.

Moreover, a supportive and productive social dialogue between all stakeholders and a highly developed trust-based industrial relations system in a country serve as general preconditions or process variables to make such a flexicurity system work. That is, at least, what the Danish flexicurity model has taught us (Jørgensen and Madsen, 2007).

The ideal-typical flexicurity pathways, which could inspire Member States in setting their own flexicurity agenda, are the following:

Flexicurity pathway 1: dealing with flexibility at the margin

The first pathway addresses the issue of flexibility at the margin of the labour market. It suggests reducing asymmetries between standard and non-standard work by promoting upward transitions in the labour market and by integrating non-standard contracts fully into labour law, collective agreements, social security and lifelong learning systems. Non-standard contracts are then treated as equal to standard contracts, following the principle of *pro rata temporis*. Alternatively, standard contracts could be made more attractive to companies by introducing an open-ended contract in which specific elements of protection are built up progressively with time, until 'full' protection is achieved. Such a contract guarantees basic but adequate protection from the start and automatically builds up 'full' protection as the working relationship continues. Social partners and governments should negotiate the terms of these arrangements.

Flexicurity pathway 2: securing transitions from job to job

The second pathway emphasises safe and successful job-to-job transitions. Built-in contractual guarantees and HRM policies should ensure timely progress into new jobs either within the company or outside the company once the necessity arises. Furthermore, it may be feasible to introduce individualised transition guarantees to redundant workers, to be borne jointly by employers, social partners and public employment services in order to prevent unemployment. A strong system of lifelong learning and vocational training may form the basis for productive labour market transitions both inside and outside companies. Such a system should allow for quick access to effective training funds and facilities at branch level. Within this pathway, strengthening *internal flexicurity* is also relevant, especially to enhance the employability and skills of workers.

Flexicurity pathway 3: access to learning and good transitions for all

This pathway recommends strengthening, on the basis of existing levels of labour market dynamism, investment in skills and R&D. The employment and security opportunities and options of specific groups in the labour market can thereby be enhanced and productivity growth boosted. A broad-ranging approach is needed to keep the labour market accessible to the low-skilled and other groups at risk, such as minorities, older workers, women and the early school leavers, of becoming long-term unemployed or excluded in other ways. Flexicurity will benefit from the possibility to conclude binding agreements at branch or regional level that combine provisions on how to address the flexibility needs of both employers and workers by investment in training. Where the institutional structures for such agreements are not yet in place, support from the social partners and government is needed.

Flexicurity pathway 4: comprehensive social security supporting transitions to regular work
This pathway starts from the urgent need to increase the employment and job opportunities of persons who are currently on social security benefits or working in the informal sector. ALMP and social security should offer sufficient opportunities and incentives, in terms of increased conditionality of benefits, to return to work and to facilitate this transition. Long-term welfare dependence could thus be prevented. Informal work can be regularised by offering flexi-secure contracts, lower payroll taxes and a skills perspective for these sectors. By formalising informal economic activities, increased financial resources can be raised for building up a more comprehensive social security system. Stronger institutional capacity needs to be developed by stimulating the social partners to negotiate key elements of working conditions and by better cooperation between labour market and benefit institutions. Social dialogue can be further developed at sector and regional level and both bipartite and tripartite dialogue can be strengthened.

1.4 OUTLINE OF THE BOOK

As stated already, this volume deals with three areas of labour market issues, which we have related in the introduction to the functions of labour market systems on the basis of Parson's AGIL scheme. The first part deals with transitional labour markets and focuses on labour market changes and policies dealing with the external labour market, the second concerns flexicurity and working time flexibility issues within internal labour markets and the third part deals with life course transitions and careers focusing on labour market dynamics and policies concerning the life course. Each part discusses certain problems and challenges as well as innovative solutions to resolve them.

In the part on *transitional labour* markets the first contribution (in Chapter 2), is by *Vandenbroucke*, minister of education, training and employment in the Flemish region of Belgium. Vandenbroucke combines a vast experience in labour market policymaking with a solid scientific background. His contribution focuses on both the necessity and the directions for labour market innovation, comparing and benchmarking Flanders to the Netherlands, the Nordic countries and the EU average. The typical labour market problems pertaining to Belgium are characterised by Vandenbroucke as a so-called compressed career model, that is people enter the labour market at a relatively high age (due to education trajectories) and retire rather early. During this fairly short spell workers are highly productive but also suffer from feelings of exhaustion. Labour market participation in the older age groups is quite low compared to EU standards. Another major issue regards, as in many other European countries, the phenomenon of outsiders in the labour market, notably older people, immigrant groups and low-skilled persons. According to Vandenbroucke innovative labour market policies should urgently enhance dynamism and need to break two 'vicious circles': (1) low economic productivity of the older age cohort, paralleled with high productivity of the middle-age cohort, resulting in high work pressure; (2) prejudices in the labour market against immigrants lead to weak incentives among these groups to invest in study and training, resulting in deficits in education and competencies, which, in turn, produces a self-fulfilling prophecy in that employers are less willing to employ these groups.

In Chapter 3 *Fouarge* and *Ester* address another key aspect of external flexibility in the labour market, namely transnational mobility or labour migration. In the current scientific and policy debate labour migration is considered both a solution, solving labour shortages in tight labour markets with insufficient national labour supply, and a potential problem in the sense that it might lead to crowding out effects, underbidding, brain drain and, all in all, to social dumping and a race to the bottom with regard to labour and social security standards. Whereas the European Commission strongly favours and encourages cross-border mobility, the earlier discussions on the EU service and posting directives and, very recently, the rulings of the European Court of Justice in the Laval,[11] Viking[12] and Ruffert[13] cases have caused quite a stir and a lot of concerns notably among unions. Yet, until recently not much was known about migration intentions and decisions across the EU and their determinants. Fouarge and Esther contribute to this knowledge, deriving rich data from the 2005 Eurobarometer Mobility Survey.

Cazes and *Nesporova* report, in Chapter 4, on labour market challenges, dynamics and flexibilisation in Central and Eastern European countries. The current debate on labour market reform and flexicurity tends to be biased towards the North-Western part of Europe. Moreover, there is a lack of acknowledgement of the variety within the Central and Eastern 'cluster' of countries, which actually does not appear to be a coherent cluster in the line of Esping-Andersen's famous typology of welfare states. From a scientific and policy point of view studies that consider the flexibility–security nexus in transition economies are highly relevant, as they can shed more light on the economic, institutional, legal and political preconditions for reconciling dynamism, stability and security. The aim of the chapter is to investigate, from a comparative perspective, whether in the light of new economic and labour market developments since the end of the 1990s new tendencies have also become manifest in labour mobility, its fluctuation across the economic cycle as well as in flexible forms of employment.

In the last contribution within this section *Muffels*, in Chapter 5, uses empirical comparative data to examine the performance of Western European countries in balancing flexibility and security goals for men and women separately. He uses the European Community Household panel to cover 13 countries during the period 1994–2001. He defines gender-based dynamic indicators on flexibility translated into a measure of occupational and contract mobility and on income and employment security to map countries and regime types on the way they seem capable of balancing flexibility and security goals. He also tries to examine the separate effects of labour market institutions on how they affect males' and females' transition patterns such as active labour market policies, employment protection legislation and the generosity of social security benefits. The chapter provides evidence on the success of various policy pathways and of the effect of specific institutions on the levels of flexibility and security in society and therewith can teach us about the salient effects of particular policy pathways and measures.

The second part of the book focuses on the employment relationship at the company level and deals with flexicurity practices and innovative working time arrangements established *within* companies, that is within the *internal labour market*, but with a proper perspective on the company's environment. *Marsden's* contribution in Chapter 6 takes as a starting-point the open-ended employment relationship, for many decades now the standard and well-established contractual form for combining great flexibility and a large degree of enforceability. Despite the fact that statistical indicators do not indicate a decline of this type of employment regulation, in certain sectors, such as the media and creative industry, a 'network economy' is emerging. This employment system is featured by project organisation and project and team work. Marsden's interest lies in exploring the challenge posed by firm's need for greater use of more transient forms of employment relations. He does so by assessing the three types of 'contract' – psychological, economic and legal – that constitute and consolidate the open-ended contract. Subsequently the author examines in what way and to what extent network employment can provide equivalents for these contracts and could possibly inspire labour market or HRM innovations.

In Chapter 7 *Kerkhofs*, *Chung* and *Ester* deal with working time flexibility, an essential form of internal numerical flexibility and adaptability as well as a key mechanism for synchronising the domain of paid labour with the private household sphere. Using the Establishment Survey in Working Time and Work–Life Balance, conducted in 21 European countries, they develop a typology of European companies based on the use and provision of working time arrangements and work–life balance facilities and the characteristics that determine these profiles. In particular the authors examine the degree to which organisations combine flexibility measures that support their operational needs with arrangements supporting and facilitating the employees' work–life balance.

Vermeylen in Chapter 8 maps out the mix of various dimensions of flexicurity – forms of flexibility and security – in the European Union, taking stock of various research projects initiated by the European Foundation for the Improvement of Living and Working Conditions and the Foundation's 4th European Working Conditions Survey. After discussing the driving forces behind the flexicurity concept, gaining a particular momentum in recent years, and the policy debate at the European and national level she investigates in detail and from a comparative perspective the different flexibility strategies (numerical, temporal, functional) that companies apply, the role of social institutions in warranting security, also in view of new social risks, and the importance of trust and the involvement of all relevant actors in developing a flexicurity model.

The contribution by *Wotschack* and *Hildebrandt* in Chapter 9 concentrates on an instrument, long-term working time accounts, that might, in an innovative way, contribute to enhancing internal flexibility in companies while simultaneously supporting individual workers' life courses by preventing or addressing discontinuities. With the latter aspect the chapter provides an introduction to the third overarching theme of the book, that is the life course. The analysis is based on a 2005 survey among German companies. The quintessence of long-term working time accounts is that hours of work provided in advance or in excess constitute availability for an equivalent number of hours of paid leave at a later point in time. Basically two forms of long-term working time accounts have emerged. On the one hand optional accounts have been created which are used during the course of the working life with withdrawals at selected points in time and for various personal purposes, and age-related accounts with take-up possibilities limited to the end of the working life (as a type of early retirement or pension provision) on the other hand. The authors point out that the diffusion of long-term working time accounts needs to be understood in the light of several related but at the same diverging tendencies in the labour market and in labour market policymaking.

As indicated, the life course is the topic of the third major theme of the book. This part starts with a contribution, in Chapter 10 by *Schmid*, the intellectual author of the concept of transitional labour markets. The core thesis of this approach, as formulated by Schmid, is that the quality of life is determined to a significant extent by people's possibility to participate in working life as long as they wish and at the same time on the opportunities they have to combine paid work with other self-determined activities. The chapter puts the emphasis on 'active aging', identifying its conditions and criteria. From a comparative view, the differences in performance by European Member States are being assessed with regard to the labour market participation of older workers in European Member States. Finally, the chapter reflects on the key aspects of positive and innovative policy strategies that increase the options for transitions from the second to the third life-phase. Among these key aspects are: the necessity to differentiate institutions according to requisite variety (that is responding to varying situations and preferences), notably by transforming unemployment insurance into a work–life insurance, the application of the normative principle of risk-sharing through an egalitarianism based on responsibility and capability, the principle of decoupling social security from discontinuities over the life course and the principle of negotiation to overcome trade-offs between flexibility and security.

Brzinsky-Fay in Chapter 11 takes as a starting-point the early stage in the life course where people make the transition from school to work, a critical stage that has a huge impact on the opportunities available in the future course of the employment and labour market career. The school-to-work transition should provide a fair amount of security in terms of employment prospects, but also allow for sufficient flexibility regarding training opportunities and the matching of individual preferences and market requirements. The objective of the study is to identify different types of school-to-work transition sequences in European countries, going beyond the study of single situations or status changes (that is one transition at a time). Thus the integrative and risk character of the entire process of labour market entry can be assessed more adequately. This more long-term approach can be an impetus for active labour market policies that currently target problem groups, such as migrant and early school leavers, that face higher risks of labour market exclusion. The longitudinal dataset used for the analysis is the European Community Household Panel.

In Chapter 12 *Román*, *Schippers* and *Heylen* argue that the process of individualisation is creating a diversification of life course patterns. Paid work may still have a central but not *per se* a predominant position within these patterns. Facilities and arrangements have been developed with the aim of enabling people to combine work with other responsibilities. There is, however, only scarce evidence with respect to the long-term effects of the use of these facilities. Are standard full-time working careers indeed becoming less the norm? Is there evidence of an increase in transitions to, on and from the labour market? The authors choose the Belgian labour market as a case to identify labour and career typologies using the Panel Study on Belgian Households, originating in 1992. Belgium represents an interesting case as it is among the few countries that has introduced an innovative and life course arrangement, the so-called career break system.

This book's explicit aim is to confront, in the next chapters, innovative labour market concepts and perspectives with the empirical and practical realities of the labour market, labour law, industrial relations and human resource management. It is only by this method that scientific and policy concepts can be tested and further developed and practices can be further improved.

NOTES

1. The distinction between function and performance is a key notion within the theory of social systems as developed by Parsons et al. (1951), Luhmann (1984) and Teubner (1993).
2. Brussels, 25.7.2001 COM(2001) 428 final.
3. This overview is based on the report of the European Expert Group on Flexicurity (2007), the European Commission's study on Europe's social realities (2007) and the joint analysis of labour market challenges and flexicurity undertaken by the European social partners (European Social Partners, 2007).
4. This first paragraph is based on Klammer et al. (forthcoming).
5. Guidelines 2005, 2005/600/EC.
6. 16201/07, SOC 523 ECOFIN 503.
7. 2007/2209 (INI).
8. 'Key challenges facing European Labour Markets. A Joint Analysis of the European Social Partners', www.etuc.org/a/4119.
9. COM (2007) 0359.
10. COM (2006) 708 final.
11. ECJ C–341/05, 18 December 2007.
12. ECJ C–438/05,11 December 2007.
13. ECJ C–346/06, 3 April 2008.

REFERENCES

Adams, M. (2006), 'Hybridizing habitus and reflexity: towards an understanding of contemporary identity', *Sociology*, **40** (3), 511–28.

Auer, P. (ed.) (2001), *Changing Labour Markets in Europe. The Role of Institutions and Policies*, Geneva: International Labour Office.

Council of the European Union (2003), 'Council Decision of 22 July 2003 on guidelines for the employment policies of the Member States', *Official Journal of the European Union*, 5.8.2003, L 197 13–L 197 21.

De Sousa Santos, B. (1995), *Toward a New Common Sense. Law, Science and Politics in the Paradigmatic Transition*, New York: Routledge.
Durkheim, E. (1960), *The Division of Labour in Society*, New York.
Elder, G.H., Johnson, M.K. and Crosnoe, R. (2003), 'The Emergence and Development of Life Course Theory', in Mortimer, J.T. and Shanahan M.J. (eds), *Handbook of the life course*, New York: Springer, pp. 3–19.
Esping-Andersen, G. and Regini, M. (eds) (2000), *Why Deregulate Labour Markets?*, New York: Oxford University Press.
Esping-Andersen, G. (2002), *Why we Need a New Welfare State*, Oxford: Oxford University Press.
European Commission (2001), *European Governance. A White Paper*, Brussels.
European Commission (2003), 'The Stockholm and Barcelona targets: Increasing employment of older workers and delaying the exit from the labour market', Commission Staff Working Paper, SEC (2003) 429, Brussels.
European Commission (2007), *Europe's Social Reality*, Bureau of Economic Policy Advisors (BEPA) document (February).
European Social Partners (2007), 'Key challenges facing European Labour Markets. A joint analysis of the European Social Partners', www.etuc.org/a/4119.
Evers, G. and Wilthagen, T. (2007), *De toekomst van de arbeidsrelatie: een essay over wederkerig risicomanagement* (The future of the employment relationship: an essay on mutual risk management), Assen: Van Gorcum.
Giddens, A. (2007), *Europe in the Global Age*, Cambridge: Polity Press.
Hall, P. and Soskice, D. (eds) (2001), *Varieties of Capitalism: The Institutional Foundations of Comparative Advantage*, Oxford: Oxford University Press.
Jørgensen, H. and Madsen, P.K. (2007), *Flexicurity and Beyond. Finding a New Agenda for the European Social Model*, Copenhagen: Djøf Publishing.
Keller, B. and Seifert, H. (2000), 'Flexicurity – das Konzept fur mehr soziale Sicherheit flexibler Beschaftigung', *WSI Mitteilungen*, **53** (5), 291–300.
Klammer, U., Keuzenkamp, S., Cebrián, I., Fagan, C., Klenner, C. and Moreno, G. (2006), *Working Time Options over the Life Course: Changing Social Security Structures*, Luxembourg: European Foundation for the Improvement of Living and Working Conditions, Office for Official Publications.
Klammer, U., Muffels, R. and Wilthagen, T. (forthcoming, 2008), *Flexibility and Security over the Life Course. Key Findings and Policy Recommendations from the Foundation Research*, Dublin: European Foundation for the Improvement of Living and Working Conditions.
Léonard, L. (2001) 'Industrial relations and the regulation of employment in Europe', *European Journal of Industrial Relations*, **7**, 27–47.
Luhmann, N. (1984), *Soziale Systeme*, Frankfurt am Main: Suhrkamp Verlag.
Mayer, K.U. (2000), 'Promises fulfilled? A review of 20 years of life course research', *Archives Européennes de Sociologie*, **XL** (12), 259–82.
Mayntz, R. and Scharpf W.F. (1995), 'Der Ansatz des akteurzentrierten Institutionalismus', in Mayntz, R. and Scharpf F.W. (eds), *Steuerung und Selbstorganisation in staatsnahen Sektoren*, Frankfurt am Main: Campus, 39–72.
Ministry of Social Affairs and Employment (the Netherlands) (2002), *Verkenning levensloop* (Exploration of life course) report. The Hague.
Muffels, R., Chung, H., Fouarge, D., Klammer, U., Luijkx R., Manzoni, A. and Wilthagen, T. (2008), *Flexibility and Security Over the Life Course: Results and Policy Implications*, Luxembourg: European Foundation for the Improvement of Living and Working Conditions, Office for Official Publications.

Muffels, R. (2007), 'Roads of "flexicurity" in Europe: how (un)equal are they?', in Jørgensen, H. and Madsen, P.K. (eds), *Flexicurity and Beyond. Finding a New Agenda for the European Social Model*, Copenhagen: Djøf Publishing, pp. 215–43.

Muffels, R. and Luijkx, R. (2008), 'Male labour market mobility and income and employment security in Europe', in Muffels, R. (ed.), *Flexibility and Employment Security in Europe: Labour Markets in Transition*, Cheltenham, UK and Northampton, MA, USA: Edward Elgar, pp. 133–168.

Parsons, T., Shils, E.A. and Tolman, E.C. (1951), *Toward A General Theory of Action*, Cambridge, MA: Harvard University Press.

Parsons, T. and Smelser, N.J. (1956), *Economy and Society: A Study in the Integration of Economic and Social Theory*, London: Routledge and Kegan Paul.

Pierson, P. (1998), 'Irresistable forces, immovable objects: post-industrial welfare states confront permanent austerity', *Journal of European Public Policy*, **5** (4), 539–60.

Rogowski, R. (2007), 'Flexicurity and reflexive coordination of european social and employment policies', in Jørgensen, H. and Madsen, P.K. (eds), *Flexicurity and Beyond. Finding a New Agenda for the European Social Model*, Copenhagen: Djøf Publishing, pp. 131–53.

Rogowski, R. and Wilthagen, T. (eds) (2004), *Reflexive Labour Law: Studies in Industrial Relations and Employment Regulation*, Deventer, Cambridge: Kluwer Law and Taxation.

Román, A., Heylen, L. and Schippers, J. (2006), *Career Breaks In Belgium: How They Affect Labor Participation and Individual Careers*, Tilburg: OSA.

Scharpf, F.W. (1997), *Games Real Actors Play. Actor-centered Institutionalism in Policy Research*, Boulder/Cumnor Hill: Westview Press.

Schmid, G. (2000), 'Transitional labour markets: a new European employment strategy', in Marin, B., Meulders, D. and Snower, D. (eds), *Innovative Employment Initiatives*, Aldershot, UK: Ashgate, 223–53.

Schmid, G. and Gazier, B. (eds), (2002), *The Dynamics of Full Employment: Social Integration Through Transitional Labour Markets*, Cheltenham, UK and Northampton, MA, USA: Edward Elgar.

Sen, A. (1985), *Commodities and Capabilities*, Amsterdam: North Holland, reprinted by Oxford University Press, Delhi.

Silva Peneda, J. and Albino De Rossa, P. (2006), *A European Social Model for the Future*, Brussels: European Parliament Report.

Sisson, K. and Marginson, P. (2002) 'Co-ordinated bargaining: a process for our times?', *British Journal of Industrial Relations*, **40**, 197–220.

Streeck, W. (1992), *Social Institutions and Economic Performance*, London etc.: SAGE Publications.

Teubner, G. (1993), *Law as an Autopoietic System*, London: Blackwell.

Traxler, F. (1994), 'Collective bargaining: levels and coverage', in OECD, *OECD Employment Outlook 1994*, Paris: OECD, pp. 167–94.

Traxler, F. (2003), 'Coordinated bargaining: a stocktaking of its preconditions, practices and performance', *Industrial Relations Journal*, **34**, 194–209.

Van den Heuvel, N., Van der Hallen, P., Van der Lippe, T. and Schippers, J. (eds) (2004), *Diversity in Life Courses: Consequences for the Labour Market*, Tilburg: OSA.

Van Lieshout, H. (2008), *Different Hands: Markets for Intermediate Skills in Germany, the U.S. and the Netherlands*, Groningen: Hanzehogeschool Groningen.

Wilthagen, T. (1998), *Flexicurity: A New Paradigm for Labour Market Policy Reform?* Berlin: WZB Discussion Paper FS I 98–202.

Wilthagen, T. and Tros, F. (2004), 'The concept of "flexicurity": a new approach to regulating employment and labour markets', *Transfer*, **10** (2), 166–86.

Wilthagen, T. and Rogowski, R. (2002), 'Legal regulation of transitional labour markets', in Schmid, G. and Gazier, B. (eds), *The Dynamics of Full Employment: Social Integration through Transitional Labour Markets*, Cheltenham, UK and Northampton, MA, USA: Edward Elgar, pp. 233–73

Wynn, M. (2000), 'European social dialogue: harmonisation or new diversity?', in Collins, H., Davies, P. and Rideout, R. (eds), *Legal Regulation of the Employment Relation*, London/Dordrecht: Kluwer Law International, pp. 491–511.

PART I

Transitional Labour Markets in Europe

2. Labour Market Policy in Flanders: How to Tackle Vicious Circles and False Beliefs

Frank Vandenbroucke

Reflecting the need for innovation in European labour market policy is challenging. What policy directions should we take? What works – in the literal sense – and what does not? What is the sense of 'innovation'? Why do we need it? Where do we need it? These are key questions indeed, both for academics and politicians. It is also challenging because of my specific policy responsibilities in the Flemish region in Belgium.

As a minister, I am responsible for education – both compulsory and higher education – and training and employment in the Flemish region, that is, roughly six million Dutch-speaking people in Belgium. The combination of education and employment in one unit is very new and exciting. Combining education and employment enables us to build bridges between the worlds of work and education. This wide scope should benefit both labour market policy and education policy. My responsibility for employment concerns placement and training, the whole 'active' side of labour market policy, but not unemployment benefits or labour law, which are federal Belgian competences. That dichotomy between activation policy and benefit policy is typical of Belgium's institutional structure, as I will explain further on. First, I will show you some figures, illustrating a sad lack of dynamism in the European labour market, and particularly in the Flemish labour market on which I will focus (Section 2.1). I will then try to explain summarily what may be behind this lack of dynamism, focussing on the dichotomy in our institutions and what I call 'false beliefs and vicious circles' that are mutually reinforcing (Section 2.2). Innovation should also target those false beliefs, in order to break vicious circles. It is important to emphasise that the Flemish labour market is very different from the Belgian labour market, behind which it is often concealed in international surveys and statistics. As a matter of fact, the Belgian labour market does not exist: Flanders, Brussels and Wallonia are characterised by very divergent regional labour markets. That is part of the Belgian policy predicament.

2.1 THE FLEMISH LABOUR MARKET: A SNAPSHOT AND A MOVIE

Globalisation, the opening up of the borders within Europe, the consequences of aging and the increasing diversification in our society, constitute major social challenges. These challenges must be met, if we want to maintain and increase our welfare. We can compare it to the climatic changes on our planet. There is growing awareness that a fundamental approach is necessary. Labour markets also need to undergo fundamental changes. It is not a matter of doom-mongering, but of facing up to the 'inconvenient truth', based on facts. Countries and regions that do not take measures or take them too slowly, will fall behind.

In what follows I want to present the current situation on the Flemish labour market, in comparison with Belgium, the Netherlands, Northern Europe which I consider as an important benchmark, and the European average. Europe refers to the old 15 EU countries. Northern Europe refers to the average of Sweden, Denmark and Finland (hence, Northern Europe). I will then look back on the past few years to illustrate the rhythm and direction of the change.

2.1.1 Snapshot: Compressed Career Pattern and Many Outsiders

The overall Flemish employment rate of 64.2 per cent is significantly higher than the Belgian figure, yet it is slightly below the European average (of the 15) of 65.9 per cent, and considerably lower than the figure in the Netherlands (74.2 per cent) and Northern Europe (73.3 per cent). The Belgian figure is pushed down by the low levels of activity in French speaking Wallonia (55.8 per cent) and Brussels (52.6 per cent).

However, the gap between Flanders and the Netherlands changes drastically when we do not use a head count, that is when we do not focus on numbers of people, but on the volume of work, say hours worked. This can be done by expressing the employment rate in terms of full time equivalents, as shown in Figure 2.1. We see that in terms of full time equivalents the employment rate in Flanders climbs above the one in the Netherlands: 58.8 per cent against 56.4 per cent. This is the same as the average in Europe (58.7 per cent).

A compressed career pattern

Figure 2.2 clearly shows our compressed career pattern, with many people in employment in the 'middle-age' cohort of 25–49 years, and relatively few in employment in the outer age groups, below 25 years, or older than 49 years. This is particularly noticeable in Flanders.

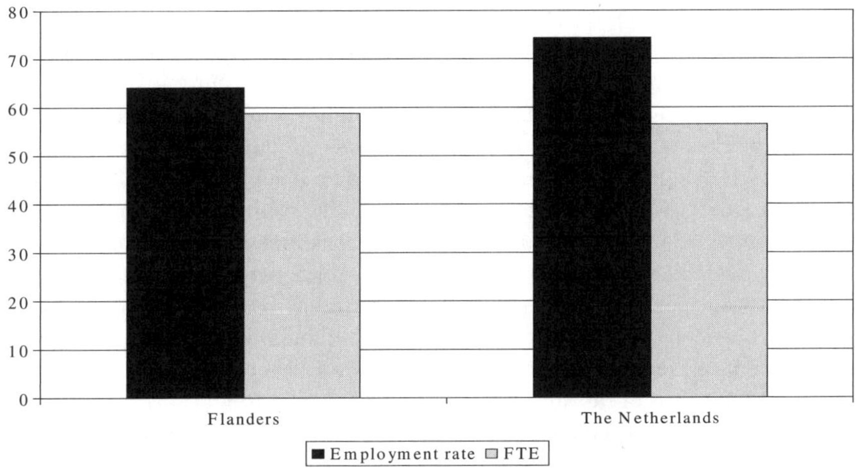

Source: Eurostat LFS.

Figure 2.1 Employment rate (in %) 25–49 years (average 2005)

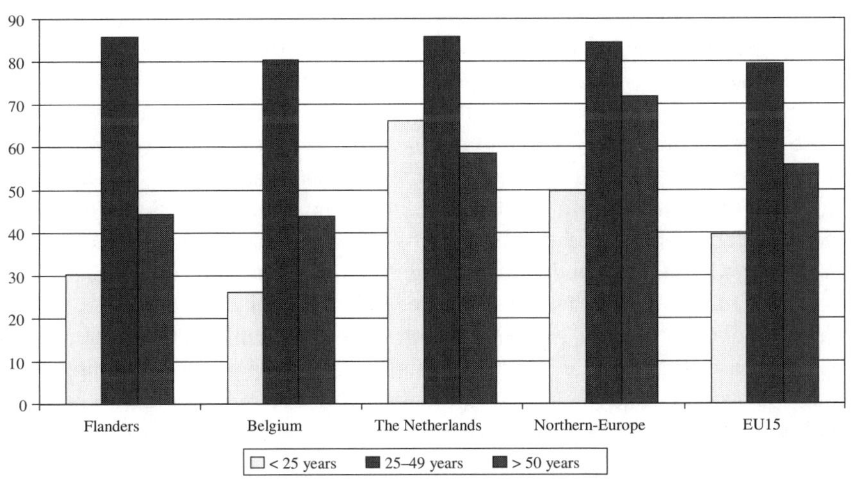

Source: Eurostat LFS.

Figure 2.2 Employment rate (in %) by age (June 2006)

The 'middle age' cohort: 25–49 years

That the overall employment rate for Flanders approaches the European average is entirely thanks to the middle age cohort: 86 out of 100 people in this middle age group work. This is as high as in the Netherlands and Northern Europe, and 6.4 percentage points higher than the European average. The high employment rate in this age group in the Netherlands is linked to the widespread part-time work in the Netherlands. The share of part-time work in the overall employment is almost twice as high in the Netherlands (39.9 per cent) as in Flanders (21.5 per cent) or in Northern Europe (14.8 per cent). Almost three-quarters (72 per cent) of all working women between 25 and 49 years in the Netherlands work part-time, against 42 per cent in Flanders, 25 per cent in Northern Europe and 35 per cent in the EU15. Many men in this age group are working part-time too: 13 per cent of working men are in part-time jobs, against 4.2 per cent in Flanders, 5.8 per cent in Northern Europe and 4.7 per cent in the EU15.

The outer age group: < 25 years

The low employment rate among under 25s in Flanders (30.3 per cent) is striking, especially in comparison with the Netherlands (66.2 per cent). Here again part-time work is very widespread in the Netherlands: 68.3 per cent of all working youngsters in the Netherlands are in part-time jobs, against 19.7 per cent in Flanders (45.6 per cent in Northern Europe and 26.3 per cent in the EU15). Although there is a difference in the youth unemployment rate between both (14 per cent in Flanders against 8.2 per cent in the Netherlands) this huge gap (and the difference in part-time work) is linked to different educational systems and different cultural patterns. In Flanders the average student is a full-time student, while in the Netherlands study and work are more often combined. This situation is a consequence of legal rules concerning social security, student jobs and educational grants. It is also the result of the typical Flemish student culture. In Flanders students travel to their university city on Sunday evening, to return to their home town on Friday evening. Dutch student careers also seem significantly longer.

If we make a hypothetical exercise and give Flanders the same youth employment rate as the Netherlands, the overall Flemish employment rate will increase to almost 71 per cent. This is almost 6 percentage points more than the actual employment rate in Flanders. Should we wish this to become reality in Flanders? As a minister for education, I doubt this. I prefer the Flemish situation, where students can concentrate fully on their studies. Simultaneously, however, I took the initiative to develop a crash programme on unemployment of low-skilled, often unqualified young people.

The outer age group: 50-plus

With just 44.4 per cent of the people over 50 working in Flanders, we are an outlier, compared to the Netherlands (58.6 per cent) or the European average (55.4 per cent) and especially to Northern Europe (71.8 per cent). Note that Flanders in this prospect is not doing any better than Wallonia (42.2 per cent) and is worse than Brussels (46 per cent). This problem is even more pronounced among the over 55s than among those aged 50 years and over.

There are only a few countries in Europe which combine a very high employment rate in the age cohort 25–49 years and a very low employment rate in the age group plus 50. In most countries both go together. Figure 2.3 shows this atypical position of Flanders in Europe. The horizontal axis gives the employment rate for the age group 25–49 years, the vertical axis for the age group 50–64 years. The cross of the axis gives the average for EU12. There is a positive correlation between countries with a high employment rate in both age groups. Flanders takes with Slovenia and Austria an atypical position. It combines a very high employment rate within the age group 25–49 years, with a low employment rate in the age group 50+.

In Flanders 26.8 per cent of the employed between 50 and 64 years are working in a part-time job, which is above the European average (20.6 per cent) and Northern Europe (18.8 per cent), but far below the situation in the Netherlands (45.8 per cent).

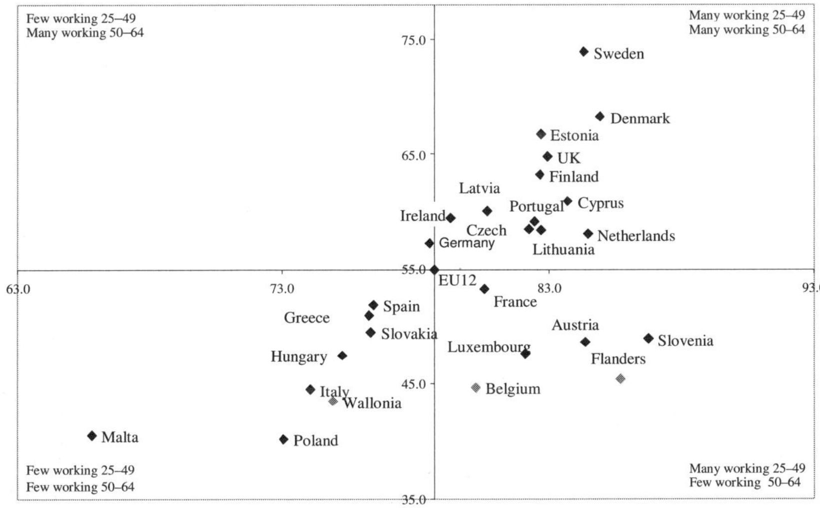

Source: Eurostat LFS.

Figure 2.3 Employment rate 25–49 and 50–64 years (average 2005–2006)

The challenge facing Flemish labour market policy is to increase the employment rate of this group drastically. Of course, the challenge of aging has been explained time and time again – and indicating its importance and urgency in figures is worth a chapter on its own – but it remains important that policymakers, scientists and public opinion realise that working longer will be an absolute necessity, if we want to prevent the labour market reservoir from running dry. Moreover, the problem of greying will manifest itself sooner and more seriously in Flanders than in other Belgian regions.

The low employment rate of the older age cohort is but one instance of the insider–outsider cleavage characterising the Flemish labour market.

Underprivileged groups

Besides the precarious situation of older people in the Flemish labour market, a number of other groups are not doing well either (see Figure 2.4).

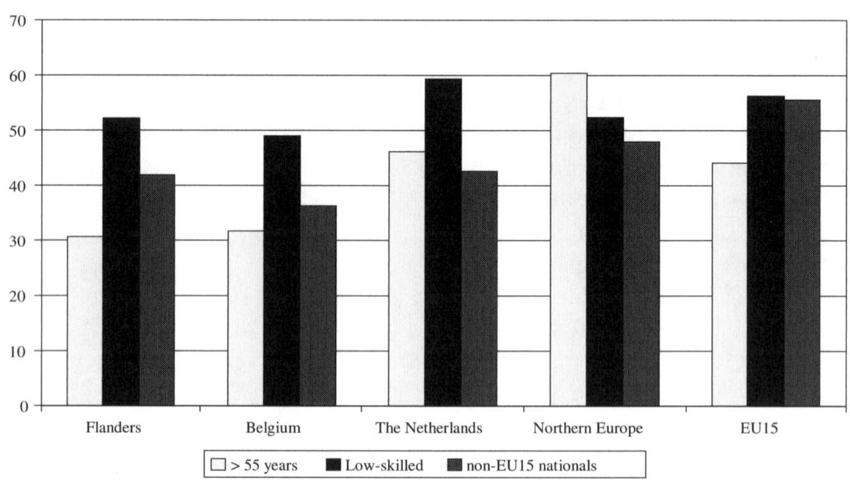

Source: Eurostat LFS.

Figure 2.4 Employment rate (in %) for 55-plus, low-skilled and non-EU 15 nationals (2005)

The employment figure for the immigrant population (defined here as non-EU15 nationals) is much lower (41.9 per cent) than the European average (55.7 per cent). The Netherlands (42.7 per cent) has a similar position in this respect as Flanders, and for Belgium the situation of immigrant groups is even worse (36.4 per cent). In Northern Europe this figure is 48 per cent.

Just over half of all low-skilled people in Flanders are working, which is nearly the same as in the Northern countries (52 per cent), under the European average (56.3 per cent) and a lot lower than the situation in the Netherlands (59.5 per cent). This is partly due to the low level of activity among the older population.

Lifelong learning
Nonetheless, the Flemish labour market is characterised by a considerable influx of well-educated youngsters: 85.1 per cent of the 25–29 year olds had at least a secondary school degree in 2005. Flanders realises the European objective (85 per cent). In the Netherlands the percentage of secondary school degrees in this age cohort is 75.6 per cent.

On the other hand, Flanders is still confronted with a persistent unqualified outflow. In Flanders 10.7 per cent of youngsters leave school without a secondary school diploma. Partly due to compulsory education up to the age of 18, this unqualified outflow in Flanders is structurally below the European average of 15.2 per cent and lower than in the Netherlands (12.6 per cent) and only slightly higher than in Northern Europe (9,8 per cent). Flanders traditionally scores well compared to other European countries and regions with regard to education performance indicators (that is the PISA indicators by the OECD).

Things are different for indicators regarding lifelong learning. Flanders is by no means the best pupil of the European class, concerning training efforts, on the contrary (see Figure 2.5).

In 2005 10.1 per cent of employed people (aged 25–64) in Flanders took part in training, compared to 11.7 per cent in Europe (EU15) on average, 17.4 per cent in the Netherlands and 23.5 per cent in Northern Europe. One possible explanation, among others, for the high rate in the Netherlands could be the high degree of transparency in the supply of adult education via the ROCs. The low participation in training in Flanders is striking and is high on the political agenda. Employers' organisations and unions both have their own views on this problem.

With regard to the training of job-seekers, Flanders is doing better than the average in Europe, respectively 14.1 per cent and 9 per cent, but worse than the Netherlands (17.5 per cent) and Northern Europe (25.6 per cent). The level of training is linked to labour participation. The OECD found a strong correlation between the initial level and additional training and labour market participation. Additional training has a positive influence on labour participation and a negative influence on the risk of unemployment. The negative correlation between additional training and involuntary turnover is the highest for low-skilled persons and older employees. For these groups, additional education ensures their productivity and therefore the chance of remaining at work. Only 3.7 per cent of all low-skilled persons in Flanders participates in training (16.5 per cent among people with a higher education), compared to 8.2 per cent in the Netherlands and 11.6 per cent in Northern Europe. The figure is slightly higher among those aged 50 and over (5.9 per cent), while 8 per cent of those aged 50–64 participate in training in the Netherlands.

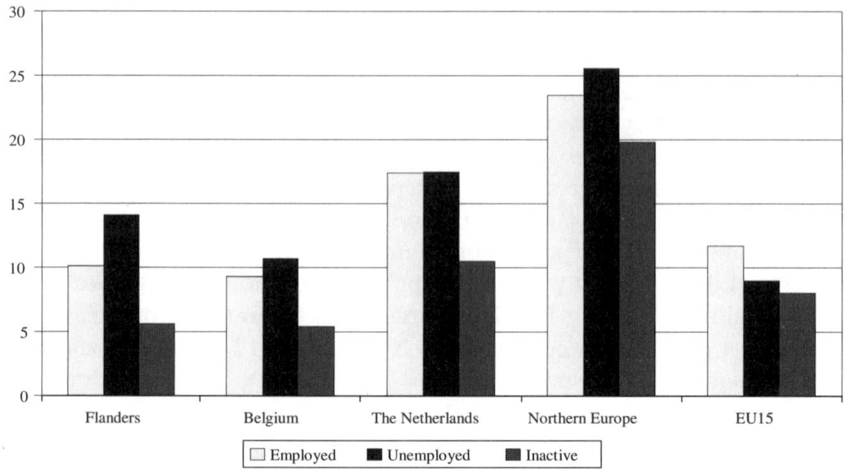

Source: Eurostat LFS.

Figure 2.5 Percentage of the population (25–64 years) participating in training by socio-economic position (employed, unemployed or inactive) (2005)

What can we conclude after this snapshot of the Flemish labour market? The so-called compressed career model is very pronounced in Flanders. And more than other labour markets the Flemish labour market is characterised by the phenomenon of 'outsiders', older people, immigrant groups and low-skilled persons (and disabled people, but there are few comparable data).

2.1.2 Movie: the Evolution Over Time

To put this snapshot into perspective, we should examine the development over time of the employment rate of the various groups compared to their evolution in Europe. Is the gap with Europe closing or is it increasing? And if it is closing, how fast is it closing? In the following Figures 2.6 to 2.10 the horizontal 0-axis is the European average. Note that this is not a fixed 0-axis, since the European average itself evolves between the indicated years. If a country's performance lies above the 0-axis, then that country is doing better on average than in Europe, under the 0-axis means the opposite. So we move from a snapshot to a movie. I will show first the movie for those aged 55 and older (Figure 2.6).

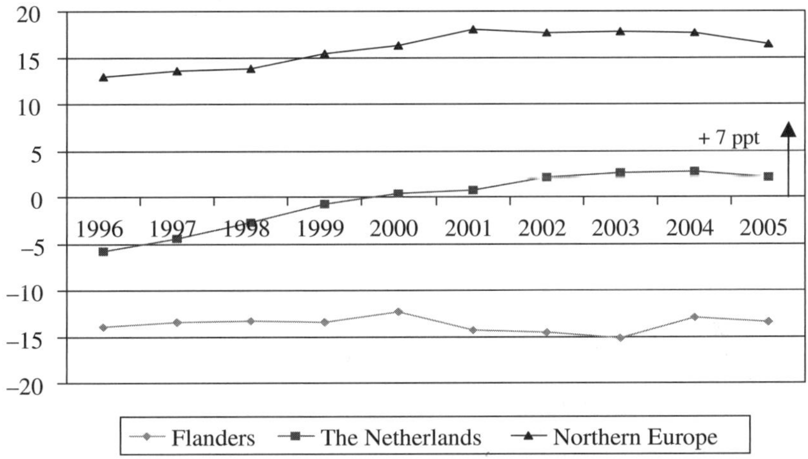

Source: Eurostat LFS.

Figure 2.6 Evolution of the gap between the employment rate in Flanders, the Netherlands, Northern Europe and EU15, concerning 55-plus (1996–2005)

With regard to the low level of activity of the plus 55s, we made hardly any progress in Flanders these past ten years compared to the European average (which itself has increased with 7 percentage points). The European average remains way ahead, and from our Flemish perspective, the European front runners have been out of sight for a long time. By contrast, from 2000 onwards the Netherlands has been able to change its poor position into a lead compared with the European average of the 1990s. The employment rate of those aged 55 and older in Flanders increased from 22.6 per cent to 30.7 per cent between 1996 and 2005, that is plus 8.1 percentage points compared to almost double the increase (15.7 percentage points) in the Netherlands (from 30.5 per cent to 46.2 per cent). Northern Europe was able to hold its strong position and even to make the gap a bit bigger.

With regard to the employment rate of non-Europeans (here as a moving average) we have hardly been able to improve our poor position compared with Europe; see Figure 2.7. During the past ten years the employment rate of non-Europeans did increase by 11 percentage points (from 29 per cent to 40.2

per cent), but the gap with Europe stayed more or less the same (as the European benchmark itself increased with 9 percentage points).

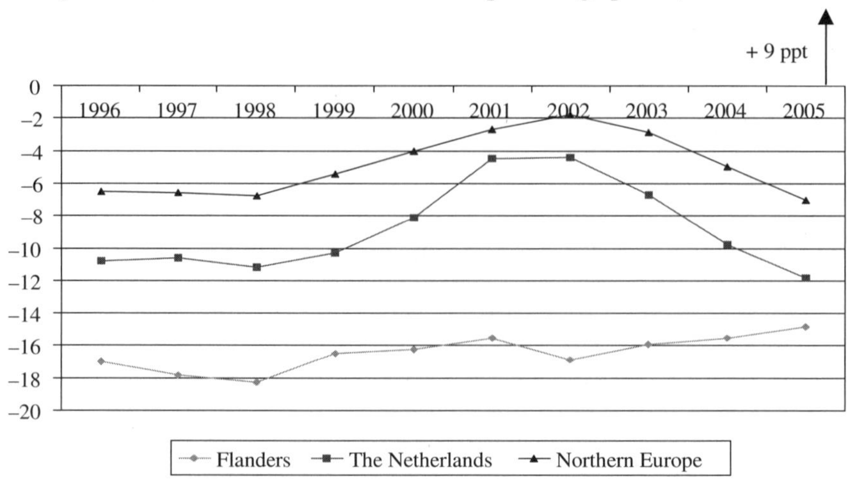

Note: * Non-EU nationals: moving average.

Source: Eurostat LFS.

*Figure 2.7 Evolution of the gap between the employment rate in Flanders, the Netherlands, Northern Europe and EU15, concerning the non-EU15 nationals (1996–2005)**

The evolution in the Netherlands and Northern Europe was more 'erratic', or cyclical. Despite a major bridging of the gap with Europe between 1999 and 2001, for the Netherlands and Northern Europe the corresponding gap increased from 2002 onwards, and in 2005 it was about as wide as in 1996. What is the explanation? Maybe, during an economic downturn the generalised principle of last in first out applies disproportionally to migrant workers. It is noteworthy that even Northern Europe displays this pattern. Or maybe, elsewhere in the EU there was an acceleration in participation of migrant groups?

In Flanders we see in Figure 2.8 that over a seven-year period (1999–2005) the share of employed people doing training has almost not moved compared to the European average, while the Netherlands has been able to consolidate its major lead compared to Europe, despite the slight relapse in the latter few years.

The situation is slightly different for training efforts of the unemployed (see Figure 2.9). Compared to Europe, Flanders shows a clear positive step forwards from 2003 onwards. There was indeed a significant effort in these years, linked to a major turn in policy doctrine and practice.

As the figures illustrate, not only does Flanders have a sharp insider/outsider duality on the labour market, which also applies to the Belgian labour market, we also see that the gap with Europe is barely closing for underprivileged groups and that the rhythm of change is too slow.

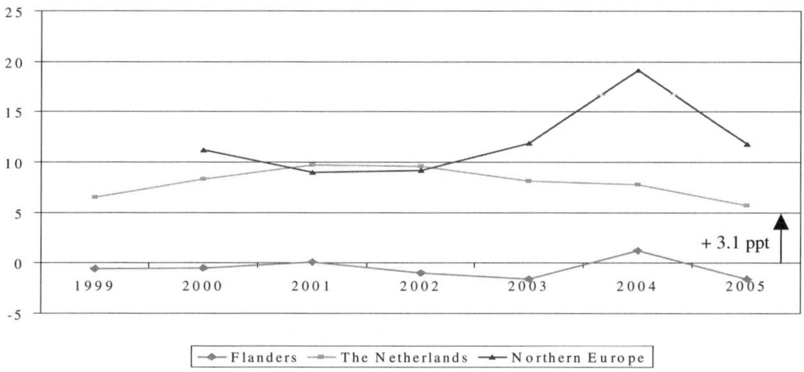

Source: Eurostat LFS.

Figure 28 Evolution of the gap between the percentages participating in training in Flanders, the Netherlands, Northern Europe and EU15, concerning the employed (1999–2005)

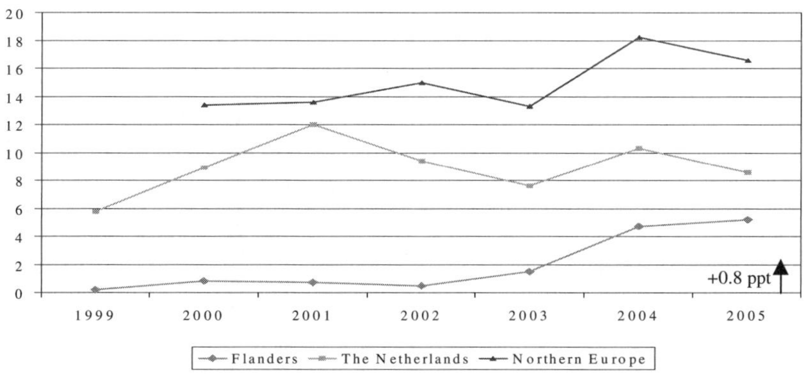

Source: Eurostat LFS.

Figure 2.9 Evolution of the gap between the percentages participating in training in Flanders, the Netherlands, Northern Europe and EU15, concerning the unemployed (1999–2005)

2.2 BREAKING VICIOUS CIRCLES

Why is there so little dynamic change on the Flemish labour market? Why do we constantly stay behind compared with the European average? In this section I will put forward some hypotheses which suggest possible answers to the challenge.

2.2.1 Labour Market Regulation

Obviously, labour market regulation is the main culprit. Labour market regulation determinates the labour market outlook. This section will briefly touch upon three issues: flexibility, early retirement and conditionality of unemployment benefits.

The OECD has developed an index which makes the so-called employment protection legislation internationally comparable between countries. The EPL index summarises the legislation on three issues: the rules concerning individual and collective dismissal and the rules concerning the use of temporary labour. The index varies from 0 to 6 points: 6 refers to the most protecting rigorous legislation. The index takes into account the legislation *sensu strictu*, but also the results of the social dialogue and the jurisprudence.

Figure 2.10 shows that Belgium is characterised by a rather rigorous legislation as well as Germany, Sweden, France and Greece. Denmark, Ireland and UK are situated on the other end of the index.

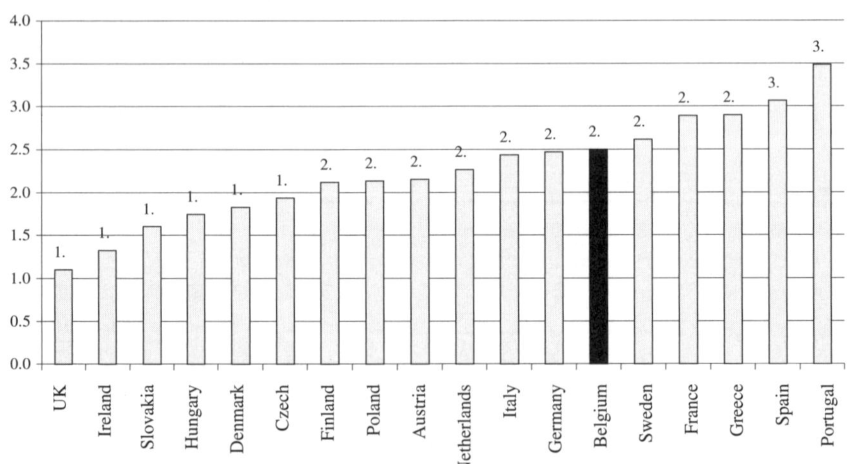

Source: OECD (2004).

Figure 2.10 Employment protection legislation index

Although there is room for much nuance on these issues, it seems fair to say that too rigorous legislation may hamper the necessary dynamism, mobility and flexibility on the labour market. Certainly, from the point of view of an individual employee a less rigorous legislation and more flexibility in the labour market can be quite threatening, especially concerning the durability of the job. This individual uncertainty cannot be neglected.

Yet, in contrast to widespread beliefs, mobility and flexibility are not necessarily enemies of a high employment rate – on the contrary. Figure 2.11 shows on the horizontal axis the employment rate; the vertical axis shows the average seniority of the employees.

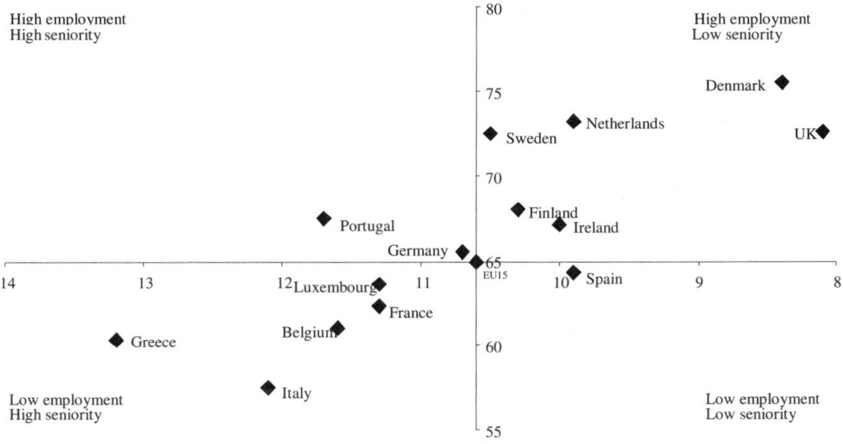

Source: HRW (2006), OECD (2005).

Figure 2.11 Average seniority–employment rate

The average seniority of the employees is considered as an indication of the mobility on the labour market. We see a rather positive correlation (although one can not make conclusion about causality): countries with a high mobility in the labour market (low seniority) are also characterised by a high employment rate and vice versa. The figure shows two rather different models of labour market flexibility: the social-democratic model in northern Europe and the Anglo-Saxon model of the UK and Ireland. Although the individual worker's perspective may be different, when we look at the labour market from a 'systemic' perspective, the conclusion that more flexibility contributes to creating jobs seems to hold.

Whilst there is room for nuance with regard to the link between flexibility and employment, there can be no doubt that generous early retirement schemes hamper job creation. Belgian has generous early exit schemes, both in the specific context of company restructuring and collective dismissals and in the normal end-of-career context. These regulations constitute both an incentive for workers to leave the labour market early, and a disincentive for companies to recruit older workers and/or to invest in older workers' human capital.

Recently the Federal Government approved a series of measures to tackle this problem within the framework of the so-called 'Generation Pact'. The intention was to increase the employment rate among older people. The measures that were taken were psychologically undoubtedly a step forward, yet significant structural measures making early retirement impossible were not taken. Although changes were made in the regulations concerning early retirement, in practice these schemes still dominate in the case of restructuring and allow people to leave the labour market at an early stage.

With regard to unemployment benefits, no significant changes have been introduced over the last ten years, except for one, important change in policy stance since 2003, which has been called the 'comprehensive approach' (in Dutch: 'sluitende aanpak'). A very passive stance was gradually replaced by a more activating approach, with unemployment benefits in practice becoming somewhat more 'conditional' on active search efforts by the unemployed themselves.

Although labour market and unemployment benefit regulation is certainly the main 'culprit' for the slow pace of change on the Flemish labour market, I will not elaborate upon these issues in this contribution. I would like to draw the attention to broader issues linked to 'policy institutions' and 'predominant beliefs' (see also Figure 2.12).

My argument is that our institutional context and persistent 'false beliefs' explain why progress has been slow, with regard to both regulatory reform and practical change on the work floor. Then, my argument will be that within my rather limited actual labour market competences (as a minister in the Flemish Government) I should endeavour to change such false beliefs.

2.2.2 Policy Institutions

Successive institutional reforms in Belgium created contradictions which hamper progress in employment policy. Following the special law of 8 August 1980 regarding the reform of institutions, the national competences regarding labour mediation and placement, vocational training and unemployment were reorganised as follows: labour mediation became a responsibility of the Regional Governments, vocational training is a matter for what we call Community (devolved) Governments – for simplicity, you may merge them with the regions – and unemployment benefits remained a matter for the Federal Government. This dichotomy is very problematic for activating labour market policy.

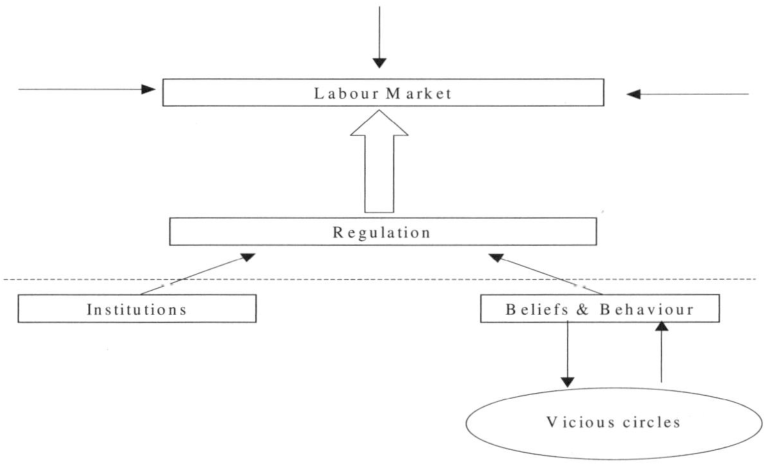

Figure 2.12 Labour market: regulations, institutions and beliefs

Activation should be implemented by one level of government to ensure a coherent and tailor-made approach of job-seekers. In view of the differences between the labour markets in the various regions, with the enormous difference between Flanders, Wallonia and Brussels concerning youth unemployment problems as a typical example, the regional level seems most appropriate.

To pursue a consistent and efficient policy it is best to keep all instruments relating to active labour market policy, carrot as well as stick, in one hand. This dichotomy was not officially considered to be a problem until the National Employment Conference of September 2003. The result of the conference was that arrangements were made between the regional public employment services and the federal unemployment office, and between the regional public employment services themselves, with regard to the activation and follow-up of the unemployed. This was certainly a step forward, and activation became a more prominent feature of employment policy. However, we are still far removed from a decisive, overall shift to activation in all the regions. The institutional dichotomy in employment policy remains a fundamental problem.[1]

2.2.3 False Beliefs

The current institutional context is a factor explaining a rather modest pace of policy adjustment in Belgium and its regions. A context of slow policy change is also an environment in which vicious circles, created by the interaction of regulation and (false) beliefs, can become entrenched. Consider, for instance, the following statements:

- We absolutely need early retirement schemes, since older workers never find jobs when they are fired.
- When immigrant workers are unemployed, it is because they lack crucial employment-related skills.
- Employers are always unwilling to hire immigrant workers, even when they have the required skills.

These statements are one-sided or exaggerated to such an extent that they should be considered untrue. They are false beliefs. They can easily be contradicted by counter-examples. Against the first statement one can also postulate that older workers have difficulty in finding a new job, precisely because of early retirement schemes. Yet, these false beliefs are persistent, because they interact with the actual outcomes of regulations, which make them seem true. Policy and belief mutually reinforce each other.

Vicious circle 1
Low economic productivity of the older-age cohort and high economic productivity of the middle-age cohort

A first example of a vicious circle is related to the 'compressed career model' as illustrated in Section 2.2.1. The compressed career model is related to a socio-economic culture, in which as much productivity, energy and creativity as possible is drawn from the people in the 'hyperactive age' category between 25 and 49, while many over 50s drop out or retire early. Such a strong contrast between the hyperactive age cohort and a totally non-active age cohort is not just an economic problem, but creates a problem for society's social cohesion.

High economic productivity of the middle-aged groups goes hand in hand with a lot of work pressure. On top of their job, a lot of workers have to combine a job with a family. As a result of this 'rat race' many people feel 'squeezed out like a lemon', and aspire to leave the labour market early, or are forced to do so. In Flanders the age that workers prefer to retire is 58 years. So we have an extensive group of older people with low economic productivity. This model is only financially sustainable if the active group realises a high economic productivity. So conceived, we have already a part of a vicious circle, with an internal, self-feeding logic (Figure 2.13).

Moreover, as a result of the tendency to early exit from the labour market, employers are reluctant to invest in the human capital of their older workers. This in turn feeds the beliefs of employers that older workers are not interesting anymore. As a result unions believe that there are not any jobs for older workers and thus that early retirement arrangements are necessary. In this way, a complete vicious circle of mutually reinforcing economic and social mechanisms and (false) beliefs is at play in the Flemish labour market. If we want to break a vicious circle it is necessary to break it simultaneously at several points. So far this has not been done with this vicious circle.

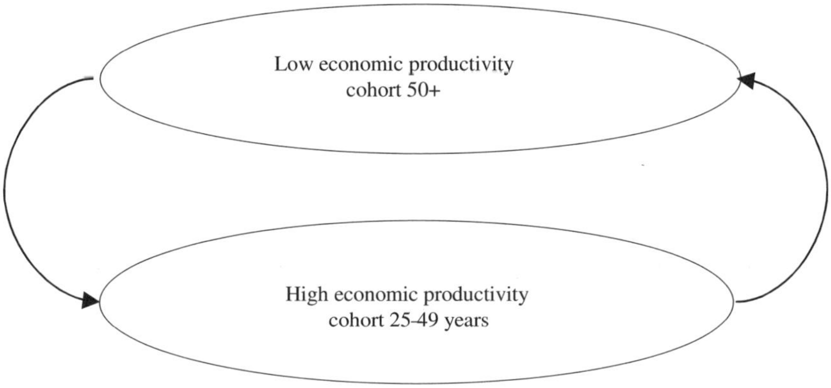

Figure 2.13 Vicious circle 1

In Flanders and Belgium the focus on the 'hard-working citizen' was explicitly on the political agenda from the mid 1990s onwards. A more relaxed career was called for, and a series of arrangements were introduced with this purpose. The signpost for this career policy is the so-called time credit system that is unique to Belgium. Under this system, employees can halt their career temporarily, completely or partially to spend time on other things such as taking care of family members or training or simply to be free to choose how to spend their time. In Flanders, in addition to the federal grant for career breaks, this amount is supplemented for a limited period by a second allowance, the so-called 'encouragement grant'. These systems were extremely successful. In 1996 32,800 people were on career breaks in Flanders. Ten years later (September 2006) 147,000 were authorised to take such breaks. On first sight these arrangements fit perfectly into the combination-idea and career-policy of the transitional labour market theory.

Looking back on this career policy I am inclined to be self-critical with regard to some of the results. I think it was a rather naïve implementation of the idea of a transitional labour market. We said we wanted to let people work longer, but in a relaxed career. We used this argument to justify the social security costs of this career policy. Because people were going to work longer, the costs of the various career arrangements would be recovered. In practice, we tried hard to offer more relaxed careers, but we did not try hard enough to make people work longer. The career policy, in this case the career break schemes, were not linked to an activating strategy vis-à-vis older people. In hindsight, this was a missed opportunity. We assumed that there was a kind of 'invisible hand' – to use an old term – that would ensure that there was causality between taking time out during a career and working longer. There is no strong empirical support for this assumption. On a macroeconomic level, the consequence is that the pressure of work and of achieving is still very high on the middle-age group and that the 'relaxation', the slowing down for some, mainly results in more pressure for others in the same middle-age cohort.

As indicated, such a vicious circle reinforces false beliefs. There are a lot of prejudices concerning older workers: they are all too often supposed to suffer burn out, or not to be flexible. Their best years in the labour market have already gone, according to this prejudice. Hence, it is understandable that employers are not inclined to hire older job-seekers. Simultaneously, trade unionists believe there are not any jobs available for older job-seekers, hence they remain convinced early retirement schemes should prevail. Reality is as much the other way round: early retirement also kills jobs for the elderly. It is important to show that the popular conviction is at least partially false. Therefore, we have to develop instruments that result in successful employment and re-employment for older people. By booking practical successes we can convince people that their beliefs are false, or at least, not entirely true. Hence, much of what I undertake with my (rather limited) competences as Flemish minister for employment is geared at creating 'success experience'.

A grant to make the re-employment of older job-seekers visible

High labour cost is one of the main reasons for the existence of so many outsiders in the Flemish labour market. This argument specifically applies to older people. Instruments to decrease wage costs are in the hands of the Federal Government. Recently, the Flemish Government created a supplementary instrument that decreases the cost for the employer when he/she recruits an older job-seeker. We introduced a substantial wage subsidy for employers hiring an older job-seeker (50 years and older). An employer can obtain a grant of up to 1,000 euro per month during one year if an older job-seeker is hired on a permanent basis. This measure was only started recently (April 2006) and still has to reach cruising speed. Up until now (May 2007) around 1,800 grants have been awarded. The objective is to help 3,750 job-seekers aged 50 and over to get out of unemployment via this grant, not by retiring, but by getting them into work. I admit, this objective is not very ambitious in quantitative terms, but the latent function of this measure is to break through the defeatist thinking concerning older job-seekers. With this measure we not only want to make clear that there are jobs for the older unemployed, but also we make them visible.

'Jobkanaal'

A specific arrangement, based on shared responsibility, has been convened between the Government and our employers' organisations in the 'Jobkanaal' (job channel) project. Jobkanaal is a specific recruitment channel where during a period of three weeks vacancies are only notified to people from underrepresented groups. The ambition and target of the scheme is to achieve 5,000 annual recruitments. On the basis of this commitment, I support the Jobkanaal project. The Flemish public employment service, VDAB, is ensuring referral of at least four valid candidates per Jobkanaal vacancy. This is not a quota system. It is an initiative where employers convince other employers to give immigrant groups, older or disabled people a fair chance of recruitment.

An agenda for competence management.

We launched the idea of a 'competence management agenda' (in Dutch: 'competentieagenda'), about which we try to build consensus among social partners and the world of education. In a sense this agenda constitutes the human capital dimension of flexicurity and the transitional labour market. Competences – 'competenties' as we say in Dutch – consist of knowledge, skills and attitudes. The core idea of our 'competence management agenda' is the following: if we are to use the talents of *all* people, including groups that are currently underrepresented in the labour market, and if we are to use people's talents throughout their entire life, then we must focus on the development of competences, in compulsory and further education, in training programmes and on the shop floor. A competence agenda encompasses education and training, it takes on board the importance of diplomas and certificates. But much more, it is about the detection, recognition and development of all competences, including those acquired through experience at work or experience in other contexts. The idea that competences can also be developed through experience at work is gaining ground. The positive appreciation of these competences is, however, not evident for all actors in the labour market, and that is why – as one element of our competence agenda – we support and organise initiatives for the assessment and recognition of competences, and for their further development. Another practical element is creating broad access to career counselling, the development of personal portfolios and – obviously – everything that relates to lifelong learning. A fundamental – yet steep – ambition is that in the end everyone in every company or organisation would have a right to personal development – but also, in a sense, a duty, since competence development is a shared responsibility. Presently, I am seeking consensus on priority actions with our Flemish trade unions and employers' organisations, and simultaneously I am introducing this agenda in education and in our public employment service. It is indeed as much an agenda for change and innovation within education, and for establishing new links between education and the labour market, as it is an agenda for innovation in the labour market.

Vicious circle 2
Failure and prejudice concerning immigrants

A dramatic vicious circle that interacts with false beliefs concerns the position of immigrants on the labour market. As a consequence of prejudices some employers discriminate against immigrants during recruitment. This weakens the position of immigrants in the labour market. As a kind of self-fulfilling prophecy people in immigrant communities have a relatively weaker incentive to study and finish formal education. ('Why do we have to study if there are not any jobs for us?') A relatively weak incentive to study is also linked to the social and economic status of the parents. A consequence of these mechanisms is that many immigrants indeed have a deficit in education (for example a language deficit). In turn, deficits in education confirm the prejudices of employers, when they are confronted with job-seekers from the immigrant population. Such negative experiences will further reduce the willingness of employers to give job-seekers from the immigrant population a fair chance to be recruited. So, a vicious circle becomes a fact (Figure 2.14).

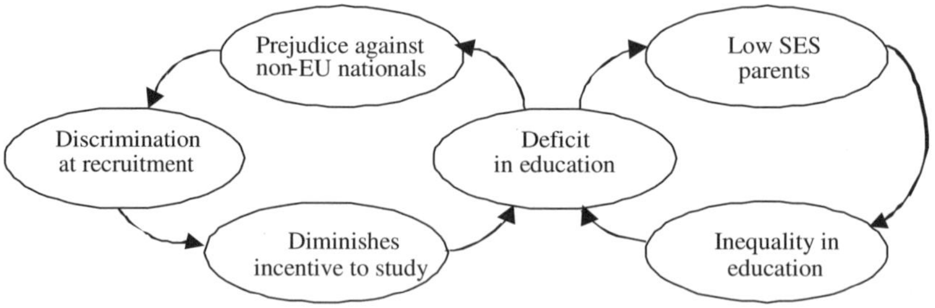

Figure 2.14 Vicious circle 2

This vicious circle feeds a whole set of false conceptions: that all employers are unwilling to recruit immigrants, that there really are no jobs for immigrants, and that when immigrants are unemployed it is always because of lack of skills.

Admittedly, this is a highly simplified story. Nevertheless, I believe we witness vicious circles of failure (actual deficits) and prejudice in our labour market. It is important to break such a vicious circle at several points simultaneously. We have to fight discrimination and prejudice, we have to show that there are jobs for immigrants and we have to invest in training and education. Aspiration has to replace unwarranted 'victimisation'. I recently took some measures especially designed to break this vicious circle. Let me give some examples.

Jobkanaal and 'diversity plans'

I have already referred to the Jobkanaal project as an initiative where employers convince each other to give immigrants, older or disabled people a fair chance of recruitment.

It is also important that people on the shop floor are given the opportunity to prove themselves as employees and to work as colleagues. Through diversity plans I therefore stimulate and support – also financially – companies to integrate various groups of employees and to adopt an HR policy with an eye for diversity. Since 2005 we reach annually about 500 companies.

Through the Jobkanaal project and the diversity plans, employers are called upon to take a social responsibility. We should not only point out that there are jobs for immigrants, we should also indicate that working with immigrants works. This is the way to break through the prejudices among employers and the despondency among the immigrants. This is the way to break the self-strengthening negative spiral of prejudice and failure.

IBO (-interim)

We also have to invest in training and in skill development. In Flanders job-seekers can follow training on the shop floor which is highly subsidised, by activating the unemployment benefit. It is called an IBO (individuele beroepsopleiding). After the training period of up to six months the job-seeker is given a permanent contract by the employer. In 2005 14,000 job-seekers started such an IBO. A first evaluation showed that immigrants were underrepresented in the IBO system. On the other hand we know that a lot of immigrants get a (temporary) job via employment agencies, but this does not always lead to durable employment. The IBOs proved to be successful on this point. With the instrument of 'IBO-interim' I try to combine the strong points of both systems. A job-seeker gets a temporary contract with an employment agency, followed by an IBO (maximum six months) and then followed by a permanent contract from the employer where the IBO was undertaken. This instrument is reserved for the unprivileged groups among the unemployed (immigrants, persons with a handicap and older job-seekers). The goal is to integrate immigrant job-seekers into the labour market and to invest in skills. A convention between the government and Federgon (organisation which represent the employment agencies) formalises their commitment.

2.3 CONCLUSION

One cannot deny that the Flemish, Brussels and Walloon labour markets need thorough reform to answer the challenges we are facing. It is obvious that Flanders is merely in the early stages of such a thorough reform process and that an increasing number of people need to become convinced that this thorough approach is necessary.

I developed some hypotheses to explain the rather modest pace of reform in the Flemish labour market, pointing to the current Belgian institutional context and vicious circles of wrong-headed regulation, hard economic and social mechanisms and false beliefs.

In order to break these vicious circles, innovating measures should not only target regulation, but also those false beliefs. The objective then is to convince people and to contribute to an overall switch in the mindset thanks to 'success experience'. Many people applaud change. For those who applaud progress everything new is good. Others fear change. They only see a series of certainties becoming more uncertain. This is in fact a normal response but it should not have a numbing effect. By focusing on success experiences, we want to overcome this fear of reform. Simultaneously, these experiences of success should illustrate that vicious circles *can* be broken, and that deeply rooted beliefs can be false indeed.

NOTE

1. On the need for institutional reform, see Vandenbroucke (2007).

REFERENCES

Eurostat LFS, *European Union Labour Force Survey* (EU LFS), Luxembourg, http://epp.euro stat.ec.europa.eu/.

HRW (2006), *Verslag 2006*, Brussel: Hoge Raad voor de Werkgelegenheid (HRW), pp. 84–5.

OECD (2004), *Employment Outlook 2004*, Paris: OECD.

OECD 2005, *Employment Outlook 2005*, Paris: OECD.

Vandenbroucke, F. (2007), 'Hoog niveau of eerlijke verdeling?', in *Naar een nieuwe sociale investeringsagenda. De toekomst van de Nederlandse verzorgingsstaat* ('A high level of fair distribution', in Toward a new social investment agenda. The future of the Dutch welfare state), Den Haag: SER, WRR, pp. 19–69.

3. How Willing are Europeans to Migrate? A Comparison of Migration Intentions in Western and Eastern Europe

Didier Fouarge and Peter Ester

3.1 INTRODUCTION[1]

The issue of geographic and labour market mobility has taken a prominent position on the EU policy agenda with the accession of new Member States to the European Union. The year 2006 was officially chosen as the 'European Year of Workers' Mobility' by the European Commission. This reflects the policy saliency of the mobility issue in Europe. At present, however, the stock of nationals from the new Member States living in an EU15 Member State is rather limited. In EU15, 7.6 per cent of the working age population is non-national: the large majority is from outside the EU (5.1 per cent), followed by nationals from other EU15 countries (2.1 per cent). Only 0.4 per cent is from one of the new Member States, relatively larger shares are observed in Ireland (2 per cent), Austria (1.4 per cent) and Germany (0.7 per cent).[2] The fear, however, is that the free movement of workers in Europe could lead to a large and uncontrolled migration flow from East to West, that is from the new Member States to the old Member States. Although the true dimension of migration is difficult to assess empirically, a number of studies attempted at doing so. An econometric study by Boeri and Brücker (2001) estimates that the stock of immigrants from the new Member States in the old Member countries might increase from less than 1 million in 1998 to some 3 to 4.5 million persons in 2030 (see also European Commission, 2001). Layard et al. (1994) expect some 3 million people from the new Member States to migrate to the EU15 in 15 years' time. A Dutch study by De Mooij (2000) estimates a migration potential of 3 to 4 million persons following the EU enlargement. Zimmerman (1995) even refers to higher estimates ranging from 5 to 50 million migrants from Eastern Europe within 10 to 15 years. Recent research based on micro data also suggests that the accession of the new EU member countries has boosted mobility intentions in those countries

(Vandenbrande et al., 2006).[3] Several other studies based on the analysis of migration intentions data also suggest that the readiness to move to another country is high in some of the new Member States (Krieger, 2004; Liebig and Sousa-Poza, 2004). See also Fassmann and Münz (2002) for an extensive overview of macro and micro econometric studies devoted to the estimation of migration flows from East to West.

There are at least two ways in which the issue of migration is linked to the theme of transitional labour markets. In the first place, globalisation of economic relations and knowledge society contribute to new dynamics on markets. Globalisation contributes to an increased mobility of labour and capital. At the same time, the rising knowledge economy is conducive to changes in the demand for labour. The demand for high-skilled labour increases while the demand for low-skilled labour decreases. This results in migratory movements of high-skilled labour to markets where the demand is relatively high. Such migratory movements induce new types of social risks (social security rights for example). In the second place, the concept of transitional labour markets refers to some idea of efficient allocation of labour within the life course of people, but also at the macro level. The underlying idea in the literature is that there are potential gains to both geographic and job mobility. Firstly, such gains are derived from the relocation of labour from regions with a surplus of workers to regions with labour shortages. Secondly, such gains result from a more efficient allocation of labour to activities and regions where they are more productive.

In this chapter we report on the migration intentions of Europeans and investigate the main correlates of such intentions.[4] This study investigates four main issues:

1. mobility intentions of people in the new and old Members States;
2. the micro and macro determinants of intended cross-border mobility;
3. the impact of past experience with mobility – and the motive thereof – on future intended cross-border mobility; and
4. the main barriers and triggers to cross-border mobility within Europe.

Because we study migration intentions, our contribution has its limits. We do not claim to forecast actual migratory movements: the study of intentions is indeed sensitive to phrasing and timing of the survey. However, because intentions are good predictors of behaviour (see Section 3.3), with these analyses, we contribute to the knowledge on cost–benefit analysis people perform when deciding whether or not to migrate. We do this using the 2005 Eurobarometer Mobility Survey (EB64.1). At the time of writing, this is the most recent Europe-wide survey on mobility intentions, including samples from all – both old and new – Member States of Europe.[5]

The structure of the chapter is as follows. Section 3.2 summarises previous research on micro- and macro-determinants of migration decisions and outlines our main expectations and hypotheses. Section 3.3 describes the data collected in the Eurobarometer Mobility Survey in some detail. Section 3.4 presents descriptive results on migration intentions in European countries. We focus explicitly on differences in migration intentions between old and new Member States. Finally, Section 3.5 summarises the major findings and sketches consequences for the current migration policy debate in Europe.

3.2 THE DECISION TO MIGRATE

According to the socio-economic literature on migration, the decision whether or not to migrate crucially depends on the individual's comparison of the costs of migrating to the benefits of it. If the expected benefits are larger than the expected costs, then the individual is likely to migrate. Generally speaking, the cost–benefit analysis depends on socio-economic characteristics (such as the labour market status, the level of human capital), demographic characteristics (such as the household composition), social and cultural characteristics (such as social ties or language), general views and perceptions on migration and its effects, the distance of the move, and specific institutional features such as portability of social security rights or other institutional barriers to migration.

The available migration literature specifies several factors that are likely to affect the decision to move. These factors can be classified into micro (individual level) and macro (aggregate) determinants of migration. These determinants include economic, social and cultural features that are likely to affect the decision to migrate. In so doing, we adopt an interdisciplinary approach to the costs–benefit analysis of migration.

Micro Level Correlates of Migration

Obviously, economic self-improvement ranks among the most influential individual-level determinants of the migration choice. Pull factors include the immediate employment and wage opportunities in the host country (Harris and Todaro, 1970). But maybe even more important are the *expected* wage and employment prospects as stated in Sjaastad's human capital theory of migration (Sjaastad, 1962). This means that the migration decision is driven by the perceived earnings growth in the host country (Chiswick, 1978). Economic pull factors also involve social security benefits in the host country (so-called 'welfare magnets': Borjas, 1999). Furthermore, the housing market in the receiving country is a decisive migration factor as well, particularly, of course, greater availability of houses and space at lower prices. Vice versa, lacking availability of affordable housing in the home country can then be seen as a major push factor (OECD, 2005).

Migration decisions are often related to demographic events as well, such as separation from one's partner. Additionally, the migration literature clearly points at the fact that migration is not just an individual decision but also and often primarily a household choice. In economic terms: a household will only migrate when utility gains of some of the household members exceed the utility loss of other household members (Mincer, 1978). Furthermore, authors have also pointed out that migration can be seen as risk-sharing behaviour (Stark, 1991). In this context, the household – rather than the individual alone – is making the migration decision in order to maximise household income and to minimise the labour markets risks for the household.

The presence and accessibility of social networks in the destination country is of crucial importance too (Massey et al., 1993, 1994; Zavodny, 1997; Hatton and Williamson, 2002). In fact, social ties have indeed a significant negative effect on the geographic mobility (Belot and Ederdeen, 2006; Belot and Ermisch, 2006). Such social networks ensure the transferability of social capital to incoming migrants and yield a better circulation of necessary information, which will foster mobility (Massey et al., 1994). Such network effects can result in either positive or negative externalities (Massey et al., 1993). Positive externalities imply that the utility of the migrant will be larger in the host country when social networks of peers are well developed and maintained. Negative externalities imply that the concentration of non-nationals has negative effects on the utility of nationals (due, for example, to increased competition). However, existing social networks in the country of origin are likely to contribute to the perceived cost of mobility. As Belot and Ermisch (2006) demonstrate, people with a tighter social network are less likely to move to another place of residence.

A further interesting finding is that future mobility is also affected by past mobility: movers tend to stay movers (Liebig and Sousa-Poza, 2004; Vandenbrande et al., 2006). Past mobility is likely to reduce the total cost of future mobility because it lowers the psychological cost of mobility as well as its actual cost due to the availability of better information. An interesting hypothesis to be tested is whether or not it matters for which reason (labour-related or socio-demographic reason) people moved in the past.

Migration and Macro Level Characteristics

At the macro level the migration literature suggests a number of socio-economic determinants of the decision to migrate. At the most general level these determinants include the current labour market situation in the home country: lack of employment opportunities or too low earnings in the home country act as incentives for migration. Moreover, the GDP level – more specifically: a low level of wealth in the country of residence – is also a migration stimulus. But it has to be added that the functional form for the effect of GDP on migration is not straightforward. As discussed by Pedersen et al. (2004), the relationship is not necessarily linear, but could also be in the form of an inverted U-shape. At low levels of wealth, out-migration is limited because people lack financial possibilities to finance their migration. As income rises, migration increases, but at high levels of wealth out-migration is less probable due to lack of pressing economic incentives to migrate (Hatton and Williamson, 2002). Pedersen et al. (2004), however, were not able to empirically verify this inverted-U relationship.

Furthermore, the taxation regime (for example excessive taxation, fiscal burden) may operate as an incentive to migrate. This will be especially true for the highly skilled who seek to maximise their net gains by moving to regions with lower taxation (Borjas, 1987), but also for welfare recipients who are expected to migrate as a response to differences in levels of welfare benefits (Borjas, 1999). Regional differences in returns to skills – for example reflected by a higher level of income inequality – have also been pointed at as an incentive to migrate for the high educated (Borjas 1987; Chiquiar and Hansen, 2002).

Despite economic incentives to migration, the literature also points to non-economic macro determinants. Differences in culture and language, for example, have been shown to be important determinants of the costs of migration (Belot and Ederveen, 2006). Other determinants such as natural disasters, war and political insecurity are important too, but remain beyond the scope of this research.

Expectations

To summarise, we expect migration intentions among European citizens to be higher if:

1. the expected returns are high (higher educated);
2. the pay-back period for costs is long (youth);
3. the household structure is such that it induces low costs (no children, single);
4. one has experience with mobility in the past;
5. one sees no language or cultural barriers;
6. one does not expect negative effects for social ties;
7. economic prospects in the home country are bad;

8. for the higher educated: when inequality in the home country is low.

3.3 DATA: THE 2005 EUROBAROMETER MOBILITY SURVEY

The data used for this study are from a special module of the Eurobarometer: the Eurobarometer Mobility Survey (EB 64.1).[6] The data collection – which was financed by the European Commission – was carried out in the 25 countries that were Member of the EU in September 2005. The countries surveyed are Austria, Belgium, Cyprus, Czech Republic, Denmark, Estonia, Finland, France, Germany, Greece, Hungary, Ireland, Italy, Latvia, Lithuania, Luxembourg, Malta, the Netherlands, Poland, Portugal, Slovakia, Slovenia, Spain, Sweden and the United Kingdom. Bulgaria and Romania that entered the EU in 2007 were not surveyed and are not considered in this research. The Mobility Survey is the most recent and the most comprehensive survey on past mobility behaviour and mobility intentions among EU countries. It is of particular interest since it gathers data on both old and new Member States.

The dataset includes some 24,500 respondents aged 15 years and over.[7] The basic sample design applied in all states is a multi-stage, random (probability) one. In each country, a number of sampling points was drawn with probability proportional to population size (for a total coverage of the country) and to population density. Use was made of face-to-face interviews and in the appropriate national language. As far as the data capture is concerned, Computer Assisted Personal Interview (CAPI) was used in those countries where this technique was available.

About 1,000 respondents were interviewed in each country. In Luxembourg and Malta only 500 people were interviewed. The samples for West and East Germany were merged so that we have some 1,500 cases in Germany. The samples for Great Britain and Northern Ireland were also merged, resulting in some 1,300 cases for the UK. When weighted, the data are representative for the national population. The analyses presented in this chaapter pertain to the population aged 18 to 64. The survey includes relevant background information of the respondent (gender, age, educational level), his or her household (marital status, children), his or her labour market status (whether working or unemployed, occupational status) and labour market experience (age at first job, number of jobs in the past). In view of the small sample size it is important to test the significance of bivariate findings. Alternatively, multivariate analysis has added value because it tests for significance while at the same time controlling for the effects of other variables. We apply both descriptive (Section 3.4) and multivariate (Section 3.5) analysis methods.

The main themes of the Eurobarometer Mobility Survey relate to geographical and labour market mobility in Europe. Of particular interest to us is the information on geographical mobility. This includes short and long distance mobility in the past and the motives for mobility. The survey also contains questions on mobility intentions (within and between countries), and encouraging and discouraging factors to move within and outside of the EU. These questions stand central in this research where we focus on people's intentions to migrate in the future. The question on intended geographical mobility was phrased as follows:

'Do you think that in the next five years you are likely to move:
1. in the same city/town/village;
2. to another city/town/village but in the same region;
3. to another region but in the same country;
4. to another country in the European Union;
5. to another country outside the European Union;
6. you don't think you will move.'

More than one answer could be given to the question. The total number of respondents (aged 18–64) that expressed their mobility intention amounts to 17,493 persons. In this chapter, we make no distinctions between people reporting the expectation to move 'to another country in the European Union' or 'to another country outside the European Union'. Only a very limited number of people who express an intention to migrate outside the EU have no intention to move within the EU. For ease of exposition, we then interpret all migration intentions as intentions to move within the EU. The main disadvantage of this special mobility module, however, is that it neither carries information concerning the location or country people intend to move to, nor on the intended duration of the stay in the destination country.

But how reliable are migration intentions data? The decision to move is a complex, multi-faceted choice. Merely measuring the intention to move as a sole indicator of the act to move ignores the complexity of the whole decision process. Following Fishbein and Ajzen's (1975) theory of reasoned action, we can state that the intention to move is a function of the attitude towards moving and existing subjective norms toward moving; the attitude towards moving is a function of beliefs about the (positive and negative) consequences of moving and the evaluations of these consequences; the subjective norm towards moving is a function of the normative (positive and negative) beliefs about moving and one's motivation to comply with those beliefs. But between the intention to move and the actual move may be a world of intervening factors: individual skills, alternative behaviours available, situational constraints, institutional barriers and so on. Nevertheless, as Manski (1990) shows, the intentions do, under certain circumstances, have a predictive value for future behaviour. The use of intention data in labour market and migration studies is well-established.[8] And empirical studies support the idea that the actual probability of moving to another place is indeed significantly larger for people who express the desire to move than for people who do not (see for example Böheim and Taylor, 2002; Gordon and Molho, 1995). From a policy perspective, understanding migration intentions is important too: future migration flows are currently probably the hottest topic on the EU policy agenda, both at the level of the EU and of the individual Member States.

3.4 MIGRATION INTENTIONS IN EUROPE

Mapping of Migration Intentions in Europe

As explained above, we consider that people who expect to move 'to another country in the European Union' or 'to another country outside the European Union' within the next five years are reporting a migration intention. Overall, 5.4 per cent of Europeans of working age is reporting such a migration intention. However, the differences across countries are large, as illustrated in Figure 3.1.

In particular citizens of Germany, Austria, Spain, Italy, the Czech Republic and Hungary express a low level of migration intentions. On the contrary, a large share of the population in Denmark, Ireland, the Baltic States and Poland expresses an intention to migrate to another country. Unfortunately, it is not possible at the time of writing to compare these migration intentions to actual migration figures.

The difference in mobility intentions in the Baltic States and Poland compared to the other new Member States is striking. But can we take these intentions on their face values? Based on previous waves of the Eurobarometer, Krieger (2004) has suggested that the percentage of people with a 'firm' intention to migrate is a third of the percentage of people expressing a general inclination to migrate.[9] With mobility intentions of 13 per cent in Lithuania and close to 10 per cent in Poland, Estonia and Latvia, this would mean that between 2.4 and 4.2 per cent of the residents of these countries have a 'firm' intention to migrate. Such intentions are significantly lower in the other new Member States. Whether or not migration intentions are realistic can also be assessed from econometric studies. Using advanced econometric methods and applying migration streams at the time of the EU accession of Greece, Spain and Portugal to a number of accessing and candidate countries, Bauer and Zimmermann (1999) report expected long-term migration ranging from 0.2 per cent for Slovenia, 6 per cent for Poland, up to almost 28 per cent for Romania in the case of free migration. The authors, however, suggest taking such simulations with caution and they hold to the overall conclusion that 'it is reasonable to expect long-run emigration rates from the East to the West of between 2–3 per cent of the population in the sending region' (Bauer and Zimmermann, 1999, p. 46).

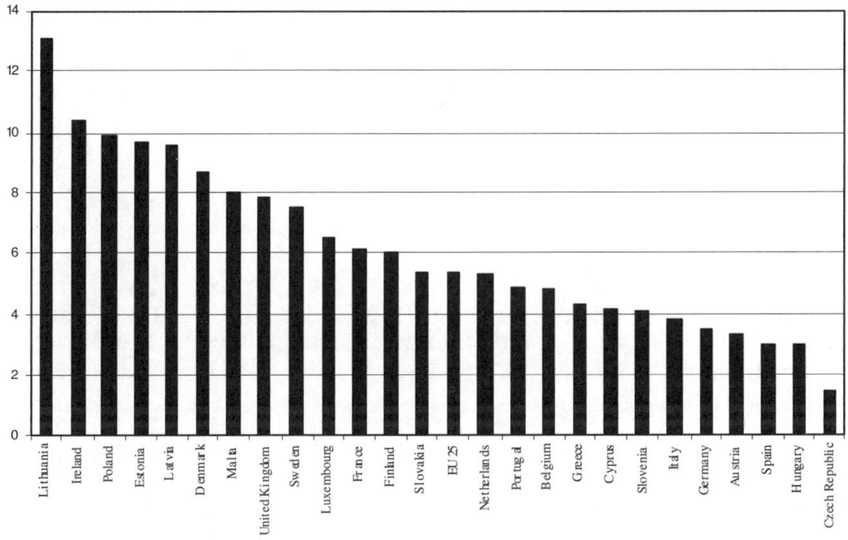

Figure 3.1 Migration intentions of Europeans (2005), percentage of people intending to move to another country within or outside the EU

Migration Intentions and Human Capital

In Table 3.1, we present a breakdown of mobility intentions by gender, age, educational level, employment status and household type. Mobility intentions for EU25 are reported as well for the old Member States and the new Member States. The new Member States are separated in two groups (see Figure 3.1): those with a low overall level of mobility intentions (Cyprus, Czech Republic, Hungary, Malta, Slovakia and Slovenia) and those with a high level of mobility intentions (Poland and the Baltic States). The table reports the percentage of people with a migration intention for each subgroup as well as the relative migration risk. The relative migration risk (rmr) is the ratio of the migration intention in a subgroup and the migration intention in the total. For example, for females in the old Member States the rmr equals 4.0/5.0 = 0.79, which says that their level of migration intentions is about 80 per cent of that in the total population. This makes the comparison of subgroup differences in migration intentions across columns more visible.

Table 3.1 Migration intentions by gender, educational level, age, employment status, and household type; percentage of people with a migration intention (%) and relative migration risk (rmr)

	EU25	Old Member States		New Member States Low intentions[a]		New Member States High intentions[b]	
	%	%	rmr[c]	%	rmr[c]	%	rmr[c]
Total	5.4	5.0	1	3.0	1	10.1	1
Gender							
Male	6.5	6.1	1.21	3.9	1.28	11.4	1.13
Female	4.4	4.0	0.79	2.2	0.73	9.0	0.88
Educational level							
Low or no	2.1	2.1	0.42	1.5	0.48	2.5	0.25
Average	4.0	3.9	0.77	2.1	0.71	6.1	0.60
High	6.6	6.1	1.21	4.4	1.45	12.3	1.22
Still studying	16.7	14.7	2.92	9.6	3.17	29.6	2.92
Age							
18–24	12.6	11.6	2.31	7.6	2.52	21.5	2.12
25–34	8.3	7.3	1.45	4.7	1.57	18.9	1.87
35–44	3.6	3.2	0.65	1.8	0.61	7.9	0.77
45–54	2.8	3.1	0.61	0.7	0.22	2.4	0.24
55–64	2.4	2.5	0.51	1.5	0.49	1.6	0.15
Employment status							
Working	4.8	4.8	0.95	1.8	0.60	7.6	0.75
Unemployed	7.8	7.1	1.40	8.2	2.72	10.4	1.03
Retired	2.0	1.9	0.38	1.0	0.32	2.9	0.28
Housewife/man	1.9	1.2	0.24	3.2	1.06	12.3	1.22
Still studying	16.7	14.7	2.92	9.6	3.17	29.6	2.92
Household type							
Couple (no child)	4.4	4.0	0.79	1.7	0.56	9.2	0.90
Couple (with child)	3.0	2.7	0.54	1.8	0.59	6.1	0.60
Single	11.4	10.8	2.15	8.3	2.76	20.6	2.03
Single parent	7.2	5.9	1.18	7.7	2.56	16.5	1.63
Divorced/separated	4.5	4.2	0.84	1.5	0.50	9.2	0.90
Widowed	4.7	4.8	0.95	0.4	0.13	7.1	0.70

Notes:

a. Cyprus, Czech Republic, Hungary, Malta, Slovakia, Slovenia.

b. Lithuania, Poland, Estonia and Latvia.

c. rmr = migration intentions in subgroups divided by migration intentions in total.

According to the literature, human capital is likely to play an important role in explaining migration (Sjaastad, 1962; OECD, 2001). The standard prediction from migration theory (see Massey et al., 1993) that the typical migrant is a young, higher educated and single male, is confirmed by the EB data. Of all European men, 6.5 per cent report an intention to move across borders compared to 4.4 per cent European women. The higher educated (6.6 per cent) and especially students (almost 17 per cent) indicate higher between-country migration proneness.[10] The high absolute level of migration intentions among students in the Baltic States and Poland (almost 30 per cent) could reflect the enhanced awareness and sensitivity of this specific group for the need to 'go international', combined with the effort of the European Union to promote cross-border mobility of students, for example through the Erasmus and Socrates programmes (Vandenbrande et al., 2006, Chapter 2). Mobility intentions of the higher educated in new Member States are also relatively higher compared to the old Member States, while migration intentions of the low educated are relatively lower. Students and the high educated from the new Member States seem to realise very well that in order to further advance their education and career opportunities Going West is a promising option.

Singles, and to a lesser extent single parents, also express the intention to migrate to another country more often than average. The readiness to migrate is especially observable among the youngest cohort of Europeans. It is not clear from these cross-sectional data – though obviously very important – whether this reflects an age or cohort (or even period) effect. Stronger intentions to cross-border migration are also observed for unemployed. A possible explanation is that for the employed, the need to migrate is relatively lower, for they already have a secured economic situation. However, this does not necessarily imply that more unemployed than employed people will actually migrate in the (near) future: the employed people – although they less often express an intention to migrate – have more chances to actually migrate, simply because they hold a job (migration is selective). Moreover, the employed is a larger group.

Although migration intentions are at a different level in new and old Member States, broadly speaking the relative differences across subgroups are more or less similar. Students in the new Member States with a low average level of migration intentions, however, do display a higher relative propensity to mobility, and so do the unemployed. In the new Member States with a high average level of migration intentions, the male–female differential in migration intentions is particularly low.

To summarise, migration intentions are most pronounced among (young) Europeans with relatively more human capital and less household responsibilities (partner, children). The intention to migrate to another country is not an exclusive feature of socially or economically deprived Europeans, on the contrary: one needs the right human resources, the right age and life course stage, and the right mind-set to seriously consider such a far-reaching step as migrating to another country.

Migration Intentions and the Economic Context

According to the literature discussed, migration is expected to be driven – at least partly – by the general macro-economic context. Poor economic opportunities and prospects could serve as direct or indirect incentives to migrate. But exactly how macro-economic features shape and reinforce the decision to move, and how the causal links between the two operate, is still not very well understood and is open to multiple interpretations. To further elaborate and illustrate the relationships between macro-economic conditions and migration readiness, correlations are presented between migration intentions and GDP per head, GDP growth rate and the rate of long-term unemployment for all 25 countries in the survey. Findings presented in Figure 3.2 show a clear U-shaped relationship between migration intentions and GDP: the inclination to migrate to another country is highest at both relatively low and relatively high GDP levels.

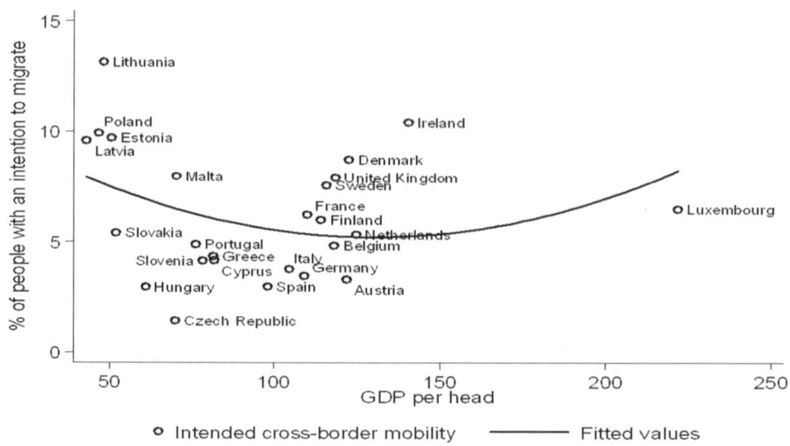

Figure 3.2 Relationship between intentions to migrate and GDP per head (EU25 = 100)

A similar relationship is found with the GDP growth rate as denoted in Figure 3.3. This result contrasts with Hatton and Williamson (2002) who expect an inverted-U relationship. However, our finding matches with the outcome obtained by Pedersen et al. (2004). No clear relationship, however, is found with respect to the rate of long-term unemployment as shown in Figure 3.4. The unemployment level is not a direct correlate of migration proneness. It can be concluded that the relationship between macro-economic conditions and migration intention is not linear: both very disadvantageous and very advantageous wealth levels function as stimuli – albeit for very different reasons – for migration readiness.

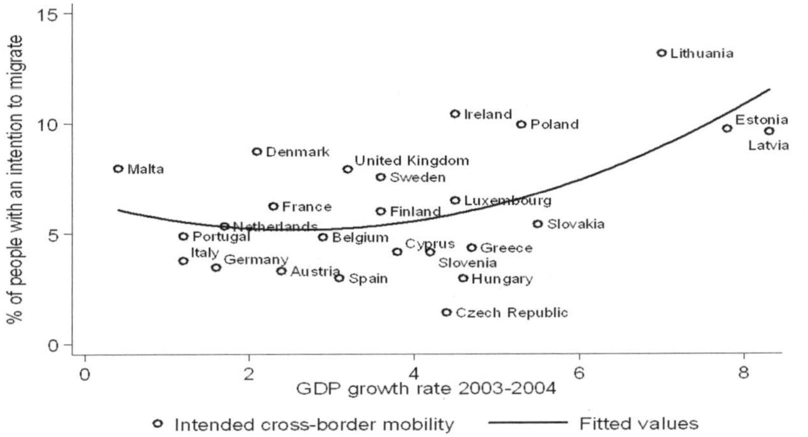

Figure 3.3 Relationship between intentions to migrate and GDP growth rate

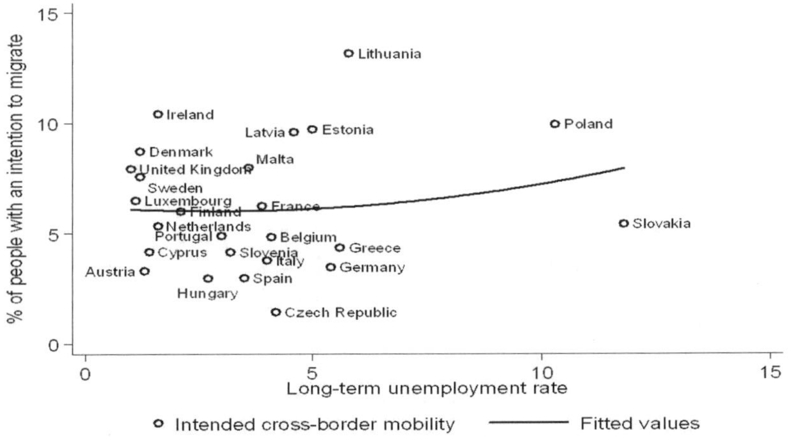

Figure 3.4 Relationship between intentions to migrate and long-term unemployment rate

As outlined in Section 3.2, migration theory has come up with quite clear hypotheses with respect to the effect of income inequality on migration as forwarded by in particular Borjas (1987, 1994), including negative self-selection (more income inequality in home country than in host country), and positive self-selection (more income inequality in host country than in home country). However, we are not able to confirm these predictions with the data at hand.

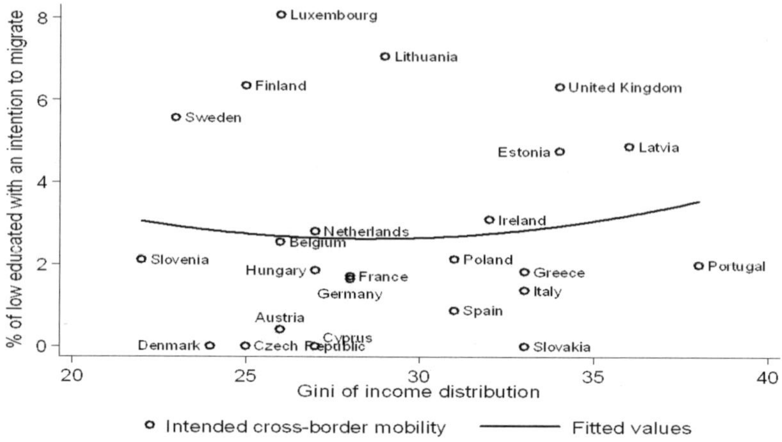

Figure 3.5 Relationship between intentions to migrate and income inequality, low educated

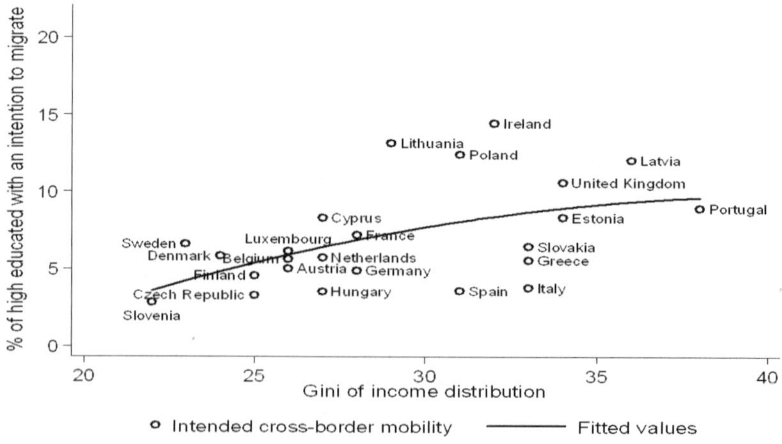

Figure 3.6 Relationship between intentions to migrate and income inequality, highly educated

Migration intentions of the lower educated do not seem to be responsive to income inequality as indicated by the findings presented in Figure 3.5.[11] For the higher educated the relationship is positive, as shown in Figure 3.6, with lower mobility intentions at low levels of income inequality and higher intentions as inequality increases.

In short: neither the negative selection hypothesis nor the positive selection hypothesis could be confirmed. We need to stress, though, that these results do not signify a 'hard' test of the Borjas hypotheses. Such a test would require to controlling for differences in relative inequality between the home and the host country. As indicated in Section 3.1, information about the host country is, unfortunately, not included in the Eurobarometer Mobility Survey.

3.5 DETERMINANTS OF MIGRATION INTENTIONS

In order to gain insight into the determinants of migration intentions, we applied multivariate analysis techniques. We estimate a logit model where the dependent variable takes the value 1 if the respondent expresses an intention to migrate to another country within the next five years, and the value 0 when the respondent has no moving intention at all.[12] Because of page limits constraints, we present highlights from the results in this section and refer the reader to Fouarge and Ester (2007) for the full results and a detailed discussion of them. Several models were estimated. The first model was estimated on all 25 EU countries. In the second, we replaced the country dummies with macro-economic characteristics of the country respondents live in. Finally, the model was estimated for respondents in the old and new Member States separately. The models include measures of:

1. human capital (a dummy variable for females, the educational level, age);
2. current employment status;
3. household structure;
4. housing tenure status;
5. country dummies (or alternatively macro characteristics of the country of residence);
6. overall view on cross-border mobility (cultural component of migration);[13]
7. past experience with geographical mobility;[14]
8. nationality;
9. perceived socio-economic and socio-cultural effects of cross-border mobility.[15]

The key findings from the analyses are reported in Table 3.2. We begin by discussing the results for the EU25 countries.

Correlates of Migration in EU25 Countries

The models do confirm the bivariate findings from the previous section: there are strong age effects on migration intentions and the educational level is a very robust determinant too. Young people are much more likely to migrate than older people, and so are the higher educated and students compared to people with an average or low educational level. This confirms our expectations 1 and 2 as outlined in Section 3.2. This is an important finding for it shows that young people are a very mobile cohort. They seem well aware of the fact that moving abroad may contribute to increasing their level of human capital. It is likely that EU policies aiming at encouraging the mobility of the higher skilled and of students are contributing to the high level of mobility intentions among these groups. Interestingly, the migration intentions of the low educated in the new Member States are significantly lower than average. This finding suggests that the fear of high migration streams of low-skilled from East to West is probably unwarranted.

The model also reveals some important life course effects. As expected, the presence of children in a household reduces the likelihood of mobility. This is probably because there are additional costs (financial and psycho-social) to migrating for parents of (young) children. Single people, however, are more prone to migrate, which confirms one of our expectations. For singles, family bounds are weaker, making it psychologically and socially more easy to migrate in order to meet new opportunities. These findings are in support of expectation 3.

Other things held equal, homeowners have significantly lower migration intentions, albeit not in new Member States with an overall low level of migration intentions. This is probably due to the fact that home ownership contributes to increasing the costs of migration. All in all, people with a positive attitude towards migration issues tend to be more prone to develop migration intentions for themselves. An explanation could be that they are more open to and perhaps also ready for new challenges and new experiences in a different country.

The model includes additional variables pertaining to long distance mobility in the past and the expected effects of future migration. Past mobility turns out to be a strong predictor of future intended mobility. This confirms earlier findings according to which long distance mobility is not a phenomenon on its own, but part of other geographic transitions people make throughout their life (Vandenbrande et al., 2006). This conclusion is also illustrated by the effect of past labour market mobility on migration intentions: people who report more changes of employer in the past are more likely to report an intention to move abroad. This evidence suggests that past experiences reduce possible reservations (due to actual practice, better information) one might have to migrate (again) in the future. This confirms expectation 4.

Table 3.2 Highlights from logit model for migration intentions in Europe, sign of significant parameters from the model

	EU25	Old Member States	New Member States; low intentions	New Member States; high intentions
Female	–	–	0	–
High educated/students	+ / ++	+ / ++	+ / ++	+ / ++
Youth	+	+	0	+
Couple with children	–	–	0	–
Single	+	+	+	0
Homeowner	–	–	0	–
Experienced long distance mobility in past	+	+	+	+
Positive views on mobility	+	+	+	+
Fears for employment/income	0	0	0	0
Fears for social ties	–	–	–	0
Language as a barrier	–	–	0	0
GDP level in home country (non-linear)	– (U-shaped)	×	×	×
Inequality in home country	0 (also for high educated)	×	×	×

Notes:
–: significant negative effect
+: significant positive effect
0: no significant effect
×: variable not included

Comparing Countries in East and West

The country effects in the model reflect the overall findings in Section 3.4. Significantly lower propensities to migrate are found in southern Europe (Spain, Italy and Portugal), in Germanic countries (Germany and Austria) and in the Czech Republic. Significantly larger propensities are found for four of the ten new Member States (Latvia, Poland, Estonia and Lithuania). Replacing the country effects by macro-level variables allows us to test the effect of institutional variables on the propensity to migrate. The estimates clearly show a U-shaped relationship between GDP per head and migration intentions already depicted in Figure 3.2. This partly confirms expectation 7. Other macro-level variables have been included in the model: the level of income inequality, the rate of unemployment, the rate of long-term unemployment, the average tax rate on labour and the poverty risk rate (all measured in the home country). None of these variables have a significant effect on migration intentions. The predicted negative relationship between the level of inequality and the migration intentions of the high educated is found in the data, but is not significant. The share of social protection spending in GDP is, however, negatively correlated with migration intentions. This could mean that people see the welfare state as a kind of risk insurance that they are not ready to revoke by migrating to another country with lesser social protection.

The variables concerning the expected effects of future migration show interesting differences between respondents in the new and the old Member States. The results show that the expected loss of social contacts due to migration fundamentally inhibits the migration intentions of people in old Member States and in new Member States with low overall migration intentions (this confirms expectation 6).[16] However, such an effect is not found for respondents in the Baltics and Poland. This either means that people there value social networks less or that they do not fear the assumed loss of social networks following migration, maybe because they do not intend to migrate permanently. These two competing explanations need further research. The results also show that respondents in the old Member States do perceive sufficient knowledge of other languages as a major difficulty for migrating in the future, but no significant effect in the new Member States. Henceforth, expectation 5 is only confirmed in EU15. A possible explanation is that the willingness of the latter to invest in acquiring new language skills is simply greater because their perceived gains from cross-border migration are greater too. Explaining this difference is also in need of further empirical exploration.

3.6 CONCLUSION

One aspect of transitional labour markets pertains to the international mobility and allocation of labour. This issue has been raised in this chapter by analysing migration intentions in Europe and trying to understand what micro and macro factors trigger such intentions. In 2004 and again in 2007 the EU was enlarged by a total of 12 countries. These successive enlargements have fed the policy and societal debates in Europe on whether or not the borders should be opened to allow the free movement of workers and on the effect of free movement of labour on the economy. A question of interest from the point of view of transitional labour markets is whether or not massive migration of people will take place all over Europe, particularly from new Member States to old Member States.

In this study we focused on migration intentions of Europeans and investigated the main determinants of such intentions. We do reckon that such intentions cannot be taken on their face value as perfect predictors of real future migration flows. Yet, studying the factors shaping these intentions is a meaningful exercise. We use data from a module on mobility of the Eurobarometer Survey (EB 64.1). The data were gathered in September 2005 in all 25 countries that were member of the EU at that time. This survey is the most comprehensive and the most recent survey on mobility in Europe.

Despite the increasing pressure of globalisation and of the knowledge economy (both developments are promoting labour migration), our findings indicate that Europeans are not that willing to move to another country. Only 5.4 per cent of the working-age population intends to move to another country within the next five years. Percentage-wise, intentional cross-border migration is not and is not expected to become a widespread phenomenon in Europe in the near future. However, this average EU percentage masks a great diversity within Europe: mobility intentions are at a higher level in Poland and the Baltic States, at a lower level among the old Member States, and at an even lower level among other new Member States. However, given the large population size of some of the countries with a relatively high level of migration intentions (for example Poland), it is conceivable that large numbers will indeed cross the borders. As suggested by various studies large numbers are indeed entering the labour markets of Western Europe (Ecorys, 2006), and the EU membership of Eastern and central European seems to have triggered these streams (Corpeleijn, 2007).

However, as Fassmann and Münz (2002) observe, the extent of labour migration from the Eastern European countries in the future will depend on the demographic development in those countries. The authors note that fertility rates in the ten new Member States have been declining over the past decade, while mortality rates have been increasing. As a result of this shrink in the population size, the younger cohorts will benefit from better chances on the labour market, which in turn might reduce their readiness to migrate.[17] In addition, the projected positive economic and labour market development in comparison to the old Member States due to increased foreign direct investment and the sustained availability of regional and structural funds will improve working and living conditions with the consequence of reduced incentives for migration.

In particular the highly educated and highly qualified workers are more likely to cross the country borders within Europe, but also students. This finding is in line with the development of a knowledge economy, and it could mean there are potential brain drain risks for some regions in Europe. However, the extent of this brain drain risk will depend on whether or not migration has a permanent character. The evidence here suggests that migration in Europe is part of a human capital investment strategy. Young Europeans are more migration prone than older Europeans, that is those countries face a combined brain and youth drain. The issue is whether this reflects an age effect or a cohort effect. If the latter were to be the case, this would of course change future migration flows in Europe quite drastically. Systematic monitoring of inter- and intra-age-cohort migration trends is essential for answering this crucial topic.

Perceived labour market opportunities are decisive motives for migration but migration has a cost to individuals too, in terms of the potential loss of social ties, socio-cultural differences and language barriers. From our analyses, it appears that these costs have a strong negative effect on the migration decision of people in the old Member States of Europe but that they play a lesser role in new Member States. The reason for this difference in costs structure is left to further scrutiny: is it due to the fact that Eastern and Central Europeans more often see migration as an investment in their human capital, because they care less about such barriers to migration, or simply because they see migration as a temporary event?

NOTES

1. We acknowledge financial support from the European Foundation (project 0336 'Analysis of Eurobarometer on mobility'). Use of the Eurobarometer data was granted by the European Commission. This book chapter is based on the report 'Determinants of international regional migration intentions in Europe', a report that we wrote for the European Foundation (Fouarge and Ester, 2007).
2. All percentages are from European Commission (2006), p. 17.
3. Between 2002 and 2005 the increase in migration intentions of new Member States' inhabitants has been a factor 2.4 larger than the corresponding increase among residents of the 'old' Members States.
4. See also Liebig and Sousa-Poza (2004) for a similar approach.
5. First descriptive results of this Mobility Survey were reported by Vandenbrande et al. (2006) in a study commissioned by the European Foundation.
6. The study was conducted in close cooperation with the European Foundation (Karppinen et al., 2006; Krieger, 2006; Vandenbrande et al., 2006).
7. Data were collected by TNS Opinion & Social. The interviews were conducted between 02/09/2005 and 06/10/2005. The survey covers the national population of citizens of the respective nationalities and the population of citizens of all the EU Member States that were residents in those countries and have a sufficient command of one of the respective national language(s) to answer the questionnaire.

8. See for example: Tidrick (1971), Finifter (1976), Faini et al. (1997), Burda et al. (1998), Ahn et al. (1999), Chiquiar and Hanson (2002), Krieger (2004), Liebig and Sousa-Poza (2004) and Hadler (2006).
9. Krieger (2004) argues that those people with a 'firm' intention to migrate could be identified with an additional question on the readiness to live in a country where the official language is different from the mother tongue. Such information is not available in our data, and it is not likely that such a scaling factor should be the same for all countries.
10. In the Eurobarometer, the educational attainment is measured by the age at which one finished full-time education. For ease of exposition, we have recoded this measure into three levels: those who stopped before the age of 16 qualify as lower educated; those who stopped between the age of 16 and 19 are said to have an average educational level; people who left full time education at age 20 or above are higher educated.
11. See Liebig and Sousa-Poza (2004) for a similar finding.
12. This means that individuals with an intention to move within the country are discarded from the analyses. Including them in the reference category would wrongly assume that they have no moving intentions at all.
13. It is computed as the sum of the answers to the five questions on whether people think mobility is a good thing for individuals, their family, the economy, the labour market and for European integration. Answers were coded 0 if the respondent is indifferent, –1 if s/he thinks it is a bad thing and 1 if s/he thinks it is a good thing. It is assumed that it captures a general notion of 'culture' of migration.
14. It is measured in terms of the longest move ever made since one left the parental home.
15. Whether people expect a loss of social contacts, a loss of employment opportunities, language or cultural barriers, or worse housing or public facilities.
16. These are people who report that 'To miss the support from family or friends' or 'To miss the direct contact with family or friends' would discourage them from moving to another country.
17. The authors also expect these countries to become immigration countries for citizens from other Eastern European countries such as Ukraine and Romania.

REFERENCES

Ahn, N., De la Rica, S. and Ugidos, A. (1999), 'Willingness to move for work and unemployment duration in Spain', *Economica*, **66**, 335–57.

Bauer, T. and Zimmermann, K. (1999), *Assessment of possible migration pressure and its labour market impact following EU enlargement to central and eastern Europe*, IZA Research Report, No. 3.

Belot, M. and Ederveen, S. (2006), *Cultural and institutional barriers in migration between OECD countries*, CPB Document, Den Haag: CPB.

Belot, M. and Ermisch, J. (2006), *Friendship ties and geographical mobility: evidence from the BHPS*, IZA Discussion Paper, No. 2209.

Boeri, T. and Brücker, H. (2001), *Eastern enlargement and EU-labour-markets: perceptions, challenges and opportunities*, IZA Discussion Paper, No. 256.

Böheim, R. and Taylor, M. (2002), 'Tied down or room to move? Investigating the relationships between housing tenure, employment status and residential mobility in Britain', *Scottish Journal of Political Economy*, **49**, 369–92.

Borjas, G. (1987), 'Self-selection and the earnings of immigrants', *American Economic Review*, **77** (4), 531–53.

Borjas, G. (1994), 'The economics of immigration', *Journal of Economic Literature*, **32** (4), 1667–717.

Borjas, G. (1999), 'Immigration and welfare magnets', *Journal of Labor Economics*, **17** (4), 607–37.

Burda, M., Härdle, W., Müller, M. and Werwatz, A. (1998), 'Semiparametric analysis of German East–West migration intentions: facts and theory', *Journal of Applied Econometrics*, **13** (5), 525–42.

Chiquiar, D. and Hanson, G. (2002), *International migration, self-selection, and the distribution of wages: evidence from Mexico and the United States*, NBER Working Paper, No. 9242.

Chiswick, B. (1978), 'The effect of Americanization on the earnings of foreign-born men', *Journal of Political Economy*, **86** (5), 897–921.

Corpeleijn, A. (2007), 'Werknemers uit nieuwe EU-lidstaten', *Tijdschrift voor Arbeidsvraagstukken*, **23** (2), 177–82.

De Mooij, R. (2000), 'Internationalisering en Europese integratie', in CPB/SCP, *Trends, dilemma's en beleid: essays over ontwikkeling op langere termijn*, Den Haag: Centraal Planbureau.

Ecorys (2006), *Evaluatie werknemersverkeer MOE-landen*, Rotterdam: Ecorys.

European Commission (2001), *The Impact of Eastern Enlargement on Employment and Labour Markets in the EU and the Member States*, Brussels.

European Commission (2006), *Report on the Functioning of the Transitional Arrangements set out in the 2003 Accession Treaty (period 1 May 2004–30 April 2006)*, Brussels: COM 2006.

Fassmann, H. and Münz, R. (2002), 'EU enlargement and future east–west migration', in IOM (ed.), *New Challenges for Migration Policy in Central and Eastern Europe*, Geneva: International Organisation for Migration.

Faini, R., Galli, G., Gennari, P. and Rossi, F. (1997), 'An empirical puzzle: falling migration and growing unemployment differentials among Italian regions', *European Economic Review*, **41**, 571–79.

Finifter, A. (1976), 'American emigration', *Society*, **13**, 30–36.

Fishbein, M. and Ajzen, I. (1975), *Belief, Attitudes, Intention and Behavior. An Introduction to Theory and Research*, Reading, MA: Addison-Wesley Publishing Company.

Fouarge, D. and Ester, P. (2007), *Factors Determining International and Regional Migration in Europe*, Dublin: European Foundation for the Improvement of Living and Working Conditions.

Gordon, I. and Molho, I. (1995), 'Duration dependence in migration behaviour: cumulative inertia versus stochastic change', *Environment and Planning*, A 27, 1961–75.

Hadler, M. (2006), 'Intentions to migrate within the European Union: a challenge for simple economic macro-level explanations', *European Societies*, **8** (1), 111–40.

Harris, J. and Todaro, M. (1970), 'Migration, unemployment and development: a two-sector analysis', *American Economic Review*, **60** (5), 126–42.

Hatton, T. and Williamson, J. (2002), *What fundamentals drive world migration?*, NBER Working Paper No. 9159.

Karppinen, J., Fernandez, E. and Krieger, H. (2006), *Geographical mobility: challenges and opportunities*, paper presented at the conference to launch the European Year of Workers' Mobility 2006: 'Workers' mobility: a right, an option, an opportunity?', Brussels, 20–21 February.

Krieger, H. (2004), *Migration Trends in an Enlarged Europe*, Luxembourg: Office for Official Publications of the European Communities.

Krieger, H. (2006), *Long distance mobility within the EU: considering the Lisbon Agenda and Transitional Arrangements*, Discussion paper presented at a Foundation seminar with stakeholders of the Governing Board in Luxembourg, 8 March.

Layard, R., Blanchard, O., Dornbusch, R. and Krugman, P. (1994), *East–West Migration: The Alternatives*, Cambridge: MIT Press.
Liebig, T. and Sousa-Poza, A. (2004), 'Migration, self-selection and income inequality: an international analysis', *Kyklos*, **57**, 125–46.
Manski, C. (1990), 'The use of intentions data to predict behavior: a best-case analysis', *Journal of the American Statistical Association*, **85**, 934–40.
Massey, D., Arango, J., Hugo, G., Kouaouci, A., Pellegrino, A. and Taylor, J. (1993), 'Theories of international migration: a review and appraisal', *Population and Development Review*, **19** (3), 431–66.
Massey, D., Goldring, L. and Durand, J. (1994), 'Communities in transnational migration: an analysis of nineteen Mexican communities', *American Journal of Sociology*, **99** (6), 1492–533.
Mincer, J. (1978), 'Family migration decisions', *Journal of Political Economy*, **86**, 749–73.
OECD (2001), *International Mobility of Highly-skilled Workers*, Paris: OECD.
OECD (2005), *Employment Outlook*, Paris: OECD.
Pedersen, P., Pytlikova, M. and Smith, N. (2004), *Selection or network effects? Migration flows into 27 OECD countries, 1990–2000*, IZA Discussion Paper, No. 1104.
Sjaastad, L. (1962), 'The costs and returns of human migration', *Journal of Political Economy*, **70**, 8093.
Stark, O. (1991), *The Migration of Llabour*, Oxford: Blackwell.
Tidrick, K. (1971), 'Need for achievement, social class and intention to emigrate in Jamaican students', *Social and Economic Studies*, **20**, 52–60.
Vandenbrande, T., Coppin, L., Van der Hallen, P., Ester, P., Fouarge, D., Fasang, A., Geerdes, S. and Schömann, K. (2006), *Mobility in Europe*, Luxembourg: Office for Official Publications of the European Communities.
Zavodny, M. (1997), 'Welfare and the locational choices of new immigrants', *Economic Review – Federal Reserve Bank of Dallas*, 2nd Quarter.
Zimmerman, K. (1995), 'Tackling the European migration problem', *Journal of Economic Perspectives*, **9** (2), 45–62.

4. Labour Markets in Central and Eastern Europe: From Transition to Stabilisation

Sandrine Cazes and Alena Nesporova

4.1 INTRODUCTION

Economic and social reforms launched since the beginning of the 1990s in the former command economies of Central and Eastern Europe have been directed towards facilitating the adjustment of the enterprise sector to the challenges of international competition; this has brought about significant labour market deregulation. Previous strong legal protection of workers against termination of their employment has gradually been weakened while newly established or restructured labour market institutions have provided laid-off workers with income support during unemployment and assistance with re-employment, including access to programmes to improve their employment prospects if necessary. While initially income support was quite generous, accelerating unemployment as a result of the deep transition crisis forced policymakers to reduce it in the hope that this would contribute towards faster re-employment of jobseekers. However, unemployment remained high due to persistent sluggish labour demand as evidenced in Cazes and Nesporova (2003).

Economic pressures on enterprises on the one hand and the trend towards labour market deregulation on the other have led towards increasing mobility of workers between different labour market statuses, among which flows from one job to another, as well as to significant changes in the characteristics of employment, including for one thing a growing incidence of flexible forms of employment. Cazes and Nesporova (2003) demonstrated with the help of labour market flow data an important rise in – mostly involuntary – labour mobility connected with enterprise restructuring. Furthermore, they pointed to its fluctuation during the economic cycle as a result of depressed demand for labour but also due to workers' behaviour, which was different from that of workers in economically advanced countries and caused by the perceived job insecurity of the former. With regard to an increasing share of flexible forms of employment they found that in the 1990s these took the form of multiple-jobs or second jobs, both formal but, even more, informal, which existed alongside primary jobs, registered unemployment or formal inactivity.

The aim of this chapter is to investigate whether in the light of new economic and labour market developments since the end of the 1990s new trends have also emerged in labour mobility and its fluctuation in the course of the economic cycle as well as in flexible forms of employment. The chapter is structured as follows. Section 4.2 analyses labour market performance in Central and South Eastern Europe and concentrates for reasons of comparison on data on positive trends, persisting problems and new challenges in the new EU member and accession countries. Section 4.3 studies recent developments in flexible forms of employment. Section 4.4 investigates labour market flow data and their correlation with GDP and employment growth. Section 4.5 presents the conclusions.

4.2 RECENT LABOUR MARKET DEVELOPMENTS: POSITIVE TRENDS, PERSISTING PROBLEMS AND NEW CHALLENGES

From the economic point of view, the period of 2000–2004 was successful for Central and South-Eastern Europe (CSEE) as all the countries finally embarked on solid economic growth (see Table 4.1), after having overcome the negative consequences of the Russian financial crisis (Baltic countries), transient economic recession (Czech Republic and Poland) and the Kosovo crisis (Balkan countries). Nevertheless, until 2004 only the five most advanced economies (Czech Republic, Hungary, Poland, Slovakia and Slovenia) and Albania managed to exceed their 1989 GDP level, albeit in the new structure of GDP. Other countries had not yet reached their pre-transition levels although, with the exception of Macedonia, on the whole they recorded higher growth rates in the period under review, thus strengthening their catching up process. The first assessments of the effects of the EU accession of the first eight CSEE countries in May 2004 point to an overall positive impact on their economies as accelerating exports contributed additionally to their growth rates for 2004 and 2005.

Economic growth, however, has not been adequately translated into employment recovery. Only Bulgaria, Latvia, Croatia, Hungary, Estonia, Slovakia and Slovenia achieved a positive, although very modest, net employment growth. All other countries of the region still face contraction of their employment (see Table 4.1).

Table 4.1 GDP and employment trends in Central and South-Eastern Europe (average annual growth rates (in per cent) in 2000–2004)

Country	GDP	Employment
Bulgaria	4.9	+1.11
Croatia	4.1	+0.67
Czech Republic	3.1	–0.24
Estonia	7.2	+0.58
Hungary	3.9	+0.46
Latvia	7.5	+1.01
Lithuania	6.7	0.28
Poland	3.1	–1.14
Romania	5.3	–1.66
Slovakia	4.1	+0.35
Slovenia	3.4	+0.63
Albania	5.8	–2.65
Bosnia and Herzegovina	4.2	–1.00
Serbia and Montenegro	4.9	–0.92
FYR of Macedonia	1.3	–3.90

Source: UNECE database, own calculations.

Thus economic growth can still be characterised as nearly jobless for the region, despite huge employment losses in particular during the transition crisis in the early 1990s. This is especially worrying for countries like Poland, Albania, Bosnia and Herzegovina, Serbia and Montenegro and Macedonia, whose labour markets are very weak. As a result, on average, the countries of Central and South-Eastern Europe have significantly lower labour market participation rates, compared with the EU15, and the difference is more profound for male than for female workers.

Figure 4.1 confirms these findings for all the 10 new EU member countries plus Croatia[1] (EU10+1) but also points to important heterogeneity among these countries: while Bulgaria, Hungary, Latvia and Slovenia recorded increasing participation rates between 2000 and 2004, three of the four countries with the highest GDP growth rates – Lithuania, Estonia and Romania – actually experienced another reduction in their participation rates.

In comparison with the participation rates, the employment rates evolved more favourably over the period 2000–2004. Comparisons with the EU15 average reveal, however, that in 2004 only Slovenia found its rate slightly above the EU15 average while all other countries had lower employment rates, including the Czech Republic and Romania, which four years before had been above or close to the EU15 average. The breakdown of the employment rates by gender reveals that the main difference between the old and the new EU member and candidate countries is in the relatively low employment of men in the latter group. None of the EU10+1 countries reached the EU15 average for males in 2004 and in Bulgaria, for example, the gap was as much as 15 percentage points.

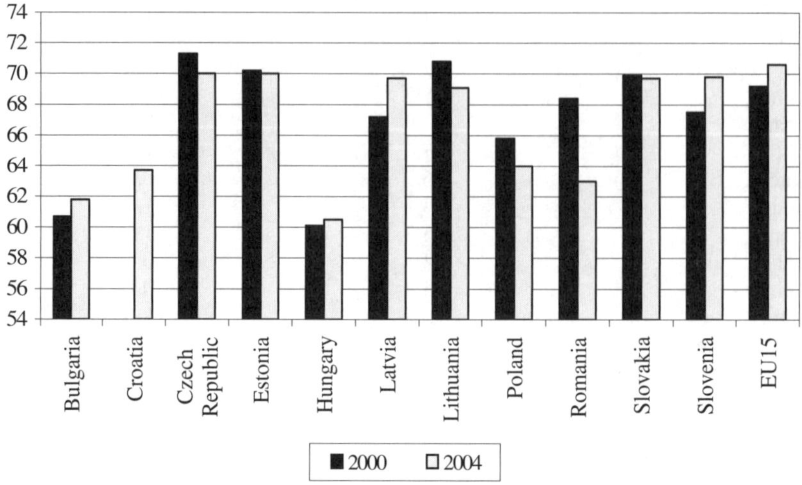

Source: Eurostat.

Figure 4.1 Labour market participation rates (population 15–64) of the EU10+1 countries

The majority of the countries in this region have recorded declining unemployment, in particular Bulgaria and the Baltic States (see Table 4.2). Nevertheless, there have been important differences across countries. In particular, Lithuania seems to be a special case. On the one hand, the steep decline in unemployment in this country was to some extent the result of a combination of continuous withdrawals from the labour market and rising employment (this issue is elaborated further later in this chapter). Part of this favourable decline in unemployment however can be attributed to people emigrating on quite a large scale after the country's accession to the EU in May 2004. Most of them were young people seeking better employment opportunities mainly in the UK and Ireland, as can be deduced from the sharply declining youth unemployment figures presented below. This also seems to be the case in Slovakia and Bulgaria as some anecdotal evidence confirms. In Latvia, Estonia, Slovenia and Bulgaria, decreasing unemployment rates are mainly connected with growing employment rates. The Czech Republic has seen both declining employment and unemployment rates due to a continuation of labour market withdrawals. In contrast, the sharp fall in employment in Romania was fully translated into the rapidly declining participation rate while relatively low unemployment only slightly increased. Changes in Hungary and Slovakia were positive but small for all the three labour market indicators. Labour market developments in Poland contrasted with the other countries in the region, with the exception of Romania. Despite healthy economic growth, employment significantly declined and led on the one hand to a rapid increase in unemployment, reaching the highest level among all these countries, and on the other hand to a further decline in the economic activity of the population. Since 2004, however, unemployment has also started rapidly declining in Poland, to a large extent also as a consequence of emigration mainly to the UK and Ireland, and the labour market situation has started improving.

Table 4.2 Aggregate (UR) and youth (YUR) unemployment rates, 2000 and 2004

	2000			2004		
	UR	YUR	YUR/UR	UR	YUR	YUR/UR
Bulgaria	16.4	33.7	2.05	11.9	24.4	2.05
Czech Republic	8.7	17.8	2.05	8.3	21.1	2.54
Estonia	12.5	23.6	1.89	9.2	21.0	2.28
Hungary	6.3	12.1	1.92	5.9	14.8	2.50
Latvia	13.7	21.4	1.56	9.8	19.0	1.94
Lithuania	16.4	30.6	1.87	10.8	19.9	1.84
Poland	16.4	36.3	2.21	18.8	39.5	2.1
Romania	6.8	17.2	2.53	7.1	21.4	3.01
Slovakia	18.7	37.1	1.98	18.0	32.3	1.79
Slovenia	6.6	16.2	2.45	6.0	14.3	2.38
EU15	7.6	15.3	2.01	8.1	16.6	2.05

Source: Eurostat, authors' calculations.

Even though total unemployment has on average fallen significantly in the EU10+1 region over the period under investigation, while slightly increasing in the EU15, it has remained well above the average of the 'old' Europe. Also the differences among countries are substantial as the Polish unemployment rate is more than three times higher than that of Hungary and Slovenia, and, what is most worrying, this particularly high unemployment rate is combined with low economic activity in Poland. In contrast, Slovenia seems to have the best labour market performance of the whole region, combining low and declining unemployment rates with relatively high and increasing participation and employment rates.

Youth unemployment rates were on average twice as high as the aggregate rates across Europe in 2000 (see again Table 4.2). However, countries with low aggregate unemployment rates like Romania and Slovenia had relatively higher youth unemployment rates (see the fourth column of Table 4.2) pointing to a disproportionately worse position of young people in these labour markets. Between 2000 and 2004 the ratio of youth to aggregate unemployment deteriorated in the majority of countries in the EU10+1 region providing evidence that improving labour demand benefited mainly the adult population at the expense of young people without work experience. Moreover, in contrast to the EU15 where youth unemployment was almost stable, the CEE countries recorded on average absolute reductions in youth unemployment but at the same time a relative deterioration of the labour market position of young people compared with adult workers. Comparisons of youth unemployment rates by sex show that in about half of these countries male rates are higher while in another half female rates are higher, climbing to 41.4 per cent in Poland.

Long-term unemployment (unemployment lasting longer than one year) remained very high in the EU10+1 region, well above the average of EU15. Moreover, unlike in the EU15, it further increased in six out of ten countries between 2000 and 2004 so that only Hungary and Latvia recorded a share of long-term unemployment in total unemployment below 50 per cent. The situation is particularly detrimental in Slovakia where two-thirds of all the jobless people and 11.7 per cent of the total labour force have been without employment for more than one year. Long-term unemployment thus represents a particular problem for the EU10+1 countries due to its very high proportion in total unemployment and its persistence which points to the fairly low attention being paid by labour market institutions to solving the labour market problems of less competitive job-seekers.

To sum up, despite the EU10+1 countries having finally embarked on sound economic growth, the majority of them have been unable to reverse the low and still declining labour market participation of their population. There is important heterogeneity among countries. Bulgaria, the Baltic States and Slovenia were the only countries to finally benefit from new job creation and to improve their employment performance while unemployment finally decreased. However, in some countries like Lithuania and Bulgaria, but also in Slovakia, some of the decline in unemployment should probably also be attributed to emigration, especially of young people, after the May 2004 enlargement of the EU. But the employment rates of all these countries still remain low compared with the EU15 average while the unemployment levels remain high for many of them. In other countries shrinking unemployment occurred as a consequence of the departure of less competitive job-seekers from the labour market. In contrast, Poland and Romania faced significant deterioration in the labour market situation in terms of economic activity, employment and unemployment. Poland and Slovakia are the two countries with the highest unemployment rates in the region. Youth unemployment and long-term unemployment remain very high for the region showing that less competitive people are seriously disadvantaged in the labour market and need intensive assistance from labour market institutions.

4.3 INCREASING FLEXIBILISATION OF EMPLOYMENT RELATIONS IN CENTRAL AND EASTERN EUROPE

The main finding of our analysis of the CEE labour market characteristics in the 1990s was a relatively low incidence of 'classical' flexible forms of employment such as part-time employment, fixed-term contracts or self-employment (this with the exception of Poland and Romania) in this region, compared with the old EU countries. Therefore it is interesting to check whether this characteristic changed in the period of economic boom after 1999.

As far as self-employment is concerned, in most countries the acceleration of economic growth led to a decline in the proportion of the self-employed in total employment (see Table 4.3). The only exceptions are the Czech Republic and Slovakia with rapidly growing self-employment and Estonia and Romania with slightly increasing shares of self-employment. In the case of Romania this was, however, combined with sharply falling employment, that is the absolute number of self-employed persons actually fell in Romania.

Table 4.3 Self-employment developments – shares in per cent of total employment by sex

	2000	2004		2000	2004
Bulgaria	11.4	10.4	Lithuania	20.0	18.4
Czech Republic	15.0	18.8	Poland	37.7	29.0
Estonia	9.0	9.6	Romania	46.2	46.8
Hungary	15.1	14.2	Slovakia	8.3	12.3
Latvia	14.9	13.3	Slovenia	18.0	16.7
EU15	14.9	14.9			

Notes:
Bulgaria: 2003 instead of 2004; Lithuania: 2002 instead of 2000; Poland: break in the series in 2003; Slovenia: 2001 instead of 2000.

Source: Eurostat.

There are major differences across the region in the percentages of self-employed persons in total employment ranging from 9.6 per cent in Estonia to 46.8 per cent in Romania. Many of these variations can be explained by a high proportion of farming in total employment and the fact that agriculture is mostly based on family farms in countries like Romania, Poland and Lithuania. With new job opportunities outside agriculture younger people are leaving small-scale farming and accepting wage employment, which contributes towards declining self-employment. This is not the case in Romania, however, where the deteriorating labour market situation in general does not allow many people to leave agriculture.

Quite frequently, self-employment conceals regular employment relations among employers and workers as employers force workers to accept civil contracts thus permitting them to avoid the payment of social contributions and occupational accident insurance and so on. Some anecdotal evidence points to increasing incidence of this phenomenon in the Czech Republic and perhaps also in Slovakia, and this could partially explain the increasing share of self-employment in both countries. There have been serious efforts by EU10+1 governments to reduce this misuse of civil contracts,[2] and this may have also contributed to an overall decline in self-employment figures. However, there have also been other factors behind this prevailing tendency towards declining self-employment in the region, such as sharp competition from the international retail trade, catering and hotel chains as well as some other services providers, which exclude local shops, restaurants and hotels, local small gardening, transportation and other firms.

The breakdown of self-employment by sex reveals that, with the exception of Romania, men are significantly more involved in self-employment than women. This is particularly true for countries with low employment percentages in agriculture. Comparison with the EU15 shows that now the EU10+1 countries tend on average to have a higher proportion of self-employed workers than the old EU member countries where this proportion stagnated after 2000. Both regions have also experienced an increasing gap between male and female self-employment levels.

An interesting development has occurred with regard to fixed-term contracts (see Table 4.4). Eight out of eleven countries have seen the growing incidence of fixed-term contracts, although the development has not been dramatic so far, with the outstanding exception of Poland. Although we have only very limited information on newly-concluded contracts, for Croatia the information suggests a sharp increase in the offer of fixed-term contracts, though their share in all contracts is growing more slowly, and to a shortening of their duration recently (in Croatia over a half of new contracts were concluded for a period of less than six months in 2002 compared with less than one-quarter five years earlier – see Crnkovic-Pozaic, 2004).

Table 4.4 Trends in the incidence of fixed-term contracts (per cent of total employment)

	2000	2004		2000	2004
Bulgaria	6.3	7.4	Lithuania	4.4	6.3
Croatia	–	12.2	Poland	5.8	22.7
Czech Republic	8.1	9.1	Romania	2.8	2.5
Estonia	3.0	2.6	Slovakia	4.8	5.5
Hungary	7.1	6.8	Slovenia	13.7	17.8
Latvia	6.7	9.5			
EU15	13.7	13.6			

Note: Bulgaria: 2001 instead of 2000.

Source: Eurostat.

Anecdotal evidence points to the existence of such a phenomenon at least in some of the other EU10+1 countries as well. These trends seem to reveal increasing labour market segmentation with a certain group of workers (usually young people and lower-skilled workers) being confined to precarious jobs of this kind with high job turnover while the majority of workers enjoy jobs with no fixed termination date and which are thus more stable and secure. The very fast development of fixed-term contracts has occurred in Poland where their share in total employment quadrupled between 2000 and 2004. This is another sign of the sharp deterioration of the Polish labour market with high economic insecurity prompting employers to resort to temporary contracts, the latter also being facilitated by changes in labour legislation – see Grotkowska et al., 2005). Even this rapid flexibilisation of employment, however, has not contributed to the significant labour market improvements expected by neo-liberal economists. Besides Poland, Slovenia is the only CSEE country which has achieved the proportion of temporary contracts in total employment above the EU15 average, while Croatia is approaching that level. Interestingly, the use of fixed-term contracts has stagnated in the old EU since 2000 while the overall tendency in Central and South-Eastern Europe is towards more temporary employment. Unlike in the EU15 where generally speaking fixed-term contracts are more often concluded with women, in the 'new' European region fixed-term employment is more frequent among men, with the exception of the Czech Republic and Slovenia.

The last flexible form of employment for which data are available is part-time employment and so far this has been under-represented in the EU10+1 countries in comparison with the EU15 (Table 4.5).

Table 4.5 Development of part-time employment as per cent of total employment

	2000	2004		2000	2004
Bulgaria	3.2	2.4	Lithuania	10.2	8.4
Croatia	–	8.5	Poland	10.5	10.8
Czech Republic	5.3	4.9	Romania	16.5	10.6
Estonia	8.1	8.0	Slovakia	2.1	2.7
Hungary	3.5	4.7	Slovenia	6.5	9.3
Latvia	11.3	10.4			
EU15	17.7	19.4			

Note: Bulgaria: 2001 instead of 2000.

Source: Eurostat.

The share of part-time employment in total employment in the EU15 region was almost double that of the three EU10+1 countries with the highest level of part-time employment being in Poland, Romania and Latvia in 2004.

Moreover, while part-time employment has further increased in the EU15, in most countries of the former region part-time employment has declined (notably in Romania) or stagnated. The only country which registered a higher increase in part-time employment was Slovenia, followed at a distance by Hungary. The main reasons for the low application of part-time employment remain the same as described in Cazes and Nesporova (2003). Employers claim that high labour taxation and other fixed labour costs make part-time employment, which allows for job sharing, unprofitable for them and that it is not viewed favourably by customers. Workers say that they cannot afford shorter working hours and corresponding wage losses because of the increasing cost of living. The low birth rate on the one hand, and the availability of long maternity and parental benefits in a situation where childcare facilities are relatively expensive, also contribute to low part-time employment since women (men only very rarely) prefer to stay at home with their children longer instead of combining early return to work and shorter working hours. In terms of gender differences, although the incidence of part-time employment is clearly higher for women than for men, the gap between both sexes is less profound than for the EU15 where the female share was five times higher in 2004. No information was available on the proportion of involuntary part-time employment.

Although data on informal employment are scanty they suggest that it is a declining tendency thanks to recent improvements in national legislation and better enforcement of legislation as well as stricter control of informal activity by labour offices and better collection of taxes by financial offices.

One can conclude from the above analysis that in the majority of the new EU member and candidate countries there is indeed a trend towards increasing flexibilisation of employment. This is mainly manifested in the growing incidence of contracts with limited duration, which are more widespread among men and in particular affect young people and low-skilled persons who often remain stuck in insecure types of employment. In contrast, part-time employment is still not popular in the region and its low availability may in fact contribute to unfavourable demographic developments as long paternal leave encourages employers to discriminate against women with smaller children who may then decide not to have more than one child. In the majority of the EU10+1 countries there has been a tendency towards declining self-employment. In fact, two opposing trends have affected the development of self-employment. On the one hand factors like (i) sharp competition from the international retail trade, catering and hotel chains and some other international services providers excluding small local firms from the market; (ii) multinational enterprises often relying on their own suppliers from abroad; or (iii) emerging better wage employment opportunities for those who had been forced earlier to turn to self-employment in the absence of good quality jobs or who wish to move out of largely unprofitable family (subsistence) farming, thus result in declining self-employment. On the other hand there are factors contributing towards an increase in self-employment such as (i) new IC technologies, which are allowing highly skilled specialists to start their own profitable businesses; or (ii) loopholes in legislation that enable substitution of labour contracts by service (civil) contracts. Informal employment seems to be still high in particular in South-Eastern Europe but the available information suggests it is a declining trend.

4.4 LABOUR MARKET DYNAMICS IN THE REGION: RECENT TRENDS

4.4.1 Declining Labour Turnover in the 2000s

Two sources of employment flow data are available to assess labour mobility and the intensity of reallocation: those based on establishment surveys (ES) and those originating from labour force surveys (LFS). Labour force surveys were introduced gradually in the region during the 1990s; and more recently, national statistical offices have begun to estimate selected aggregate flow data regularly and provide them to Eurostat. Additional LFS flow data have been provided by researchers based on their own calculations.[3] As establishment surveys only cover enterprises exceeding a certain size, they may exclude an important segment of the enterprise sector as well as certain categories of workers with irregular contracts. Hence, we have based our analysis on LFS, whenever possible.[4]

Labour turnover based on the former source is calculated as a sum of recruitments and separations by individual establishments over a given year divided by their initial or average employment levels for that year. Labour turnover based on LFS flow data is a sum of the aggregate accession and separation rates. The accession rate is calculated as a sum of aggregate flows from unemployment to employment, from inactivity to employment and from one employment to another, divided by initial or average employment in a given year.[5] The separation rate is a sum of aggregate flows from employment to unemployment, from employment to inactivity and from one employment to another, divided by initial or average employment in a given year.

The available data from both sources indicate a general stabilisation – and in some countries even a decrease – of labour turnover in the region over the 1999–2003 period, which seems to correspond to a phase of enterprise stabilisation (see Figure 4.2). Bulgaria, though, is an exception with outstanding labour mobility rates,[6] as explained in more detail below. Another remarkable pattern is the convergence of separation and accession rates in recent years; moreover, while in the 1990s separation rates exceeded hiring rates (mostly due to the downsizing of large enterprises), the reverse can be observed since the early 2000s in Bulgaria, the Czech Republic and Hungary.

In Poland the dynamics of the labour market weakened quite significantly after 1998. Separation rates and turnover data from both sources show that job destruction, but also labour churning,[7] dominated labour market dynamics. However, data and patterns diverged between ES and LFS for accession rates, in particular over the last five years: they suggest that, unlike in the 1990s, the job creation capacity of small enterprises (which are better captured by LFS) has slowed down significantly since 1998. As detailed in Grotkowska et al. (2005), the Polish labour market has been characterised by a fall in participation and employment rates during the past five years; changes in the level of employment were also combined with changes in employment structure, with three groups in particular being hit on the labour market: workers in the public sector, own account workers and employers whose numbers dropped respectively, by 28.6 per cent, 12.8 per cent and 10.6 per cent. In addition, employment in firms employing 1–5 persons decreased between 1998 and 2004.

Bulgaria experienced very high labour mobility rates over the 1990s, indicating massive job destruction in large and medium-sized enterprises. As indicated previously, the establishment of the Currency Board in 1997 forced the government to accelerate the privatisation of large state enterprises; this led to restructuring and major downsizing, particularly in 1999. Simul-

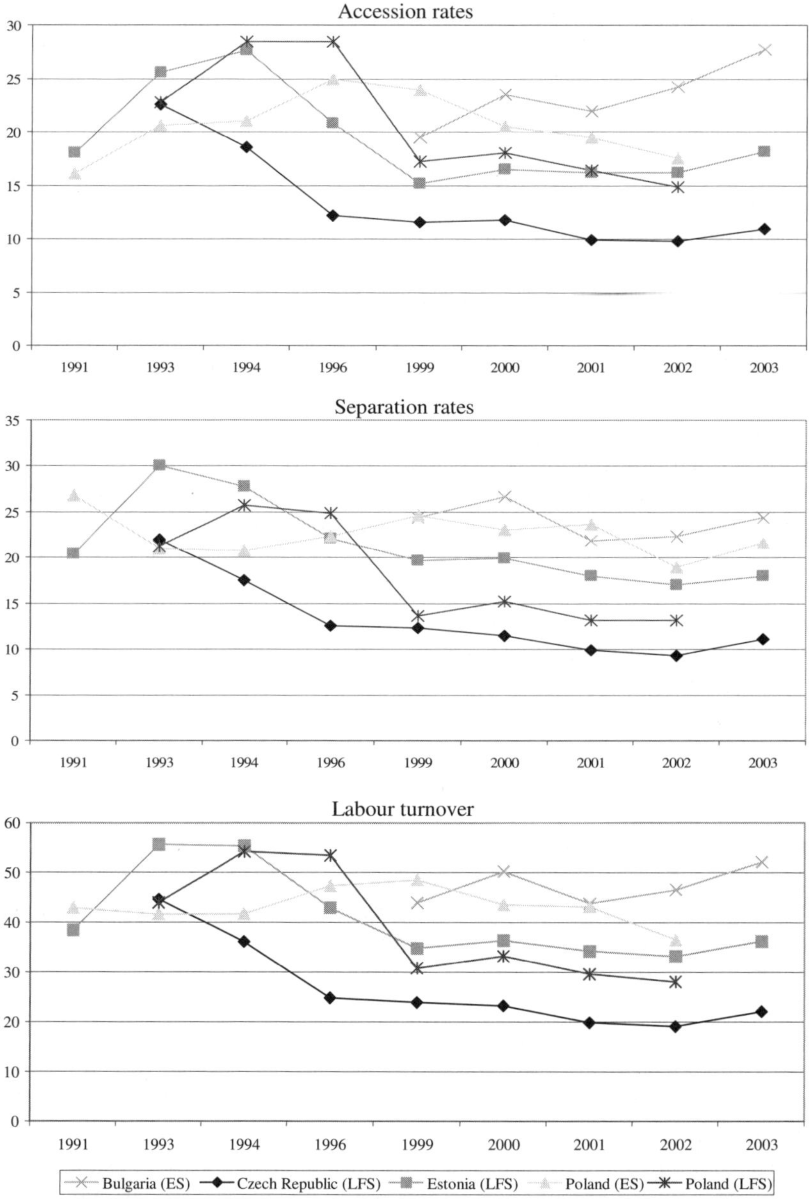

Source: Authors' calculations.

Figure 4.2 Accession rates, separation rates and labour turnover for selected CSEE countries, 1990–2003

taneously, the hiring rate increased substantially, pointing to strengthening structural changes with a positive effect on economic growth. In 2001, for the first time, the hiring rate exceeded the separation rate, but the reason was a sharp decrease in the separation rate compared with the – also declining – hiring rate. Since then, both rates have been increasing again, with hiring rates accelerating in 2003. Macroeconomic stability and positive economic growth over recent years (over 4 per cent for 2000–2003) have created a favourable environment for increased job creation and a high demand for labour. This led to a positive impact on employment[8] and a general improvement in labour market outcomes after 2000.

Estonia and the Czech Republic recorded the lowest labour turnover in the early 2000s.[9] Moreover, turnover continued to decline, indicating further stabilisation of the labour market there. In Estonia, the accession rate slightly outnumbered the separation rate for the first time in 2003, after massive restructuring of the enterprise sector and intensive reallocation of labour over the whole transition period. The overall effect of structural changes translated into a slight improvement in labour market performance.

In the Czech Republic, accession and separation rates have followed a quasi-similar (synchronised) pattern, in level and tendency. The Czech employment growth rate was negative for the 2000–2004 period despite economic recovery but this level was still one of the highest in the region. Turnover data for Croatia, Hungary and Lithuania have only recently become available. They point to an overall stabilisation of the labour dynamics of these countries, with some differences in their relationship between accession and separation rates. In Hungary,[10] hiring and firing rates have been synchronised but at rather low levels, with the former always outnumbering the latter. This has happened in Lithuania only since 2002 and in Croatia since 2003. Declining separation rates – in particular outflows from employment to unemployment – reflected the recovery of the Lithuanian economy (which began in year 2000); they were followed by a slight decrease in unemployment levels.

4.4.2 Labour Turnover, Job Tenure and Employment Outflows

How is labour turnover affected by economic fluctuations? In industrialised countries labour turnover typically accelerates in periods of economic growth: enterprise start-ups and expansions create new jobs, attracting newcomers to the labour market and increasing the hiring of unemployed job-seekers. At the same time, though dismissals for economic reasons decline, the growing number of job opportunities encourages more people to change their jobs voluntarily. In contrast, in economic downturns, labour turnover declines: enterprises seek to cut costs by reducing hiring and by resorting to redundancies, while the consequent sharp reduction in voluntary quits more than counterbalances the increase in dismissals. Hence, largely for supply-side reasons, labour turnover tends to behave pro-cyclically (Boeri 1995; ILO, 1996). An important finding of Cazes and Nesporova (2003) was the counter-cyclical behaviour of labour turnover in CEE countries during the transition decade. Table 4.6 presents the correlation coefficients of labour turnover to both GDP and employment growth rates for a new set of CSEE countries, which slightly differ from our previous research; hence results are not fully comparable. Cross-country comparisons are impaired by the fact that the labour turnover data series are rather short for some countries and the results therefore have to be interpreted with caution. Bearing these caveats in mind, the same correlations have been calculated with a time lag of one year, as labour adjustment to new economic performances may take a certain time.

Table 4.6 Correlations between GDP and employment dynamics (E) versus labour turnover (LT), selected countries, 1999–2003

Country	LT vs GDP	LT vs GDP (–1)	LT vs E	LT vs E (–1)
Bulgaria	0.6295	–0.3167	0.1625	0.3672
Croatia[b]	–0.4914	–0.7893	–0.7279	–0.9063
Czech Republic	0.1995	–0.8682	–0.6459	– 0.8162
Estonia	0.1248	–0.5330	–0.1878	– 0.4233
Hungary	0.2471	0.0719	0.9762	0.2660
Lithuania[a]	–0.7461	–0.0339	0.3158	–0.7675
Poland[b]	0.7984	0.7031	–0.2803	–0.2163

Notes:
a. 2001–2003.
b. 1999–2002, LFS.

Source: Own calculations based on labour turnover data from Figure 4.2 and GDP data from UNECE, 2005.

Figures provided in the second column of Table 4.6 do not indicate clear-cut patterns: correlation coefficients of labour turnover to GDP indicate a negative correlation for Croatia and Lithuania and a significant positive correlation for Bulgaria, Hungary and Poland. For the other countries there seems to be no significant correlation between the two indicators. However, the time-lagged coefficients in the next column show the correlation to be negative for almost all the countries – with the exception of Poland (the correlation being non-significant for Hungary). Correlations with employment growth (see last two columns) confirm this pattern, in particular with the time-lagged variable, which is more strongly correlated to labour turnover. These findings suggest that in general labour reallocation has been more responsive to employment changes than economic ones, and they point to a weaker link between economic and employment fluctuations; while strong economic performance did not translate into more significant employment creation, it did contribute to a decrease in unemployment. Poland again is an exception with a strong pro-cyclical labour turnover on the one hand and a mild counter-cyclical fluctuation of turnover to employment growth on the other. This result could be explained by labour churning, in a context of depressed demand for labour.

In Croatia, negative correlations exist between employment growth and labour turnover, on the one hand, and between economic growth and labour turnover, on the other. The same goes for Hungary, though the correlations are in this case positive. This pattern suggests a rather strong relationship between economic and employment developments. For all other countries, the overall picture is less clear-cut as said before: labour turnover may be positively correlated to GDP and negatively to employment growth or vice versa, suggesting a rather peculiar link between economic and labour market developments. However, when a time lag is introduced, a strong negative correlation emerges between labour turnover and the employment dynamics in all countries, except in Hungary and Bulgaria (last column of Table 4.6). The pro-cyclical behaviour of turnover in these two latter countries can be explained by the recent improvement of their labour market outcomes, in particular the growing labour force and employment rates.

Overall, the calculations presented in Table 4.6 invite the tentative conclusion that labour turnover still tends to have a counter-cyclical development in the region, with the exception of Hungary and Bulgaria, and this continues to contrast with the situation in industrialised countries. This pattern coincides with the simultaneous decrease of accession and separation rates, with a stronger deceleration for the latter. As indicated previously, the explanation can be found in a certain stabilisation of the labour markets since 2000s, as defensive restructuring[11] and massive withdrawals from the labour markets have come to an end. Enterprises are not dismissing workers more, but they have not opened new positions, as the continuing rather poor employment performance indicates.

The distribution of employment by job tenure,[12] as well as average tenures, provide a general summary of job stability across countries. Table 4.7 presents these indicators for some countries in 2003. Unfortunately data on job tenures are quite scarce in the region. Average job tenure in these countries was 9.0 years in 2003, below the average of 10.6 years for the European Union (EU 14)[13] and 12.2 years for Japan in 2002, but above the average for the United States (6.6 years in 1999). Table 4.7 shows the differences between countries in average tenure. The two Baltic States and Bulgaria have the lowest job tenure of 7.3 years for Estonia, 7.6 years for

Bulgaria and 7.7 years for Lithuania (slightly above the US level of 6.6 years, but still below the UK level of 8.1 years) followed by Hungary and the Czech Republic with tenures below ten years (levels similar to Denmark and the Netherlands).[14] The longest average tenure is still to be found in Poland.

Table 4.7 Distribution of employment by job tenure, 2003 and comparison with 1999 (%)

	Bulgaria	Croatia	Czech Rep	Estonia	Hungary	Lithuania	Poland	Unweighted average	OECD[b]
Job Tenure (%)									
Less than 6 months			5.7			6.7	7.0		
6 to 11 months	16.9[c]	n.a	5.3	18.0[c]	13.3[c]	6.3	5.0		
1 to less than 2 years[a]	8.6		16.1[a]	12.0	8.7	11.3	7.8		
2 to less than 5 years[a]	23.2		14.3[a]	23.0	26.6	18.2	17.1		
5 to less than 10 years	21.6		25.4	24.0	20.8	29.3	19.3		
10 to less than 20 years			21.1			19.6	22.0		
More than 20 years	29.7[d]		12.2	23.0[d]	30.6[d]	8.7	21.8		
Total	100	n.a	100	100	100	100	100		
Average tenure (years)									
in 2003	7.6	11.0	9.0	7.3	8.7	7.7	11.7	9.0	10.6
in 1999	n.a.	n.a.	8.2	6.9	8.8	7.6	11.9	8.7	10.5
Under 1 year (%)	16.9	n.a.	11.0	18.0	13.3	13.0	12.0	13.5	14.8
Over 10 years (%)	29.7	n.a	33.3	23.0	30.6	28.3	43.8	31.8	41.5

Notes:
a. The breakdown provided by the Czech Statistical Office differs slightly for two sub-periods, as it refers to 1–3 years and 3–5 years.
b. 2002: for average tenure: European Union, the United States and Japan; for the distribution of employment by tenure: European Union and the United States.
c. Under one year.
d. Over ten years.

Source: Eurostat; Czech data from the *Statistical Yearbook of the Czech Republic*, 2004; data in Auer et al. (2005).

Cross-country differences are even more pronounced when the distribution of employment across some job tenure classes is considered, and notably the share of workers with long tenures. There are significant differences in the proportion of workers with ten or more years of tenure, between Poland (43.8 per cent) and the Baltic States (23.0 per cent in Estonia and 28.3 per cent in Lithuania in 2003). As detailed in Cazes and Nesporova (2003), these striking differences can be partly explained by the sectoral distribution of job tenure. A comparison of average tenure data between 1999 and 2003 points to a slight lengthening of job tenure, except for Poland, where it decreased slightly from 11.9 to 11.7 years.

We also collected data on outflows from employment by destination (exit to another job, to unemployment and to inactivity) and tested their fluctuation during economic cycle. As already mentioned, demand for labour increases in Western industrialised countries in periods of economic upswing and employers tend to offer higher wages in order to attract new and more qualified workers. The latter, in turn, are more inclined to avail themselves of better job opportunities so that, besides new labour market entries and re-employment of previously unemployed persons, job-to-job moves also accelerate. In contrast, in periods of economic decline workers become more hesitant to change their jobs voluntarily in fear of eventually remaining jobless. Enterprises endeavour to cut production costs in order to maintain or restore their competitiveness, and resort if necessary to redundancies, use of early retirement schemes and similar measures to cut their workforce.

Table 4.8 presents the correlation between GDP growth rates and flows from employment to each of the three destinations. As job-to-job moves are usually voluntary, while outflows from employment to unemployment and to inactivity are mostly involuntary (forced withdrawals from employment, de-registration from unemployment, early retirement and so on), one would expect positive correlation of the former flows and negative correlation of the two latter flows with economic cycle. Again, as employment protection rules may delay outflows from employment to unemployment and to inactivity, the same correlations have been calculated with a time lag of one year.[15]

In line with expectations, Table 4.8 shows a strong negative correlation between GDP growth and exits to unemployment for all countries under review. The correlation is even more pronounced if exits to unemployment are correlated with lagged GDP. The general picture for moves from employment to inactivity is less clear-cut: correlations tend to show a counter-cyclical pattern in Croatia and Lithuania, and in the Czech Republic for the time-lagged variable; in contrast the pro-cyclical pattern seems to characterise outflows to inactivity in Estonia and Poland. Job-to-job moves present also contrasting patterns: correlations are in conformity with our previous conclusion on counter-cyclical behaviour of job-to-job flows for Croatia, Estonia and Lithuania (Cazes and Nesporova, 2003). In Poland and the Czech Republic however, job-to-job flows increase with economic upswing; these developments of job-to-job flows have to be interpreted differently in the two countries, reflecting, in Poland, a large amount of labour churning as indicated before, but rather voluntary moves in the case of the Czech Republic.

Table 4.8 Correlation coefficients of GDP and outflows from employment by destination for selected countries, 1999–2003

Country	E–E vs GDP	E–I vs GDP	E–I vs GDP–1	E–U vs GDP	E–U vs GDP–1
Croatia	–0.3125	–0.8223	–0.7711	–0.2509	–0.9916
Czech Republic	0.4677	0.1151	–0.8507	–0.2123	–0.9199
Estonia	–0.4757	–0.0429	0.8001	–0.2217	–0.7897
Lithuania	–0.2533	–0.9162	–0.9226	–0.9162	–0.9226
Poland	0.6417	0.9947	0.5101	–0.5945	–0.5233

Notes:
E–E is a flow from one job to another; E–I a flow from employment to inactivity; and E–U from employment to unemployment.

Source: Own computations.

These results do not differ widely from our findings for the 1990s period. They point to the generally counter-cyclical movements of labour market flows: higher outflows from employment in periods of depressed demand for labour and lower outflows during employment upswings. Clearly, the economic recovery that characterised the region over recent years, contributed to a significant decrease in flows into unemployment; however, due to the weak link between economic and employment growth, outflows to inactivity and/or employment have differed among countries. Poland displays a particularly worrying picture with high levels of (positive) correlations between outflows both to inactivity and other employment with the economic cycle.

4.5 CONCLUDING REMARKS

Our comparative analysis has revealed that despite robust economic growth, coinciding with declining unemployment, employment has so far increased only in five of the CSEE countries and even there only modestly. Economic growth is thus still almost jobless but there are differences among countries. The fall in unemployment has continued to feed inactivity more than employment: labour market participation is still on the decline in the majority of these countries, including two of the five countries with improving employment performance. The persistent long-term inactivity of the working age population combined with very high long-term unemployment and an increasing ratio of the youth to average unemployment rate indicate important barriers to labour market (re-) entry, especially for young persons, older workers, ethnic minorities, low-skilled workers, women returning from maternity leave and persons with health problems. Some of them have to take informal jobs to make ends meet.

The share of temporary employment has accelerated. However, unlike in the 1990s, it has taken the form of fixed-term and short-term contracts rather than civil contracts, the number of which has declined as a result of a stricter stance taken by labour market and financial institutions in many countries. A much higher incidence of time-limited contracts among newly concluded contracts compared with their much lower and only slowly increasing share in all contracts indicates important labour market segmentation. In contrast, part-time employment has remained limited. In the majority of the countries there has been a tendency towards declining self-employment. Although data on informal employment are scarce they also indicate a certain contraction in informal employment.

Labour turnover has declined since 2000, indicating a certain stabilisation of labour markets. Both the accession and separation rates have fallen, which suggests that enterprises are no longer resorting to mass redundancies (or forced 'voluntary quits') but are unable to create many new positions either, and employment performance remains poor. This limited availability and frequent precariousness of new jobs explains why people are reluctant to quit their old jobs during economic upswings, which is reflected in a continuing tendency towards counter-cyclical development of labour turnover found by our analysis. The link between economic and employment growth has remained weak in the 2000s, and economic recovery has only brought a significant decrease of flows from employment into unemployment, while we have not found any significant correlation between economic growth and outflows from employment to inactivity or flows from one employment to another.

Stabilisation of the labour market has also been confirmed by a slight lengthening of average job tenures. An analysis of the employment distribution by duration of job tenure revealed that between 1999 and 2003 this distribution polarised towards a higher share of short-term (below one year) and long-term (above ten years) job tenures, which is more evidence of the above-mentioned tendency towards labour market segmentation.

All these issues have to be tackled by well-designed employment policy. The most important objective is to address the challenge of jobless growth and translate economic growth into positive and sufficiently high net job creation resulting in higher employment of good quality. This calls for a sound, balanced macroeconomic policy, which would stimulate sustainable economic development through interventions on the supply and demand sides of the economy. At the same time it has to be combined with good education and training policy as well as with effective labour market policy in order to create more and better employment opportunities for the population, improve the matching of labour demand with labour supply in terms of level but also structure, and to ensure that all the social groups have equal employment opportunities. Social dialogue with the involvement of the governments at all levels – national, regional and local – and the social partners, but also partnerships with other institutions concerned, is indispensable for formulating and implementing employment and labour market policies of this kind and for ensuring that these have the desired positive impact on labour market performance of these countries. All these different elements call for comprehensive and better-balanced policies, which would combine flexibility and security in the labour markets of CSEE countries. In Cazes and Nesporova (2007) we look into how this can be achieved through the flexicurity approach and show how 'activation' of labour market policies and social dialogue can be the keys to success.

NOTES

1. Due to lack of data and problems with their comparability for the countries of South-Eastern Europe we limit our analysis to this group of countries so as to benefit from comparable Eurostat data.
2. Recently, the Hungarian Government introduced new rules on the use of independent contractors and on so-called 'labour loan' arrangements (workers being lent by one company to perform work for another company) as of 1 January 2006. Among others, these rules explicitly define the differences between regular contracts and independent/civil contracts, which can be concluded only for the provision of one precise product or service. Those contravening the labour law can be fined up to HUF 20 million.
3. For example, Haltiwanger and Vodopivec (1998), Arro et al. (2001), Kwiatkowski et al., (2001) and Vecernik (2001), who provided data calculated by themselves for Estonia, Poland and the Czech Republic. More recent data for these countries as well as for Hungary and Slovenia have been gathered and kindly provided to us by departments responsible for labour force surveys in the National Statistical Offices.
4. For a comprehensive presentation of data and sources, as well as their characteristics, see Cazes and Nesporova (2003).
5. Similarly as in the case of establishment surveys a vague definition of job-to-job changes may be an important source of data distortions especially in comparative studies. For this reason we were unable to use all the available data, in particular when there was a strikingly wide difference between the results of establishment surveys and labour force surveys, as in the case of Slovenia.
6. Data for Bulgaria, from ES, however, do not seem fully comparable with other figures.
7. Labour churning refers to labour mobility connected with non-structural factors.
8. However, in 2004 employment in Bulgaria remained still below its 1992 level.
9. It is important to note that labour turnover data for the Czech Republic are not fully comparable with those for other countries, as they underestimate job-to-job moves. For methodological reasons it was not possible to separate job-to-job moves from continuous employment for some 20 per cent of persons covered by the LFS – see Vecernik (2001). Moreover, unlike Poland, where calculations sum up quarterly flows, the data for the Czech Republic as well as for Estonia are annual and do not take into account multiple changes during the year. The data therefore underestimate aggregate labour market flows.

10. Small enterprises not taken into account.
11. 'Defensive restructuring' includes enterprises' reforms engendered by the imposition of discipline with results largely in labour shedding while 'strategic restructuring' should lead to the revival of the firm through innovations, with possible new recruitments.
12. Defined as the length of time currently employed individuals have spent with their present employer.
13. EU14: Germany, Belgium, Denmark, Finland, France, Greece, Ireland, Italy, Luxembourg, Netherlands, Portugal, Spain, Sweden and the United Kingdom.
14. According to Eurostat the average job tenure was 8.4 years in Denmark and 9.9 years in the Netherlands in 2002.
15. Again, these results should be taken with caution, due to rather short and incomplete data series, with differences among countries.

REFERENCES

Arro, R., Eamets, R., Järve, J., Kallaste, E. and Philips, K. (2001), *Labour market flexibility and employment security: Estonia*, Employment Papers Series, No. 25, Geneva: International Labour Office.

Auer, P., Berg, J. and Coulibaly, I. (2005), 'Is a stable workforce good for productivity?', *International Labour Review*, **144** (3), 319–443.

Boeri, T. (1995), *Is job turnover counter-cyclical?* EUI Working Papers in Economics Series, No. 12, Florence: European University Institute.

Cazes, S. and Nesporova, A. (2003), *Labour Markets in Transition: Balancing Flexibility and Security in Central and Eastern Europe*, Geneva: International Labour Office.

Cazes, S. and Nesporova, A. (2007), *Flexicurity: A Relevant Approach in Central and Eastern Europe*, Geneva: International Labour Office.

Crnkovic-Pozaic, S. (2004), *Flexibility and security in the labour market: Croatia's experience*, Flexicurity paper No. 1, Budapest: International Labour Office, Sub-regional Office for Central and Eastern Europe.

Czech Statistical Office (2004), *Statistical Yearbook of the Czech Republic, 2004*, Prague: Author.

Grotkowska, G., Socha, M. and Sztanderska, U. (2007), 'Poland', in Cazes, S. and A. Nesporova, *Flexicurity: A Relevant Approach in Central and Eastern Europe*, Geneva: International Labour Office, pp. 181–211.

Haltiwanger, J. and Vodopivec, M. (1998), *Gross worker and job flow in a transition economy: an analysis of Estonia*, University of Maryland (mimeo).

International Labour Office (ILO) (1996), *World Employment 1996/97: National Policies in a Global Context*, Geneva: International Labour Office.

Kwiatkowski, E., Socha, M. and Sztanderska, U. (2001), *Labour market flexibility, employment and social security: Poland*, Employment Papers Series, No. 28, Geneva: International Labour Office.

United Nations Economic Commission for Europe (UNECE) (2005), *Economic Survey of Europe 2005*, No. 2, New York and Geneva: United Nations.

Vecernik, J. (2001), *Labour market flexibility, employment and social security: Czech Republic*, Employment Papers Series, No. 27, Geneva: International Labour Office.

5. Pathways to Flexicurity in Europe: Do They Affect Male and Female Labour Market Transition Patterns?

Ruud Muffels[1]

5.1 INTRODUCTION

The notion that modern labour markets perform better if they are capable of maintaining a balance between labour market flexibility and employment security is gaining ground in the European policy arena. In European social policy terms it boils down to improving the adaptability of the labour market by avoiding rigidities caused by legal or institutional constraints, while simultaneously maintaining or increasing existing levels of income and employment security. This is coined in the literature under the heading of 'flexicurity'. There is ample evidence now that the way European labour markets appear capable of creating a more or less balanced mix between labour market flexibility and income and employment security is showing a large heterogeneity (European Commission, 2006, 2007). In an earlier publication we concluded that there is no one-size-fits-all approach but that there are clearly distinct roads or pathways in Europe (Muffels, 2007).

In this chapter we examine the relationship between labour market flexibility, indicated by labour market mobility and income and employment security across Europe from an empirical perspective using the data of the European Community Household Panel (ECHP) for the period 1994–2001.

Compared to previous work in which we focused on men only we will deal in this chapter also with women and compare their mobility patterns and 'flexicurity' outcomes with those of men. But, because we are including women we need to take account of the factors that might explain the specific transition patterns of women in the labour market compared to men such as female's working times, caring duties and household formation patterns. The main research questions pertain to the 'what' and 'why' questions: we ask ourselves not only which countries or pathways perform better or worse in balancing flexibility and security for males and females separately, but also why they perform better or worse. For the latter part we examine in particular the impact of institutions and policies on males' and females' mobility patterns controlling for compositional differences across countries. First, we examine to what extent labour market mobility patterns of men and women are affected by common factors such as human capital endowments and life course events (childbirth, divorce) and second we view the impact of labour market policies and specific labour market institutions such as the availability of (flexible) working time options (WTO), the degree of activation in labour market policies (ALMP) and the generosity of unemployment benefit systems (UIB) on males' and females' transition patterns in Europe.

Outline

In the first part we report on how countries perform in safeguarding high levels of 'flexibility and income and employment security' for males and females distinctly using the dynamic outcome measures. In the next part we try to explain the various forms of labour market mobility we distinguish and primarily examine the effects of specific macro-level institutions compared to regime type. In the end we formulate some conclusions and points of discussion.

5.2 THE THEORETICAL RELATIONSHIP BETWEEN FLEXIBILITY AND SECURITY AT THE MACRO LEVEL

The main thrust of our approach is constituted by the so-called 'flexicurity' quadrant, based on the theoretical relationship between flexibility, indicated by our dynamic outcome indicators for mobility and income and employment security (see Muffels and Luijkx, 2008a). The trade-off thesis suggests that the relationship between mobility and security is negatively sloped, whereas the flexicurity thesis argues for a positive relationship, implying that either of both poles are high (flexicurity) or low (inflexicurity). The trade-off thesis points to the existence of a zero-sum game between flexibility and security, whereas the 'flexicurity' thesis presumes a positive-sum game. From a theoretical viewpoint we would expect that if the 'flexicurity' thesis holds, country's scores would lie around the positively sloped 45° line drawn in Figure 5.1 and when the 'trade-off' thesis holds that they would lie around the negatively sloped 45° line.

In reality countries can of course be located anywhere left or right of both lines. There might be as many combinations as there are countries though according to the welfare regime and 'Varieties of Capitalism' literature (Albert, 1991; Estéves-Abe et al., 2001; Hall and Soskice, 2001) we expect that particular combinations cluster in a limited number. These clusters reflect regime types or pathways in Europe. In Figure 5.1 we try to locate the various welfare regimes distinguished in the literature (see Esping-Andersen, 1999; Ferrera et al., 2000; Muffels and Luijkx, 2006).

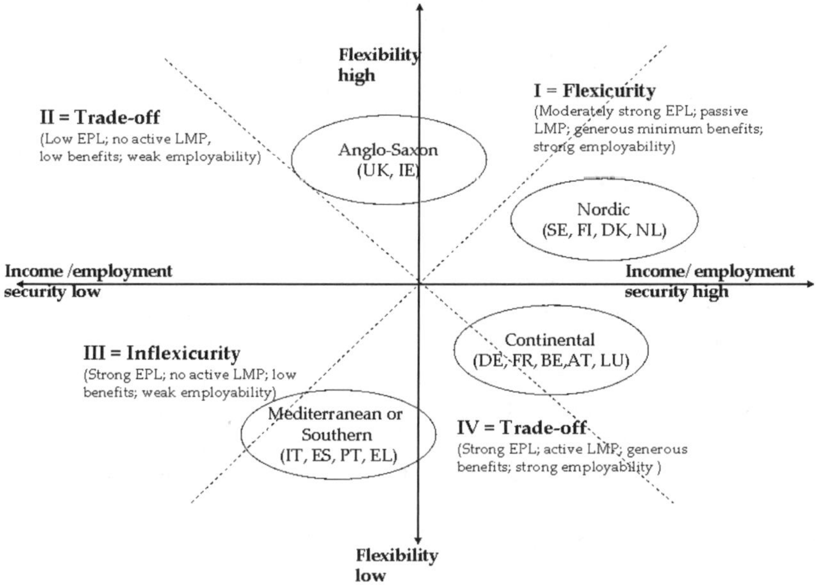

Source: Muffels and Luijkx (2008).

Figure 5.1 The 'flexicurity' quadrant and regime type

Since the ECHP lacks information on the transition countries in Eastern Europe we had to limit our regime analyses to four regime types only, though according to other information sources the transition regime type set itself clearly apart (Philips and Eamets, 2007). The Nordic regime is presumed to attain a moderate level of institutional flexibility on the labour market and at the same time provide much income and employment security due to generous benefits, a strong focus on employability policies and active or activating labour market policies. The Anglo-Saxon or Liberal regime combines a high level of numerical flexibility (low employment protection), with a low level of functional flexibility (employability) and also a weak record on safeguarding income and employment security (low benefits, no active labour market policies) whereas the Continental regime performs rather poorly as regards labour market flexibility (strong employment protection) but fairly well in terms of safeguarding income (high benefits) and employment security (active labour market policies and a strong focus on employability). Although the Southern European regimes are very dissimilar in many respects they combine a low level of flexibility (strong employment protection) with low levels of income (low benefits) and employment security for outsiders (no active labour market policies and a weak employability record). However, income security as well as flexibility is not primarily attained in these countries through formal arrangements but through informal settings. There is no regime that perfectly fits the 'flexicurity' quadrant though the Nordic and Anglo-Saxon regimes seem the best candidates.

Theoretical Underpinnings

The relationship between flexibility and security has been studied – though framed in very different wordings – in various strands of the economic and sociological literature. It is common among economists to speak about a 'zero-sum game' or the inevitable trade-offs when viewing the relationship between efficiency and equity to which the flexibility–security issue refers.

In institutional economics the so-called unified theory of Blau and Kahn (2002) should be mentioned in which it is argued that due to the existing wage rigidities in European labour markets as caused by the wage-setting institutions, the adjustment to asymmetric economic shocks will be not through wage flexibility but through high unemployment levels of the low-skilled worker. This is due to the 'knowledge economy' in which the process of skill-biased technological change lowers the demand for the low-skilled in favour of the demand for the high-skilled causing downward pressures on real wage levels of the low-skilled and to heightened unemployment risks (Acemoglu, 2003). However, DiPrete et al. (2006), reviewing the evidence for the US and Europe, showed that the adaptation process to asymmetric macro-economic shocks will in their view not result in high unemployment levels in Europe or in high wage inequality as in the US as the 'unified theory' (Blau and Kahn, 2002) predicts, but in reduced employment security due to increasing shares of workers in insecure non-standard jobs. If this proves to be correct the theory implies that women who are generally lower skilled will be overrepresented in these insecure non-standard jobs. However there is another reason to suspect that women will occupy these non-standard jobs more often because it might better fit to their working time preferences.

Also sociologists engaged in social stratification research showed that globalisation and social stratification processes affect particularly the weakest groups on the labour market: workers in low status jobs, with low skill levels and human capital endowments which are increasingly exposed to rising employment instability and income insecurity (Blossfeld and Mills 2003; Blossfeld et al., 2006; Breen, 1997; DiPrete et al., 1997; Goldthorpe, 2001). This therefore seems to suggest that according to the 'globalisation' thesis women are more likely to experience heightened employment and income risks.

Further to this, the 'scarring thesis' should be mentioned that has become increasingly popular among sociologists. According to this thesis, experiences of non-employment or employment in low-level jobs, as a partly result of flexibilisation, have an enduring negative effect on the workers' future career in terms of employment stability and earnings (Booth et al., 2002, 2003; DiPrete et al., 1997; Gangl, 2003, 2006; Golsch, 2003; Kalleberg, 2000; Muffels and Luijkx, 2006). Again, these 'scarring' effects will affect women in particular more than men.

However, the advocates of the flexicurity thesis challenge the view that such trade-offs between flexibility and security need to exist. They refer to organisational sociology and management literature dealing with the changes occurring in the employment relationship as a consequence of the alleged flexibility trend that is delineated as an ongoing shift 'from lifetime employment to the boundaryless career' (Stone, 2005). They talk about the 'new' employment relationship in which job security offered through lifetime employment and the 'internal labour market' is substituted by employment security offered through investments in the 'employability' of workers by providing for training and learning opportunities which raises the 'general' skill level (Collins, 2005). The underlying hypothesis is that the 'new worker' will change jobs and employers more frequently provided that sufficient investments are made in skill formation during the job. By marketing his newly acquired skills on the external labour market the worker is better capable of safeguarding his or her employment security. The currently very prominent metaphor of 'flexicurity' in European policy circles (European Commission, 2007; Wilthagen, 1998; Wilthagen and Tros, 2004) resembles the views of these management theorists. The underlying idea is that when institutions are properly designed to activate employers and employees to facilitate investments in workers' 'employability', this will also contribute to a high level of mobility raising the workers' productivity and therewith employment security. The other side of the coin is that lack of investments in the 'employability' of workers can lead to a low level of mobility and hence of flexibility. When this is accompanied with a tightly regulated, segmented labour market excluding particular groups, the attained level of employment security is also low reflecting a situation of 'inflexicurity'. The flexicurity thesis therefore suggests that women compared to men face lower employment and income risks in Nordic countries and heightened risks in regulated Continental and Southern labour markets.

5.3 RESEARCH QUESTIONS AND HYPOTHESES

The main research questions addressed in this chapter deal 1) at the macro level with the extent by which the various pathways in Europe seem capable of balancing flexibility and security, for males and females separately, and 2) at the micro level to what extent labour market mobility patterns of men and women in the various countries can, apart from common factors, also be explained by specific institutions and labour market policies.

Macro-level Hypotheses

We firstly assumed that the observed differences across countries in the attained levels of flexibility and security for males and females can be explained by the impact of particular labour market and social security institutions and policies. We also assumed that these institutions are likely to affect men's and women's labour market behaviour in a rather dissimilar way. We included Active Labour Market policy expenditures as a percentage of GDP (ALMP), the net replacement rates of the unemployment benefits including social assistance for the various years (UIB) and, a novelty compared to other research, the share of companies in each country having working time options made available to their employees since we believe that these latter arrangements are especially important for women (see the chapter by Kerkhofs, Chung and Ester in this volume).

We assume that:

- Countries with more active labour market policies are more successful in getting men and women back to permanent work by creating more employment opportunities for unemployed workers and workers in temporary contracts.
- Countries with more generous benefit levels might confront higher disincentives to work and hence lower occupational and contract mobility rates, higher exit rates out of work and lower (re-)entry rates into work. A contrasting hypothesis might however be that it also increases the mobility from temporary into permanent jobs while generous welfare states allow people to wait and to search for the best job.
- Countries with more working time options for their employees are likely to be more successful in keeping men and especially women at work in families with young children or after childbirth by providing options which allow women but also men to take up caring duties to combine work and private life.

- We further suspect that the Nordic regimes provide more working time options for their employees and also more income and employment security due to their active labour market policies and generous benefits. The Anglo-Saxon regimes will grant fewer opportunities to combine work and private life and therefore confront higher employment exit rates especially of women in families with young children or after childbirth. Due to the absence of employment protection regulations these unregulated countries face higher occupational mobility rates, more exits but also higher re-entry rates. The Southern and Continental regimes due to their segmented labour markets and high level of protection will face low mobility and low exit rates but also low re-entry rates.

Micro-level Hypotheses

In our transition models we include micro-level variables which are derived from the social stratification literature on job and occupational mobility (Blossfeld and Mills, 2003; Blossfeld et al., 2006; DiPrete et al., 1997), from human capital theory (Becker, 1975) and from life course approaches (Elder and Pavalko, 1993). We suspect that the mobility patterns of males and females are significantly different due to differences in their life courses with respect to combining work and private life. For women working time options are very important to be able to combine work and care, for which reason we included an institutional variable reflecting the availability of these options in companies and only consider the options which are considered to accommodate the needs of employees instead of employers. This means that we included a variable measuring the percentage of companies (weighted with the number of employees) in a country that has made the following set of options available to their employees: part-time work, care leave, education leave and other leave options, flexible working time arrangements and early and phased retirement (Chung and Muffels, 2007; see the chapter by Kerkhofs et al. in this volume). We further assumed that women's transition patterns are affected by household formation events such as divorce and childbirth. We therefore defined a life cycle variable indicating the life stage the household is currently in (single person household versus couples with or without children, further disaggregated into singles and couples with young or older children or the empty nest family) and we constructed a childbirth variable indicating whether a child was born in the preceding year. The idea is that for women the occurrence of a childbirth event during their life course impacts significantly their future career and work–life balance. We further included a variable indicating whether women take up part-time work for caring reasons or for other reasons. From other research in the field (Fouarge et al. 2006; Uunk et al., 2005) we also know that the welfare state institutions providing income and employment support to females have a significant effect on the labour force participation and working hours of women after childbirth. Therefore, we also included benefit replacement rates (including social assistance) for various household types and information on active labour market policies.

We included human capital variables like age, job tenure and education level, signalling the skill level and work experience of the job-seeker. Bad health is supposed to lower someone's productivity and human capital endowments for which reason he is less likely to move into a better job and more likely to move into a worse job. We further included some control variables such as the level of economic resources in the household of the respondent, the occupational class of the worker in each year, the characteristics of the job the worker currently occupies (number of hours, industrial sector, firm size), life-course-related variables such as marital status and number and age of children, the country's time-varying unemployment rate and year dummies to take account of changes in the business cycle. The definition of the variables included is summarised in Table A5.1.

5.4 DEFINING INSTITUTIONAL AND DYNAMIC OUTCOME MEASURES

To define labour market flexibility we use an economic definition as the degree to which the labour market is capable of creating opportunities for employers and employees to meet their demands for qualified workers and jobs and to respond properly and timely to economic shocks and changes in labour market conditions. A flexible labour market operating efficiently exhibits high levels of mobility on the internal (functional flexibility) as well as the external labour market (numerical flexibility). It means that employers have more leeway either due to lack of institutional constraints or to opportunities offered by the terms of law to adapt the workforce to changes in demand. For workers and the unemployed it means that they rapidly acquire the job they are looking for and for which they are qualified, but also that they can adapt their labour input according to their needs throughout the life course (Schmid, 1995; Schmid and Gazier, 2002).[2] The meaning of security is rather straightforward and boils down to assuming that properly working labour markets safeguard equal opportunities or chances to maintain fair levels of income and employment security to all workers over the entire career.

To map the countries on the flexibility–security dimension we first calculated some time-varying institutional and dynamic outcome indicators.

They were elaborated in previous work using truly comparative panel data for the period 1994–2001 and applied here again (Muffels and Luijkx, 2008).

Institutional indicators are the strictness of employment protection regulation (EPL) and the generosity of the unemployment or social assistance benefits (Muffels, 2007). We use the overall EPL indicator being a composite measure for the strictness of the country's employment protection legislation with respect to standard and temporary employment and dismissal procedures as developed by the OECD for the late 1990s. For the generosity of the social security system we use the OECD overall five years replacement rates (including social assistance) which are given for every two years, and we calculated the average of the year preceding and the following year for the years that were missing. With respect to the supporting labour market institutions we included active labour market policies (ALMP) which we also included as a time-varying construct and the availability of working time arrangements at the company level within each country for the only year for which we had information, 2004/2005.[3] We used the information of the establishment survey on working time and work–life balance in 21 countries for that year. We assumed that the cross-country differences for that particular year will also reflect the differences in working time options for the earlier period for the late 1990s. Whereas the ALMP and UIB are included as time varying, due to lack of information the EPL and WTO institutional indicators were not (Muffels et al., 2008).

Dynamic outcome indicators are the indicators as elaborated in Muffels and Luijkx (2008) and Muffels (2008). Labour market mobility is defined as the sum of the mobility within work (indicated by OM = occupational mobility) and between work (indicated by CM = contract mobility, that is the mobility between permanent jobs, flexible contracts and self-employment).[4] Occupational mobility is defined as the mobility between jobs of different professional level and is considered a proxy for job mobility. A change in occupational status always involves a job change but some people remaining in the same occupational status still experience a job change either within or outside the firm. Therefore occupational mobility slightly underestimates the amount of job mobility in society.

Dynamic employment (ESD) and *income security* (YSD) are calculated from the European Community Household Panel (ECHP). The starting point is the annual transition matrix of the various employment (permanent contract, flexible contract, self-employed, unemployed, inactive) and poverty statuses (in or out of poverty). The annual transitions are however cumulated over the six pairs of years. The ESD measure is the summation of the yearly staying probabilities in employment plus the entry rate into employment minus the exit rate out of employment. They are calculated separately for males and females. As such, the ESD measure is a gender-based indicator for employment exit and (re-)entry mobility. The income security measure is defined as the yearly staying probabilities in non-poverty plus the exit rate out of poverty minus the entry rate into poverty (YSD). We first calculated the poverty threshold on the total population and then calculated the fraction of men and women respectively earning an income below that threshold.

5.5 DATA AND MAIN DEFINITIONS

ECHP Data

We use the available eight waves of the European Community Household Panel (ECHP) covering 14 countries of the European Union during the years 1994–2001. Sweden was excluded from the sample due to the data being cross-sectional. For substantive reasons we restricted our sample to persons of working age, that is men and women between 16 and 65 years old.

We weighted the data and calculated adjusted longitudinal weights. These were calculated as the product of the cross-sectional weights and the inverse of the survival probabilities between two consecutive waves. The weights were adjusted to take account of the differences in population and sample sizes across countries. The ECHP contains information on the type of contract, on occupation (2-digit ISCO 1988 code) and the branch of industry (NACE). Unfortunately, there is lack of information on the employer and hence on job changes involving an employer's change. We focus on year-to-year changes in employment contract, labour market status and occupational class. The dependent variables are defined using the information as reported for the preceding calendar year. For estimation we pooled the information for the seven transition rates for each individual in the sample and consider changes in statuses between year t and year t+1. The independent variables are all measured at time t. The total number of observations in the seven year-by-year transition panel data sets is 860,690 of which about 50 per cent is female. Because of the clustering of transitions over time within countries and the clustering of individuals over countries we used robust estimation of the model parameters by adjusting the standard errors for the clustering across time and countries. Our parameter estimates are therefore rather conservative to ensure that the effects found are robust.

5.6 RESULTS OF THE DESCRIPTIVE ANALYSIS

First, we looked into the scores of our mobility and security measures by gender. The results are given in Table 5.1.

Table 5.1 Contract, occupational mobility and dynamic income and employment security for males and females, by country (per cent)[5]

	Males					Females					ΔESD	ΔYSD	ΔM
Country	CM	OM	M	ESD	YSD	CM	OM	M	ESD	YSD	F–M	F–M	F–M
Denmark	7.6	5.9	13.5	62.2	76.5	5.8	4.7	10.5	45.8	73.0	–16.4	–3.5	–3
Netherlands	7.5	9.1	16.6	63.3	70.9	5.4	7.3	12.7	21.5	65.9	–41.8	–5	–3.9
Belgium	4.9	12.5	17.4	57.0	68.4	4.5	7.3	11.8	28.3	60.2	–28.7	–8.2	–5.6
France	3.7	1.7	5.4	52.2	64.6	2.0	1.0	3.0	28.9	62.1	–23.3	–2.5	–2.4
Ireland	6.7	10.1	16.8	52.6	55.9	5.1	6.8	11.8	28.2	51.8	–24.4	–4.1	–5
Italy	6.2	6.2	12.4	42.1	54.4	3.2	2.8	5.9	15.6	51.7	–26.5	–2.7	–6.5
Greece	7.5	3.3	10.8	53.8	54.1	3.4	1.6	5.0	17.9	51.3	–35.9	–2.8	–5.8
Spain	9.0	11.7	20.7	38.9	54.2	4.4	5.8	10.2	9.1	51.3	–29.8	–2.9	–10.5
Portugal	7.8	9.3	17.0	61.0	59.3	4.7	6.8	11.5	35.6	55.1	–25.4	–4.2	–5.5
Austria	5.9	8.9	14.8	58.6	73.0	4.5	5.8	10.3	39.1	66.9	–19.5	–6.1	–4.5
Finland	5.3	3.7	9.1	50.2	69.5	4.6	3.9	8.5	39.3	69.1	–109	–0.4	–0.6
Germany	5.8	6.3	12.1	50.9	73.2	4.6	5.3	9.9	31.4	67.5	–19.5	–5.7	–2.2
Luxembourg	5.4	3.6	9.1	69.6	71.8	3.3	2.0	5.4	32.9	69.2	–36.7	–2.6	–3.7
UK	5.2	11.4	16.6	61.8	62.8	3.9	8.9	12.8	43.5	50.5	–18.3	–12.3	–3.8
Total	6.0	7.3	13.3	51.3	63.8	3.9	4.9	8.8	27.5	58.4	–23.8	–5.4	–4.5

Notes:
CM = contract mobility; OM = occupational mobility; M = Labour market mobility (M = CM + OM), ESD = Dynamic employment security; YSD = Dynamic income security. ΔESD/ΔYSD = ESD/YSD for females minus ESD/YSD for males.

Source: ECHP 1994–2001.

In the last three columns we present the differences between the ESD, YSD and M scores for females compared to males. The results for women are very dissimilar to those of men especially on the employment security indicator (ESD). Note the low mobility rates in France and the high mobility rates in the UK and Ireland but remarkably also in Belgium, Spain and Portugal. In Spain a high mobility is coupled to a low level of employment security. It resembles in particular the high contract mobility in southern countries, though occupational mobility rates are relatively high too. Denmark scores extremely high with respect to employment security but for these years not better than the EU average on mobility. Contract mobility seems high but occupational mobility is rather low especially for males in Denmark. The unregulated regimes of UK and Ireland appear capable of maintaining high levels of occupational and contract mobility and simultaneously and unexpectedly high levels of employment security whereas the continental countries such as Germany, Austria, France and

Belgium show a mixed picture. France exhibits the lowest mobility levels of all for both sexes coupled with just above average employment security. The regulated southern countries Italy and Greece share rather poor levels of occupational mobility and employment security both for males and females. Viewing the evidence on income security and comparing it with the employment security evidence, the UK and Belgium in particular perform rather differently with a very good employment security record but a rather poor income security record, especially for women.

5.7 MODELS TO TEST OUR MAIN HYPOTHESIS

To test the 'flexicurity' and trade-off theses for males and females separately in a multivariate way, we have estimated multi-level models to explain the variation in flexibility/mobility and security levels across males and females and countries.

Model I deals with occupational class mobility being the mobility from a current occupational class position at t into another position at t+1. The ECHP enables the construction of only a very crude indicator, consisting of four classes: professional worker; low white-collar worker; upper manual worker and lower manual or personal service workers. The ranking was based on the calculation of hourly wages for male and female workers separately working more than 15 hours. Using this ranking we are able to make a distinction between lateral (staying in the same class), upward and downward job mobility. The reference category is staying in the same occupational class.

Model II on contract mobility examines the mobility from a flexible contract or a temporary job (origin state) into a permanent job, into unemployment/inactivity or into self-employment (destination states). The ECHP contains information on whether workers are occupied in a permanent job or in a temporary job, a casual job or another job with a different kind of contract (like an on-call or a freelance contract, the so-called other arrangement) as of 1994. We also added workers in training contracts working more than 15 hours a week. The reference category is staying in a flexible contract across both years that we consider a lateral move.

Model III and IV on exit and (re-)entry mobility examines the mobility from permanent employment into unemployment and inactivity (Model III: exit) and from non-work into employment (Model IV: re-entry).

All models are estimated for males and females separately. In these models we try to test the impact of institutional characteristics in two different ways.

In the first institutional model we use the constructed company's working time options (WTO) measure to account for the different working time preferences of women due to caring. We also used other direct institutional measures such as the EPL indicator, the ALMP (active labour market policy) and the UIB (benefit generosity) indicator (replacement rates) that we used also in an earlier paper (Muffels, 2007).

In a second regime type model we applied the seminal Esping-Andersen regime typology (EA) to examine to what extent the institutions model is able to explain the cross-country variations nearly as well as the regime model. We did not define our own typology for two reasons: firstly because the flexicurity picture does not seem to be very different from EA's typology, especially if we leave out a few country outliers like Portugal; secondly because all welfare regime and 'Varieties of Capitalism' typologies result in more or less the same typology as Esping-Andersen's for which reason it is the theoretical benchmark with which we want to compare our empirical findings.

5.8 RESULTS OF MODEL ESTIMATIONS

Model I: Occupational Mobility

The results from the first multinomial model on occupational mobility which we see as a proxy for job mobility are reproduced in Table 5.2. We will report briefly on the control variables which are age and age squared, life course stage, education level, occupational class, unemployment history, tenure, industrial sector, working hours and firm size, and we will focus on the variables where our main interest went to, the various institutional variables and the economic cycle effects represented by the unemployment rate and the year dummies. Most of the results on the controls seem also to confirm our prior assumptions.

Controls

We observe a U-shaped pattern for age, with a positive effect of age and negative effect of age squared on upward mobility for women. Single fathers and mothers have higher odds to move downwards on the job ladder and lower odds to move upwards compared to couples without children. Childbirth impacts, not surprisingly, only on females' mobility while it raises women's chances to move downwards on the job ladder. The caring reason for working part-time has no effect on females' careers possibly because the effect is already captured in the other life course variables.

The education effects confirm what we expected, a low (high) education increases (reduces) the odds to move downwards and it reduces (increases) the odds to move upwards compared to people with intermediate education.

The effects are stronger for females than for males for downwards moves on the job ladder. A high education shows no positive impact on the odds of women for upward moves, which effect might reflect the 'glass ceiling' feature of their career. Bad health increases the chances of downwards moves for males and females. Unemployment history increases (reduces) the odds of downwards (upwards) moves. The longer the tenure is the more likely it is for male and female workers to stay in their current job and not to move. Other income resources of the person or the household seem to prevent downward moves and to raise the odds of upward moves. It might allow people to wait and to search for a job with favourable career prospects.

The effects for the other variables confirm our expectations: upward and downward mobility are higher (respectively lower) in the public sector for males and females. The longer working hours are, especially for men, the less likely they are to move downwards. The occupational class effects confirm the existence of bottom and ceiling effects for males and females.

Economic cycle

The *year effects*, signalling the economic cycle effects, are all positive in both models, indicating that the improved economic conditions during the 1990s raise the likelihood of upward as well as downward mobility, although the time trend is not particularly strong. The unemployment rate has a similar effect, reducing upward and downward mobility in the institutional model, both for males and for females. In the regime model the effects of the year dummies are similar but the unemployment rate effect is taken over in the males' and females' model by the regime type effect.

Institutional variables

In the institutional model the effects are particularly strong for the level of institutional flexibility indicated by the strictness of the employment protection legislation (the overall EPL). The stricter the protection rules are, the lower the odds of upward and downward occupational mobility for both male and female workers. The negative effect on upward mobility is stronger than on downward mobility again, both for men and women. Employment protection appears to inhibit the mobility on the labour market for males and females and therewith reduces the level of flexibility.

It is further shown that the five-years replacement rates of unemployment insurance have no effect on downward or upward occupational mobility. For the two other institutional variables we also find significant effects though slightly at odds with our conjectures beforehand. The more countries spend on active labour market policies the higher downward and upward mobility tend to be, especially for females.

Table 5.2 Occupational class mobility: institutional (model Ia) and regime model (model Ib), males and females, 1994–2001

	Ia: Institutional model				Ib: Regime model			
	Males		Females		Males		Females	
	Downward	Upward	Downward	Upward	Downward	Upward	Downward	Upward
Life course	coeff.	coeff.	coeff.	coeff.	coeff.	coeff.	coeff.	coeff.
Age	–0.085***	–0.038	–0.014	0.024**	–0.090***	–0.043*	–0.017	0.022*
Age sq/100	0.081***	0.027	0.009	–0.055***	0.088***	0.034	0.013	–0.051***
Life course phase/HH-type (ref. couple no children)								
Couple yngst								
– child 0–5	0.106	–0.081	–0.059	–0.148	0.101	–0.090	–0.073	–0.169
– child 6–16	0.049	–0.041	0.110	0.067	0.060	–0.025	0.115	0.084
Single								
– no child	0.014	0.004	–0.064	0.004	0.001	0.009	–0.044	0.024
– with children	0.297***	–0.188*	0.134*	0.071	0.301***	–0.134	0.162**	0.109
Number of children	–0.027	–0.025	0.023	–0.049	–0.022	–0.018	0.037	–0.042
Childbirth	0.096	–0.081	0.300**	0.204	0.069	–0.091	0.274**	0.198
Part-time for caring			0.106	–0.103			0.115	–0.051
Socio-economic variables								
Education level (ref. Intermediate)								
Education								
– low	0.450***	–0.498***	0.526***	–0.516***	0.529***	–0.500***	0.623***	–0.486***
– high	–0.853***	0.166**	–0.762***	0.017	–0.762***	0.263**	–0.653***	0.064
Unemployment history	0.434***	–0.089	0.289***	–0.132***	0.491***	–0.024	0.319***	–0.110**
Tenure current job	–0.001*	–0.002*	–0.002***	–0.002***	–0.001**	–0.002**	–0.002***	–0.003***
Bad health	0.135*	–0.028	0.162	–0.124*	0.119	–0.013	0.190	–0.089*
Personal non-labour inc./10^3	–0.008**	0.005	0.013***	0.009**	–0.011***	0.001	0.012***	0.007*
Other HH labour inc./10^3	–0.005***	0.005***	–0.004*	0.002	–0.004**	0.006***	–0.004	0.002**
HH non–labour inc./10^3	0.002	0.007***	0.000	0.001	0.003	0.009***	0.000	0.001
Job characteristics								
Hours worked	–0.009***	0.001	–0.004	0.004	–0.007**	0.002	–0.001	0.006
Occupational class (1 = low 4 = high)	1.004***	–1.166***	1.196***	–1.065***	1.020***	–1.173***	1.212***	–1.076***

Table 5.2 (Continued)

	1a: Institutional model				1b: Regime model			
	Males		Females		Males		Females	
	Down-ward	Up-ward	Down-ward	Up-ward	Down-ward	Up-ward	Down-ward	Up-ward
Sector (ref. Industry + services)								
Sector								
– primary	0.477***	–0.347***	0.814***	–0.246*	0.481***	–0.335***	0.826***	–0.275**
– public	–0.361***	0.198***	–0.556***	–0.218***	–0.395***	0.147**	–0.588***	–0.220***
Firm size	–0.017	–0.004	–0.005	0.000	–0.011	0.006	–0.001	0.007
Institutions/policies								
ALM Policies	0.385**	0.305	0.429**	0.515**				
Flexible WTO for employees	–4.166***	–4.219***	–5.408***	–3.629***				
Net RR 5 yrs (une + sa)	–0.003	–0.004	0.007*	0.000				
EPL overall	–0.504***	–0.605***	–0.432***	–0.642***				
Regime type (ref. Continental)								
Anglo-Saxon					0.469***	0.831***	0.457**	0.989***
Nordic					0.218	0.725**	0.267	0.751**
Southern					0.359	0.535**	0.263	–0.075
Male/Female UR	–0.039**	–0.063**	–0.016	–0.032***	0.027	0.024	0.010	0.021
Year dummies (ref. = 1994)								
1995	0.030	–0.211	–0.111	0.076	0.052	–0.160	–0.140	0.044
1996	1.592***	1.522***	1.139***	1.468***	1.607***	1.561***	1.100***	1.435***
1997	1.069***	0.946***	0.938***	1.155***	1.128***	1.036***	0.897***	1.147***
1998	1.040***	0.652**	0.808***	0.969***	1.088***	0.756**	0.714**	0.910***
1999	1.227***	0.891***	0.973***	1.290***	1.341***	1.068***	0.915***	1.291***
2000	1.232***	0.899*	0.902***	1.052***	1.439***	1.188**	0.895***	1.159***
Constant	–1.628*	4.024***	–4.383***	2.083***	–5.264***	–0.405	–7.367***	–1.265***
R squared	0.148		0.132		0.140		0.125	
N	129,524		78,613		129,524		78,613	

Notes:
* p < 0.10, ** p < 0.05, *** p < 0.01.

Source: ECHP, 1994–2000.

The finding seems to suggest that active labour market policies raise the mobility on the labour market though the effect is not particularly strong. This makes sense if one assumes that the unemployed worker who will be placed in a job replaces somebody else who subsequently either moves upwards or downwards. The availability of working time options in the company which meet the needs of employees (WTO), seem to have the opposite effect, and reduces both upward and downward mobility. The negative effect on downward mobility is stronger and for upward mobility weaker for females than for males. It might indicate that if more working time options are available for employees in a country, that workers feel less need to move into other jobs to meet their working time preferences. Better working time options seem to increase the job match and to reduce downward mobility for women. It also shows that it is not mobility per se that matters but also which transitions are encouraged and which not. The distinction made in the TLM approach between 'good' and 'bad' transitions seems therefore to make sense.

The regime model shows a lower explanatory power than the institutional model. The Anglo-Saxon regime exhibits higher odds of downward and upward mobility compared to the Continental regime, confirming our hypothesis of higher mobility levels in unregulated regimes. The Nordic regime performs significantly better in terms of increasing upward mobility compared to the Continental regime but not, as we expected, better on reducing downward mobility. Remarkably though, also the Southern countries appear to exhibit higher upward mobility than the Continental countries and confirms the earlier descriptive results reported in Table 5.1.

Model II: Contract Mobility

In Tables 5.3 and 5.4 we report on the findings of the institutional and regime model, respectively, with respect to contract mobility, the movement out of a flexible contract into a permanent job, self-employment or non-work. The results on the control and economic cycle variables in both models are very similar for which reason we report the outcomes on these variables for the institutional model only. In Table 5.4 we therefore only discuss the effects of the regime type dummies.

Institutional model (IIa): control variables

For age and age squared we again observe for males and females a U-shaped pattern with opposite signs for the within-work and exit transitions. The presence of a young child lowers the odds of moving into a permanent job or into self-employment but only for women living in a couple. Single fathers with young children have lower odds of moving into a permanent job or self-employment but, remarkably, single mothers with young children do not. However, childbirth tends to push women more into unemployment whereas no effect was found for men. Trainees constitute a special group while the odds of a transition into permanent employment are lower for trainees than for non-trainees. Their odds for a transition into inactivity are also lower both for men and women compared to the odds for the other categories.

If women work shorter hours for caring reasons the odds of moving into a permanent job or into self-employment are larger than for women who work part-time for other reasons for example because they could not find a permanent job, or who do not work at all. The odds of moving into unemployment are similarly smaller for these women than for the other categories of women.

The effects of low education are similar for men and women and show that a low education reduces the odds of moving into a permanent job or self-employment. Unexpectedly, we find that higher educated men are less likely to move into a permanent job but more likely to move into self-employment. Higher educated men also exhibit clearly lower odds to move into unemployment or into inactivity than men with intermediate education. These findings corroborate the findings of other research (Dekker, 2007; Hernanz et al., 2008; Muffels, 2007) signalling probably a selection effect because the higher educated occupy the better temporary jobs and are therefore more critical in the choice of a permanent job that they want to move to. The effect is not found for high educated women signalling their weaker labour market position. A person's bad health seems to inhibit the movement into a permanent job though only for men but clearly raises the odds for exit into unemployment. A higher occupational class seems to exert a negative impact on the odds of unemployment, at least for males, but also on the females' odds to move into inactivity.

Longer tenure in a temporary job tends to increase the odds of moving into a permanent job and to lower the odds of moving into unemployment or inactivity both for males and females. Contrary to what we expected we found that male temporary workers in the primary as well as the public sector are less likely to move into permanent jobs but more likely to move into self-employment. Females working in the public sector are also less likely to move into a permanent job but also less likely to move into unemployment.

The availability of other income resources in the household leads to higher odds of moving into unemployment and inactivity especially for females. The longer working hours are the higher the odds of moving into employment and the lower the odds of exit into unemployment, especially for women. Occupational class reduces the odds of moving into unemployment or inactivity. Finally, a larger firm size has no effect on moving into a permanent job which contradicts our prior expectations.

Economic cycle

Again, the unemployment rate exerts a negative effect on moving into a permanent job and self-employment, both for men and women, and it raises the odds of exit into unemployment for women and into inactivity for men. Most of the year effects turn out to be insignificant both for males and females. The few significant effects found are for males exhibiting lower odds of movements into unemployment over time.

Table 5.3 Contract mobility (transitions out of temporary contract): institutional model for males and females (model IIa)

	Males				Females			
From flex contract into:	Permanent	Self-empl.	Un-empl.	In-act.	Permanent	Self-empl.	Un-empl.	In-act.
Life course								
Age	0.087***	0.130*	–0.003	–0.198**	0.144***	0.194***	0.021	–0.060
Age sq/100	–0.112***	–0.162	0.033	0.266**	–0.199***	–0.202***	–0.022	0.073
Life course phase/ HH-type (ref. couple no children)								
Couple, yngst								
– child 0–5	–0.120	–0.136	0.081	–0.105	–0.141	1.020*	0.068	0.381***
– child 6–16	–0.093	0.107	0.156	–0.208	–0.231**	0.213	–0.124	–0.061
Single								
– no child	–0.080	–0.660**	0.597**	0.419**	0.017	0.110	–0.149	–0.343**
– with children	–0.344**	–0.890***	0.404**	0.304	–0.103	0.582	–0.078	–0.360***
Number of children	0.063	–0.204**	0.098	–0.062	–0.035	–0.224	–0.024	–0.039
Childbirth	0.168	–0.011	0.167	–0.254	0.201	0.647*	0.530**	0.277
Trainee/apprenticeship	–0.611*	–0.356	–0.345	–0.726***	–0.539***	–0.196	–0.055	–0.391**
Part-time for caring					0.230***	0.636**	–0.449***	–0.005
Socio-economic variables								
Education level (ref. Intermediate)								
Education								
– low	–0.517***	–0.380**	–0.161	–0.544***	–0.268***	–0.707***	–0.300*	–0.208**
– high	–0.166**	0.260*	–0.310***	–0.255*	–0.177**	0.037	–0.374*	–0.171
Unemployment history	–0.312***	–0.561***	0.545***	–0.536***	–0.055	–0.370*	0.660**	–0.145
Tenure current job	0.005***	0.002	–0.013***	–0.011***	0.005***	–0.002	–0.014***	–0.008***
Bad health	–0.320***	0.325	0.738***	0.464	–0.076	0.059	0.256*	0.170
Personal non-labour inc./10^3	–0.005	–0.005	0.001	0.020**	–0.020	–0.115**	0.034***	0.036***
Other HH labour inc./10^3	0.003	0.009	–0.006	0.002	0.000	0.002	–0.010**	0.000
HH non-labour inc./10^3	–0.001	–0.003	0.000	–0.001	–0.001	0.044**	0.003	0.008*

Table 5.3 (Continued)

	Males				Females			
From flex contract into:	Permanent	Self-empl.	Un-empl.	In-act.	Permanent	Self-empl.	Un-empl.	In-act.
Job characteristics								
Hours worked	0.007	0.032***	–0.006	–0.036***	0.005***	0.031***	–0.002	–0.038***
Occupational class (1 = low 4 = high)	0.038	0.066	–0.257***	0.046	–0.063	–0.010	–0.228***	–0.232***
Sector (ref. Industry + services)								
Sector								
– primary	–0.619***	0.639***	–0.259	–0.085	–1.014**	0.145	–0.287	–0.072
– public	–0.496***	0.314**	–0.063	–0.174	–0.303***	–0.428***	–0.143**	–0.051
Firm size	0.036	–0.401***	–0.127***	–0.036**	0.047***	–0.505***	–0.107***	–0.078***
Institutions/policies								
ALM Policies	–0.398*	–0.724***	–0.095	–0.486	0.068	0.107	0.078	0.215
Flexible WTO for employees	2.943***	1.578	3.068***	6.332***	0.354	0.476	2.165	0.687
Net RR 5 yrs (une + sa)	–0.009*	–0.025***	0.001	–0.006	–0.009**	–0.018**	0.015***	–0.016***
EPL overall	–0.183**	–0.314**	0.199	–0.030	–0.296***	–0.104	0.378***	–0.455***
Economic cycle								
Male/Female UR	–0.089***	–0.027	0.068***	0.006	–0.056***	–0.038*	0.044***	–0.010
Year dummies (ref. = 1994)								
1995	0.073	–0.038	–0.050	0.093	–0.228*	0.709***	–0.182	0.095
1997	0.122	–0.119	–0.146	–0.385**	0.072	0.100	–0.171	0.197
1998	–0.162	–0.913***	–0.347**	0.045	–0.127	0.123	–0.280	0.008
1999	–0.191	–0.242	–0.241	–0.367	–0.204	–0.189	–0.336	–0.136
2000	–0.218***	–0.132	–0.005	–0.171	–0.537***	0.199	–0.359	–0.136
Constant	–0.611	–1.947	–2.867**	1.705	–0.517	–5.159***	–3.479***	3.845***
R squared	0.093				0.078			
N	15,008				12,311			

Notes:
* $p < 0.10$, ** $p < 0.05$, *** $p < 0.01$.

Source: ECHP, 1994–2000.

Table 5.4 Contract mobility (transitions out of temporary contract): regime model for males and females (model IIb)

	Males				Females			
From flex contract into:	Perma-nent	Self-empl.	Un-empl.	In-act.	Perma nent	Self-empl.	Un-empl.	In-act.
Regime type (ref. Continental)								
Anglo-Saxon	0.850***	1.651***	–0.300	0.637**	0.595***	0.371	–0.815***	0.958***
Nordic	0.235	0.298	–0.518***	–0.086	0.410***	0.387**	–0.396*	0.789***
Southern	–0.041	0.939***	0.557**	0.701**	–0.049	0.430	–0.731***	0.097
R squared	0.093				0.077			
N	15,008				12,311			

Notes:
* p < 0.10, ** p < 0.05, *** p < 0.01.

Source: ECHP, 1994–2000.

Institutional variables

Countries which spend a larger share of their GDP to active labour market policies entail lower odds for temporary workers to move into permanent jobs or into self-employment though only for males. Countries with more employees' accommodating working time options (WTO) show higher odds to move into permanent jobs but also higher odds to exit into unemployment and inactivity. The latter effect might be related to the options for flexible and partial retirement allowing workers to leave the labour market early. These effects are found for men but unexpectedly not for women. Further inspection shows that the main effect of active labour market policy spending (when the WTO variable is left out) is insignificant for males and females whereas the WTO variable (if the ALMP variable is left out) remains significant and becomes even stronger. Including an interaction term shows that the main effects of ALMP and WTO are positive for males but that the interaction between ALMP and WTO is significantly negative, suggesting that countries with priority to both policies perform less well than countries with priority to only one. Since the correlation between active labour market policies and working time options for employees is positive and strong (0.7), countries showing a higher working time options' availability also have more active labour market policies (see also the European Commission, 2007). Though the evidence is not straightforward, 'activating' policies in the form of either active LM policies or WTO policies seem to exert a positive effect on the transitions of male temporary workers to permanent jobs although such an effect is unexpectedly not found for females.

High benefit replacement rates exert a disincentive effect for these temporary workers since they lower the odds of moving into a permanent job or into self-employment though the effects are not particularly strong. For female temporary workers, high unemployment benefits also raise the odds of moving into unemployment.

The findings for EPL show that the more regulated labour markets are, due to strict employment protection rules, the lower the odds for male and female workers in temporary contracts to move into permanent jobs. This is associated with the stronger protection rules in regulated regimes for permanent jobs. For female temporary workers, the stricter the protection rules are, the higher the odds to move into unemployment although not into inactivity. These findings corroborate the hypothesis about the adverse effects of EPL on mobility.

Contract mobility: regime model

The results of the regime model (IIb) are reported in Table 5.4. We leave out the results of the control variables because they are very much similar to the ones found in the institutional model. The unregulated Anglo-Saxon countries, both for males and females, and the Nordic countries, though only for females, exhibit the highest transition rates into permanent jobs compared to the other regimes. The Anglo-Saxon countries and the Southern countries show larger odds for transitions into self-employment than the Continental countries but only for males. Remarkably, though, not the Southern but the Nordic countries seem to exhibit higher odds than the other regimes for the transitions of females into self-employment. The odds for male temporary workers to move into unemployment or inactivity are larger in Anglo-Saxon and lower in Nordic and Southern countries compared to the Continental countries. However, for females these odds are higher in Anglo-Saxon as well as in Nordic countries.

Model III: Exit Mobility

In Table 5.5 we report on the institutional (model IIIa) and regime model (model IIIb) for exit mobility out of a permanent job. Because the findings for the controls are generally very similar (although with opposite sign) to what we found in model III on contract mobility we will not present their effects.[6] We restrict the discussion to the effect of institutions and regime type and the economic cycle effects represented by the gender-specific unemployment rate. Viewing the unemployment rate, first, higher unemployment in a country reduces the odds of moving out of a permanent job into a temporary job but raises the odds of moving into unemployment both for males and females.

Table 5.5 Institutional and regime model for exit mobility: transitions out of permanent job into temporary jobs, self-employment, unemployment or inactivity

Model IIIa: Institutional model for transitions out of permanent job								
Institutions/ policies	Males				Females			
From permanent into:	Temporary	Self-empl.	Un-empl.	In-active	Tempo rary	Self-empl.	Un-empl.	In-active
Male/Female UR	-0.089^{***}	-0.027	0.068^{***}	0.006	-0.056^{***}	-0.038^{*}	0.044^{***}	-0.010
ALM Policies	0.968^{***}	0.526^{***}	0.430^{*}	-0.147^{*}	0.774^{***}	-0.186	0.354	-0.114
Flexible WTO for employees	-3.962^{***}	-4.075^{***}	-1.163	2.208^{***}	-1.886	-2.187	0.083	1.859^{***}
Net RR 5 yrs (une + sa)	0.001	-0.013^{***}	0.020^{***}	-0.011^{***}	0.002	-0.007^{*}	0.019^{***}	-0.011^{***}
EPL overall	-0.041	-0.225^{***}	0.238^{**}	-0.025	-0.051	-0.152	0.196	-0.112^{*}
Model IIIb: Regime model for transitions out of permanent job								
Male/Female UR	-0.062^{***}	-0.008	0.039^{*}	0.009	-0.029^{**}	-0.032^{*}	0.021^{**}	0.025
Regime type (ref.= Continental)								
Anglo-Saxon	-1.068^{***}	0.115	-1.026^{***}	0.165^{***}	-0.619^{***}	0.629^{***}	-0.922^{***}	0.380^{***}
Nordic	0.340^{**}	0.378^{***}	-0.455^{**}	0.060	0.254	0.652^{***}	-0.237	0.038
Southern	-0.022	0.854^{***}	-0.719^{***}	0.063	-0.310	0.880^{***}	-0.727^{**}	-0.097

Notes:
* $p < 0.10$, ** $p < 0.05$, *** $p < 0.01$; Male/ Female UR = Unemployment Rate for males and females respectively.

Source: ECHP, 1994–2000.

Viewing the impact of active labour market policies and working time options availability on exit mobility the results are again slightly puzzling. Notwithstanding the high positive correlation between the two (0.64), the effects of both are opposite in sign. Inclusion of an interaction effect, which is significant and positive, turns the main positive ALMP effect to become insignificant and the negative WTO effect to become even more negative but only for males. It shows that in combination WTO and ALMP have a positive effect on exit from a permanent job into a temporary job but the availability of WTO alone reduces exit into a temporary job at least for males. The effects are insignificant for females which begs for more scrutiny into the issue. Further it is shown that the higher the net replacement rates are in a country the higher the odds of exit into unemployment and the lower the odds of exit into inactivity both for males and females.

The unemployment rate in the regime model, presented in Table 5.5, exhibits exactly the same effect as in the institutional model although the odds are smaller showing that part of the effect is captured by regime type. Anglo-Saxon regimes perform relatively best in keeping workers in permanent employment and preventing them from switching into a more insecure temporary job or into unemployment compared to Continental countries. The Southern and Continental countries protect permanent workers better than the other two regimes from exits into a more insecure job, although the Southern countries show lower odds than the Continental countries for workers ending up in unemployment possibly due to ungenerous benefits. For that reason people in Southern regimes seem to prefer exiting into self-employment than into unemployment. These results confirm most of our prior conjectures about the possible impact of regime type on exit mobility.

Model IV: Re-entry Mobility

In the last part of this chapter we look into re-entry into employment from unemployment or inactivity. This type of mobility is particularly relevant within the Transitional Labour Market model because it entails the critical role of activating labour market policies as well as of the business cycle on re-entry into the labour market. The outcomes of the institutional (model IVa) and regime model (model IVb) are respectively presented in Table 5.6 and Table 5.7. Again, we leave out in these models the effects of the control variables except for the unemployment rate to capture the economic cycle effects. Viewing the effects of some of the controls, we observe again that more children inhibit re-entry into work for males and females. It is also shown that women engaged in domestic chores have lower odds of re-entry into employment but also for men, it inhibits accepting a temporary contract. The results convincingly show the importance of job search behaviour for re-entry, for males and females. The odds of searching are even larger for re-entry into a flexible contract than into a permanent contract. Notice also the strong effects of the discouraged worker variable for the re-entry into permanent employment which are, not surprisingly, particularly large for women but also for men.

A high education has a strong positive impact on re-entry whereas a low education inhibits the transition into a permanent job. The odds are even higher for women than for men although the odds of re-entry into self-employment are lower for women. Again the results show that bad health inhibits re-entry into work both for men and women and that the availability of other income resources acts as a disincentive to work.

The institutional variables show again some mixed evidence. The effects of ALMP and WTO have unexpected negative and positive signs on re-entry into permanent work, though only for males notwithstanding their high positive correlation. For re-entry into temporary work ALMP has a positive and WTO a negative effect, both for males and females.

Table 5.6 Re-entry mobility (transitions out of non-work): institutional model for males and females (model IVa)

	Males			Females		
	Perma-nent Coeff.	Flex ctr. Coeff.	Self-empl. Coeff.	Perma-nent Coeff.	Flex ctr. Coeff.	Self-empl. Coeff.
Life course						
Age	0.274***	0.122***	0.345***	0.272***	0.124***	0.253***
Age sq/100	–0.409***	–0.229***	–0.453***	–0.416***	–0.235***	–0.312***
Life course phase/HH type (ref. Couple no child)						
Couple, yngst child 0–5	0.152	–0.144	0.035	–0.102	–0.415**	–0.037
Couple, yngst child 6–16	0.282*	0.164	0.049	–0.106	0.077	–0.188***
Single no child	–0.562***	–0.468***	–0.283	–0.232*	–0.017	0.028
Single with child	–0.571***	–0.392***	–0.351	–0.028	–0.068	–0.108
Number of children	–0.150***	0.000	0.003	–0.106**	–0.109	0.057
Childbirth	0.131	–0.028	0.211	–0.116	0.032	–0.416***
Socio-economic variables						
Job search behaviour						
Domestic work (yes, no)	–0.557	–1.067***	–0.101	–0.926***	–0.904***	–0.205*
Job search (yes, no)	0.937***	1.087***	0.706***	0.783***	1.028***	0.345***
Discouraged worker (yes, no)	–0.472***	–0.429**	–0.409***	–0.665***	–0.270*	–0.132
Education level (ref. Intermediate)						
Low education	–0.334**	0.061	–0.071	–0.246***	0.056	–0.281*
High education	0.384***	0.343***	0.694***	0.483***	0.476***	0.378***
Unemployment history	–0.145	0.211**	–0.153	–0.015	0.301***	–0.189
Bad health	–1.071***	–0.648***	–0.434**	–0.776***	–0.471**	–0.642***
Pers. non-labour inc./1000	–0.045**	–0.043***	–0.029	–0.020*	–0.005	–0.059***
Other HH labour inc./1000	–0.005*	–0.004***	–0.006	–0.004	–0.005	–0.001
HH non-labour inc./1000	–0.022***	–0.010**	–0.017	–0.010**	–0.011***	–0.005
ALM policies	–0.474**	0.523***	–0.226	–0.053	0.540**	0.123
Flexible WTO for employees	2.639***	-3.151***	-3.438***	0.715	–2.819**	-7.815***
Net RR 5 yrs (une + sa)	0.010***	0.012***	–0.013***	–0.002	0.009*	–0.004*
EPL overall	–0.031	–0.256***	–0.208**	–0.238	–0.231**	–0.211***
Male/Female UR	–0.090***	–0.009	–0.037**	–0.089***	–0.011	–0.040***

Table 5.6 (Continued)

	Males			Females		
	Permanent Coeff.	Flex ctr. Coeff.	Self-empl. Coeff.	Permanent Coeff.	Flex ctr. Coeff.	Self-empl. Coeff.
Year dummies (ref. = 1994)						
1995[a]	–0.204*	–0.150***	0.006			
1996[a]				–0.117**	0.184***	0.097
1997	0.240**	0.183	–0.127	0.193**	0.314***	–0.041
1998	–0.076	0.170***	–0.060	–0.072	0.473***	–0.151
1999	–0.098	0.136	–0.233	0.012	0.382***	–0.087
2000	–0.125	0.163***	–0.166	0.140	0.476***	–0.038
Constant	–4.631***	-3.941***	-7.103***	–4.729**	-3.495***	–4.219***
R squared	0.169			0.155		
N	56,757			118,389		

Notes:
* $p < 0.10$, ** $p < 0.05$, *** $p < 0.01$.
a. The year dummy for 1995 is removed in the model for females and the year dummy for 1996 in the model for males.

Source: ECHP, 1994–2001.

Inclusion of an interaction term shows that only the WTO variable still has a positive impact on re-entry into permanent work for males. For re-entry into temporary work and self-employment, the combination of ALMP and WTO has a positive effect, whereas WTO itself exerts a negative effect both for males and females. It appears that in countries with more working time options, preferences for working times are better met in permanent jobs than in temporary jobs or self-employment. The evidence on net replacement rates exhibit strong positive effects on transitions into permanent and temporary work especially for males. This seems awkward but further inspection shows it just reflects that countries with high benefits have low unemployment rates and therefore larger odds for non-working people to switch into employment.

Re-entry mobility: regime model

The regime model findings presented in Table 5.7 tell a similar story as before and confirm our hypotheses on pathways or regime effects: the Anglo-Saxon regime outperforms the other regimes in showing larger odds of re-entry into permanent employment after unemployment or inactivity whereas the Southern regimes perform even worse than the Continental regimes in this respect. However, the Southern regimes perform even better than the

Anglo-Saxon regimes in reintegrating jobless people into self-employment jobs, whereas the Nordic regimes are outperforming the others with a view to improving re-entry into non-standard jobs. The record of the Continental countries seems therefore rather poor with a view to re-entry. The results are similar for males and females except for the poor performance of Anglo-Saxon countries to reintegrate females into self-employment jobs.

Table 5.7 Re-entry mobility (transitions out of non-work): regime model for males and females (model IVb)

	Males			Females		
	Perma-nent Coeff.	Flex ctr. Coeff.	Self-empl. Coeff.	Perma-nent Coeff.	Flex ctr. Coeff.	Self-empl. Coeff.
Male/Female UR	–0.069***	0.057*	–0.023*	–0.054***	0.024	–0.024
Regime type (ref. Continental)						
Anglo-Saxon	0.457***	–0.009	0.763***	0.660***	0.179	0.236
Nordic	0.134	0.820***	0.241**	0.162	0.726***	0.010
Southern	–0.590***	–0.158	1.147***	–0.448	–0.283	1.149***
R squared	0.167			0.153		
N	56,757			118,389		

Notes:
* $p < 0.10$, ** $p < 0.05$, *** $p < 0.01$.

Source: ECHP, 1994–2001.

5.9 CONCLUSIONS AND DISCUSSION

This chapter examines the gender-specific performance of policy routes or pathways in Europe to balance flexibility and income and employment security. We particularly focus on the effects of regime type and specific labour market institutions on this balance. We show in the first part that the mobility patterns are very dissimilar between men and women and across the various countries. We find that the mobility and security levels attained are generally lower for females than for males, but also that the relative income and employment security performance of a country is sometimes different, such as in Greece, Luxembourg, the UK and the Netherlands.

In the second part of the chapter we tried to explain the various mobility patterns by gender: occupational mobility, contract mobility and exit and re-entry mobility. The main question posed deals with the impact of specific labour market institutions and pathways for males and females separately after controlling for a number of explanatory factors such as human capital endowments, life-course-related factors (childbirth, divorce) job characteristics, working time preferences and personal and household characteristics.

The main hypothesis tested is that a trade-off between mobility/flexibility and income and employment security does not necessarily exist, but that policies aimed at strengthening both might have positive effects on balancing economic and social goals. This resembles the notion of 'flexicurity' that has become a prominent metaphor in the current European policy debate on employment and social issues.

The Role Of Specific Labour Market Institutions

The extent of labour market mobility for males and females seems affected by the level of flexibility as measured by the strictness of the employment protection legislation (EPL), and to a lesser extent also by the OECD overall replacement rate and the availability of working time options (WTO), although for the latter two we find somewhat mixed evidence. Rather solid evidence was found that the stronger EPL is, the more segmented the labour market is and the more it reduces the occupational mobility for both sexes in a country. It also reduces the mobility from a temporary into an open-ended contract. Countries with the highest mobility/flexibility both for males and females due to absence of strong EPL also seem to perform rather well in safeguarding income and employment security, but not unconditionally. These effects show up only when such policy is coupled to policies to maintain income security and 'employability' policies to activate the unemployed. Countries which either focus on active labour market policies or on creating flexible working time options at the workplace seem to impact positively on the transition from non-standard jobs into standard jobs, though not in combination. The effects of net replacement rates also interact strongly with the unemployment rate showing that countries with high benefits have low unemployment rates and therefore showing a positive effect on re-entry into permanent work. The availability of working time options seems to affect males' transition patterns more than those of females which is puzzling and needs more scrutiny. More recent data covering more countries in Europe such as SILC (Statistics on Income and Living Conditions) might provide more answers here. The results seem to provide some support to the premises underlying the transitional labour market and 'flexicurity' approach.

Regimes and Pathways

Compared to the more flexible labour markets of the Anglo-Saxon and the Nordic regimes the more tightly regulated labour markets of the Continental and Southern regimes perform worse for males and females with respect to maintaining the balance between flexibility and income and employment security. The Nordic and Anglo-Saxon regimes or pathways differ markedly in terms of labour market structure, institutional set-up and socio-political background, whereas in terms of outcomes they seem more equal. Both pathways, however, share their caveats with the Nordic regime to safeguard the employment security of its workers in non-standard employment contracts and for the Anglo-Saxon regime in safeguarding the income security of people with weaker ties to the labour market, in particular females with caring dutics.

In the Continental and Southern pathways the high level of employment protection created a segmented labour market of insiders and outsiders and had distorting effects on the balance attained between flexibility and security equally for males and females during the 1990s, though with different consequences. Whereas the Continental countries were able notwithstanding their low mobility to maintain high levels of income and employment security both for males and females, the Southern countries seem to have had serious problems in maintaining the income security of outsiders, especially young people entering the labour market in non-standard contracts and female workers with interrupted careers due to childbirth and caring duties.

Therefore we conclude that European social policy entails various roads and pathways, each with its own caveats, and even though Europe shows 'unity in diversity' the premise of creating a balance between flexibility and security, between an efficient and fair society, belongs unquestionably to the sets of shared values and beliefs.

NOTES

1. Part of the research for this chapter was carried out in the framework of a research project sponsored by the European Foundation for Living and Working Conditions in Dublin. We gratefully acknowledge their invaluable support and contribution to the project. Some findings reported here were already published in the summary report (Muffels et al., 2008a).
2. This definition of flexibility/mobility certainly covers only a subset of the various flexibility forms, that is numerical flexibility, and not functional flexibility. We also do not deal explicitly with wage flexibility although our measure of occupational mobility captures part of the wage variation over time.
3. The company information is derived from the Establishment Survey of the European Foundation for the Improvement of Working and Living Conditions for the year 2004/2005.
4. We make no distinction between voluntary and involuntary changes because what matters is the total amount of mobility: even when people's job change is involuntary, what matters is that the labour market allowed them to find another job.
5. The mobility measures range from 0 (nobody moves) to 100 per cent (everyone moves) whereas the dynamic employment and income security measures range from –100 to +100 per cent. They are minus 100 per cent when every unemployed or poor person stays unemployed or poor and all employed or non-poor persons entered unemployment and

poverty respectively. They are plus 100 per cent when nobody stayed unemployed or poor and every unemployed or poor person moved into employment or escaped poverty.
6. However, not all effects of the control variables are exactly the same in both models. The unanticipated result for high education in the contract mobility model is not found here. Higher educated workers, although only males, have lower chances to move from a permanent into a temporary job. Occupational class also exhibits stronger effects for males and females on contract and exit mobility.

REFERENCES

Acemoglu, D. (2003), 'Patterns of skill premia', *Review of Economic Studies*, **70** (2), 199–230.

Albert, M. (1991), *Capitalisme contre capitalisme*, Paris: Editions du Seuil.

Becker, G. (1975), *Human Capital: A Theoretical and Empirical Analysis, with Special Reference to Education*, New York: National Bureau of Economic Research.

Blau, F.D. and Kahn, L.M. (2002), *At Home and Abroad: US Labor Market Performance in International Perspective*, New York: Russell Sage Foundation.

Blossfeld, H.P. and Mills, M. (2003), *Globalization and Job Mobility over the Life Course of Men: the Role of Country-Specific Institutions*, Bamberg: Bamberg University.

Blossfeld, H.P., Mills, M. and Bernardi, F. (2006), *Globalisation, Uncertainty and Men's Careers*, Cheltenham, UK and Northampton, MA, USA: Edward Elgar.

Booth, A.L., Francesconi, M. and Frank, J. (2002), 'Temporary jobs: Stepping stones or dead ends?', *Economic Journal*, **112** (480), F189–F213.

Booth, A.L., Francesconi, M. and Frank, J. (2003), 'A sticky floors model of promotion, pay, and gender', *European Economic Review*, **47** (2), 295–322.

Breen, R. (1997), 'Risk, commodification and stratification', *Sociology*, **31** (3), 473–89.

Chung, H.J. and Muffels, R.J.A. (2007), *Contract Flexibility and Working Time Arrangements: Constructing a Typology*, Tilburg: universiteit van Tilburg.

Collins, H. (2005), 'Flexibility and stability of expectations in the contract of employment', *Socio-Economic Review*, **26** (4), 139–53.

Dekker, R. (2007), *Non-standard Employment and Mobility in the Dutch, German and British Labour Market*, Ridderkerk: Ridderprint.

DiPrete, T.A., De Graaf, P.M., Luijkx, R., Tahlin, M. and Blossfeld, H.P. (1997), 'Collectivist versus individualist mobility regimes? Structural change and job mobility in four countries', *American Journal of Sociology*, **103** (2), 318–58.

Elder, G.H. and Pavalko, E.K. (1993), 'Work careers in men's later years – transitions, trajectories, and historical change', *Journals of Gerontology*, **48** (4), S180–S91.

Esping-Andersen, G. (1999), *Social Foundations of Post-Industrial Economics*, Oxford: Oxford University Press.

Estéves-Abe, M., Iversen, T. and Soskice, D. (eds) (2001), *Social Protection and the Formation of Skills: A Reinterpretation of the Welfare State*, New York: Oxford University Press.

European Commission (2003), *Employment in Europe 2003*, Luxembourg: Office for Official Publications of the European Communities.

European Commission (2006), *Employment in Europe 2006*, Luxembourg: Office for Official Publications of the European Communities.

European Commission (2007), *Employment in Europe 2007*, Luxembourg: Office for Official Publications of the European Communities.
Ferrera, M., Hemerijck, A. and Rhodes, M. (2000), 'Recasting European welfare states for the 21st century', *European Review*, **8** (3), 427–46.
Fouarge, D., Luijkx, R., Manzoni, A. and Muffels, R. (2006), *Careers of Working Mothers after First Childbirth*, Dublin, Tilburg: European Foundation, OSA-Tilburg University.
Gangl, M. (2003), 'The only way is up? Employment protection and job mobility among recent entrants to European labour markets', *European Sociological Review*, **19** (5), 429–49.
Gangl, M. (2006), 'Scar effects of unemployment: an assessment of institutional complementarities', *American Sociological Review*, **71**, (December), 986–1013.
Goldthorpe, J.H. (2001), *Globalisation and Social Class*, Mannheim: University of Mannheim.
Golsch, K. (2003), 'Employment flexibility in Spain and its impact on transitions to adulthood', *Work Employment and Society*, **17** (4), 691–718.
Hall, P. and Soskice, D. (eds) (2001), *Varieties of Capitalism: The Institutional Foundations of Comparative Advantage*, Oxford: Oxford University Press.
Hernanz, V., Origo, F., Samek Lodovici, M. and Toharia, L. (2008), 'Dreaming of a Permanent Job: the Transitions of Temporary Workers in Italy and Spain', in Muffels, R.J.A. (ed.), *Innovating Labour Markets in Europe*, Cheltenham, UK and Northampton, MA, USA: Edward Elgar, pp. 79–106.
Kalleberg, A.L. (2000), 'Nonstandard employment relations: part-time, temporary and contract work', *Annual Review of Sociology*, **26**, 341–65.
Muffels, R. (2007), 'Roads of "Flexicurity" in Europe: How (un)equal are they?', in Jørgensen, H. and Madsen, P.K. (eds), *Flexicurity and Beyond. Finding a New Agenda for the European Social Model*, Copenhagen: DJØF Publishing, pp. 215–43.
Muffels, R. (2008), *Flexibility and Employment Security in Europe, Labour Markets in Transition*, Cheltenham, UK and Northampton, MA, USA: Edward Elgar.
Muffels, R.J.A. and Luijkx, R. (2006), 'Globalisation and Male Job Mobility in European Welfare States', in Blossfeld, H.P., Mills, M. and Bernard, F. (eds), *Globalisation and Uncertainty of Men's Careers*, Cheltenham, UK and Northampton, MA, USA: Edward Elgar, pp. 38–72.
Muffels, R. and Luijkx, R. (2008), 'Labour market mobility and employment security of male employees in Europe: "trade-off" or "flexicurity"?', *Work, Employment and Society*, **22** (2), 221–42.
Muffels, R., Chung, H., Fouarge, D., Klammer, U., Luijkx, R., Manzoni, A., Wilthagen, T. and Thiel, A. (eds) (2008), *Flexibility and Security over the Lifecourse*, Luxembourg: Office for Official Publications of the European Communities, pp. 56.
Philips, K. and Eamets, R. (2007), *Approaches to Flexicurity: EU Models*, Luxembourg: Office for Official Publications of the European Communities: European Foundation.
Schmid, G. (1995), 'Institutional incentives to prevent unemployment: unemployment insurance and active labor market policy in a comparative perspective', *Journal of Socio Economics*, **24** (1), 51–103.
Schmid, G. and Gazier, B. (2002), *The Dynamics of Full Employment: Social Integration Through Transitional Labour Markets*, Cheltenham, UK and Northampton, MA, USA: Edward Elgar.

Stone, K.V.W. (2005), 'Thinking and doing – the regulation of workers' human capital in the United States', *Socio-Economic Review*, **26** (4), 121–38.

Uunk, W., Kalmijn, M. and Muffels, R. (2005), 'The impact of young children on women's labour supply: a reassessment of institutional effects in Europe', *Acta Sociologica*, 41–62.

Wilthagen, T. (1998), *Flexicurity: A new paradigm for labour market policy research*, Berlin: WZB Discussion Paper FS I 98–202.

Wilthagen, T. and Tros, F. (2004), 'The concept of "flexicurity": a new approach to regulating employment and labour markets', *Transfer*, **10** (2), 166–86.

APPENDIX

Table A5.1 Model variables and summary statistics by gender (mean)

Variables	Description	Men	Women
Life course			
Age	Age in years.	39.5	40.0
Age squared/100	Age squared divided by 100.	17.4	17.8
Life course phase/ Household type	Dummies for: couple with child of 0–5 years (2); couple with child 6–16 (3); single without children (4), single with children 0–5 or 6–16 years (5). Reference is couple without children (1).	0.31 (1) 0.14 (2) 0.18 (3) 0.26 (4) 0.07 (5)	0.34 (1) 0.14 (2) 0.18 (3) 0.24 (4) 0.09 (5)
Number of children	Number of children below 17 years of age in the household.	0.51	0.54
Childbirth	Whether a child was born during the observation period 1994–2001.	0.027	0.027
Part-time for caring	Working part-time for caring reasons. Based on ECHP question about the main reasons why people work less than full-time.	0.003	0.003
Job search behaviour			
Domestic work	Dummy for reporting housework as main activity status (1 = yes, 0 = no).	0.01	0.24
Job search	Dummy for searching actively for a job (1 = yes, 0 = no).	0.18	0.18
Discouraged worker	Dummy for not looking for a job because one cannot find a job.	0.03	0.07
Socio-economic characteristics			
Education level	1. primary education; 2. lower and medium level of vocational training plus high school (reference category); and 3. higher vocational training and university. Level 2 is taken as the reference group.	2.15	2.23
Low education	Dummy for low education.	0.38	0.44
High education	Dummy for high education.	0.24	0.20
Unemployment history	Dummy for whether people experienced an unemployment spell in the five-years preceding the current job (1 = yes; 0 = no).	0.20	0.19
Tenure	Duration of employment in months in current job.	50	50

Table A5.1 (Continued)

Variables	Description	Men	Women
Socio-economic characteristics (continued)			
Bad health	Dummy for bad health, which is a subjectively assessed measure for one's personal health (1 = bad health; 0 = not in bad health).	0.07	0.09
Personal non-labour income	Personal net non-labour income in 1000 euros per year, corrected for price increases and purchasing power parities (ppp) differences.	2.57	2.11
Other net labour income in household	Net household labour income of other household members is the summation of the annual net labour incomes of all other persons between 25 and 65 years in the household in the calendar year preceding the interview year, ppp corrected and in 1000 euros per year.	6.48	7.35
Net non-labour income in household	Net non-labour household income is the net household income from social security transfers and/or from wealth (excluding income from imputed rent). Incomes are deflated and made comparable across countries using the purchasing power parities as calculated by Eurostat for the various countries, ppp corrected, in 1000 euros per year.	10.91	15.94
Job characteristics			
Trainee/ apprenticeship	Engaged in fixed-term training contract of 15+ hours or apprenticeship.	0.02	0.01
Number of working hours	Weekly working hours are the total number of actual working hours a worker usually worked throughout the past calendar year.	43.61	34.4
Occupational class	To take account of bottom and ceiling effects we included the initial *occupational class* position consisting of either three categories as in Model I; or four categories as in Models II, III and IV (1 = low, low manual; 2 = upper manual; 3 = low white collar; 4 = high, professional).	2.8	3.1
Primary sector Service sector Industry Public sector	Dummies for industrial sector as derived from the two-digit NACE-code, recoded into four dummies for: the primary sector; the services/trade sector; the industrial sector; and the public sector. Reference category is industry plus services.	0.05 0.16 0.24 0.13	0.02 0.14 0.07 0.20
Firm size	Firm size measuring the number of employees in seven classes in the firm: (0; 1–4; 5–19; 20–49; 50–99; 100–499; 500+).	3.95	3.91

Table A5.1 (Continued)

Variables	Description	Men	Women
Institutions/policies			
Active labour market policies (ALM policies)	Expenditures to active labour market policies in per cent of GDP for the years 1994 to 2001.	1.02	1.01
Employment protection legislation	Strictness of employment protection legislation as constructed by OECD for the late 1990s. Is weighted sum of EPL for permanent and temporary workers and for dismissal procedures.	2.38	2.38
Generosity of the unemployment insurance benefits	Net Replacement Rates Unemployment benefits over five year period, including social assistance and averaged over several household types and pay levels (67% and 100 per cent of the average production worker wage) for all years between 1993–2000. Missing years imputed by taking the average between adjacent years.	60.97	60.84
Regime type	Dummies for regime type: Anglo-Saxon, Nordic, Southern, Continental (reference).	0.16 0.07 0.44 0.33	0.16 0.07 0.44 0.33
Male/female annual unemployment rate	Annual unemployment rates for males and females.	8.8	12.3
Year dummies	We included year dummies to account for economic cycle effects. The reference year is the first year of the observation period (1994 for all models except for model III, that is 1995)		

PART II

Flexicurity and Working Time Arrangements

6. 'Project-based Employment' and Models of the Employment Contract

David Marsden

6.1 INTRODUCTION

The full development of the so-called 'network economy' depends upon establishing suitable forms of contracting between firms and workers. The classical employment relationship, open-ended as to both its task content and its duration, came to assume near universality in the advanced industrial world during the 20th century because it succeeded in aligning employees' psychological expectations, performance incentives and a supportive legal framework. This gave rise to a contractual form which has combined great flexibility and a good deal of enforceability: hence the popularity of the open-ended employment relationship. It has worked so successfully in the past because it has evolved a number of incentive mechanisms, for shorthand referred to as three types of 'contract' (psychological, economic/incentive and legal), all of which seek to deal with the non-codified elements of the relationship that underpin its flexibility. These are complementary and mutually supportive. However, these are embedded within structured patterns of entry and employment progression for a wide range of activities and occupations, and they establish this largely on the expectation of a long-term relationship.

The European Commission's Supiot Report (1999) was among the first to call attention to the fundamental changes occurring in labour markets and the need to develop alternative forms of regulation rather than to try to push back the tide by reinforcing existing patterns of regulation. Supiot and his colleagues sought to reconcile discontinuity of employment with continuity of activity in a chosen occupation, and concentrated on legal mechanisms. In this contribution, I should like to focus more on the incentive and institutional mechanisms that underpin the open-ended employment relationship and how these articulate with legal norms in order to understand better the challenge posed by firms' need for greater use of more transient forms of employment relationship.[1] I should like to focus particularly on collaborative work with a team output rather than the traditional system whereby predetermined tasks are put out to freelancers such as in translation or publishing (Fraser and Gold, 2001). In the latter cases, a specific product can be defined. The former case is much closer to the spirit of the open-ended employment relationship because teamwork requires adaptive and flexible roles, thus preserving something of the spirit of the open-ended employment relationship as concerns its task content, but without the implied open-ended duration. Such ideas are at the heart of the so-called network economy.[2]

Sydow and Staber (2002) identify project organisation and project net works as key organisational features of the 'network economy' as it is developing in certain economic sectors, such as the media industries. One might say that the project rather than the firm emerges as the focus of workers' activity. With this sector in mind, Jones and Walsh (1997) characterised the career system of workers as comprising three elements: movement between employers; validation from the labour market rather than the employer, and use of extra-organisational networks and information. A project might comprise an advertising campaign, a film, a CD or a book for example, on which a temporary team of people might work, bringing together a mix of business management, technical and creative expertise.

Baumann (2002) argues that project production and small companies have flourished in the media industries because:

- Media products, especially fiction and entertainment, resemble fashion items with constant audience demand for novelty and innovation;
- There is a high element of one-off creation of new material (as in fashion) which is highly risky as the outcome is uncertain;
- Once produced, the product is easily and cheaply reproduced (as contrasted with reproduction of models in such industries as automobiles where reproduction is highly capital and labour intensive);
- Dominance of one-off creation as opposed to continuous reproduction.

Although these can be handled within large organisations, as was the case when large studios and large broadcasters dominated production, there are clear advantages to organising such activities by means of small firms and project teams. Indeed, although the initial impulse for dispersing production work in Britain and Germany owed much to their respective governments' competition programmes, it was not reversed when the immediate political pressures subsided (Tempest et al., 1997).

The emphasis on project organisation is not confined to the media sector. It has long been a feature of large-scale construction activities where each project is unique, and demands a unique mix of labour skills. In several countries, this feature of the industry is recognised in employment law (for example Calan, 2001). Indeed, Calan argues this model should be extended to small and medium-sized firms that engage in large orders because employing labour for such 'projects' enables them better to cope with the risks involved. Project work and project networks have also figured largely in accounts of work and business organisation in 'Silicon Valley' (for example Saxenian, 1996; Carnoy et al., 1997; Scott, 1998,). Similar pressures prevail there as innovation often takes place around new projects set up to exploit a new idea. University research is also often organised on a project basis, as is university collaboration with private firms, for example on scientific ventures (Lam, 2003). In England and Wales, for example, there is a strong correlation between universities' scores in the national Research Assessment Exercise (RAE) and the percentage of non-tenured academic staff, with the top-rated Cambridge, London and Oxford universities having 50 per cent or more of their academic staff in fixed-term employment.[3]

The relevance to other sectors is also stressed by writers, such as Cappelli (1999) and Osterman (1996). They have argued that the business environment has become more fluid and less predictable in recent years so that the offer of long-term employment has become increasingly costly to firms. Commonly cited reasons include rapid technical change, the expansion of knowledge-intensive activities, greater competition and social change, all of which mean that employment models developing within sectors such as media and information technology are likely to be of interest to other sectors where similar pressures may exist but in less severe forms. Especially in the latter sectors, the absence of a widely recognised contractual framework that all parties trust is likely to be a barrier to the development of more flexible patterns of economic organisation.

Despite these pressures, statistical indicators of a shift from the established pattern of open-ended employment contracts suggest only limited change. OECD (2000) figures for 1997 indicate that self-employment in industry and services remained at about one worker in ten, increasing only slightly despite two decades of 'deregulation' in the 1980s and 1990s, and there was no uniform direction of change across countries. Likewise, the OECD average share of temporary workers increased very moderately between 1985 and 2000, and remained in the region of one employee in ten (OECD, 2002). In a similar vein, long-term jobs have not disappeared: an OECD (1997) study highlighted that although perceived job insecurity had increased among workers, long-term jobs remained the dominant pattern of employment.

Project employment is not a panacea. It is wise to remember the reasons commonly given for the rise of the open-ended employment relationship at the start of the last century, and why it displaced the many forms of labour contracting. Writing in 1919, Slichter stressed the deficiencies of the 'drive system' whereby contractors had little incentive to train workers, share information and improve quality, and bargaining entered into every point in the relationship between the business and the human resources it mobilised.

In a masterly survey of contractual forms before the rise of the open-ended employment relationship, Mottez (1966) contrasted the enthusiasts for hierarchies of sub-contractors who saw that 'the eye of the master' was at every point in the transaction with the risk that the haggling of the market intervened at every point making the control of complex production systems extremely difficult. Such pressures came to be held in check by the development of the open-ended employment relationship.

Since then, production systems and workers' skills have increased in complexity, witness the growth in the college graduate workforce, and the virtual disappearance of the 'unskilled' category from employment statistics in many advanced industrial economies. Hence the search for new contractual models of employment cannot simply go back to the nineteenth century. What is often not appreciated, however, is the extent to which the open-ended employment relationship relies on a whole system of incentives to secure its effectiveness. Management does not direct workers to new tasks by fiat, nor do workers passively sign up to a system that allows their exploitation. Section 6.2 outlines some of the key incentive structures that enable it to function, and in doing so, highlights how far employment duration is built into these. If there is a trade-off between numerical and functional flexibility it works only because of the incentive structures that surround it. In particular, it is argued that it has succeeded in aligning workers' psychological expectations, economic incentives and legal supports – metaphorically, the psychological, economic and legal contracts. Section 6.3 then looks at project-based forms of employment and explores some functional equivalents of these incentive structures. Their lesser development outside certain sectors may help explain the limited growth of this contractual model in other sectors. It is also suggested that this weaker development has also been accompanied by what might be called tournament type entry and progression processes within these occupations to which many aspirants are attracted, and compete for access to the high prestige positions within them (Marsden, 2007). Section 6.4 contains some conclusions.

6.2 THE STANDARD EMPLOYMENT RELATIONSHIP: INCENTIVES AND SANCTIONS FOR COOPERATION

The rise of the open-ended employment relationship is remarkable when one considers the system of contracting that it gradually displaced. At a time when most industrial workers would have been familiar with the haggling and low trust relations of the 'drive system', to endow that same management with the authority to determine the content of work after the price has been agreed might seem a recipe for exploitation. Yet given free labour markets, its attractiveness to employers could only be realised if workers also found it a suitable framework for their exchange and cooperation. Evidence of its effectiveness can be seen in its continued wide popularity (see for example Auer and Cazes, 2000).

By substituting an employment relationship for a series of open-market transactions, in the manner Coase (1937) observed, one does not eliminate the sources of conflict and opportunistic behaviour. Rather, the employment relationship has developed a platform of rules that helps to contain these so that both parties can achieve a reasonably effective degree of cooperation despite divergent interests. In doing so, it has transformed the firm from a coordinator of market contracts into an employing organisation. Around this platform has developed a set of employee expectations and beliefs, systems of incentives and a system of legal rules which reinforce its operation and effectiveness.

The basic structure of the employment relationship can be understood as the resolution of two sets of constraints: that the terms of the transaction between the worker and the firm should be enforceable, and that they should be productively efficient. In terms of workers' task obligations to the employer, two broad approaches have evolved: one relating workers' jobs to families of tasks they can be expected to undertake, and one relating them to functions within the enterprise. Resolving the link between firms' job demands and workers' competences, one can either start from the job demands and 'mould the man to the job not the job to the man' in the words of a US production engineer (Piore, 1968), the 'production approach', or one can organise work and define task obligations on the basis of workers' skills, the 'training approach' (Sengenberger, 1987). These are summarised in Table 6.1, together with some common examples of work rules associated with each solution.

Table 6.1 The contractual constraints and common employment rules

		Job demands identified by:	
		Production approach	Training approach
The focus of enforcement criteria	Task-centred	'Work post' rule, common in bureaucratic work organisation	'Job territory'/ 'tools of trade' rule, common in craft organisation
	Function-centred	'Competence rank' rule common in Japanese work systems	'Qualification' rule, common in skilled work in Germany

Source: Marsden (1999, Chapter 2).

The work rules resolve the all-important problem of enabling the parties to determine boundaries to their respective obligations, but they do not eliminate all sources of opportunistic behaviour. Controlling these helps to make the employment relationship more effective as a framework for labour service transactions. The next paragraphs consider some of the more common ones, and seek to show how they are supported by the actors' beliefs and expectations, by incentive structures and by legal rules. It will be argued that these solutions are premised on long-duration employment, and hence are difficult to apply to more transient forms of employment such as might occur in project-based work. These concern problems relating to job performance and its evaluation, work assignments and the treatment of unanticipated and unusual tasks; risk-sharing and employment continuity; and training and knowledge sharing.

In all cases, opportunistic behaviour may result from either party, and often the problem is to persuade one party that the other can be trusted to refrain from it. How each contributes to containing these four areas of opportunism is summarised in Table 6.2, which also provides the template for the analysis in this chapter. Much has already been written about these areas individually. I should like to concentrate on two points of special relevance for the development of more transient forms of employment: the complementarities between the three types of process, and the importance of time, or duration, in making the various control mechanisms effective.

6.2.1 Psychological Contracts

The notion that there is a 'psychological contract' governing the employment relationship, which can enable its open-ended nature to function positively and hold opportunistic behaviour at bay, has gained wide currency in recent years (for example Guest et al., 1996; Guest, 1998). The most thorough analytical presentation of the concept has been given by Rousseau (1995). She summarises the psychological contract between A and B as comprising the following elements:

- Individual A's belief in:
  a. Reciprocal obligations between A and B following;
  b. B's prior promise to the initial consideration of the exchange.
- Both B's promise and A's consideration are subjective.
- A's belief in a psychological contract rests on a belief that B is acting in good faith, fairly, and in trust.

Although framed in terms of subjective perceptions of obligations, the latter relate to a number of social conventions that transcend the individual

Table 6.2 Psychological, incentive and legal 'contracts' and opportunism in employment

Type of contract and problem area	Protections against opportunism
Psychological contract	
Performance and pay (valuation of the product)	Shared employee beliefs about the purposes of the relationship and the nature of mutual obligations with the employer. These converge with the duration of the relationship (Rousseau, 1995).
Work assignments and unusual/unanticipated tasks	'Citizenship' to motivate undertaking unusual tasks: concept brings perceived obligations and rights (van Dyne and Dienesch, 1994).
Risk-sharing and employment continuity	Organisational commitment, loyalty to the organisation, as a form of risk-sharing (Meyer and Allen, 1997).
Training and knowledge sharing	Shared beliefs about the contribution of training and knowledge to the inherent quality of the service provided (for example teachers).
Economic/incentive contracts	
Performance and pay (valuation of the product)	Widespread use of long-term incentives: deferred pay and career/promotion opportunities (Lazear, 1995).
Work assignments and unusual/unanticipated tasks	Work rules and job classifications to delimit employees' work obligations and reduce job idiosyncrasy (Marsden, 1999).
Risk-sharing and employment continuity	Stable wage and employment with risk of lay-off managed through agreed lay-off procedures. Continuous employment a basis for 'tit-for-tat' cooperation (Axelrod, 1984).
Training and knowledge sharing	Cost-sharing for investment in occupational skills; seniority incentives to invest in firm-based skills (Becker, 1975).
Legal contracts	
Performance and pay (valuation of the product)	Concepts of 'implied terms' and 'goodwill' enable some legal norms to bind on incomplete contracts (Collins, 2001).
Work assignments and unusual/unanticipated tasks	Anti-discrimination laws require clear procedural rules for work allocation and access to on-the-job training and promotion opportunities (Sorensen, 1994).
Risk-sharing and employment continuity	Legal provisions over dismissal and discrimination (for example to prevent discriminatory risk shifting).
Training and knowledge sharing	Legal basis for participation can strengthen knowledge sharing by excluding unilateral withdrawal by management.

relationship. Promising involves the social or moral convention that one ought to keep one's promises. Such obligations are more than mere expectations of probable outcomes. The same is true of acting in 'good faith' and 'fairly'.

Given that human beings are subject to bounded rationality, then it is reasonable to suppose that they will operate with a limited number of categories of relationships, each with its own set of behaviour rules. Thus, employees will seek to identify the type of relationship they are in and attribute the appropriate set of obligations to the other party. Although individual workers often have their own idiosyncratic ideas of what their employer owes them, it is clear that the more widely held such ideas are, the more effectively they can be enforced. Rousseau suggests that common enforcement mechanisms include a decline in an employee's motivation and morale, and the threat of 'exit' (Rousseau, 1995, p. 135). Thus, those that correspond most closely to widely used social categories of types of employment relationship and their respective obligations will be the most potent. From the other side, employers can also seek to influence employee behaviour by the way they shape the reciprocal obligations of the psychological contract; for example, to encourage employee commitment by getting them to identify theirs as a long-term relationship with the organisation.

Turning to the common types of opportunistic behaviour that need to be held in check, employee beliefs about the type of relationship can be important, as can be those of managers acting on behalf of the company. For example, shared beliefs in providing a professional, or public, service may hold many employees back from providing the minimum effort they can get away with, or hold managers back from fiddling performance valuations to save money. These beliefs may be inculcated during training and socialisation at work, and then underpin strong psychological beliefs about the mutual obligations that apply within an employment relationship. Likewise, taking a broad attitude to the content of one's job, or sticking with an organisation during bad times, or being willing to train and share knowledge with new employees, are all behaviours that make the open-ended employment relationship viable, and are commonly supported by shared beliefs about the purpose of the joint activity. A notable feature of such shared beliefs and perceptions is that they take time to develop within an organisation.

The importance of duration is illustrated by Stone's (2001) comparison between the' old' and the 'new' psychological contracts in the US (Table 6.3). Lack of detail about the precise content of an employer's commitment could be resolved by applying certain benchmarks to the employer's behaviour, for example on the provision of job security or promotions, and observing these over time. Under the 'new' psychological contract, the behavioural benchmarks are less clear and the intended duration of the relationship is shorter, so there is less time to learn about one's business partner's behaviour.

Table 6.3 'Old' and 'new' psychological contracts

'Old' psychological contract	'New' psychological contract
Job security	Employability security
Firm-specific training	General/transferable training
Deskilling	Upskilling
Promotional opportunities	Networking opportunities
Command supervision	Micro-level job control
Pay and benefits linked to job tenure	Market-based pay
Collective bargaining and grievance arbitration	Dispute resolution procedures for individual fairness claims

Source: Stone (2001).

6.2.2 Economic and Incentive 'Contracts'

Many of the most widespread incentive reward mechanisms in employment both support and use its open-ended duration for their effectiveness. They also reinforce the employee beliefs and expectations about the relationship and the types of performance that are expected of them. For example, to deal with the performance and risk-sharing issues, two common features of employee reward systems stand out: the offer of stable wages and the use of incremental pay scales and promotion systems.

An almost universal feature of wage and salary systems is that pay is relatively stable compared with the fluctuations in the market value of employees' output. This element of risk-sharing with the firm provides a valuable benefit to employees. It also provides the employer with a platform on which other incentive systems can be built. Taking the first area of potential opportunistic behaviour (following Table 6.2 above), incentive systems play a large part in regulating performance by employees and the delivery of rewards by their employers. Many of these are of a long-term nature. For example, so-called 'efficiency wage' systems, whereby an employer pays above the market-clearing rate for a given category of workers in order to secure higher productivity, depend upon a flow of rewards to the employee. The longer the anticipated period of enhanced earnings, the greater the employee's corresponding loss if dismissed for poor performance, and arguably, too, the greater the 'quasi-gift exchange' to encourage above average performance.[4] If the 'efficiency wages' related to the current period only, then their value as a sanction would be greatly reduced.

Incentive pay systems that rely on deferred pay, by definition, make use of the time dimension. A closer look at their dynamics, however, also reveals the complexities of how time is used to moderate pressures for opportunistic behaviour. A common feature of career pay systems is that employees are initially hired with pay above their productivity while they learn the job. In mid-career, their productivity exceeds their pay, which serves both to pay back the cost of training, and to build up an investment in the firm. In their late careers, employees reap the return on this investment as their pay exceeds their productivity. The firm gains considerable advantages from this, as it provides incentives to undertake training that the firm needs, to work flexibly and loyally for the firm's benefit, and it gives the firm a useful sanction in the event of persistent poor performance. The key purposes of such systems are to motivate employees to learn the skills their employers need and to work cooperatively. However, as Lazear (1990) has shown, the key to a good working relationship is a clear date for termination. In the latter years, when pay exceeds productivity, there is a conflict of interest as prolongation brings a net benefit for the employee and a net cost for the employer. With a clear termination date, retirement, each party knows where it stands. Employees can tell easily if the employer is reneging on its promise, and the employer is protected from employees demanding unwarranted extensions to their period of employment. Employees in their early careers can also gauge how trustfully their employer is behaving with regard to those currently coming to the end of their careers.

The risk-sharing component of employment similarly rests on a balancing of time-related benefits and rules that will withstand opportunistic manipulation. This component has been analysed by a number of economists under the guise of 'implicit contracts' (for example Stiglitz, 1984) and the 'économie des conventions' (for example Salais, 1989). It rests on the insight that by providing a steady wage, the firm is taking on the risk element arising from fluctuations in product demand. During good times, the value of workers' output would exceed their wage, this amount being retained by the employer as a payment into the implicit insurance fund. During bad times, the employer would honour the implicit agreement and retain workers and maintain their level of wages. For the 'conventionalists' the firm also gains a stable platform for coordinating complex production activities. However, firms do not have the resources to provide unlimited guarantees of job security, so the risk is shared with employees by the opportunity to lay-off some of them when conditions become too severe. As a theory of voluntary unemployment, implicit contract theories may not have succeeded, but the essential insight into the dynamics of risk-sharing in long-term employment relationships is surely correct.

Given that there has been experimentation using wage flexibility as a means of extending employment security, as in the historic Volkswagen agreements in 1993/94,[5] one might ask why risk-averse workers should apparently continue to prefer stable wages with a higher risk of lay-off instead of a combination of more flexible wages and less risk of job loss. The answer would seem to lie in the difficulty of enforcing contracts in which pay tracks the market value of workers' output. If the firm has best access to the necessary information, then it is in a position to deceive workers about the true value of their output, and state that conditions are worse than they really are in order to gain a larger than necessary pay cut. To do so costs the firm little, and would increase profits. Even if their current employer were honest, many workers would suspect that the incentive to cheat is too strong and so they would be leery of this kind of contract.[6] In contrast, declaring that business conditions are bad enough to warrant lay-offs means that the firm must also cut capacity and output which will reduce profits. Hence, the type of contract that best fits both parties is one containing a mix of a stable wage, which can be easily monitored by employees, and a risk of lay-off which is unpleasant for the worker, but also costly to the employer. This can also be monitored by agreed lay-off procedures. Although this may be a second best solution for both parties, given limited trust and the incentives to cheat, it emerges as the chosen contractual model because it is enforceable. Indeed, it is largely self-enforcing.

There are no doubt other reasons also why firms may prefer stable wages and deferred pay such as administrative simplicity, the fear of losing their most marketable workers to other firms and providing a framework for investing in skills, but mostly they complement the risk-sharing argument. Nevertheless, the importance of these examples is that they highlight the role of such incentive systems in supporting the employment relationship as an open-ended framework by building sanctions against kinds of opportunistic behaviour that would undermine it.

6.2.3 Legal Contracts

The nature of the employment relationship as an open-ended agreement places it in a special position with regard to employment law. An 'incomplete contract' cannot be enforced by the courts in the normal way because its breach is not like that of other contracts where one can simply compare what was agreed and what has been delivered. This means that the law cannot get into the detail of the employment transaction. Rather, it provides a framework for cooperation and focuses on certain key points in the relationship which it can enforce, such as procedures for termination, or very clear failures to carry out certain duties. However, as will be argued in this section, the mechanisms by which employment law underpins the employment relationship are adapted to long-term relationships and are much less adapted to more transient forms such as might prevail in project-based employment.

In recent decades, the debate among economic policy analysts on labour market regulation has tended to focus on the 'constraining' rather than the 'enabling' features of employment law. This was the sense of the OECD's review of labour market regulation measures in its review (OECD, 1999, Ch. 2). In contrast, Commons (1924) makes the case for the enabling function of law powerfully in his 'Legal Foundations of Capitalism'. There, he shows how legal recognition of certain economic concepts made it possible to write legally enforceable contracts. For example, legal recognition of the exchange value of 'goodwill' and of 'non-corporeal capital' opened the way for new forms of economic organisation, including much of the modern business enterprise, just as it also opened up new sources of taxation.[7] In the domain of employment, arguably the smaller economic stakes in individual transactions have meant that greater reliance could be placed upon collectively agreed rules than in other business areas. Nevertheless, the development of a suitable legal framework that was adapted to the risks inherent in the employment relationship gave it a considerable boost, as will be explained below.[8]

Commons (1924) argued that within the employment relationship, workers offer their 'goodwill' to their employer to apply their skills and talents within their jobs. Moral hazard would amount to reducing or withdrawing such 'goodwill' once the relationship had been established. With an incomplete contract, one might ask how the law can help enforceability. The solution, as stressed by Collins (2001) under English law and by Stone (2001) for US law, lies in the concept of 'implied terms' – what was reasonably intended at the time of engagement. Implied terms require some kind of benchmark. In many organisations, the use of job classifications provides workers, management and outside third parties with a guide as to the type of work and performance that can be expected from people with goodwill hired into certain positions. 'Implied terms' and job classifications also give employees some protection against excessive or unreasonable work demands.

Employees from more vulnerable groups in the labour market might fear that, with an incomplete contract, their employers would take advantage of their greater difficulties to find alternative employment to drive them harder or reward them less. Anti-discrimination legislation gives some protection in this area, but again, job classification plays an important part in enabling the parties concerned, and the law, to identify cases of unfair treatment. With the US experience in mind, Sorensen (1994) shows how the application of equal worth provisions depends heavily upon job classifications. These depend on stable organisations.

Renegotiation of the terms of employment has to occur periodically within employment relationships in order to take account of evolving job demands. The problem, as Teulings and Hartog (1998) argue, is how to engage this process without undermining the boundary between issues that are subject to bargaining and those subject to coordination by management authority. Major renegotiation often occurs during times of restructuring, such as when redundancies (dismissals for economic reasons) are being sought. Knowing that employees are concerned about the future of their skill and other investments they have made in their jobs, an employer could seek to exaggerate the extent of a downturn in order to impose worse terms than necessary on its employees. By means of collective bargaining, workers and firms have developed their own private means of resolving such issues so they can contain the risk of 'hold-ups' by either side. Indeed, the precursors to much continental European legislation in this area can be found in such collective agreements as those in the Lorraine steel industry in the late 1960s (Reynaud, 1969). The law has helped generalise this approach to all sectors, including those where collective bargaining is much weaker.

Much continental European employment law has long established procedures by which firms may conduct the renegotiation that goes with restructuring. Under French and German law, for example, employer and employee representatives must agree a 'social plan' which details measures to minimise straight lay-offs, making full use of alternative measures where practical, and involving a considerable degree of consultation. In these countries, and in Britain, the law establishes certain minimum levels of financial compensation for employees losing their jobs. Both the procedural and the financial elements help to reduce the risk that redundancies are used simply to pressurise employees into conceding better terms to their employers. All these provisions presuppose that employment is a long-term relationship. Redundancy compensation is proportionate to length of prior service, and much employment protection is subject to a time threshold before employees become eligible. Consultative procedures for agreeing a 'social plan' work best with a stable workforce. To echo Stone's (2001) analysis, employment law is well-adapted to reinforcing the 'old' but not the 'new' psychological contract.

6.2.4 Articulation Between the Three Kinds of 'Contract'

One may consider the three different approaches as focusing on complementary processes that underpin the employment relationship, and in this respect they can be mutually reinforcing. Nevertheless, they are distinct from each other as they rely on different enforcement mechanisms. Incentive contracts can steer performance in certain directions. However, they are unlikely to be completely effective because monitoring can never be wholly effective whether related to inputs of employee effort or to outputs of their performance. Motivation with regard to shared values and beliefs, and shared perceptions of mutual obligations, as expressed by the metaphor of the psychological contract, often provide an essential back-up. Incentives can also reinforce psychological contracts, for example by communicating the kinds of performance that management values, and the kind of rewards on offer, for example deferred pay and promotion schemes, convey an expectation of durable employment.

The law sets wider parameters than either of these two processes, but it can reinforce them by making certain key elements of the relationship enforceable by third parties. For example, redundancy provisions protect a key aspect of long-term employment and limit the threat of dismissals as a tactic to force concessions from employees.

Each of the three processes relate also to processes outside the firm. This is especially true of employment laws that must be consistent with wider legal principles. An illustration of this can be seen in both Commons' (1924) and Supiot's (1994) accounts of the emergence of key legal concepts underpinning the employment relationship.[9] The legal system's first response to newly emerging economic relationships was to seek to apply established legal principles, and then gradually to adapt them. As Supiot put it, contracts originally related to exchanges of property and the human element of labour never quite fitted. Gradually the practice emerged of integrating a special status and special rights for workers into the contract: 'englober un statut dans un contrat'. This is because systems of laws need internal consistency if they are to command the respect and confidence of citizens. Similar influences apply to the psychological contract, which, it was argued, will relate to a limited repertoire of possible relationships, mostly drawn from a pre-existing range of possible types of relationship. These will be the ones best understood by the parties.

What consolidates the position of the open-ended, long-duration employment relationship currently is that it lies at the intersection between these three types of 'contract': psychological, economic and legal. This gives it great stability as a social institution, and great predictability for the employers and workers who adopt it as the contractual frame for their relationship. For the long-term relationship, all three elements provide compatible incentives and enforcement mechanisms. The next section explores whether they function as effectively to support more transient forms of employment.

6.3 REGULATING PERFORMANCE IN NETWORK EMPLOYMENT

It was suggested at the start that with network organisation, the firm gives ground to the project as the primary focus of employment activity. An old-fashioned way of thinking about this would be to suggest that with more transient relationships, both workers and firms will invest less in the current transaction, and the sanction of non-renewal of contracts will return to the fore. The problem of the long-term employment relationship, as Malcomson (1997) and Teulings and Hartog (1998) stress, is that the investments by both parties, for example in training and specific skills, make each vulnerable to 'hold-ups' by the other side. With a return to shorter-term market transactions for labour services, do we not simply avoid these difficulties?

Project employment has developed in a number of sectors where creative activity is important. A brief consideration of some of the performance and product valuation issues will show that the incentive problems noted in the open-ended employment also occur in project organisation, albeit in a slightly different form. For example, a common feature of project-based work is that it resembles small batch or customer-centred production so that intensive supervision is often not a feasible option. Although there is a stronger focus on the final output and each team member's contribution to that than under the standard employment relationship, substandard performance may often not be detected until after the project is complete and the team disbanded. Likewise, abuse of the product by the coordinator may not become apparent until afterwards, when the collaborators can no longer easily apply sanctions. Collaborators may want to hold back their best or most creative ideas and use them to gain a position in a future project. They may also pick up ideas from others during the collaboration, and wish to exploit them themselves later on. The coordinator may seek to derive extra income from further exploitation of the collaborators' creative work, perhaps without telling them, or possibly by commercialising it in a way that damages their artistic reputation. Such tensions were highlighted by Paul and Kleingartner's (1994) study of Hollywood, by the British Film Institute's (BFI, 1997) study of the industry in Britain and by Haunschild's (2003) study of the German theatre industry.

Thus, even though the collaboration may be of finite duration during the project, the quality of the creative input and subsequent commercialisation ensure that the economic consequences extend well beyond. Whereas a dissatisfied employee or employer can use the quit or dismissal threat and loss of potential future rewards as sanctions, once the project is complete, there is limited come-back for either side apart from legalistic disputes over contract terms which are slow and expensive.

What mechanisms exist to control some of these tensions within more transient forms of employment? A first clue is that many self-employed and fixed-term workers, albeit imperfect proxies for project employment, are to be found in professional and skilled occupations. Looking across France, Germany, the UK and the US, the share of managerial and professional occupations among the self-employed in industry and services ranged between about one-fifth and one-third (OECD, 1992, Ch. 4), and the strongest growth in self-employment has been among these occupations (OECD, 2000). In the UK, over half of those on fixed-term contracts are in the managerial, professional and associated professional categories (Sly and Stillwell, 1997). Many others have office qualifications, for example agency temps in clerical and secretarial jobs. In other words, the skill base of such employment is provided by means of transferable skills and educational qualifications, in line with the 'training approach' to work organisation and regulation outlined in Table 6.1 above. Tolbert (1996) made a similar observation when surveying the growth of 'boundaryless careers' in the US.

Taking the occupation as a base provides a foundation for considering the three types of 'contract' as they might apply within project-based organisation. The occupation can provide a basis for a 'psychological contract' by means of the shared values learned during training and developed during practice as a member of an occupational group. Reputation within an occupational group can provide a functional equivalent to one's reputation among one's peers and superiors within a firm, and some legal support may be provided by measures of occupational licensing and entry regulation. Much of this, however, is premised upon the existence of formalised occupations whereas the evidence from studies of the media and software industries suggests that the occupational basis is often of a more informal nature, hence the use of such terms as 'occupational communities' and 'communities of practice' (Tolbert, 1996).[10]

6.3.1 Social Networks as Bearers of 'Psychological Contracts'

Compared with long-term employment, project working has to rely on alternative motivational and monitoring devices that lie outside the organisation. Within a firm, both good and bad performance contribute to one's reputation with one's peers and with management (see Table 6.2 above). In more transient forms of employment, one's reputation outside the firm will be the key factor. In a competitive environment, reports about other people's performance are notoriously unreliable, as they may be gossip, or even malicious, intended to undermine the standing of a potential competitor. One therefore needs to couple these with information about one's informant's likely motives. Often, this can be derived from social networks, hence the importance of what Granovetter (1973) described as 'weak ties' such as might exist among alumnus groups, members of an association or among those who often collaborate together (Dex et al., 2000). It is not just that one might trust reports from such people more, but if they are dishonest, the chances are that that information will feed back into the network.

Reputation functions in two ways: as information about past, and hence likely future, behaviour; and as an indication of one's commitment to certain occupational norms and standards. There has been much emphasis on the first, in the tradition of Williamson (1985), but the social and professional groups that support networks also carry norms of correct behaviour for their members. Saxenian (1996) stresses that the networks for sharing ideas and getting jobs within the occupational communities of Silicon Valley are also social networks, and so will carry some measure of shared identity and values. Likewise, in the German media industry, Sydow and Staber (2002) stress the social and legitimating role of networks as a support to coordination by underpinning certain standards of behaviour. In the case of craft and professional skills, norms of pride in one's trade guide both parties as to the level and quality of performance that can be expected (Scullion and Edwards, 1988). In return for this, management often do not supervise craftsworkers closely, but equally, one can see that if individual craftsworkers repeatedly failed to perform, they would be seen as letting down their colleagues.

This last example highlights an additional feature of the obligational side of reputation, namely, that reputation for good and reliable performance is also a collective good of the whole occupational community. Thus poor performance not only damages one's own standing, but it also gradually undermines that of the whole occupational community. Given the informal nature of many such communities, moral rather than contractual sanctions have to apply.

Thus one can see reputation functioning both as an informational incentive, and as a sign that one accepts the obligational ties that underpin 'psychological contracts'. It informs the individuals concerned as to the appropriate expectations and obligations of the relationship – in the above craft example, obligations of good performance by the worker, and respect of autonomy by management.

6.3.2 Functional Equivalents of Deferred Rewards in Transient Employment

In the open-ended employment relationship, procedures for sharing the fruits of collaboration are one of the foundations of financial incentive systems. Similar incentive issues arise in project work, as noted above. In particular, it can be difficult for project coordinators to motivate their collaborators to give of their best, for example in creative work where there is often an incentive to hold back one's best ideas for future projects (for example BFI, 1997).

Two functional equivalents of 'deferred salary' have received much attention in sectors with a high degree of transient employment, although their coverage of workers in the sectors is far from universal. The first concerns royalty-type incomes, and the second various forms of employee share ownership, such as stock options. In their study of Hollywood, Paul and Kleingartner (1994) found that 'residual incomes' make up about 45 per cent of total earnings for member of the Screen Actors' Guild. These were analogous to royalty incomes derived from additional commercial exploitation of an artistic work, for example use of Disney film logos in marketing children's merchandise. Such payments helped to smooth actors' incomes in between jobs, especially important given the uncertainty about the timing of future work. However, it also provides an important incentive because the film's success will determine its usefulness for marketing other products, and hence the flow of residual incomes. Thus media workers can have an incentive to share their most creative ideas because it will boost their future residual incomes.

Stock options, which have been very popular in Silicon Valley, provide another form of deferred income (Sesil et al., 2002). Like the royalty-type payments, stock options can be seen as an incentive scheme to motivate workers to perform well while working in transient employment relationships. The value of employee output may not become apparent until after the relationship has ended, so the employers have few punitive sanctions at their disposal. In so far as the value of employees' contribution is reflected in the company's value, then a stock option provides a way of linking their future wealth to the quality of their current work input.

Although often discussed with reference to top management pay, stock options have also spread among other employees. Sesil et al. (2002) cite current estimates of use of 'broad-based' schemes in 'new economy' activities in the US as involving 30–40 per cent of all firms, with a sizeable additional percentage of firms considering their adoption. Subject to some important reservations, the authors find that use of broad-based stock options was associated with higher productivity, but not apparently with faster knowledge creation (as measured by patents). Looking more widely, there are signs that performance-related pay may be suited to more transient employment: as a substitute for promotional incentives and commitment mechanisms that were based on the implicit promise of long-term employment. Because it is able to operate over a much shorter time span, it can be integrated into shorter duration employment relationships.

6.3.3 Employment Stability and Training within an Occupational Community

Just as hiring and firing by the firm play a part in incentives to perform, so gaining access to, and losing one's place in, an occupational community can serve as important sanctions. The functional equivalent to a stable job in a firm is regular access to employment by virtue of membership of an occupational community. Many years ago, Kerr (1954) contrasted the modes of entry into 'craft' and 'industrial' (enterprise-based) labour markets, in the first case based on the worker's decision to train and in the second on the employer's hiring decision. Indeed, he likened the craft labour market to a hiring hall. These two models also gave rise to contrasted patterns of income and employment security.

The traditional path into a craft or a professional occupation has been through some kind of apprenticeship. In this, trainees typically share the cost of training with their employer by working, during the training period, for a low wage, below the value of their output thus enabling the employer to recover some or all of the cost of training (Becker, 1975). A variety of mechanisms exist for such investments ranging from formally organised programmes of training, as in apprenticeships, to the practice of gaining experience while working long hours for low pay as new entrants compete for access to professional work (for example Landers et al., 1996). In the German media industry, employers have managed to establish an effective formal apprenticeship for some occupations, although the turnover among project-based organisations meant that many firms lacked the resources and continuity to support the traditional model of a three-year apprenticeship (Baumann, 2002).

In the absence of a well-developed formal apprenticeship, in the British film industry it appears that many young workers in the media sector, who work very long hours on low earnings, do so as a means of gaining access to subsequent employment (BFI, 1997). This is consistent with the large dispersion of earnings within the media sector (the BFI reported roughly 7:1 for the top to the bottom decile in 1996), with many of those on low earnings likely to be aspiring members of the occupational community, paying for their experience and access by long hours on low pay. Jones and Walsh (1997) observe analogous career processes in the network-based US film industry as workers compete to move towards the 'inner core' of better paid more interesting work. Recognising the value of such investments by workers, unions in Britain in the media industries and in contingent employment have been reinvigorating their activities over such issues as regulation of training, licensing and employment risks (Heery et al., 2000).

Such investments underpin occupational communities. They create both a common occupational identity and a shared economic resource to which access is secured by occupational membership. The shared investment gives all members a common interest in maintaining performance standards, which assures the future supply of work to the whole occupation. Peer recognition within the group ensures individual access to future work, and hence continuity of employment. In this respect, there is a parallel with the continuity of employment provided by the standard employment relationship, and loss of one's reputation has a parallel in dismissal. Finally, the career process of progression towards more interesting and better-paid work observed by Jones and Walsh (1997) suggests a functional equivalent to the deferred pay mechanisms discussed earlier.

6.3.4 Representative Institutions, Credible Commitments and Contract Enforcement

One way in which employment law underpins collaboration within the open-ended employment relationship is to make enforceable certain key items that have been agreed. These enable the parties to make credible commitments, which the other party knows can be enforced if necessary. These depend to a large extent on being able to identify certain critical procedures and actions, and although the legal concept of 'implied terms' provides some flexibility to deal with non-codified commitments, there are limits to how far it can reach. One of the recurring features of project-based employment highlighted in recent research has been its informal organisation, and hence the difficulty of using the law to underpin collaboration.

Collins (2001) has argued that one of the barriers to more flexible employment patterns generally is the limited scope employers have to make credible promises to their employees. He was particularly concerned about the difficulties of enforcing promises in relation to such concepts as training for 'employability', which make no specific commitment to a particular kind of training. The concept of 'implied terms', he suggests, does not stretch sufficiently far, in English law at least, to enable the courts to enforce such promises. Stone (2001) has highlighted similar difficulties under recent US law. She cites additionally a number of cases where the American courts have upheld employer claims over restrictive covenants concerning use of knowledge of potential customers, and on human capital. These would make promises by individual employers even less credible in the eyes of their collaborators.

Might the law play a role by supporting representative institutions, and so reinforce the procedures underpinning expectations and incentives within project working, rather than underpinning substantive outcomes? Networks often need an institutional basis particularly if they are to control access and to exclude unreliable elements. For example, in the English private security industry, which practices a wide variety of contractual structures, occupational licensing has been used as a means to promote staff training, raise quality and to eliminate criminal elements (Home Office, Great Britain, 1999). In this example, the occupational closure introduced by licensing is intended to foster a stronger institutional organisation of the sector, for example in matters of training and quality improvement, and to eliminate 'free-riders' that trade on the reputation of better firms.

In Paul and Kleingartner's study, the Screen Actors' Guild played a key role in the negotiation of artists' contracts and in keeping track of residual payments. This naturally placed them at the nerve centre of social networks in that sector. At a very minimum, they needed to maintain an up-to-date list of addresses and members' financial details. In the UK media and related industries, Heery et al. (2000) stress the growing union role in providing an institutional support to inter-organisational employment systems. In Silicon Valley, Saxenian (1996) and Tolbert (1996) stress the key role played by major research universities, which vet the reputations of the professors they employ, and filter the students they select. University positions also provide professors engaged in commercial research projects with an independent career structure and stable employment. Like the unions in Hollywood, these provide an essential anchor for social networks which can, in turn, help to make promises about employment conditions and quality of service more credible.

6.3.5 Articulation of the Three Types of 'Contract' for the Network Economy

This contribution has argued that the open-ended nature of the standard employment relationship rests on a closely articulated set of incentives and sanctions, and that duration has been built into the core of many of these. Thus if project-based employment is to spread more widely as a contractual form in modern economies, it has to find both functional equivalents of these incentives, and a new articulation of the processes underlying the psychological, economic/incentive and legal/institutional 'contracts', which would reinforce their individual effectiveness. It has been argued that functional equivalents have been achieved in a limited number of economic sectors. However, conflict, lack of articulation, between these 'contracts' is common, particularly when they are strongly influenced by the dominant conventions regulating employment, such as in employment law.

Often the presumptions of employment law conflict with the patterns of expectations required for project employment. Calan (2001), a leading member of one the French employers' associations, and himself head of a small firm, expressed the difficulty for small firms in taking on large projects when the 'psychological contract' was adapted to long-term employment. This presumption is built into and reinforced by French employment law. Small employers may have the legal right to lay-off for economic reasons such as the loss of a major customer, but how do you manage this as an employer when those to be laid off may be relatives of other employees, and dismissal, even for economic reasons, has a connotation of fault, if not in the initial cause, then in the reason for selecting particular employees for lay-off? Apart from the immediate effect on the employees concerned, is damage to the morale of those remaining. Could not French law be adapted so that it would send a different signal about the implied relationship between employer and employee in such circumstances? Both Calan and Supiot suggest that it could. Indeed, in January 2004, after a series of major conflicts in the media sector, the French government proposed new legislation introducing special contracts for project employment (Code du travail: la précarité normalisée: *Le Monde* 17.1.2004).

In the cases of Hollywood and Silicon Valley, the types of reward system used also gave a distinct signal to collaborators and employees about the expected duration of the relationship: royalties signal income after completion of the work, and stock options signal a continued financial relationship because it is envisaged from the outset that the flow of economic rewards will outlast the flow of labour services. However, the biggest study of the British film industry, which included information on earnings levels (BFI, 1997), makes very little reference to innovative reward systems that might support new patterns of working, despite their prominence in US studies, suggesting that piece contracts and pay for time worked remain widespread. In other research, when performance issues are discussed, the reported emphasis is on reputation and access to future work as the key incentives (for example Blair, 2001).

Given the reputed informality of much project-based employment, one might expect that norms of good performance, such as those learned during training, would be mobilised in order to reduce the risk of moral hazard by the parties. This brings the issue of occupational communities very much to the fore as the key incentives to regulate the performance and behaviour of coordinators and collaborators. It is also the most difficult element to replicate because of the number of different actors involved in their creation. The examples found in the media industries point to diverse historical origins: Hollywood with the break-up of the large studios and the discovery of a new role by the leading unions; in the German and British television industries, with deregulation and the break-up of the dominance of the large producing companies. In each of these cases, a body of skills had been built up around major employers, arguably solving some of the collective action problems in founding multi-employer occupational training systems (Johansen, 2000). In Silicon Valley, and other high-technology 'industrial districts' such as in south-east France, government programmes and research universities have provided the seedbed on which a skilled community could develop. In other words, these communities seem to function because they build on pre-existing institutional arrangements. Taking stock of the resurgence of small firms, Piore and Sabel (1984) stressed the need to revive neo-craft patterns of union organisation to encourage inter-organisational skill formation and labour mobility. Nevertheless, the primary focus of unions in both the US and the UK remains on the enterprise, treating that as the most effective basis for mobilisation, so most have been ill-adapted to support occupational communities. Thus, in each of these respects, the three types of 'contract' appear to conflict with rather than support each other for the growth of project-based and other types of more transient employment.

Finally, one feature of many of the occupations in which project-based employment has flourished in recent years appears to be increased inequality of rewards, and a more accentuated distribution of employment insecurity. Considering evidence from the British New Earnings Survey panel data (NESPD) for 1975 to 2002, it appears that in the occupations in which transient employment relations have developed the most, there has been an increase in the relative rewards of the most successful, the top 5 percent of earners and above, compared with the least successful 10 per cent (Marsden, 2007). In particular, while access to the entry levels of these occupations has become easier, with the expansion of secondary and higher education, competition for access to the more secure and prestigious levels has become more intense. As a consequence, one can trace out different types of career paths: of those who do well in the entry tournaments, gain peer recognition and move on upwards, and those who become trapped in the entry positions, and spend their careers on low incomes and with unstable employment conditions. A factor driving this process is that with more transient employment relationships, there is less incentive for employers to invest in their employees' skills, which shifts the burden of building up skills, contacts and reputation onto the individuals. In order to gain access to such opportunities, aspirants accept very low pay on short-term commissions, while they wait for their 'break'.

Despite its long time series which is needed for identifying such changes which tend to occur gradually, the NESPD has a number of limitations for tracing this segmentation pattern in terms of the way earnings are measured, the exclusion of self-employed earnings and change of occupational classification in mid-period. So, some caution is needed in interpreting these results. However, they are consistent with findings of others who have worked on the film industry and on journalism and who have noted a similar segmentation developing (Jones and Walsh, 1997; BFI, 1997; and Sutton Trust, 2006) between those who become established in particular occupational communities and those who remain for most of their lives on the fringes. It has been suggested, notably by the Sutton Trust, that the initial entry competition can be socially regressive because the prolonged periods of work on low income. While building up contacts and a reputation, aspirants need a high degree of parental support, which favours those from more wealthy families who can support them.

6.4 CONCLUSIONS

Compared with the 'standard' employment relationship, one might consider project-based employment as being open-ended in terms of collaborators' task obligations, but not so in relation to its temporal duration. People may well collaborate on successive projects, but the implicit promise of open-ended duration employment is absent, and renewed collaboration is contingent on getting new commissions. In this respect, project-based employment differs also from many common forms of freelance work where the parties contract for a specific product, such as translating a document.

This chapter has treated the employment relationship as a cooperative framework for the supply of labour services. Its success and diffusion during much of the twentieth century owed much to the development of three convergent and mutually reinforcing processes: employee expectations, incentives, and legal and institutional support. These focused around a presumption of a long-term relationship of indefinite duration. This met the needs of both employers and employees in the many activities in which cooperation centred on a common workplace bringing together both capital and labour services. There, long-term employment provided a platform for the development of skills, and distinctive organisational capabilities. In recent years, as recognised by the Supiot Report, changing product markets, technologies and patterns of service have increasingly challenged this model by undermining the widespread presumption of long-term employment.

Employers may be able to impose short-term, unstable employment on vulnerable groups in the labour market and on those competing for entry into attractive occupations, but for those with marketable skills and talents, this can only be done at a cost, such as compensatory higher pay, and even then, the organisational model may be inappropriate and inhibit cooperation. This chapter has looked at employment relationships in sectors using project-based models of organisation, some of which have done so for a long time, in order to understand how workers and firms have solved problems of cooperation. There, it was shown that they have developed a number of mechanisms that help to control opportunism and foster a zone of shared interests in order to strengthen cooperation. Nevertheless, these functional equivalents to the mechanisms governing the established employment relationship were often less well developed, and tensions between them undermined their influence. There is some evidence also that compared with occupations which have more structured entry and careers, those in which project-based employment is more developed are characterised by a more unequal distribution of earnings and of economic security.

All of this suggests that project-based employment has a long way to go before it could displace the standard open-ended employment relationship from its pre-eminent position in the world of work. Nevertheless the challenge to develop new contractual forms remains. As Osterman (1996), Cappelli (1999) for the US and Grimshaw et al. (2002) for the UK have argued, it is increasingly difficult for firms to use internal labour markets as a means of assuring functional flexibility among their workforces. Project-based employment offers a framework that is open-ended with regard to work content but not duration, and so offers a possible solution to this problem. As argued in this chapter, outside certain sectors key elements of this contractual form are still lacking, and even within those sectors it seems that the degree of complementarity among the three incentive processes, and the extent to which they are mutually reinforcing, remains short of that achieved for the standard employment relationship. There are also important questions about whether they may increase inequality and reduce inter-generational economic mobility.

NOTES

1. I should like to thank participants at the Conference on 'Innovating Labour Market Policies', Amsterdam 2006, the anonymous referees, and the editors for valuable comments on the early draft of this contribution. This contribution is a substantially reworked version of Marsden (2004). The author and editors are grateful to the publisher, Blackwell, for permission to use this material.
2. The chosen theme of the IIRA congress 'Beyond Traditional Employment: Industrial Relations in the Network Economy', Berlin, September 2003.
3. These figures were extracted from the university performance league tables for 2000, published by the *Times Higher Education Supplement* in its issue of 14.4.2000. The median percentage of non-permanent staff across Britain's 97 universities was about 40 per cent. Overall, there is a correlation of 0.77 between university research ratings in the national Research Assessment Exercise (RAE) and the percentage of non-permanent staff. The RAE is one measure of success in the competition for research funds, and it also serves as a quality index in the search to attract overseas students.
4. For a discussion of different concepts of efficiency wage, see Akerlof and Yellen (1986).
5. 'VW drive for four-day week'. *European Industrial Relations Review*, 239, December 1993, pp. 15–16.

6. Should such levels of distrust seem implausible, one has only to reflect on the large number of public sector employees who thought that their management manipulated performance appraisal scores in order to avoid paying performance-related pay (Marsden and French, 1998).
7. The judgements he considers relate to whether the state should uphold the right of citizens to redress for loss of potential income rather than just loss of physical assets. In the 1872 case, the State of Louisiana had granted a corporation a monopoly to maintain the slaughterhouses in New Orleans, and regulated the charges made to other butchers. The latter contested the law on the grounds that it deprived them of their property without due process of law, a right established under the Fourteenth Amendment. The case hinged on whether 'property' meant physical assets, use value, which they had not lost, or whether it covered the exercise of their trade, exchange value, of which they argued they were deprived. In that case, the Supreme Court ruled by majority in favour of the older notion of property. However, by 1897, in the Allegeyer case, the Supreme Court recognised property as exchange value, including liberty of access to markets.
8. In fact, Commons devotes considerable space to arguing how the employment relationship should be understood as an exchange of goodwill, and how the recognition of non-corporeal capital also covered workers' ability to earn a living from their skills: both essential elements of 'at will' employment. This was workers' 'earning power'. A restraint of trade, such as a restrictive covenant limiting where they can work in the future, could deprive them of the earning power of their skills even though it did not remove their 'use value'. Although 'at will' employment is often associated with the employer's right to hire and fire at will, the employee likewise remains in the relationship 'at will'.
9. Deakin (1998) makes a similar evolutionary argument for Britain.
10. Tolbert (1996, p. 339) defines a 'community of practice' as: individuals who actively share a core body of tacit knowledge that is necessary for the execution of concrete, everyday work tasks ... provide the foundation for occupations'.

REFERENCES

Akerlof, G. and Yellen, J. (eds) (1986), *Efficiency wage models of the labor market*, Cambridge: Cambridge University Press.

Auer, P. and Cazes, S. (2000), 'The resilience of the long-term employment relationship: evidence from the industrialised countries', *International Labour Review*, **139** (4), 379–408.

Axelrod, R. (1984), *The evolution of cooperation*, New York: Basic Books.

Baumann, A. (2002), *Path-dependency or convergence? The emergence of labour market institutions in the media production industries of the UK and Germany*, unpublished doctoral thesis, Florence: European University Institute.

Becker, G.S. (1975), *Human capital: a theoretical and empirical analysis, with special reference to education*, Chicago: University of Chicago Press.

BFI (1997), Pettigrew, N., Willis, J., Paterson, R. and Dex, S., *British Film Institute Television Tracking Study: Second Interim Report*, London: British Film Institute.

Blair, H. (2001), '"You're only as good as your last job": the labour process and labour market in the British film industry', *Work, Employment & Society*, **15** (1), 149–69.

Calan, D. (2001), 'Comment', in Marsden, David and Stephenson, Hugh (eds), *Labour law and social insurance in the new economy: a debate on the Supiot Report*, Centre for Economic Performance, Discussion paper, No. 500, July, London: London School of Economics.

Cappelli P. (1999), *The new deal at work: managing the market-driven workforce*, Cambridge MA: Harvard Business School Press.

Carnoy, M., Castells, M. and Benner, C. (1997), 'Labour markets and employment practices in the age of flexibility: a case study of silicon valley', *International Labour Review*, **136** (1), 27–48.

Coase, R.H. (1937), 'The nature of the firm', *Economica*, November, 386–405.

Collins, H. (2001), 'Regulating the employment relationship for competitiveness', *Industrial Law Journal*, **30** (1), 17–47.

Commons, J.R. (1924), *Legal foundations of capitalism*, New York: Macmillan.

Deakin, S. (1998), 'The evolution of the contract of employment, 1900–50: the influence of the welfare state', in Whiteside, N. and Salais, R. (eds), *Governance, industry and labour markets in Britain and France: the modernising state in the mid-twentieth century*, London: Routledge.

Dex, S., Willis, J., Paterson, R. and Sheppard, E. (2000), 'Freelance workers and contract uncertainty: the effects of contractual changes in the television industry', *Work, Employment and Society*, **14** (2), 283–305.

Dyne, L. van and Dienesch, R. (1994), 'Organisational citizenship behavior: construct redefinition, measurement, and validation', *Academy of Management Journal*, **37** (4), 765–802.

Fraser, J. and Gold, M. (2001), '"Portfolio workers": autonomy and control amongst freelance translators', *Work, Employment & Society*, **15** (4), 679–97

Granovetter M. (1973), 'The strength of weak ties', *American Journal of Sociology*, **78** (6), 1360–80.

Grimshaw, D., Ward, K.G., Rubery, J. and Beynon, H. (2001), 'Organisations and the transformation of the internal labour market', *Work, Employment & Society*, **15** (1), 25–54.

Guest, D.E. (1998), 'Is the psychological contract worth taking seriously?', *Journal of Organizational Behavior*, **19** (Special issue), 649–64.

Guest, D., Conway, N., Briner, R. and Dickman, M. (1996), 'The state of the psychological contract in employment', Institute of Personnel and Development, *Issues in People Management*, No. 16.

Haunschild, A. (2003), 'Managing employment relationships in flexible labour markets: the case of German repertory theatres', *Human Relations*, **56** (8), August, 899–929.

Heery, E., Conley, H., Dlebridge, R. and Stewart, P. (2000), *Beyond the enterprise? Trade unions and the representation of contingent workers*, Working Paper, No. 7, ESRC Future of Work Programme, ISSN 1469–531.

Home Office, Great Britain (1999), *The Government's Proposals for Regulation of the Private Security Industry in England and Wales*, Parliamentary papers, CM 4254, London: Stationery Office.

Johansen, L.-H. (2000), *Transferable training and the collective action problem for employers: an analysis of further education and training in four Norwegian industries*, PhD Thesis, University of London.

Jones, C. and Walsh, K. (1997), 'Boundaryless careers in the US film industry', *Industrielle Beziehungen*, **4** (1), 58–73.

Kerr, C. (1954), 'The Balkanization of labor markets', in Bakke (ed.), *Labor Mobility and Economic Opportunity*, Cambridge MA: MIT Press, pp. 92–110.

Lam, A. (2003), 'Organizational learning in multinationals: R&D networks of Japanese and US MNEs in the UK', *Journal of Management Studies*, **40** (3), 673–703.

Landers, R., Rebitzer, J. and Taylor, L. (1996), 'Human resources practices and the demographic transformation of professional labour markets', in Osterman, P. (ed.), *Broken ladders: managerial careers in the new economy*, New York: Oxford University Press.

Lazear, E.P. (1990), 'Pensions and deferred benefits as strategic compensation', *Industrial Relations*, **2** (29), 263–80.

Lazear, E. (1995), *Personnel economics*, Cambridge MA: MIT Press.

Malcomson, J. (1997), 'Contracts, hold-up, and labor markets', *Journal of Economic Literature*, **35** (4), 1916–57.

Marsden, David. W. (1999), *A theory of employment systems: micro-foundations of societal diversity*, Oxford: Oxford University Press.

Marsden, David W. (2004), 'The "Network economy" and models of the employment contract', *British Journal of Industrial Relations*, **42** (4), 659–84.

Marsden, David W. (2007), 'Labour market segmentation in Britain: the decline of occupational labour markets and the spread of "entry tournaments"', *Économies et Sociétés, Série 'Socio-Économie du Travail'*, AB, **28** (6), 965–98.

Marsden, David W. and French, S. (1998), *What a performance: performance related pay in the public services*, Centre for Economic Performance, Special Report, London: London School of Economics.

Meyer, J.P. and Allen, N.J. (1997), *Commitment in the workplace: theory, research and application*, Capelli and Oaks, California: Sage.

Mottez, B. (1966), *Systèmes de salaire et politiques patronales: essai sur l'évolution des pratiques et des idéologies patronales*, Paris: Centre National de la Recherche Scientifique.

OECD (1992), *Employment Outlook 1992*, Paris: Organisation for Economic Cooperation and Development, Chapter 4.

OECD (1997), *Employment Outlook, June 1997*, Paris: Organisation for Economic Cooperation and Development, Chapter 5.

OECD (1999), *Employment Outlook 1999*, Paris: Organisation for Economic Cooperation and Development, Chapter 2 and 4.

OECD (2000), *Employment Outlook 2000*, Paris: Organisation for Economic Cooperation and Development, Chapter 5.

OECD (2002), *Employment Outlook 2002*, Organisation for Economic Cooperation and Development, Paris, Chapter 3.

Osterman, P. (ed.) (1996), *Broken ladders: managerial careers in the new economy*, New York: Oxford University Press.

Paul, A. and Kleingartner, A. (1994), 'Flexible production and the transformation of industrial relations in the motion picture and television industry', *Industrial and Labor Relations Review*, **47** (4), 663–78.

Piore, M.J. (1968), 'The impact of the labor market on the design and selection of productive techniques within the manufacturing plant', *Quarterly Journal of Economics*, **82** (4), 602–20.

Piore, M.J. and Sabel, C.F. (1984), *The second industrial divide: possibilities for prosperity*, New York: Basic Books.

Reynaud, J.-D. (1969), 'La convention sociale de la sidérurgue lorraine', *Droit Social*, **4**, 219–27.

Rousseau, D. (1995), *Psychological contracts in organisations: understanding written and unwritten agreements*, Thousand Oaks, CA: Sage.

Salais, R. (1989), 'L'analyse économique des conventions du travail', *Revue Économique*, **40** (2), 199–240.

Saxenian, A. (1996), 'Beyond boundaries: open labor markets and learning in Silicon Valley', in Arthur, M. and Rousseau, D. (ed.), *The boundaryless career*, New York: Oxford University Press.

Scott, A.J. (1998), 'Multimedia and digital visual effects: an emerging local labor market', *Monthly Labor Review*, **121** (3), 30–38.

Scullion, H. and Edwards, P. (1988), 'Craft unionism, job controls and management strategy: "Premier Metals" 1955–1980', in Terry, M. and Edwards, P. (eds), *Shop floor politics and job controls: the post-war engineering industry*, Oxford: Blackwell.

Sengenberger, W. (1987), *Struktur und Funktionsweise von Arbeitsmärkten: die Bundesrepublik Deutschland im internationalen Vergleich*, Frankfurt: Campus Verlag.

Sesil, J.C., Kroumova, M.K., Blasi, J.R. and Kruse, D. (2002), 'Broad-based employee stock options in US "New Economy" firms', *British Journal of Industrial Relations*, **40** (2), 273–94.

Slichter, S. (1919), *The turnover of factory labor*, New York: Appleton.

Sly, F. and Stillwell, D. (1997), 'Temporary workers in Great Britain', *Labour Market Trends*, September, 347–54.

Sorensen, E. (1994), *Comparable worth: is it a worthy policy?* Princeton: Princeton University Press.

Stiglitz, J. (1984), *Theories of wage rigidity*, Paper presented to the Centre for Labour Economics, London School of Economics, April.

Stone, K.V.W. (2001), 'The new psychological contract: implications of the changing workplace for labor and employment law', *UCLA Law Review*, **48** (3), 519–661.

Supiot, A. (1994), *Critique du droit du travail*, Presses Universitaires de France, Paris.

Supiot, A. (Chair) (1999), *Au-delà le l'emploi: rapport pour la Commission européenne*, Paris: Flammarion.

Sutton Trust (2006), The *educational backgrounds of leading journalists*, London: The Sutton Trust.

Sydow, J. and Staber, U. (2002), 'The institutional embeddedness of project networks: the case of content production in German television', *Regional Studies*, **36** (3), 215–27.

Tempest, S., Starkey, K. (1997), 'Diversity or devide? In search of flexible specialization in the UK televison industry', Industrielle Beziehungen (German Journal of Industrial Relations), **4** (1), 38–57.

Teulings, C. and Hartog, J. (1998), *Corporatism or competition? Labour contracts, institutions and wage structures in international comparison*, Cambridge: Cambridge University Press.

Tolbert, P. (1996), 'Occupations, organizations, and boundaryless careers', in Arthur, M. and Rousseau, D. (eds), *The boundaryless career: a new employment principle for a new organizational era*, New York: Oxford University Press, pp. 331–49.

Williamson, O.E. (1985), *The economic institutions of capitalism: firms, markets and relational contracting*, New York: Free Press.

7. Working Time Flexibility across Europe

Marcel Kerkhofs, Heejung Chung and Peter Ester

7.1 INTRODUCTION

The need for more flexibility is a key notion in the current policy debate on the present and future of the European economy and labour market. Europe, so the European Commission holds, has to be less rigid in terms of its institutions, regulations, culture and policies in effectively addressing the radical impacts of accelerated processes of globalisation, increased competition, and rapid changes in the demand and supply dynamics (European Commission, 2005).[1] These new challenges will deeply affect European employer–employee relationships, if only because flexibility directly impacts existing working time regimes and practices as well as the forms of contracts. Both employers and employees need to take their share of flexibility challenges. In the words of the European Employment Taskforce (2003, p. 27): 'Flexibility is not just in the interest of employers. Modern workers also have a need for flexible working arrangements and modern work organisations to help them combine work and care, to make time for education and to respond to their personal preferences and lifestyles'. This becomes clear if one looks at flexibility arrangements that are presently in vogue: companies aim to gain a competitive edge by making production time and opening hours more flexible, for example by means of non-standard working times, overtime and flex-contracts, whereas workers want more flexibility of their working time through arrangements such as flexitime, part-time work and various leave schemes.

Although there is a substantive scholarly literature on flexibilisation and a growing number of empirical studies on the national level for several European countries, there is a surprising lack of comparative data on flexibility trends across Europe (Huys, 2006; Vinken and Ester, 2006). This is particularly true for flexibility trends at the level of firms and organisations, and less so for employees' working time preferences for balancing work life and private life. The way companies across Europe have addressed the need for more flexibility is simply not very well-known, particularly due to the lack of cross-national (longitudinal) data. In 2004 the European Foundation for the Improvement of Living and Working Conditions has launched a major survey to tackle this pressing data deficit: the Establishment Survey on Working Time and Work–life Balance (ESWT). This survey, conducted in 21 European countries (EU15 and six new member states) among more than 21,000 companies, covers a wide array of working time arrangements including: flexible working hours, overtime, part-time work, non-standard working hours, family-related leave arrangements and other long leaves, phased and early retirement, and work–life balance facilities. A unique feature of the ESWT study is that both management and employee representatives are interviewed. Riedman et al. (2006) provide an extensive overview of the survey.[2] In this chapter we use the information in the ESWT survey to explore the different ways in which firms organise working time at the work place. More specifically, this study aims at identifying a typology of organisations reflecting how working time arrangements and work–life balance facilities are used or provided by European firms. Of particular interest is the degree to which organisations combine flexibility measures that support their operational needs with arrangements supporting the employees' work–life balance. Both types of practices increase flexibility but in different ways and for quite different reasons.

In Section 7.2 we discuss the ESWT survey and the working time arrangements that will be considered for this analysis. This section also discusses the Latent Class methodology that is used to construct the flexibility profiles. Section 7.3 presents the outcomes of this analysis, particularly the typology of working time flexibility of organisations. This typology is then used to compare working time flexibility across European countries in Section 7.4. In Section 7.5 we investigate which observed characteristics – such as the line of business, size and composition of the workforce and the geographical location – determine the flexibility profile of an organisation. This section focuses on characteristics that are potential determinants of the flexibility profile of an organisation. In Section 7.6 we relate the flexibility profile of an organisation to indicators of economic performance, employment relations and some specific HRM themes. Section 7.7 presents the main conclusions.

7.2 DATA AND METHODOLOGY

In 2004 the European Foundation for the Improvement of Living and Working Conditions launched a large-scale survey in establishments in 21 European countries: the 15 'old' Member States of the European Union

(EU15) and six of the new Member States (the Czech Republic, Cyprus, Hungary, Latvia, Poland and Slovenia). In more than 21,000 establishments[3] personnel managers and – where available – formal employee representatives (for example shop stewards, works councils) were interviewed about working time arrangements and work–life balance issues in their companies. Interviews for the survey were carried out via telephone in the autumn of 2004 (EU15) and the spring of 2005 (six new Member States).

The data of the European Establishment Survey on Working Time and Work–life Balance (ESWT) are representative for all establishments with ten or more employees in the above-mentioned countries. The survey covers private and public establishments from practically all sectors of activity.[4] Table 7.1 shows the indicators of working time flexibility in the ESWT. For each topic that was distinguished in the questionnaire, one or more indicators were constructed.

The main objective of this analysis is to investigate whether a typology of firms can be distilled from the observed patterns of working time flexibility. Rather than for a typology of arrangements – which could be derived from a factor analysis on the observed arrangements – this requires a method that focuses on the establishments and the complete mix of working time arrangements by which these are characterised. Moreover, neither the types of firms that can be distinguished nor their number are known beforehand and they will be constructed on the basis of the observed working time arrangements and practices in the ESWT dataset. Latent Class models (Vermunt, 2003) are most appropriate for this purpose. Modelling the flexibility profiles of firms as latent classes, we single out groups of establishment that are similar in terms of the working time arrangements they do or do not use, but differ substantially from the other establishments. This comparison will be based on a subset of the indicators in Table 7.1.

Denote the vector of m indicators by Y and the latent class by C, which may be a number ranging from 1 to the number of clusters N_C. We now define the probability distribution of the observed values of the indicators Y_i for organisation i as:

$$\mathrm{pdf}(Y_i) = \sum_{j=1}^{N_C} \Pr(C_i = j) \cdot \mathrm{pdf}(Y_i | C_i = j) \tag{7.1}$$

This type of model is a Latent Class model.[5] The name actually refers to a fairly general class of models which has the advantage that it can deal with very different types of indicators – continuous measures, unordered categories, ordered categories, event histories, count data – by using the best applicable specifications as sub-models for each indicator, and linking their outcomes by referring to the latent class to which an organisation is assigned. In our application all indicators are dichotomous and all sub-models are logit specifications. The cluster membership probabilities are estimated simultaneously with the parameters determining the probability distribution of Y in each cluster. The model is estimated by means of the maximum likelihood.

Table 7.1 Indicators for working time flexibility and work–life balance in the ESWT

Topic	Dichotomous indicators (= 1 if applicable, 0 otherwise)
Part-time work	part-time workers
	part-time workers (≥20% of the employees)
Irregular hours	irregular working hours
	work at night
	work on Saturday
	work on Sunday
	work at night (≥20% of the employees)
	work on Saturday (≥20% of the employees)
	work on Sunday (≥20% of the employees)
	shift system
	shift system (≥20% of the employees)
Flexible working time	flexible working hours
	flexible working hours (≥20% of the employees)
	working time accounts
Overtime	overtime
	overtime (≥20% of the employees)
Leave arrangements	parental leave
	long-term leave available
	leave for care or illness in family
	leave for education
	leave for other purposes
Early and phased retirement	early retirement possible
	phased retirement possible (and relevant)
Measures for work–life balance	measures to facilitate work–life balance
Flexible contract workers	workers on flexible contracts
	fixed-term contracts
	temporary agency workers
	freelance workers

This type of model is a Latent Class model.[6] The name actually refers to a fairly general class of models which has the advantage that it can deal with very different types of indicators – continuous measures, unordered categories, ordered categories, event histories, count data – by using the best applicable specifications as sub-models for each indicator, and linking their outcomes by referring to the latent class to which an organisation is assigned.

In our application all indicators are dichotomous and all sub-models are logit specifications. The cluster membership probabilities are estimated simultaneously with the parameters determining the probability distribution of Y in each cluster. The model is estimated by means of the maximum likelihood.

The number of latent classes is not known beforehand and is determined on the basis of a 'goodness of fit' criterion from statistical decision theory expressing how well the resulting clusters fit the data. Moreover one has to inspect whether model assumptions are violated, which is usually the case if the number of latent classes is too small, and whether each cluster still contains a substantial number of firms. For the comparison of the models that pass this validity check the Bayesian Information Criterion (BIC) is probably the most commonly used 'goodness of fit' measure. We will follow this standing practice.

In this first step of the analysis – the derivation of the latent flexibility profiles – we only use the observed indicators and not the other observed organisation characteristics. This step results in a marginal distribution of the N_C latent classes and their profiles, as characterised by the conditional probability distribution of Y in each class. Next we can analyse what observed characteristics determine a firm's flexibility profile. For this purpose we use the estimates of model (1.1) to compute the posterior probability that a given organisation has a specific flexibility profile:

$$\Pr(C_i = j \mid Y_i) = \frac{\Pr(C_i = j) \cdot \text{pdf}\ (Y_i \mid C_i = j)}{\sum_{k=1}^{N_C} \Pr(C_i = k) \cdot \text{pdf}\ (Y_i \mid C_i = k)} \tag{7.2}$$

Using these probabilities we assign each firm to the flexibility profile that has the largest posterior (modal assignment). Knowing what 'type' an organisation is, we can relate the typology of working time flexibility to firm characteristics such as country, size or sector.

7.3 A TYPOLOGY OF WORKING TIME FLEXIBILITY

In this section we apply the data and methodology discussed in the previous section to derive the typology of working time flexibility. For this purpose we have used the following set of indicators:

1. Part-time work: whether 20 per cent or more of the employees are part-time workers.
2. Irregular hours: whether there are employees in the establishment that regularly work at night or during the weekend.

3. Flexible working hours: whether 20 per cent or more of the employees can to some extent determine when they begin or finish their working day.
4. Overtime: whether 20 per cent or more of the employees have worked any overtime in the preceding months.
5. Parental leave: whether employees have been on parental leave in the last three years.
6. Long-term leave: whether long-leave arrangements – other than parental leave – are available in the establishment.
7. Early retirement: whether employees have the option to retire before the statutory retirement age.
8. Work–life balance facilities: whether the establishment offers special services to support domestic commitments of the employees.
9. Non-standard employment: whether the establishment currently employs workers on fixed-term contracts, agency workers or freelancers.

On the basis of the Bayesian Information Criterion the optimal number of latent classes turns out to be six. The model outcomes for this number of classes do not violate the assumptions underlying the statistical model and the classes each contain at least 5 per cent of the establishments. A range of alternative specifications was analysed, using various combinations of the indicators in Table 7.1. The results of these analyses were quite similar.

Where possible we prefer the use of 20 per cent threshold indicators, as these allow a sharper distinction between firms and profiles, while still comparing groups that are sufficiently large in size. The main reason for using a percentage of workers as a threshold is that the meaning of the indicators will otherwise be affected by the size of the workforce. In sectors or countries with few part-time workers, most of the smaller establishments will report no part-time workers, while almost all of the larger firms will employ some part-time workers, although the number of those workers may be relatively small. Applying the 20 per cent thresholds accounts for this conceptual bias.

The outcomes of the latent class analysis are summarised in Table 7.2. The first line shows the percentage of organisations in each cluster. Below these percentages are the average indicator scores in that cluster. For the indicator of part-time work, it shows for example that 33 per cent of establishments in the first cluster have 20 per cent or more part-time workers, whereas this applies to 89 per cent of establishments in the sixth cluster and 25 per cent of all establishments.[7]

The first cluster includes 22 per cent of all establishments surveyed in our data. These establishments have above-average use of all the options for working time flexibility considered here, with the exception of flexible working hours, for which the take-up is lowest of all clusters derived. Cluster 5, which covers 14 per cent of all establishments, also consists of establishments that have an above-average take-up of most of the arrangements covered, with the exception of irregular working hours. Both clusters therefore represent organisations with a high level of working time flexibility.

Table 7.2 The cluster profiles

	Cluster 1	Cluster 2	Cluster 3	Cluster 4	Cluster 5	Cluster 6	Overall
% of organisations	22	21	18	18	14	7	100
Indicators (%)							
part-time work	33	6	0	31	32	89	25
irregular hours	70	20	42	33	37	56	42
flexible working hours	14	20	31	37	97	49	37
overtime	57	0	90	41	66	49	49
parental leave	76	36	34	44	80	43	53
long-term leave	70	39	34	89	78	37	59
early retirement	67	31	30	96	68	37	56
work–life balance	11	2	3	15	10	9	8
non-standard employment	95	59	61	66	84	43	70

The main difference between these two clusters is the use of flexible working hours (lowest percentage of all for cluster 1, highest for cluster 5) and irregular hours (highest percentage of all for cluster 1 and below average for cluster 5). On the other side of the flexibility spectrum stands the second cluster, which accounts for 21 per cent of all establishments in our analysis. This cluster consists of organisations with a below-average take-up rate for all the flexibility options in this analysis, especially for overtime which shows as 0 per cent. The remaining three clusters can be interpreted as showing intermediate levels of flexibility and work–life balance measures, differing in which arrangement is emphasised more than the others.

The two most flexible clusters differ most clearly in their use of flexible working hours and irregular working hours. On the other aspects considered here, the differences are smaller and take-up rates are above the sample average for both clusters. Stressing these differences, one could conclude that both clusters are highly flexible, but that the first cluster focuses on arrangements that are more driven by companies' operational needs, such as irregular hours and non-standard workers. On the other hand, the fifth cluster shows higher levels of flexible working hours schemes and long-leave arrangements and somewhat higher take-up of overtime and parental leave, all of which, maybe with the exception of overtime, are arrangements that put a greater weight on workers' work–life balance needs. For this reason, within the two high-flexibility clusters, we distinguish between worker-oriented flexibility, cluster 5, and company-oriented flexibility, cluster 1.

Similarly, we can distinguish between the three clusters with intermediate levels of flexibility by highlighting the elements of flexibility that figure more or less prominently in each. First of all, cluster 4 shows an exceptionally high proportion of establishments that have arrangements for early retirement and longer periods of leave and offer various services to facilitate the work–life balance of its workers. This cluster also shows high scores for part-time work, while having low levels of irregular hours, overtime and parental leave. For this reason, we will refer to this cluster as the life course flexibility profile, underlining its emphasis on arrangements for the work–life balance throughout the worker's life course. On the other hand, the cluster 6 shows low percentages of establishments having leave and retirement schemes, but has the highest take-up of part-time work, high levels of irregular hours and overtime, and a slightly above-average score for providing measures to facilitate the work–life balance. Looking at the total package of arrangements that are overrepresented in this cluster, it makes sense to assume that it will mainly consist of companies that face short-term variability of the workload (within a day or within a week), thus needing part-time work and flexible working hours, but not temporary contracts which are more suitable for dealing with workload variation over longer periods of time. Accordingly, this cluster will be referred to as the day-to-day flexibility profile. Cluster 3 shows very low levels of all arrangements with the exception of overtime and irregular hours: 90 per cent of establishments in this cluster has more than a fifth of its employees working overtime on a regular basis, and their use of extended and unusual hours is at the average level for all European companies. We refer to this cluster as the *overtime* profile. Finally, cluster 2 is labelled the low flexibility profile, as it shows the lowest use of irregular hours, flexible working hours, overtime and work–life balance services of all clusters, and the scores on all the other flexibility items are far below average.

Table 7.3 summarises the typology. The profiles are rearranged from more to less flexible and the table shows for each profile which aspects of working time flexibility occur more and which aspects less than in the average European organisation. Deviations of 10 per cent or more are denoted by '+' or '–', deviations of 25 per cent or more are shaded.

Table 7.3 The typology of working time flexibility

	Working time flexibility profiles					
	High		Intermediate			Low
	Worker-oriented	Firm-oriented	Life course	Day-to-day	Over-time	
% of organisations	14	22	18	7	18	21
Indicators						
part-time workers	+	+	+	+	–	–
irregular hours	–	+	–	+		–
flexible working hours	+	–		+	–	–
overtime	+	+	–		+	–
parental leave	+	+	–	–	–	–
long-term leave available	+	+	+	–	–	–
early retirement option	+	+	+	–	–	–
facilities for work–life balance	+	+	+	+	–	–
flexible contracts	+	+		–	–	–

Notes:
Shading indicates deviation of 25% or more from the average EU21 organisation.
+ = 10% or more above the average.
– = 10% or more below the average.

Before elaborating on the typology, it has to be noted that the typology is data-based and therefore depends on the possibilities and the limitations of the data that were used. Primarily, the typology is a means of compressing or summarising the information on the practices regarding working times as reported by the establishments in the survey. However exploratory this may be, it also allows an assessment of the flexibility strategies of firms on the dimensions covered by the survey. The scope of such an assessment is, however, limited by the information that was used to derive it. Wider application would require further scrutiny of the internal and external validity of the typology, in which the internal validity refers to the robustness of the typology with respect to the use of alternative indicators on the topics covered, and external validity refers to its robustness to the use of indicators on a wider range of flexibility themes (for example internal numerical and functional flexibility) and its relation to the insights from more theoretical and institutional research. The clusters derived above demonstrate that the observed diversity of company practices on the topics in the ESWT survey can be successfully captured by a typology distinguishing six types of companies. Moreover, this typology makes strikingly clear that the profiles that can be distinguished in this way not only differ in the amount of flexibility, but also in their focus on the two main reasons for adopting more flexible practices. Summarising the discussion in the previous paragraphs, one could tentatively summarise this point as in Figure 7.1, where each of the six clusters is positioned according to the extent and the focus of working time flexibility. The amount of flexibility is denoted by the distance from the origin. The position relative to the 45° line through the origin indicates the focus of the mix of flexible practices. Closer towards the horizontal axis are profiles that focus on supporting a better work–life balance for workers, closer to the vertical axis are profiles that put more weight on flexibility for the purpose of the company's adaptability to external shocks.

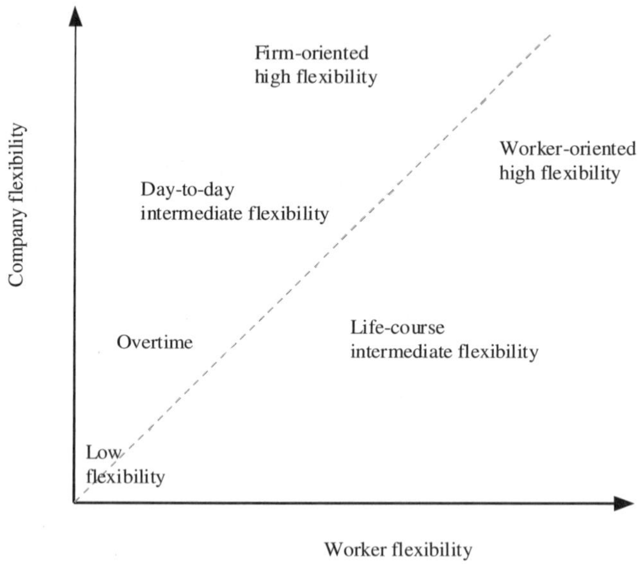

Figure 7.1 Focus and extent of the six working time flexibility profiles

7.4 COUNTRY DIFFERENCES

Now we examine the distribution of the six different flexibility profiles within the 21 European countries in the ESWT. Based on the previous studies on welfare state regimes and flexibility regime typologies, one may expect differences between countries and clustering of countries depending on how the establishments in the country organise their working time and work–life balance options. In this section, we therefore examine how the six flexibility profiles regarding working time flexibility and work–life balance issues are represented within each country and whether the typology of establishment aggregates to a typology of countries. This clustering of countries may – among other things – reflect cultural differences as well as differences in institutional settings.

First we examine the proportion of each of the six company types within each country. Table 7.4 shows the percentages of each type of organisations in the 21 countries in the ESWT dataset. The countries have been ordered by the type of organisation that covers the largest proportion of the establishments, that is the modal type of organisation in the country (shaded percentages).

Table 7.4 Distribution of the six types of organisations in the 21 ESWT countries (in %)

	Types of working time flexibility						
	High		Intermediate			Low	Total
	Worker-oriented	Firm-oriented	Life course	Day-to-day	Over-time		
Overall	14	22	18	7	18	21	100
Country							
Finland	33	26	24	2	8	7	100
Sweden	32	25	11	7	14	11	100
France	14	29	16	5	18	19	100
Czech Republic	17	27	26	1	12	16	100
Belgium	11	26	17	6	14	26	100
United Kingdom	17	26	21	12	14	10	100
Poland	12	21	35	3	7	22	100
Netherlands	14	24	30	10	11	11	100
Latvia	13	24	28	5	9	22	100
Denmark	19	21	23	5	18	14	100
Austria	13	13	9	11	32	22	100
Ireland	12	17	21	10	29	12	100
Germany	17	19	15	12	23	13	100
Greece	5	17	13	2	13	51	100
Hungary	7	17	20	3	12	41	100
Spain	8	15	15	4	19	40	100
Portugal	7	24	14	1	15	39	100
Italy	11	18	6	5	26	35	100
Cyprus	3	22	15	4	24	33	100
Slovenia	12	23	16	2	22	27	100
Luxembourg	13	21	17	4	22	23	100

Note: Shading indicates the modal type of organisation, that is the most prevalent type of organisation in a country.

Overall 36 per cent of all firms in Europe can be categorised as high-flexibility organisations. This proportion is much higher in Finland and Sweden, where the largest proportion of companies is of the worker-oriented high-flexibility type and the second largest group is the firm-oriented high-flexibility organisations. These are the two most flexible organisation profiles regarding working time and the work–life balance, and combined account for 59 per cent and 57 per cent of all establishments in Finland and Sweden.

France, the Czech Republic, Belgium and the United Kingdom also have large proportions of organisations of the firm-oriented high-flexibility type, but in these countries the proportions of worker-oriented high-flexibility organisation are only slightly above or even below the European average.

The next distinctive group of countries is those which have a large proportion of organisations that are of the low-flexibility type. The Mediterranean countries – Greece, Hungary, Spain, Portugal, Italy, Cyprus and Slovenia – along with Luxembourg and Belgium can be placed in this category. One thing to note is that for most of the countries included here, the next biggest proportion of its organisations is either of the overtime flexibility type or of the firm-oriented high-flexibility type. Organisations that are of the overtime flexibility type are characterised by an exceptionally high use of overtime, but as most of the other arrangements are used considerably less than in the average European organisation, this type of organisation could equally well be called a low-flexibility type. In this respect it is not surprising that the two company types go together. What is interesting is that the next most prevailing type of organisations in these countries is the firm-oriented high-flexibility type. This means that in these countries most companies do not use many flexibility or work–life balance options, but if they do, they usually take up arrangements which serve the organisation's flexibility needs rather than flexibility needs of the workers.

For the overtime flexibility type, Austria, Ireland and Germany are the countries in which this type of organisation is larger than any of the other five types.

A fifth group of countries is characterised by a large proportion of companies which are of the remaining two intermediate level flexibility types, and particularly the life course type of flexibility as the day-to-day type of flexibility is not the dominant type of organisation in any of the 21 countries considered. For the life course type of intermediate level of working time flexibility, Poland, the Netherlands, Latvia and to some degree Denmark and the Czech Republic have large proportions of organisations that belong to this type.

Focussing on each type separately, the prevalence of that type in each country is shown graphically in Figure 7.2. The first type we examine is the worker-oriented high-flexibility company.

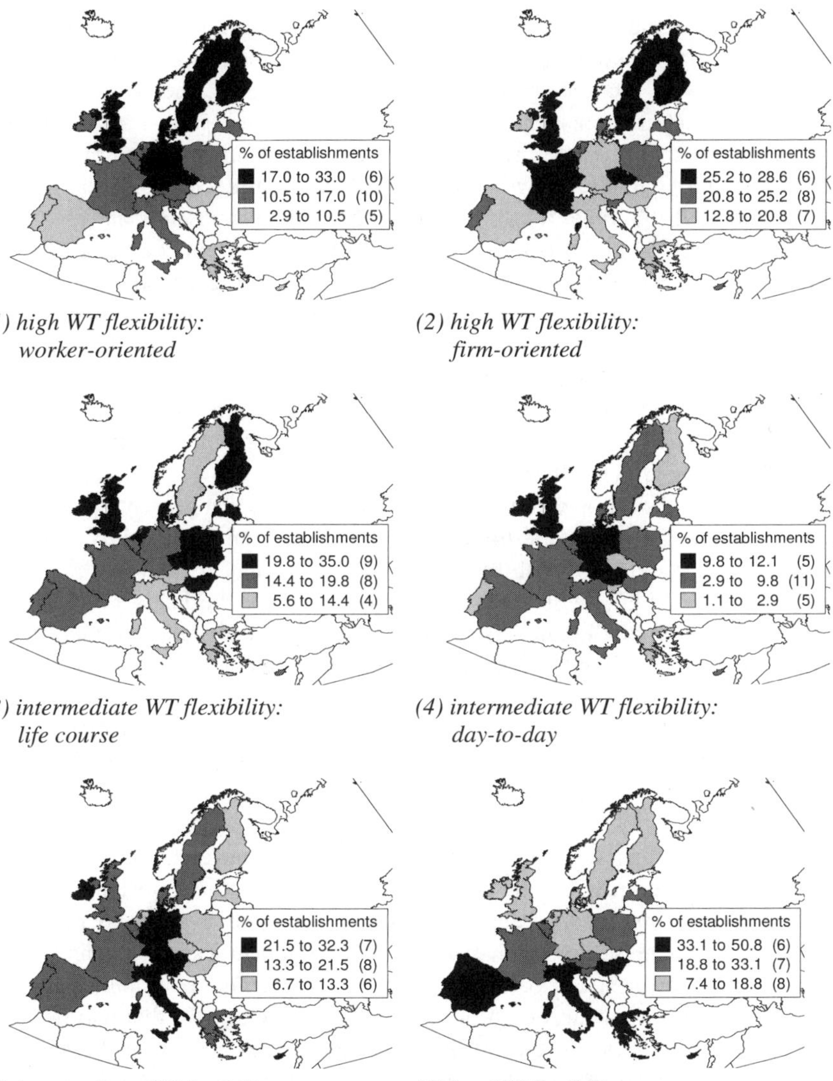

(1) high WT flexibility: worker-oriented

(2) high WT flexibility: firm-oriented

(3) intermediate WT flexibility: life course

(4) intermediate WT flexibility: day-to-day

(5) intermediate WT flexibility: overtime

(6) low WT flexibility

Figure 7.2 Distribution of flexibility profiles of organisations across Europe

As we can see from the first panel, Sweden, Finland and Denmark have the highest percentages of companies that can be categorised as being of this type, however the Czech Republic, Germany and the UK show above average shares of companies with worker-oriented flexibility arrangements as well. Most of the Mediterranean countries such as Cyprus, Italy, Greece, Spain, Portugal, and in addition Hungary show the lowest proportion of companies with worker-oriented flexibility. Examining the distribution of companies that are considered to be of the firm-oriented high-flexibility type we can see that the Nordic countries, except Denmark, and the Czech Republic and the UK show high proportions, while Germany has lower proportions of this type of companies. France, the Netherlands and Belgium also show high levels of firm-oriented high-flexibility type companies, while the southern European countries together with Hungary still show low percentages. These outcomes mirror the results for the proportion of companies which have overall low levels of flexibility, where the southern European countries and Hungary now show the highest shares of this type of companies. In addition, Slovenia and, somewhat surprisingly, Belgium also have higher levels of companies that do not use much or any flexibility measures compared to other countries.

Even for the proportion of companies with arrangements aimed at supporting life course work–life balance – the life course flexibility type – it is the Nordic countries, with the exception of Sweden, that show the higher percentages. Along with these countries, the Netherlands, the Czech Republic, Latvia and Poland also show above average shares of organisations that focus on providing life course directed arrangements.

The Netherlands, Germany, Austria, the UK and Ireland have higher percentages of organisations with a day-to-day flexibility profile, while Germany, Austria, Ireland, Cyprus and Italy are the countries with higher percentages of companies who use overtime but have overall low levels of flexibility.

The picture that emerges from these graphs is more subtle than if you characterise countries by the most prevailing type of organisation as this would clearly ignore differences and similarities with respect to the other types of companies. To summarise the information in Table 7.4 and Figure 7.2 we have performed a so-called hierarchical cluster analysis comparing the entire distribution of the flexibility profiles in a country. In this way we can see which countries are closest in the sense that the distribution of their organisations across the six flexibility types are similar. Table 7.5 summarises the grouping that results from this analysis.

This country grouping shows some resemblance to the Esping-Andersen (1999) typology of welfare state regimes with the exception that there is no separate liberal cluster (as the UK and Ireland are not in the same group), and Denmark and the Netherlands are not included in the Nordic cluster.

Table 7.5 Summary of country profiles

Group	Characteristics	Countries included
Nordic	High flexibility + worker oriented	Finland, Sweden
Central 1	High/intermediate flexibility + worker oriented	Denmark, The Netherlands, UK, Czech Republic, Latvia, Poland
Central 2	Low/intermediate flexibility + firm oriented	Germany, Austria, Ireland, France, Belgium, Luxembourg, Slovenia
South	Low flexibility + firm oriented	Italy, Spain, Portugal, Greece, Cyprus, Hungary

7.5 MULTIVARIATE ANALYSIS OF FLEXIBILITY PROFILE OF AN ESTABLISHMENT

The previous section showed that the types of firms differ considerably between and also within countries. One may expect that other organisation characteristics, such as sector, size and composition of the workforce, are also important determinants in explaining how working time and work–life balance options are organised. Based on the Latent Class analysis each establishment can be uniquely assigned to one of the flexibility profiles. This makes it possible to study the background characteristics of the highly flexible firms and compare them to less flexible firms. Conversely, one can study for specific groups of organisations – for example large organisations or organisations that face a lot of workload variation – how the share of each flexibility type differs from the average. Such analyses are exploratory and one should be careful to not to interpret a correlation as a causal relationship going one way or the other.[8] More flexible arrangements may attract different types of employees. But the existing composition of the workforce may also require the firm to have arrangements that better suit the needs and capacities of its current employees.

As we can see from Figure 7.3, the services sector has higher shares of the high-flexibility types of companies, both worker and company oriented, and to some degree of the life course and day-to-day types of moderately flexible companies. In the industry sector there is a higher proportion of companies which do not have much flexibility, that is the overtime and low flexibility types. This may have to do with the fact that establishments in the services sector, having less standardised work processes, have more opportunities to reorganise their working times. This may also be due to the fact that some forms of working time flexibility – such as irregular working and opening hours – are needed in the services sector to suit customer needs.

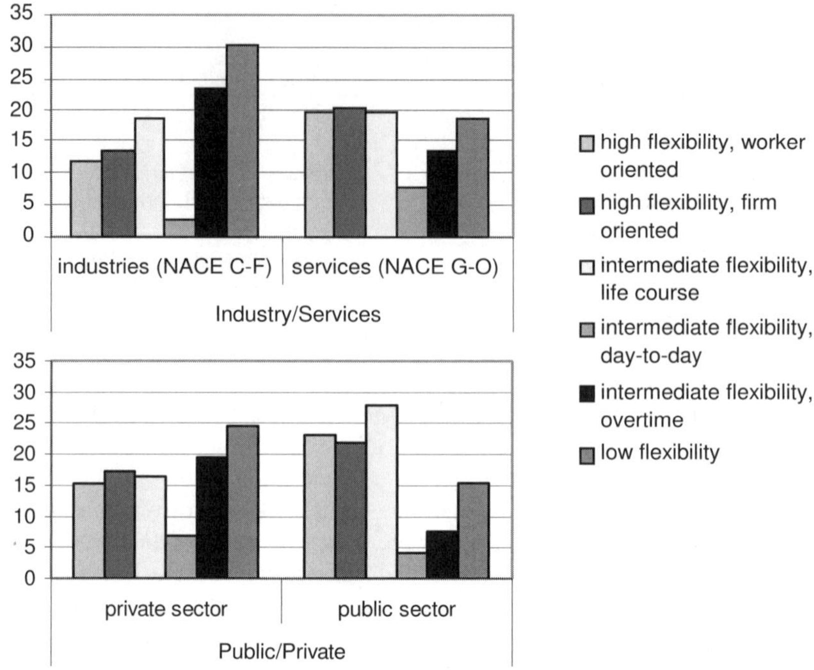

Figure 7.3 Distribution of company types within industry and services sector, and within public and private sector

Comparing the private and public sector, we see that in the public sector there are higher proportions of the three more flexible types of organisations: the two high-flexibility types and the life-course-oriented moderately flexible type. The differences are largest for the two flexibility profiles in which organisations focus on working time arrangements to facilitate the employee's work–life balance. This means that public sector companies appear to fair better in facilitating the work–life balance by providing more flexible working time arrangements to their workers than private sectors companies.

Next, we compare the distribution of flexibility types for various workforce sizes (see Figure 7.4). Here we distinguish four size classes, namely 10–19 employees, 20–49, 50–149 and 150 and over. As we can see from Figure 7.4, the shares of companies that are of either of the two high-flexibility types is larger among larger firms. Only a quarter of all small companies (10–19 workers) can be categorised as highly flexible, whereas more than three-quarters of the larger companies (150 or more employees) can be categorised as being one or the other high-flexibility company type.

On the other hand, the shares of other company types fall as the size of the company increases. The low-flexibility profile accounts for approximately 27 per cent of the smallest organisations, while it accounts for only 8 per cent of the largest organisations. The same goes for all of the intermediate flexibility types, whose shares are substantially larger in the smaller company categories.

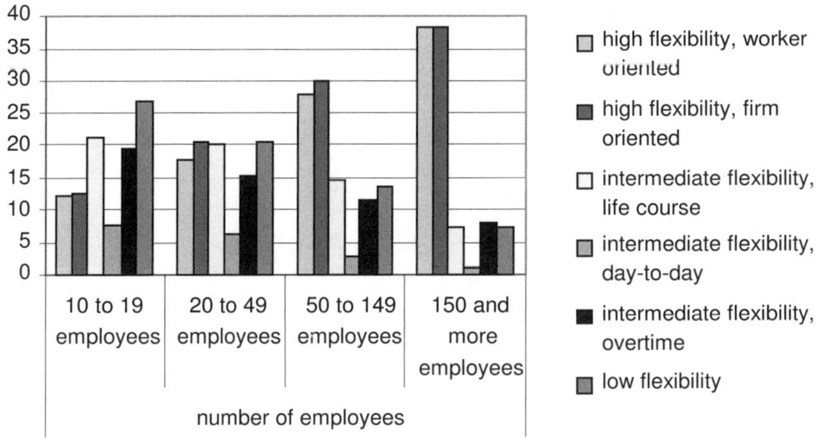

Figure 7.4 Distribution of company types within various company sizes

To better understand how these and other firm characteristics are related to the flexibility profile of an organisation, we have estimated a multinomial logistic model that describes how the probability that a firm belongs to one of the six flexibility types depends on a range of firm characteristics. Included characteristics were country, size, sector, workforce composition (percentages of female, skilled, young and older employees), workload variations, the length of the normal working week, the presence of collective agreements related to working time, being part of a multi-site organisation and the extent to which a firm feels responsibility for the work–life balance of its employees. The ESWT data also contains some indicators of firm performance and HRM issues. As these variables are more likely to be affected by the firm's decisions regarding working time flexibility, these are considered separately in the next section. The distinction between the characteristics as being determinants or effects is only suggestive and is a distinction in degree, rather than a distinction in kind.

Judging by the size and the statistical significance of the parameter estimates, the country in which the organisation is located and the size of its workforce have the strongest effect. The line of business (distinguishing 12 sectors of economic activity) ranks third as determinant of the flexibility profile of an organisation. The other characteristics have a smaller impact. Table 7.6 summarises how the flexibility profiles are related to some of these characteristics.

Table 7.6 Typology of working time flexibility by determinants

	Sector	Size	Other
High flexibility			
– worker oriented	Commercial Services, Government	50+ employees	Foreseeable variation of workload, more high-skilled
– firm oriented	Health Services, Transportation	50+ employees	More low-skilled, more young employees
Intermediate flexibility			
– life course	Education	10–19 employees	
– day-to-day	Hotels and Restaurants		
– overtime	Industry, Transportation	10–49 employees	Unforeseeable variation of workload, more males
Low flexibility	Construction, Industry	10–19 employees	Little variation of workload, less young employees

The estimated marginal effects of the country in which an establishment is located are very similar to the country differences in the previous section (Table 7.4), but are on average somewhat lower. This indicates that the other characteristics in the multivariate analysis can help to explain some of the differences between countries, but leave a substantial amount of variation unexplained. The important role of the country as determinant of a firm's flexibility strategy definitely deserves further research. The differences between countries may reflect how institutional and cultural differences affect the ability of firms to respond to the various needs for working time flexibility. Another explanation of the differences between countries may be that institutional and cultural differences determine what aspects of working time flexibility are left for the firm to answer. National child care provisions may alleviate the demand for specific parental leave arrangements within companies. The observed differences between the flexibility strategies adopted by firms in different countries may therefore be affected by differences in the scope within which organisations have control or discretion over these arrangements, as well as by differences in the demands that firms face.

Size matters: larger firms are often more flexible firms, both of the firm-oriented and the worker-oriented type. The four other types of firms are therefore more likely to be found in the smaller sized firms. This relationship with firm size is particularly strong for the probability that a firm is of the low-flexibility type. A similar relation to the flexibility profile of an organisation is seen for the variable indicating whether a firm is part of a multi-site – usually larger – organisation. Establishments that are part of multi-site organisations are more often of one of the two most flexible types of firms.

The Construction sector is characterised by an overrepresentation of the low-flexibility type of firms. The typical worker-oriented high-flexibility sectors are Public Administration, Financial Intermediation, Real Estate, Renting and Business activities, Electricity, Gas and Water Supply and Other Services. Health and Social Work stands out as the firm-oriented high-flexibility sector, with a 20 percentage points higher probability of being this type than in the Manufacturing Industry and Mining, but the sector Transport, Storage and Communication, and the sector Hotels and Restaurants also show a relatively large percentage of these firms. The life-course-oriented moderately flexible type of firms are overrepresented in the Education sector. The day-to-day flexibility type accounts for the lowest share of all firms. Therefore the variation across sectors is also lower than for the other types. Nevertheless, we can see that this type of companies is overrepresented in the Hotel and Restaurant business and in the Other services sector. The type of firms for which working time flexibility mainly concerns overtime is most frequently found in the Manufacturing Industry and the Transport sector. Overall, we can see that the services sectors have more organisations with a higher flexibility profile and the industrial sectors have more organisations with a lower flexibility profile. After controlling for the differences between sectors, the difference between public and private companies is only small, the main differences between the public and the private sector being captured by the sector differences.

The larger the proportion of female employees the smaller the probability that the firm is of the moderately flexible 'overtime' type. All other flexibility profiles show no relation to the proportion of female workers or the relationship is non-monotonous. The latter most distinctly holds for the probability that a firm is of the worker-oriented high-flexibility type. The probability of having that flexibility profile firm is largest if the percentage of women in the workforce is between 20 and 59 per cent. However, the probability of being a firm-oriented high-flexibility type of firm is highest when the share of females in the workforce is 60 per cent or more. This result deviates from our prediction that organisations with a worker-oriented flexibility profile would have more (or attract more) female workers, as these organisations offer more opportunities to facilitate the work–life balance. Although this reasoning may still be valid, it could be that the organisations in which the majority of the employees is female are typically in a line of business with poorer working conditions, making it less likely to have a worker-oriented flexibility profile.

Worker-oriented flexibility is more often encountered in firms with a large share of skilled workers, while firm-oriented flexibility and low flexibility are more common in firms in which the percentage of skilled workers is low. This complies with our hypothesis that organisations that provide more worker-oriented working time arrangements fare better in attracting and maintaining a skilled workforce.

The age composition of the workforce has little relation to the flexibility profile. Firms with a larger percentage of young workers are however significantly more likely to be firm-oriented high-flexibility firms and less likely to be low-flexibility firms.

Firms for which a general agreement dealing with working time issues applies are more often of one of the two high-flexibility types and less often have a low-flexibility profile. Also, organisations in which managers perceive work–life balance needs of their workers as a responsibility of the organisation are more likely to be a worker-oriented high-flexibility type of organisation, and less likely to have a low-flexibility profile or a firm-oriented high-flexibility profile. The relationship between workload variations and type of working time flexibility is also interesting. Firms that experience variations of workload – whether these are short-run or long-run fluctuations – are more likely to be a firm-oriented high-flexibility firm and less likely a low-flexibility firm. This effect vanishes however if it concerns long-term fluctuations that are not foreseeable. If short-term variations are unforeseeable this raises the probability of being an overtime type of firm.

7.6 FLEXIBILITY AND PERFORMANCE

Flexibility is generally seen as a ‘good practice’, raising adaptability and thereby productivity, profitability and growth. The truth of this common perception and particularly its applicability in specific situations is still open to debate. Although there is consistent empirical evidence on the macro level – comparing economic performance of countries and flexibility referring to legal and institutional settings – these results are not easily translated to the level of individual firms and firm-specific arrangements, such as the take-up of various working time practices studied in this report. As mentioned before, flexibility of working times serves various goals. Flexible opening hours may serve customers or business relations and would – provided costs and benefits are traded off correctly – be beneficial for the firm’s results. A similar reason holds for overtime. Leave arrangements aim to facilitate the work–life balance of the employees. By attracting high-quality workers, raising workers' motivation and long-run productivity this could also have a positive effect on the firm's performance. One could overall argue that flexible working time practices, bearing organisational and financial costs, will only be adopted if these costs are outweighed by benefits. This line of reasoning, however, fails if these practices are imposed by laws or binding general agreements.

A direct causal relationship between flexibility and performance at the level of firms may be hard to measure in practice. Both the cause and the consequence are in this case concepts that are typically hard to measure. Moreover, flexible working conditions are part of the mix of employee benefits, making it difficult to separate variations in working time flexibility from variations in other facilities and forms of compensation. Also, the adoption of flexible working time arrangements is likely to be affected by the firm-specific characteristics, which may in turn be related to the organisation's economic performance. In highly competitive surroundings, profit margins are typically low and workload variations will induce firms to make more extensive use of flexibility measures such as flexible contracts, that is fixed-term contracts, agency workers and freelancers. Comparing these firms to firms that operate in a more stable and shielded market environment, one could falsely conclude that flexible contracts are bad for profitability. In order to avoid this fallacy one should account for an organisation's idiosyncrasies, which is easier said than done and in fact hardly possible on the basis of cross-section data for a heterogeneous population of firms like the ESWT. When studying the relationship between flexibility and firm performance one should therefore be careful in interpreting this relation as a causal effect going one way or the other.

Bearing all this in mind, it is still interesting to relate the flexibility profile of an organisation to indicators in the ESWT for economic performance and personnel management problems, such as difficulties in hiring or retaining staff. As can be seen from Table 7.7, the percentage of establishments that refer to the economic situation of the firm as 'very good' is higher for 'high-flexibility' firms than for the other types. At closer inspection, those 'high-flexibility' firms that are categorised as worker-oriented fare better than those that are company-oriented. Particularly the moderately low-flexible firms only using overtime score lower than all the other types. The differences are small, however, and are more or less evened out if we consider both firms with a 'very good' and those with a 'quite good' economic situation.

The picture is similar for personnel growth. The share of firms for which the number of employees has increased (over a period of three years) is largest for firms with a high-flexibility profile and for intermediately flexible firms focussing on life course aspects of working time flexibility. Firms with below-average working time flexibility do however not show a larger percentage of shrinking firms, but more often stay about the same in size.

Table 7.7 Working time flexibility and the firm's performance and bottlenecks

	Economic situation very good	Personnel size increased
Type of establishment		
High flexibility		
– worker oriented	19	37
– firm oriented	17	37
Intermediate flexibility		
– life course	15	35
– day-to-day	16	32
– overtime	13	32
Low flexibility	15	32
All establishments	16	34

The first three columns of Table 7.8 refer to indicators for problems that organisations may experience in the HRM field. On all three categories of personnel problems in this table, the least flexible type of firm reports experiencing less problems than the average firm. One possible explanation for this unexpected pattern is that flexibility may be adopted to deal with already existing problems. Firms that do not experience problems do not need such a cure, making the cure an indicator of the existence of problems, although these are hopefully somewhat reduced by it. More importantly, the figures show that it may not be the extent of flexibility that makes the difference, but rather the way flexibility is implemented. Low motivation of the staff and difficulties in finding and retaining employees are highest for the 'firm-oriented high-flexibility' type of firms. In addition, the organisations that use relatively few arrangements for working time flexibility, but use overtime intensively – arguably one of the most firm-oriented flexibility profiles – can be seen to experience more than the average amount of problems, specifically related to staff recruitment and low motivation of the staff. In the other high-flexibility type of organisations, in which the flexibility profile is worker-oriented, the share of the companies reporting any of these problems is just about average.

In the interviews with the employee representatives, the respondents were asked to evaluate the relationship between themselves and the management. On average, for one in five establishments this relationship is characterised as being 'quite strained' or 'very strained'. With 26 per cent this share is largest for the least flexible firms and the firms in which working time flexibility consists mainly of overtime. Of the other four types of firms, this percentage is highest for the most flexible firms in which flexibility is firm-oriented, reporting a strained relationship in 20 per cent of the companies. On the other hand, life course intermediate-flexibility and worker-oriented high-flexibility firms show relatively high shares of companies for which the employee representative considers the relationship with the management to be 'very cooperative'. If we consider both the 'very cooperative' and 'quite cooperative' categories, the day-to-day flexibility type of firms does even slightly better.

Table 7.8 Personnel management problems by working time flexibility profile

	Problems finding skilled staff	Problems retaining staff	Low motivation of staff	Social climate very strained	Work–life balance very hard
Type of establishment					
High flexibility					
– worker oriented	36	8	16	2	4
– firm oriented	42	12	22	4	8
Intermediate flexibility					
– life course	28	8	12	3	6
– day-to-day	32	6	13	2	1
– overtime	42	8	17	10	9
Low flexibility	31	8	13	4	5
All establishments	35	9	16	4	6

Employee representatives were also asked to indicate how difficult it is for the employees of the establishment to combine their work with other activities and obligations outside work. The percentage of firms for which this was reported to be 'hard' or 'quite hard', is highest for the moderately flexible firms mainly using overtime and the highly flexible firms in which the working time flexibility profile is more firm-oriented. For the least flexible firms, the percentage in which the work–life balance is considered to be problematic is almost equal to the average for all firms. Again, the worker-oriented high-flexibility types and life-course-oriented intermediate flexibility show the highest shares of companies where it is considered 'very easy' to combine work and life needs. Here again, the real difference is not between more and less flexibility, but rather between the different types of flexibility.

7.7 CONCLUSIONS

Flexibility is a key concept in the European policy debate. Considering this role, the empirical basis of the concept of flexibility still is surprisingly weak, particularly regarding the flexibility strategies of organisations. In this chapter we have used a recent establishment survey in 21 European countries to study working time arrangements and related flexibility strategies. On the basis of a range of indicators we have developed a typology of organisation strategies regarding working time flexibility and the work–life balance. This typology is based on a Latent Class cluster analysis of the observed practices in the establishments in the survey. The resulting typology discerns six flexibility profiles – two very flexible, three moderately flexible and one relatively inflexible – and is seen to distinguish organisations and organisation strategies by the degree of flexibility as well as the focus of the flexibility profile. The two most flexible profiles have a relatively high take-up of most of the arrangements involved, but one puts more weight on the aim of supporting the workers' work–life balance and the other on accommodating to workload variations and preferences of customers and business relations. This clearly shows that working time flexibility should not be treated as a one-dimensional concept ranging from low to high flexibility.

Each of the six profiles covers a considerable proportion of the European establishments. The most widespread profile – having a high level of working time flexibility, mainly focused on the organisation's operational needs – applies to 22 per cent of the European organisations, still leaving 78 per cent for the other five profiles. The smallest profile – the day-to-day type of moderate working time flexibility – applies to 7 per cent of the organisations. These findings imply that in terms of working time flexibility, Europe is rather heterogeneous. It is not the case that one flexibility profile dominates, or in other words that European firms tend to favour one form of flexibility in particular.

Although this typology of working time flexibility refers to establishments, it easily translates into a typology of European countries if we consider the dominant flexibility profiles of the organisations in a country. This demonstrates that cultural and institutional differences can explain some of the observed differences between flexibility strategies of organisations, but that the differences within countries are also substantial. A multivariate analysis, relating the flexibility profiles to other characteristics of the organisation – such as its line of business and the size and composition of the workforce – shows that the country in which it is located and the size of the establishment are the strongest determinants of the flexibility profile of the organisation. The next strongest determinant is the sector of the firm's main activity. The important role of the country as a determinant of the flexibility strategy of organisations definitely deserves further research, as it encompasses institutional and cultural differences, and may reflect both differences in the span of control of organisations and differences in the demands that organisations face.

In the final section we have also considered how the six flexibility profiles differ as regards economic performance and experienced personnel bottlenecks. There is some evidence that social and economic problems particularly arise in the highly flexible organisations that prioritise operational needs and in the intermediately flexible organisations that adopt overtime and irregular working hours; the least problems are observed in worker-oriented high-flexibility organisations and in low-flexibility organisations. Thus again, it is the type and not so much the level of flexibility that matters. But differences are generally small and the direction of causality definitely deserves further research, preferably using longitudinal data.

All in all these outcomes are relevant for the European policy debate on working time flexibility. Considering the role that flexibility plays in the socio-economic policy debate in Europe, it is important to develop flexibility concepts that (1) do justice to the variety of flexible working time practices, (2) allow monitoring of the flexibility trends in European countries and (3) encourage more rigorous study of the effects of the adoption of these practices. The present study has shown the strength, both scientifically and policy-wise, of comparative company surveys. In order to monitor Europe's performance on a global and highly competitive market, with a workforce that wants to balance work life and private life, we need to know how European companies are doing comparatively. This requires a much more sophisticated European data infrastructure, including (repeated) comparative company surveys (preferably on a panel basis) in all EU countries, that allows researchers to make cross-national comparisons and trace the development of companies over time. If not, the debate on flexibility of European economies will remain very speculative. Flexibility is too important and complex an issue to do without sound empirical insights.

NOTES

1. This chapter reports on research commissioned by the European Foundation for the Improvement of Working and Living Conditions. See Chung et al. (2007) for a more detailed discussion.
2. See also Anxo et al. (2007a,b), Kümmerling and Lehndorff (2007) and Leber and Wagner (2007) for studies of specific working time arrangements based on the ESWT survey.
3. Although the observation units in the survey are establishments, we will use the terms 'firm', 'company', 'organisation' and 'establishment' interchangeably in referring to the observation units in the ESWT.
4. Excluded are the sectors 'Agriculture', 'Forestry', 'Private households' and 'Extraterritorial organisations'. In these sectors the number of establishments with ten or more employees is

negligible in the countries surveyed. The sample is a stratified sample with unequal sampling probabilities but random sampling within the strata defined by sector and number of employees. In the analyses the observations are weighed by establishment weights to account for the sampling design.

5. In statistics and econometrics this type of model is also referred to as mixed models or random effects models. The model is estimated using the LatentGold software (Magidson and Vermunt, 2004).
6. In statistics and econometrics this type of models is also referred to as mixed models or random effects models. The model is estimated using the LatentGold software (Magidson and Vermunt, 2004).
7. See Chung et al. (2007) for detailed estimation results.
8. A causal interpretation of such relationships requires analysis based on longitudinal data or availability of suitable instrumental variables.

REFERENCES

Anxo, D., Fagan, C., Letablier, M., Perraudin, C. and Smith, M. (2007a), *Part-time Work in European Companies*, Report for the European Foundation for the Improvement of Living and Working Conditions, Dublin.

Anxo, D., Fagan, C., Letablier, M., Perraudin, C. and Smith, M. (2007b), *Parental Leave in European Companies – Establishment Survey on Working Time and Work–life Balance arrangements 2004–2005*, Report for the European Foundation for the Improvement of Living and Working Conditions, Dublin.

Chung, H., Kerkhofs, M. and Ester, P. (2007), *Working Time Flexibility of European Companies*, Report for the European Foundation for the Improvement of Living and Working Conditions, Dublin.

Esping-Andersen, G. (1999), *The Social Foundations of Post-industrial Economies*, Oxford: Oxford University Press.

European Commission (2005), *More and Better Jobs: Delivering the Priorities of the European Employment Strategy*, Joint Employment Report 2005/2006.

European Employment Taskforce (2003), *Jobs, Jobs, Jobs. Creating More Employment in Europe.*

Huys, R. (2006), *Organisation Surveys in Europe as a Data Source for WORKS*, Paper presented at 'Measuring changes in work. International workshop quantitative pillar of the WORKS project', Leuven, Belgium.

Kümmerling, A. and Lehndorff, S. (2007), *Extended and Unusual Working Hours of European Companies*, Report for the European Foundation for the Improvement of Living and Working Conditions, Dublin.

Leber, U. and Wagner, A. (2007), *Early and Phased Retirement in European companies: Establishment Survey on Working Time 2004–2005*, Dublin: European Foundation for the Improvement of Living and Working Conditions.

Magidson, J. and Vermunt, J.K. (2004), 'Latent class models', in Kaplan, D. (ed.), *The Sage Handbook of Quantitative Methodology for the Social Sciences*, Thousand Oaks: Sage Publications, pp. 175–98.

Riedmann, A., Bielenski, H., Szczurowska, T. and Wagner, A. (2006), *Working Time and Work–Life Balance in European Companies: Establishment Survey on Working Time 2004–2005*, Dublin: European Foundation for the Improvement of Living and Working Conditions.

Vermunt, J.K. (2003), 'Applications of latent class analysis in social science research', *Lecture Notes in Artificial Intelligence*, 2711, 22–36.

Vinken, H. and Ester, P. (2006), *The Need for European Company Surveys. Some results from panel surveys in the Netherlands and Germany*, Paper presented at the First WORKS Conference, Chania, Greece, September 21–22.

8. Mapping Flexicurity in the EU

Greet Vermeylen

8.1 INTRODUCTION

The concept of flexicurity comprises a series of reflections on different social systems and their capacity to respond to the current challenges facing our society and economy, at European and at Member State level. Globalisation is one of the main contextual factors behind this drive to make labour markets more flexible while at the same time not jeopardising the security of workers.

This chapter tries to reflect on the different elements that together constitute the concept of flexicurity.[1] It looks at how different countries implement a different mix of these elements, how to create more flexibility combined with new forms of security. It is based on findings from different research projects undertaken by the European Foundation for the Improvement of Living and Working Conditions. Particular emphasis is given to some findings from the fourth European Working Conditions Survey (2007).

This contribution addresses furthermore the issue of responsibility for flexicurity. Better solutions can be found where all actors, including social partners, are involved in the whole process of shaping and implementing these policies at all levels.

8.2 MAIN DRIVERS OF FLEXICURITY

What are the forces creating the need for flexicurity-type solutions? Several factors are often cited.[2] One principal factor is the economic challenge posed by a growing global economy that is increasingly integrated and competitive (globalisation). Other factors include the demographic challenge of a rapidly ageing society and the increasing feminisation of the workforce.

Regarding the impact of globalisation on the flexicurity debate, it is clear that global trade is increasingly defined by fast-changing markets and increased competitive pressures, requiring greater responsiveness on the part of businesses to variations of demand in the business cycle. These pressures have consequences for companies in the first instance but also for societies as a whole, as they affect the wealth-generating capacity which in turn underpins our traditions and levels of social provision.

While the European social model is characterised by a diversity of national social systems, nevertheless a number of shared values can be identified that define the model: universal access, solidarity and equality/social justice. These common elements have contributed to the development of a modern welfare state whose original objective was to mitigate the negative consequences of industrialisation.

These factors put pressure on social and economic systems to adapt. Demographic change means that Europe will have to face the growing economic pressures with a stable or shrinking cohort of working age individuals. This implies a necessity to boost employment rates. Both for current and future working-age individuals, it is important to encourage a climate in which people can combine work with having a family.

The increasing numbers of women in the workforce should prompt reflection on the use of time, both working and non-working time. It may, for example, necessitate a greater individualisation of workers' rights; women should no longer have to depend on the social security rights of a 'male breadwinner'. At a more general level, there is a need to assess which rights are individual and which rights exist at the household level.

One policy response has been the articulation of a life course perspective, which is based on the fact that individuals have different economic and time needs at different phases of their life and that systems can be adapted to reflect the increasing diversity of such needs (Naegele, 2003).

Companies would like to avail themselves of greater flexibility in order to be able to respond more rapidly to competition in a globalised world. Flexibility, especially with regard to labour, is a necessary part of enhancing this capacity, though it is also clearly the case that Europe cannot maintain international competitiveness in the low wage and low skill segment of the global labour market. The ultimate objective of a more flexible labour market should be to improve European capacity at the top end of the international value chain.

There are different ways of becoming more flexible at company level: quantitative/qualitative, internal/external flexibility. In practice, companies use a combination of different forms. With regard to, for instance, working time flexibility in companies, companies tend to implement diverse measures. In an analysis of the results of the Establishment Survey on Working Time and Work–Life Balance, the different measures and packages were mapped. The combination of these measures can be either more employer- or more employee-friendly (Chung et al., 2007). There has been an evolution in labour legislation in all Member States to deal with this issue. It is in the context of discussing the associated risks and changes in society that the term of flexicurity has emerged.

8.2.1 Policy Debate at the European Level

The concept of flexicurity has been on the policy agenda for over a decade and has gained a particular momentum in recent years. The Green Paper on Partnership for New Organisation of Work (European Commission, 1997) was already making relevant references: 'the key issue for workers, management, the social partners and policymakers alike is to strike the right balance between flexibility and security. This balance has many aspects. The reorganisation of work often causes uncertainty.'

Another more recent example can be found in the report of the Employment Taskforce (2003):

> Better responsiveness of EU economies to change requires a high degree of flexibility in labour markets, in particular through modern work organisation and a diversity of contractual and working arrangements. This can only succeed if combined with adequate security for workers in terms of their capacity to remain and progress in the labour markets. Since flexibility is in both employers' and workers' interest, social partners' involvement is desirable.

Indeed, of all of the above-mentioned actors, it is clear that the social partners in particular have a crucial role in the roll-out of new forms of work organisation via processes of collective bargaining, and so on. It is also the case that many of the challenges confronting our societies require coordinated reflection both in the labour market and the social protection spheres.

The European Employment Strategy also dedicates attention to the promotion of more flexicbility combined with security. At the same time, the social protection strategy[3] contributes to the European debate by a coordinated reflection on modernisation of social protection systems. Both processes have been streamlined since 2005, feeding into the general discussion of the broad economic policy guidelines at the annual Spring Council. How to 'promote flexibility combined with employment security and reduce labour market segmentation' is one of the issues discussed extensively in all the committees.

In 2006, the Commission issued a Green Paper on labour law in which it invited reflections on how labour law might be modernised. The paper specifically addressed issues related to different kinds of contracts and the flexicurity challenge. An Expert Group on Flexicurity (2007) indicated that indeed very different forms can be chosen for flexicurity in each country, based on a set of common principles to be agreed upon by all Member States.

They also map different alternative and complementary pathways to flexicurity: flexible and secure contractual arrangements, upgrading active labour market policies to strengthen transition security, systematic lifelong learning systems, modern social security systems and a supportive and productive social dialogue.

The next step consisted of a Commission communication outlining these pathways and determining the principles on which they should be built (European Commission, 2007). The aim of this communication was to guide the discussion in all policy circles, including the employment and social committees. This could allow the Council to embark upon this concerted political process.

8.2.2 Different National Formulas

There are indeed different national formulas for flexicurity. They can be divided into two groups, even though they are not mutually exclusive and could be combined.

A first approach is the flexibilisation of the whole workforce. This includes the 80 per cent of workers in traditional, permanent work or with 'typical contracts'. There are two main ways of implementing this flexibilisation: through new ways of organising work, through more diverse or flexible working time arrangements or through a higher turnover of the workforce. At the same time, this should be complemented with some form of employment security.

The Danish system is a well-known example of such an approach. It combines comparatively relaxed employment protection legislation with a high level of unemployment benefits paid by the government and very active labour market policies (ALMP). The security element of flexicurity is mainly provided by the government, not by the employers. 'Protect workers, not jobs' is the simplified message of the philosophy behind this model. The Austrian reforms also focus on that element, with the creation of a severance pay fund which is transferable and not linked to one employer only.

The second approach is the normalisation of the rights of 'atypical' workers (for example fixed-term contracts, temporary contracts, part-time contracts) while retaining the flexibility of these forms of contract.

The Dutch system tries to incorporate this idea by providing more social protection rights for non-standard workers (in particular part-timers but also non-permanent contracts) and by improving their entitlements (social security, pension and so on) to reach levels comparable to those of their permanent counterparts in the labour market. Other countries have very similar patterns and are considering how to increase the rights for their 'atypical workers'.[4]

Different national approaches have to take account of very different starting points. In particular, the proportion of 'atypical' or non-standard workers varies significantly between Member States.[5]

The choice of a particular form of flexicurity is linked primarily to the historical development of labour markets, collective agreements and the role of the government in these, as well as to basic considerations of public policy in the employment and social protection areas. Policy development depends very much on national traditions as well as on the capacity of countries to generate the resources to pay for the chosen solutions.

The economic and political situation in each country is different and has a bearing on the way changes can be implemented and what choice will be made by the countries. The impact will also be different in each of the countries. The reflection is being undertaken currently in all the member states of the European Union. There are however very big differences in how the debate is undertaken in old or new Member States, but also in each of the member states itself.[6]

The starting point in the reflection in each system is quite important: tenure could create a feeling of security in most cases, but in some cases one could be locked in a bad quality job with no alternative of change (Auer, 2007). Hence, the idea, put forward by Auer, that the lack of security or stability of a job could be balanced out with some upward mobility: transforming lower quality jobs into higher quality jobs. The whole discussion on a balance between EPL, flexibility and security should be re-read in the context of the economic situation and changes in the labour market in each of the systems.

It is important to recall that a system in place in one country cannot be easily transferred to any other Member State, as policies are embedded in a specific national context. Potential reforms need to take into account the different levels of application (worker, household, enterprise, sector, national) as well as their interactions.

Nonetheless, an 'open reflection' on an integrated policy is useful. This could lead to a new approach, encompassing the whole set of social policies, including labour market policies and social protection systems in a wider sense.

8.3 THE FLEXIBILITY/SECURITY MIX

In order to tackle the issue of flexicurity, it is worth looking first at its different elements. A framework for reflection has been proposed by Wilthagen. The 'Wilthagen Matrix', also used by the Employment Committee, describes some possible avenues for the combination of flexibility and security and points to some possibilities for reforms at different levels (company and institutions), see Table 8.1.

Table 8.1 The Wilthagen matrix: examples of the instrumental variables for flexicurity policy

Flexibility	Job security	Employment security	Income security	Combination security
External numerical flexibility	–Types of employment contracts –Employment protection legislation –Early retirement	–Employment services/ALMP –Training/ lifelong learning	–Unemployment compensation –Other social benefits –Minimum wages	–Protection against dismissal during various leave schemes
Internal numerical flexibility	–Shortened work weeks/part-time arrangements	–Employment protection legislation –Training/life-long learning	–Part-time supplementary benefit –Study grants –Sickness benefit	–Different kind of leave schemes –Part-time pension
Functional flexibility	–Job enrichment –Training –Labour leasing –Subcontracting –Outsourcing	–Training/life-long learning –Job rotation –Teamwork –Multi-skilling	–Performance related pay systems	–Voluntary working time arrangements
Labour cost/wage flexibility	–Local adjustments in labour costs –Scaling/reductions in social security payments	–Changes in social security payments –Employment subsidies –In-work benefits	–Collective wage agreements –Adjusted benefit for shortened work week	–Voluntary working time arrangements

Source: (EMCO, 2006, p. 5).

In their comprehensive definition, Wilthagen and Tros (2004) describe flexicurity as:

> (1) a degree of job, employment, income and 'combination' security that facilitates the labour market careers and biographies of workers with a relatively weak position and allows for enduring and high quality labour market participation and social inclusion, while at the same time providing (2) a degree of numerical (both external and internal), functional and wage flexibility that allows for labour markets' (and individual companies') timely and adequate adjustment to changing conditions in order to maintain and enhance competitiveness and productivity.

In this context, there might be different ways to achieve a 'flexicurity mix' based on the compromises achieved between workers, companies and governments. This implies a key role for social partner negotiation in the framework of established institutional settings and bargaining systems.

8.4 FLEXIBILITY STRATEGIES OF COMPANIES

The first element to tackle is flexibility. Nowadays, many medium-size companies use a combination of many flexibility strategies. The following four-way subdivision of flexibility (see Table 8.2) may serve as a useful mapping of company practice (Atkinson, 1984; Goudswaard and De Nanteuil, 2000).

Table 8.2 Subdivisions of flexibility

	Quantitative flexibility	Qualitative flexibility
External flexibility	Employment status (types of contract – fixed duration, temporary, work on call, and so on)	Production systems (subcontracting, use of freelance labour)
	Numerical/contractual flexibility	Productive/geographical flexibility
Internal flexibility	Working hours (overtime, part-time, weekend working, irregular/variable hours)	Work organisation (job rotation, multitasking, making workers responsible for planning and budgeting, and so on)
	Temporal/financial flexibility	Functional/organisational flexibility

Source: Goudswaard and De Nanteuil (2000, p. 20).

It is often the case that different types of flexibility may overlap, thus affecting what kind of security might be offered (Atkinson, 1984). An example: a part-time employee may also have an annual working time account or be asked to work in different geographic units of the same company and might have variations in income (variable pay). This combination of flexibility may apply only to a subgroup of workers, often the more precarious workers (young workers, women or immigrants), resulting in segmentation of a company's workforce. On the other hand, flexibility can also be introduced more generally for all workers, for example via internal flexibility through new forms of work organisation.

It is important to underline that flexibility, while so far largely employer-driven, may also arise as a result of employee demands. This can be for a variety of reasons, such as the desire to better combine family and work or to take breaks for either care or study leave. Different needs at different phases of the life course may result in a variety of career trajectories with fluctuations in the volume of working hours or with career breaks (Anxo et al., 2007a; Muffels et al., 2007).

8.4.1 Numerical or Contractual Flexibility

Numerical or contractual flexibility consists of the recourse to non-permanent contracts by companies as a way of having a more flexible workforce. The most common forms of non-permanent contract are fixed-term contracts (including seasonal work), temporary work (including temporary agency work) and work on call.

Table 8.3 illustrates how diverse the incidence of fixed-term contracts is across Member States. It also shows that in the majority of countries it is a growing proportion of overall employment. There are interesting exceptions, notably Ireland, the UK and Denmark, where labour markets have a higher degree of flexibility which may reduce the need for fixed-term contracts.[7]

Table 8.3 Percentage of fixed-term contracts in total employment

	1995	2000	2005		1995	2000	2005
EU Total	11.7	12.6	14.5	LT	na	4.4	5.5
EU Male	11.1	12.0	14.0	LU	4.1	5.3	5.3
EU Female	12.4	13.4	15.0	HU	6.6	7.1	7.0
BE	5.4	9.1	8.9	MT	na	4.1	4.5
CZ	6.7	8.1	8.6	NL	11.4	13.7	15.5
DK	11.6	9.7	9.8	AT	6.8	8.0	9.1
DE	10.5	12.7	14.2	PL	4.8	5.8	25.7
EE	2.1	3.0	2.7	PT	11.6	19.9	19.5
EL	9.4	13.5	11.8	SI	na	13.7	17.4
ES	35.2	32.2	33.3	SK	na	4.8	5.0
FR	12.4	15.2	13.3	FI	18.1	16.3	16.5
IE	10.0	5.9	3.7	SV	14.7	15.8	16.0
IT	7.4	10.1	12.3	UK	7.2	6.9	5.7
CY	na	10.7	14.0	BG	na	6.3	6.4
LV	na	6.7	8.4	RO	na	2.8	2.4

Notes:
EU aggregates are for EU25. Some national figures cited in the 1995 row refer to 1996/97 as earlier data are not available.

Source: European Commission (2006a).

Research by the European Foundation for the Improvement of Living and Working Conditions shows that workers on temporary contracts are exposed to poorer working conditions than those on permanent contracts, in particular lower levels of access to training and job autonomy (Goudswaard and De Nanteuil, 2000).

8.4.2 Temporal or Financial Flexibility

With temporal or financial flexibility companies can secure greater levels of flexibility through more flexible working time or pay arrangements. These could include for example overtime, part-time work, weekend work, irregular or variable hours.

The Foundation's Establishment Survey on Working Time 2004–5 looked at a series of flexible working time arrangements which are offered by companies (Riedmann et al., 2006). The different forms of working time arrangements can be grouped according to whether they are led more by employers or employees. Some schemes fall into both categories and the effect of business cycles may reverse this categorisation. What may favour one party during an upturn of the business cycle may be less advantageous during a downturn. What appears to be a right may turn out to be a risk.

Part-time work, flexible working time schedules, phased retirement and early retirement may suit both companies and employees. Unusual working hours (night shift, Saturday or Sunday shifts or shift work in general), overtime and temporary employment (including fixed-term contracts, temporary agency work and freelance work) are generally more at the request of the employer, while parental leave and other leave schemes (care, education, sabbaticals) and working time accounts are generally more at the demand of the employee. Annual working time accounts can be at the demand of either employer or employee but are often associated with fluctuations in workload and business cycle variations (Chung et al., 2007).

As with fixed-term work, the incidence of part-time work varies considerably from country to country. Research has shown that the quality of work of part-time workers is often lower than that of comparable full time workers, notably in terms of access to training, career development and promotion possibilities (Anxo et al., 2007b). This issue, however, is being carefully reflected on in the European debate among social partners and the European legislation. The last point which has to be considered is how to smoothen the transition from full-time to part-time work and vice versa.

8.4.3 Functional Flexibility

Functional flexibility consists of forms of work organisation such as job rotation, multitasking, involvement of workers in planning or budgeting (team autonomy).

These forms of work organisation are primarily meant to make work within the company more flexible, allowing workers to change places as needed (job rotation). However, this can also lead to more skills development in the sense that workers can update their skills in a way that is beneficial for them individually as well as for the company. This would increase both their job and employment security. Workers would be empowered to carry out more tasks within the job and the company (enhancing their job security), but they would also increase their employability in terms of subsequently finding another job (in or outside the company).

Secondary analysis of the European Working Conditions Survey data reveals that functional flexibility has an important impact on learning, problem-solving and innovation at the organisation level. Four different types of work organisation were identified (Lorenz and Valeyre, 2004; Arundel et al., 2006).[8] Of the four types identified, two tend to increase the (internal) flexibility of (the workers within) the company: 'learning organisations' and 'lean or high performance organisations'. In companies with such forms of work organisation, employees are involved in problem solving and decision making. They have more possibilities for self-development in the job. There is also a close connection between the way people work and learn in a company and the way the company can innovate, although in terms of innovation, learning organisations tend to have an advantage over lean organisations.

Employment security is enhanced: in order to prepare and equip workers to deal with necessary changes and possible transitions over their working careers it is important to emphasise the updating of skills, both through training and work organisation.

The fourth European Working Conditions Survey shows that there is no improvement in levels of training in European companies: less than one in three workers in the EU reports having received paid training in the previous twelve months. Over time, the number of employees who say that they have received training provided for or paid for by their employer has not increased, and has actually decreased for old member states, but is even lower in new member states. This level has decreased from 30 per cent in 1995 and 2000 (EU15) to 27 per cent in 2005 for EU15 (and 26 per cent for EU27).

It is also true to note that there are significant differences in the level of access to training between countries, both with regard to levels of training provided for by employers in general but also with respect to changes over time (see Figure 8.1).

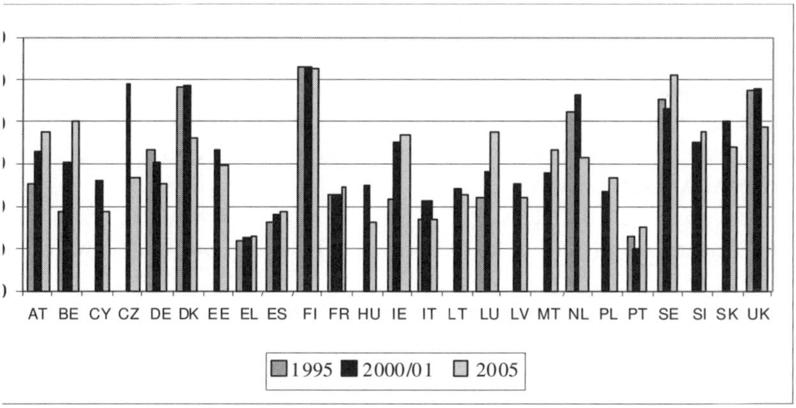

Source: European Working Conditions Survey (2007), trends over time, employees only.

Figure 8.1 Country differences in levels of training provided by employer: percentage of workers who received training, differences over time (%)

The last notable difference is between low/high skilled workers and between workers with different types of employment contracts (see Figure 8.2). Initial education seems to have a strong bearing on the possibilities of further training in the labour market, which raises the prospect of increasing polarisation between those with access to training and those without access.

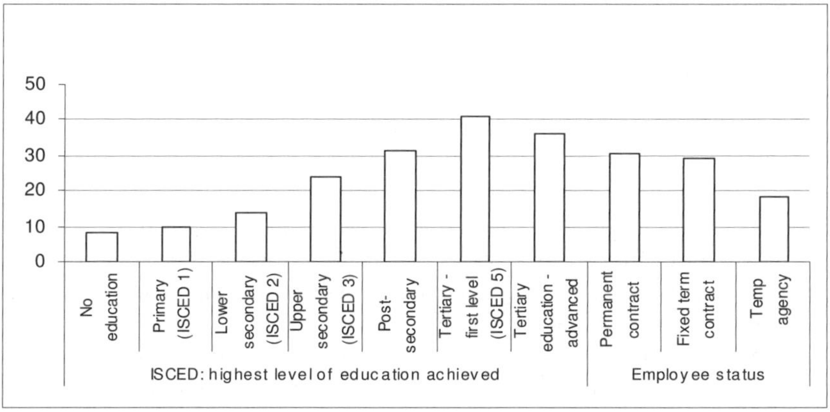

Source: European Working Conditions Survey (2007).

Figure 8.2 Paid training received in last twelve months, by educational attainment (%)

Another way to increase skills levels in the European Union is through learning on the job, through work organisation (for example teamwork) and through job rotation and multi-skilling (see Table 8.4). Such competence development develops both adaptability at the individual level and flexibility at the company level and will generally be useful in a longer term perspective for individual workers.

Table 8.4 Functional flexibility and teamwork (employees only, EU27)

Employees whose job involves rotating tasks with colleagues		47.7	
			of total
	Tasks require different skills	77.8	37.1
	Manager decides division of tasks	71.6	34.1
	Team decides division of tasks	51.0	24.3
Employees whose job involves doing part of all work in teams		60.0	
			of total
	Team members decide division of tasks	52.1	31.3
	Team members select head of team	28.8	17.3

Source: European Working Conditions Survey (2007).

One step further could be to develop 'competence development' into a more general 'right to learn', adapted to each individual's capability. The idea is to equip people to deal with change over their life, both in work and out of work.[9]

8.5 ROLE OF THE SOCIAL INSTITUTIONS IN SAFEGUARDING SECURITY

Security, according to the Wilthagen Matrix (see Table 8.1), can take very different forms: job security, employment security, income security, combination security. These forms of security for the different forms of flexibility can be safeguarded through a number of measures, which could be undertaken or institutionalised by different actors.

Companies play a very important role in the development of the employability of their employees. Recent research from the Foundation (2007c) shows that there is a business case for companies to engage on this issue. When determining work arrangements, both in form and content, they can create some possibilities for security, especially by means of increased functional flexibility through job enrichment, training, work organisation and possibly pay differentiation. They can also determine the choice of type of employment contract and working time arrangements. However, what companies are able to offer depends also on the national and sectoral level. Both legislation and social institutions, both social protection and social infrastructure, are important elements with an influence on how much security there is for workers.

8.5.1 Labour Market Institutions

Labour market institutions play an important role. Employment protection legislation (EPL) is a barrier to the easy 'hire and fire' culture which is one way of introducing flexibility for all workers. One offshoot of EPL is the possible development of a dual labour market, in which a core of permanent workers has a very strong protection against dismissal: this predisposes employers to make greater use of non-permanent contracts in order to impact on their strategy of numerical flexibility (the so-called insider–outsider effect).

In order to achieve the necessary level of security, active labour market policies (ALMP) can play an important role. These help to ensure that people who lose their job or who choose to follow the 'flexible route' are helped to find another job where necessary. Two of the principal functions of an active labour market policy are to provide extra training in 'in-between periods' and to help in matching the supply and demand of labour. However, these roles are clearly facilitated by the presence of certain conditions. First of all, the labour market and economic performance of a country should be such as to have a reasonable volume of work and jobs for employment agencies to carry out their matching function. At the same time there should be substantial investment in public employment services and ancillary agencies. The creation of such an institutional framework requires significant expenses of both time and money.

One core element of an active labour market policy, whose importance is undiminished by variations in national economic situations, is an emphasis on continuous updating of skills and competences. Lifelong learning is indeed one of the building blocks of the European Employment Strategy. While special efforts might be needed to make transitions between unemployment and employment and/or between different employment contracts[10] smoother, a continuous updating of skills will generally make a worker 'more flexible'.

8.5.2 Social Protection Systems

The impact of more flexibility in the labour market (whether for all workers or for a group of more precarious workers) should be thoroughly examined. It can also be considered as a new form of social risk. The benefits of flexibility in creating more jobs and employment could be complemented by social protection systems to manage the risks of individual workers, a concept that is close to the basic idea of flexicurity. Social protection systems play a central role in the overcoming of risks, which is why they play such an important role in the social model in the European Union. They therefore have a clear complementary role in dealing with the unemployment risk of a more flexible labour market.

Social protection systems have two main aims: decommodification on the one hand and employability on the other. Decommodification describes the degree to which individuals and families can maintain a socially acceptable standard of living without participation in the labour market (Esping Andersen, 1990, 2002). One could also add as a third aim the achievement of social justice or redistribution. However, for simplicity, the emphasis here lies on the first two with their short- and long-term consequences (Table8.5).

Table 8.5 Short- and long-term objectives of social protection systems

	Short-term	Long-term
Decommodification	Temporary income to protect people from precarious situations (for example unemployment benefits)	Continuation of income in the case of structural or long-term events (for example disability benefits, pensions not linked to previous labour market activity)
Employability	Re-employment, 'secondary status' contracts such as fixed-term contracts, integration schemes in companies	Development of personal projects that are not necessarily immediately profitable in the short term on the labour market, skills development

Source: Vielle and Walthery (2003, p. 85).

Welfare states (or social protection systems) have always played an important role as instruments of decommodification (Vielle and Walthery, 2003). In practice, the European social model is based on the idea that states compensate for possible events relating to loss or reduction of earned income in the case of a number of risk events occurring (unemployment, illness, advancing age, maternity, invalidity, death) or the occurrence of exceptional burdens, for example medical or family expenses (Dupeyroux and Ruellan,

1998). Most states also have mechanisms to assist those who are incapable (temporarily or permanently) of securing their own livelihoods.

The second major aspect of social protection systems is related to employability, in which employment has been considered as the main means to ensure an income and also as a foundation of individual well-being. This aspect also plays an important role in the economic strategy of the European Union in which high employment has been considered as one of the main goals.

With regard to flexicurity, the role of social protection systems is therefore still an important instrument to deal with social risks in the short and long term. It allows recipients the means to overcome periods without employment. These benefits should not constitute a trap for individuals, for example in the form of overgenerous or unlimited unemployment benefits, which can trap people in unemployment in certain cases. The emphasis is therefore on 'making work pay' without losing sight of the necessity to give people the means to overcome periods in which they cannot work for some reason.

Different social protection systems put the emphasis on different sets of benefits and ways of financing social protection systems. Many welfare state typologies have been put forward. The one which guides the debate most often is the one developed initially by Esping-Andersen (1990), who identifies three types of welfare state (the corporatist/conservative welfare state, the liberal welfare state and the social democratic welfare states), complemented by a fourth model, the mediterranean welfare state (Ferrera, 1996). All systems however have adapted to changes in policies and have become more hybrid models. It is also difficult to classify the new Member States using this typology. However, based on the typology, some constraints for each of the systems can be identified.[11] These should be taken into account in the debate on flexicurity for each of the social protection systems.

New social risks and possible avenues for change

When European social protection systems were conceived, they were based on the 'male breadwinner model' characterised by a single income in the family (the male breadwinner), with family/household organisation being the principal responsibility of the wife. Workers often stayed in the same job for the duration of their entire working life. With the growth of female participation in the labour force as well as the spread of more episodic, discontinuous career trajectories there has been a renewed focus on different possibilities of organising working time over the life course. A key element that needs to be considered is the consequence of the above trends for access to social protection entitlements.

The impact of working time arrangements over the life course should be considered from the point of view of their effect on the social protection rights, access to different elements of social security systems, the level of income and/or compensating benefits and, ultimately, the financial sustainability of the social security systems (Klammer et al., 2006).

Some possible avenues for changes in social protection systems should be explored in a systematic way in order to take into account the impact of more flexibility and flexicurity on individuals and systems. One way to do this could be to consider what has been done for the coordination of social security rights for migrant workers[12] and base the changes on the same important principles:

- Equality of treatment (such as in the Dutch model between part-time and full-time contracts).
- Legislation for rights encompassing 'transitions' between different employment status/contracts/spells (for example between employment and self-employment, between different contracts and with unemployment spells).
- Aggregation of insurance periods, maintenance of rights (for example pension building rights).
- Transferability of rights, especially during transitions: maintenance of acquired rights (this might be the most difficult, as some of the rights built up are inherently linked to the contract, for example access to (supplementary) health care).

Another important aspect to consider when analysing the consequences of more flexibility for individuals is the global 'package' of social rights. It is, for example, important to reflect on all social protection rights, not only first pillar schemes but also second pillar schemes, for example occupational schemes.[13]

The question to be considered in this context is whether the necessary guarantees are built into the systems in order to avoid loss of rights. Another question is the articulation between minimum qualifying periods and the length of contracts. Any potential reforms should take into account these often hidden elements.

8.5.3 Social Infrastructure

Besides labour market and social protection policies, other social institutions at the national level play a role in the way flexicurity, flexibility, employability and employment participation can work together. Employment choices may also be determined by the availability of social infrastructure. An example of this is how child-bearing and care is institutionalised in a society. The same holds true for care of the elderly.

The participation of working parents, and in particular working mothers, in the labour market may depend on the availability of childcare facilities and after-school care, provision of which varies very much from country to country (Elniff-Larsen et al., 2006). Opening hours, quality and cost of these provisions, whether they are public, private or publicly funded, have a big influence on the choices of working parents.

Parents may opt to stay home for a longer time when their children are young (parental leave). Here the choice is often influenced by the availability, duration and generosity of benefits (Anxo et al., 2007a). For more extended leave periods, it is important to facilitate the return to work (whether full-time or part-time).

In some countries, recourse to part-time employment, particularly for women, is a common way of reconciling work and private life. In the Netherlands, for example, a sizeable majority of working women work part-time.

Hence, countries and citizens respond in very different ways to the combination of work and family: from withdrawal from the labour market to extended leave periods (parental leaves) to a combination of working and childrearing (where availability, cost and quality of care facilities become critical factors).

8.5.4 Flexicurity at the Household Level

Another complexity is that even though flexicurity is primarily an issue concerning the relationship between employers and the workforce, flexibility, and in particular security, are elements with obvious repercussions at the household level.

The most important measurement of income is often at the household rather than the individual level. This can also be the case in terms of allocation of time, working and non-working, on the part of adults with dependents. For this reason, household composition is an important element to bear in mind when reflecting upon the consequences of flexible forms of work as it, too, influences the possibilities for labour market attachment over the life course (Riedmann et al., 2006).

Income insecurity is detrimental not just for an individual worker but also for his or her household situation. In the Foundation's analysis of working poverty, one can see that there is a clear association between household composition, non-permanent contracts or interrupted career paths and greater vulnerability (Pena Casas and Latta, 2004). Hence, one should be aware of possible flexicurity traps resulting in more in-work poverty.

8.6 THE IMPORTANCE OF TRUST

8.6.1 Trust as a Prerequisite of Flexicurity

In order to make flexicurity work, it is important to reflect upon the consequences for all parties involved: for the individual (worker), for the society, for companies. The key element to make this link is trust.[14] Trust should exist at different levels, as outlined below.

If people believe in the future, they may be willing to take more risks with regard to their employment status, may be willing to work more 'flexibly' (contractual, working time, functional flexibility) and combine work with having a family.

People should also be able to trust in changes: they should not consider change intrinsically negative and should be confident that the means are there to adapt to emerging circumstances. One example of this is the fact that comparatively weak employment protection legislation in Denmark coexists with a high level of employment turnover: 25 per cent of Danish workers change job each year. This is an accepted trade-off as there is a strong confidence in finding another, equivalent job in a reasonable amount of time, due to both the general economic performance of the country and as a result of Danish active labour market policies.

People should be able to trust in work: workers should be able to plan over their life without too many inconveniences and risks for their career/pensions. Job/employment interruptions and transitions need to be organised in such a way that workers have the necessary support structure to combine working and non-working life. Transitions should be smoothened to take place over the life course between full-time and part-time, between different forms of employment status and to overcome spells of unemployment.

In order to create this society of trust, European systems have to be adapted to this new reality: social protection systems, labour market systems and social infrastructure. There is no 'one size fits all' solution which can be transferred readily from one country to another.

An important element in the reflection is the financial and institutional situation of each Member State which has an impact on reform possibilities. It should also be underlined that all reforms require not only a good deal of political courage but might also require time for them to bear fruit, depending on specific economic context. The possible transferability of other 'ideas' on flexicurity depends on economic capacity and policy institutional capacity, including veto actors, preferences, economic viability and political will to accept these reforms at different levels.

8.6.2 A Role for All Partners

Mutual trust is very important between all actors involved in this configuration, including trust between social partners and government. Also, it takes time to implement and achieve results from any reforms. Social partners can be involved at very different levels. They can be involved at the level of shaping (national) policies, be it labour market or social protection policies. The role of social partners at that level varies considerably between countries. It can range from cross-sectoral partnership agreements (for example in Ireland), to consultation (for example more or less systematic consultation for all relevant pieces of legislation, for example Belgium) to social partner initiatives at national or sectoral levels which might be endorsed by national policy makers, for example the agreement on lifelong learning by the social partners in France.

Furthermore, at the company level, social partners can play a very important role in both the acceptance but also in the shaping of any changes to be introduced at company level (and also at the sectoral and national level). If social partners can agree upon a way to deal with these difficult issues, they might try and develop good practice in this area. Trade unions should be willing to accept less job security in the short term in order to have a more dynamic labour market and greater employment security in the longer term (Madsen, 2006).[15] If they are included in the process of decision making and implementation, this could enhance the trust element. Discussions at all the relevant levels can lead to a better compromise between flexibility and security.

Given the multidimensional nature of flexicurity, it is important to strive for an integration of different policy areas. A more coherent policy to tackle the issue, increased interaction between the different elements and between different policies (labour law, labour market policies and social protection systems), is needed to create sustainable employment and social cohesion.

There is no one way to do it, whether it is the Danish model with more flexibility for all workers, or a more 'transitional labour market' approach such as the Dutch model in which people move in and out of the labour market. However, it is important in all systems to have all actors involved and committed at the relevant levels in a tripartite setting.

8.7 CONCLUSIONS

Flexicurity has the potential to substantially enhance the competitiveness of the European economy and create higher levels of employment. However, to make this possible, companies, workers and society have to be able to agree and trust in flexicurity. The element of security is a vital aspect in creating this trust. Security should be based on employment security, not job security, and contains a mix of rights and tools.

With regard to rights: they should be seen in a wider context over the life course and might require some reforms of national labour market, employment and social protection systems. The rights could be reconsidered in order to guarantee some coordination over the life course for flexible workers and could be grounded on certain principles, such as equal treatment, legislation for (national) transitional labour markets, aggregation of insurance periods and transferability of rights. It is important to reflect on all social protection rights, including not only first pillar schemes but also second pillar schemes, namely occupational schemes.

With regard to tools, it is vital to equip workers to deal with change to make flexicurity work: this should include a more consistent debate on how skills building throughout the career can be implemented. This includes a mix of different actors who are involved in this: workers learn new things in work through innovative forms of work organisation (so-called 'learning organisations', multi-skilling, job rotation), through training offered by their employer, sectoral funds initiatives, regional development funds and active labour market policies. The way this is organised depends a lot on sectoral and national institutions and choices, as well as on economic circumstances at national level.

Specific attention should be given to the more vulnerable workers, who might have fewer possibilities to training because of a series of circumstances, be it their personal situation or because the training is not adapted to the needs of both workers and companies. There is a risk of creating new categories of worker for whom this 'upward mobility' might not work, a new group of working poor. This group needs specific attention in the reflection on flexicurity.

As with any process of change, it is quite clear that for the process of flexicurity, trade-offs have to be made at all levels. This implies a key role for dialogue, in particular social dialogue, on the content of changes needed and on the manner of implementation of these changes.

Flexicurity is a big challenge for the years to come and needs serious reflection on the part of all actors involved, at all levels in each Member State and at the European level. However, it has the potential to contribute actively to a more competitive and productive labour market with higher levels of employment while still adhering to the basic tenets of the European social model.

NOTES

1. The author is research manager in the Monitoring and Survey Unit of the European Foundation of the Improvement of Living and Working Conditions. This chapter is based on research undertaken by the Foundation and is a revised version of the background paper for the hearing in the European Parliament on 21 March 2007 on 'Varieties of flexicurity: reflections on key elements of flexibility and security' (with co-author John Hurley) and of Foundation Findings 'Flexicurity – Issues and Challenges'.

   The views expressed in this chapter do not necessarily reflect those of the European Foundation for the Improvement of Living and Working Conditions. The author is grateful to the colleagues of the European Foundation for the Improvement of Living and Working Conditions, and in particular John Hurley, Agnès Parent-Thirion, Sylvie Jacquet and Willy Buschak for their input and comments on an earlier version of this chapter.
2. These factors have been studied and commented on widely in the literature and in the policy background documents from OECD (Employment Outlook), European Commission (Employment in Europe, Communication on demographic change and so on).
3. Social protection in general remains a national competence. But since 1958, the competence for coordination of social security elements with regard to mobility of workers and people is at European level (European Treaty).
4. There is some debate about the terms 'atypical' or 'non-standard', particularly in light of their relatively high share in some countries. 'Atypical' in this chapter refers to all workers who do not work in a full-time permanent job. This would include part-time workers, fixed-term workers, seasonal workers, temporary agency workers and so on.
5. Both the UK and the Netherlands have high rates of part-time work, particular amongst working women. In Spain, fixed-term contracts represent over 30 per cent of the entire workforce. However, recent major labour market reforms have attempted to redress some of the disadvantages associated with this (for example excessive labour market segmentation, declining levels of per head productivity), in the form of new provisions to safeguard and promote the rights of atypical workers and to create incentives for employers to convert atypical to typical contracts.
6. A good overview of the debate in new Member States can be found in Cazes and Nesparova (2007) and Council of Europe (2007).
7. The low level of non-permanent contracts in these countries could be explained by a lower level of employment protection legislation (EPL) allowing for the easier hiring and firing. OECD, ILO and the European Commission have extensively studied the impact of such legislation concluding that lower EPL in itself is not guaranteed to lead to more flexicurity.
8. The four 'types' of organisational forms are labelled: 'learning', 'lean', 'taylorist' and 'traditional' form of work organisation. Valeyre et al. are exploring this issue further with new data of the 4th EWCS in a forthcoming publication (Valeyre et al., 2008, forthcoming).
9. This idea could be linked to Amartya Sen's 'capabilities' theory. This was also developed by Supiot in what he called 'social drawing rights' whereby individuals get some 'credit' for this type of rights (Supiot, 2001; Vielle and Walthery, 2003).
10. This should be read as covering a wide range of possible situations and also include movement between self-employment and employment, between part-time and full-time, between temporary and permanent contracts and going in both directions. This might be important in the light of a life course perspective, see Muffels et al., (2007).
11. The different constraints for each of the systems are for corporatist systems: financing pensions without increasing labour costs disproportionately; for liberal systems: dual system engendered by the difficulty in achieving a return to full employment and the phenomenon of young unemployed and single parents; for social democratic systems: how to increase work availability, especially for the unskilled, without challenging the egalitarian principle of social democracy; for Mediterranean systems: how to increase flexibility while ensuring some economic security for employees.
12. Coordination regulation 1408/71 on social security for migrant workers.
13. The first pillar scheme is the basic social security system as provided by the state. Second pillar schemes are supplementary, occupational schemes, usually provided at company or

branch level. Second pillar schemes are common in most countries for supplementary pension schemes and/or supplementary health care.

14. This idea of trust is widely reflected upon in the literature, particularly in the reflections on the reasons for the success of the Danish system. Another example is the 'square of trust' idea as proposed by Ton Wilthagen, presentation at the Foundation Seminar Series, European Foundation, Dublin, May 2006.
15. Also Per Madsen's speech at the conference on Transitional Labour Markets and Flexicurity, Amsterdam, December 2006.

REFERENCES

Anxo, D., Fagan, C., Smith, M., Letablier, M. and Perraudin, C. (2007a), *Parental Leave in European Companies*, European Foundation for the Improvement of Living and Working Conditions, Luxembourg: Office for Official Publications, http://euro found.europa.eu/pubdocs/2006/87/en/1/ef0687en.pdf.

Anxo, D., Fagan, C., Smith, M., Letablier, M. and Perraudin, C. (2007b), *Part-time Work in European Companies*, European Foundation for the Improvement of Living and Working Conditions, Luxembourg: Office for Official Publications, www.eurofound.europa.eu/pubdocs/2006/102/en/1/ef06102en.pdf.

Arundel, A., Lorenz, E., Lundvall, B. and Valeyre, A. (2006), *The Organisation of Work and Innovative Performance: A Comparison of the EU-15*, DRUID Working Paper, No. 06-14, Aalborg University, Danish Research Unit for Industrial Dynamics, September, www.ceerecherche.fr/fr/fiches_chercheurs/texte_pdf/valey re/wp0614.pdf.

Atkinson, J. (1984), 'Manpower strategies for flexible organizations', *Personnel Management*, **16**.

Auer, P. (2007), 'In search of optimal labour market institutions', in Jørgensen, H. and Madsen, P.K. (2007), *Flexicurity and Beyond. Finding a new agenda for the European Social Model*, Copenhagen: DJØF Publishing Copenhagen, p. 83.

Cazes, S. and Nesporova, A. (2007), *Flexicurity: A Relevant Approach in Central and Eastern Europe*, Geneva: ILO.

Chung, H., Ester, P. and Kerkhofs, M. (2007), *Flexibility at the Firm Level: A Typology of Working Time Flexibility*, European Foundation for the Improvement of Living and Working Conditions, Luxembourg: Office for Official Publications.

Council of Europe (2007), 'Reconciling labour flexibility with social cohesion, the experiences and specificities in central and eastern Europe', *Trends in Social Cohesion 17*, Strasbourg.

Dupeyroux, J. and Ruellan, R. (1998), *Droit de la sécurité sociale*, Paris: Dalloz.

Elniff-Larsen, A., Dreyling, M. and Williams, J. (2006), *Employment Developments in Childcare Services For School-Age Children*, European Foundation for the Improvement of Living and Working Conditions, Luxembourg: Office for Official Publications, www.eurofound.europa.eu/pubdocs/2006/32/en/1/ef0632en.pdf.

EMCO working group on Flexicurity (2006), *Flexicurity*, European Commission, May. http://ec.europa.eu/employment_social/employment_strategy/pdf/emco_workgrou pflexicurity06_en.pdf.

Employment Taskforce (2003), *Jobs, Jobs, Jobs. Creating More Employment in Europe*, Report of the Employment Task Force, chaired by Wim Kok, Luxembourg: Office for Official Publications, www.europa.eu.int/comm/em ployment_social/ employment_strategy/task_en.htm.

European Commission (1997), *Partnership for a New Organisation of Work, Green Paper*, COM(97) 128, Bulletin of the European Union, supplement 4/97, Luxembourg: Office for Official Publications, http://ec.europa.eu/employment_social/labour_law/docs/wo_greenpaper_en.pdf.

European Commission (2006), *Modernising Labour Law to Meet the Challenges of the 21st Century, Green Paper*, COM (2006) 708 final, Brussels, 22 November, http://ec. europa.eu/employment_social/labour_law/green_paper_en.htm.

Europen Commission (2006a), *Employment in Europe 2006: Statistical Annex*, Luxembourg: Office for Official Publications of the European Communities, http://digitalcommons.ilr.cornell.edu/.

European Commission (2007), *Towards Common Principles of Flexicurity: More and better jobs through flexibility and security*, COM(2007) 359 final, Brussels, 27 June, http://ec.europa.eu/employment_social/employment_strategy/pdf/flex_comm_en.pdf.

European Foundation for the Improvement of Living and Working Conditions (2007a), *Varieties of Flexicurity: Reflections on Key Elements of Flexibility and Security. Background Paper*, Hearing on the Commission's Green Paper, 'Modernising labour law to meet the challenges of the 21st century', European Parliament Committee on Employment and Social Affairs, 21 March, 18 p.

European Foundation for the Improvement of Living and Working Conditions (2007b), *Foundation Findings, Flexicurity – Issues and Challenges*, Dublin: European Foundation for the Improvement of Living and Working Conditions.

European Foundation for the Improvement of Living and Working Conditions (2007c), *Attractive workplace for all, database of company cases*, www.eurofound.europa.eu/areas/qualityofwork/betterjobs/search.php.

European Working Conditions Surveys (2007), own calculations on base of 1995, 2000/2001 and/or 2005 data, European Foundation for the Improvement of Living and Working Conditions.

Esping-Andersen, G. (1990), *The Three Worlds of Welfare Capitalism*, Princeton, NJ: Princeton University Press.

Esping-Andersen, G. (2002), *Why we Need a New Welfare State*, Oxford: Oxford University Press.

Expert Group on Flexicurity (2007), *Flexicurity Pathways*, Interim report from the rapporteur (Wilthagen), presented at the Stakeholder Conference on Flexicurity, Brussels, 20 April, http://ec.europa.eu/employment_social/employment_strategy/pdf/flex_interimexpertrep_en.pdf.

Ferrera, M. (1996), 'The Southern Model Of Welfare In Social Europe', *Journal of European Social Policy*, 17–37.

Goudswaard, A. and De Nanteuil, M. (2000), *Flexibility and Working Conditions: A Qualitative and Comparative Study in Seven EU Member States*, European Foundation for the Improvement of Living and Working Conditions, Luxembourg: Office for Official Publications, www.eurofound.europa.eu/publications/htmlfiles/ef0007.htm.

Klammer, U., Keuzenkamp, S., Cebrián, I., Fagan, C., Klenner, C. and Moreno, G. (2006), *Working Time Options Over the Life Course: Changing Social Security Structures*, European Foundation for the Improvement of Living and Working Conditions, Luxembourg: Office for Official Publications, www.eurofound.europa.eu/pubdocs/2005/101/en/1/ef05101en.pdf.

Lorenz, E. and Valeyre, A. (2004), *Organisational Change in Europe: National Models or the Diffusion of a New 'One Best Way'?*, DRUID Working Paper, n°04–

04, Danish Research Unit for Industrial Dynamics, Aalborg: Aalborg University, www.druid.dk/wp/pdf_files/04-04.pdf.

Madsen, P. (2006), *Flexicurity: A New Perspective on Labour Markets and Social Protection Policies in Europe*, Paper presented at the conference on 'Transitional Labour Markets and Flexicurity', Amsterdam, www.tilburguniversity.nl/faculties/frw/research/schoordijk/flexicurity/ILP/events/programme1/permadsenpaper.pdf.

Muffels, R., Chung, H., Fouarge, D., Klammer, U., Luijkx, R., Manzoni, A. and Wilthagen, T. (2007), *Flexibility and Security over the Life Course: Results and Policy Implications*, European Foundation for the Improvement of Living and Working Conditions, Luxembourg: Office for Official Publications.

Naegele, G. (2003), *A New Organisation of Time Over Working Life*, European Foundation for the Improvement of Living and Working Conditions, Office for Official Publications, Luxembourg, http://eurofound.europa.eu/publications/html files/ef0336.htm.

Pena Casas, R. and Latta, M. (2004), *Working Poor in the EU*, European Foundation for the Improvement of Living and Working Conditions, Luxembourg: Office of Official Publications, www.eurofound.europa.eu/publications/htmlfiles/ef0467.htm.

Riedmann, A., Bielenski, H., Szczurowska, T. and Wagner, A. (2006), *Working Time and Work–Life Balance in European Companies: Establishment Survey on Working Time*, European Foundation for the Improvement of Living and Working Conditions, Luxembourg: Office of Official Publications, www.eurofound.europa.eu/publications/htmlfiles/ef0627.htm.

Supiot, A. (2001), *Beyond Employment, Changes in Work and the Future of Labour Law in Europe*, New York: Oxford University Press.

Valeyre, A., Lorenz, E., Cartron, D., Czizmadia, P., Gollac, M., Illéssy, M. and Makó, C. (2008, forthcoming), *Work Organisation in the European Union*, European Foundation for the Improvement of Living and Working Conditions.

Vielle, P. and Walthery, P. (2003), *Flexibility and Social Protection*, European Foundation for the Improvement of Living and Working Conditions, Luxembourg: Office for Official Publications, www.eurofound.europa.eu/publications/htmlfiles/ef0355.htm.

Wilthagen, T. and Tros, F. (2004), 'The concept of "flexicurity": A new approach to regulating employment in the labour market', *Transfer*, **10** (2), 166–86.

Wilthagen, T. (2006), *Dutch Flexicurity Policies: Normalisation of Atypical Work*, paper presented at 'Foundation Seminar Series on Flexicurity and Employability', Dublin: European Foundation for the Improvement of Living and Working Conditions, http://eurofound.europa.eu/docs/events/fss/060522/Wilthagen_pres.pdf.

9. Working-life Time Accounts in German Companies: New Opportunities for Structuring Working Hours and Careers?

Philip Wotschack and Eckart Hildebrandt

9.1 INTRODUCTION

A constant increase in labour flexibility remains an essential competitive strategy of enterprises. One component of this process is the expansion of time volumes and the extension of time horizons with respect to the redistribution of individual working time. Such a development alters not only the day-to-day work–life balance, but also the entire life course of employees. Our contribution presents preliminary results from a current empirical research project at the Social Science Research Center Berlin (WZB) on the preconditions and practices of long-term working time accounts in Germany.[1] The main questions asked are how long-term working time accounts change the dynamics of company working time policy, and whether or not they help to stabilise discontinuous life courses. The chapter first introduces the basic concept and functioning of long-term working time accounts and discusses major trends and related risks and opportunities. We then present a preliminary overview of the distribution and use of long-term working time accounts in Germany. This overview is based on initial analyses of a representative company survey that was carried out in 2005. The main questions concern the individual options and opportunities offered by long-term working time accounts and the characteristics of their distribution. With regard to the latter aspect, we examine effects of firm size, sector, demand fluctuations, economic performance, personnel policy, industrial relations and workforce composition.

9.2 LONG-TERM WORKING TIME ACCOUNTS: RATIONALE, CHARACTERISTICS AND CURRENT TRENDS

The basic aim of working time accounts in companies is to enable employees to redistribute their working hours. In other words, the purpose of working time accounts is the regulation of deviations from normal working hours, which essentially amounts to the regularisation of flexible working time. To this end, the working hours (both plus and minus hours) that deviate from the company's formal regulations are deposited in a working time account that has specified limits as regards volumes and balancing periods. The procedures for depositing time credits (with respect to volumes and sources) and for withdrawing them (with respect to volumes, designated uses and withdrawal requests) are usually agreed at the company level.

Working time accounts are organised according to the basic principle of compensatory time off. They allow employees to temporarily work longer hours and (less commonly) to temporarily work shorter hours; the employee balances the account within a specified period of time and thus eventually works the total hours laid down in the relevant collective contract or works agreement. Depending on the length of the balancing period, we can distinguish between short-term, long-term and lifetime accounts, whereby as the duration of the balancing period is extended, so too is the potential volume of the account (see Figure 9.1). What is unique about working time accounts – unlike other instruments for increasing working time flexibility, such as paid overtime or temporary part-time work – is that hours of work provided in advance or in excess of contractually agreed hours constitute eligibility for an equivalent number of hours of paid leave at a later point in time; in other words, the concept seeks to preserve time over the life cycle under conditions of greater flexibility. Time for life, for recuperation, for family, education and leisure thus becomes a determining factor of company working time policy.

Long-term working time accounts have the following four characteristics:

1. The accounts remain open for at least one year and often for an employee's entire tenure with a company or for the full length of his/her working life (if he/she enters retirement from the company managing the account or if the account is transferable). There is usually no stipulated point in time at which an account must be emptied before being built up again.
2. Long-term accounts are built up on the basis of direct deposits in the form of time and money and, occasionally, on the basis of transfers from other, short-term accounts.

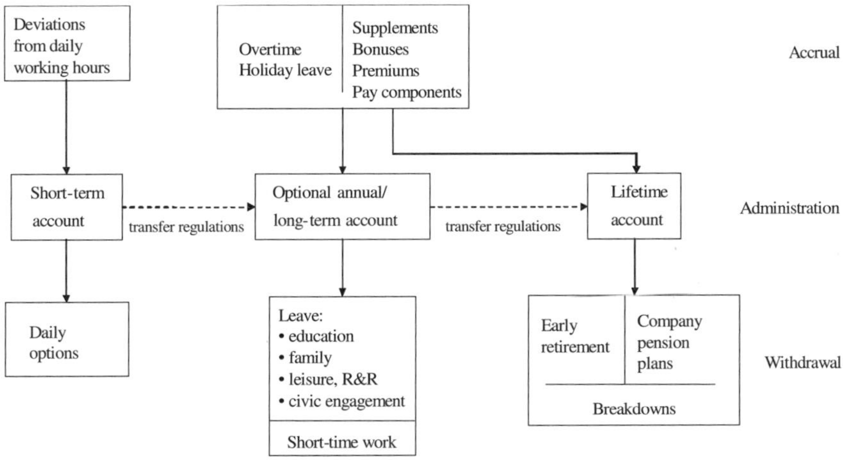

Figure 9.1 Types of working time accounts

3. As regards withdrawals, two kinds of long-term accounts with qualitatively different characteristics can be distinguished. Optional long-term accounts are used during the course of the working life for withdrawals at selected points in time and for various personal purposes that can be determined by the employee but also by the company. Age-related long-term accounts, on the other hand, only mature at the end of the working life, either in the form of early retirement or semi-retirement, or as a supplementary pension provision. Some company models run the two types of account under the generic name of 'long-term working time account'.
4. Unlike short-term accounts, a minimum volume is specified for time withdrawals (depending on the purpose of withdrawal).

The diffusion and the characteristic features of long-term working time accounts are shaped by four current trends:

First, the economic environment has changed significantly for employees over the last decade. Trade union demands for compensatory time off in exchange for overtime hours arose within the context of the goal of increased humanisation of work and a more important role for leisure time and were intended, especially, to serve the aim of health protection. But this did nothing to change the fact that overtime pay remained an important income component for many workers, who were accustomed to using the additional earnings to cover extraordinary expenses. This preference for cash in lieu of time off was mitigated to some extent by a high level of employment stability and steady income growth. Over the last ten years, however, average real incomes from dependent employment have not risen and employment security has decreased. The majority of employees are now likely to react to this development by increasing their cash preference and by pushing for rapid disbursement of overtime pay.

Second, the fact that a share of an employee's due remuneration can be deposited in a working time account enables allocation of a combination of time and money values – mainly in the form of deposits (for example, of performance-related bonuses), but also in the form of withdrawals (in the event of company 'breakdowns' or under company pension plans). This changes the original character of working time accounts, as is expressed by the new term 'time-value account'. In addition to regulating compensatory time off, the accounts now also function as a basis for financial compensation or savings mechanisms (for example, deferred compensation under the company pension scheme). A consequence is that one of the aims of working time accounts – to increase employees' sovereignty over their time – is thus curtailed. On the other hand, other motives for the use of the accounts, such as interest accrual and tax benefits, gain in significance. As far as employees are concerned, this shift in emphasis will reinforce their savings and security incentives, but it will also tend to slow down learning processes regarding time management in working life; the network of mutual interaction will become more complex.

Third, where working time accounts have been implemented, there is currently a tendency to extend both the volume of the account and the balancing period until the end of the employee's working life. In addition to flexitime accounts and annual working time accounts (which are both already widespread), we now also have long-term and lifetime working time accounts (Seifert, 2005a). Mechanisms are being created for transferring credits between the different types of accounts, which is leading to the dissolution of the boundaries between day-to-day flexibility and life cycle flexibility. However, the configuration of the new boundaries is dealt with in a variety of different ways. At one extreme is the total separation of short-term flexibility and long-term saving; at the other is the greatest possible use of short-term savings processes for building up long-term accounts. The difference between long-term and lifetime accounts becomes more relevant in this context. Given that age-related long-term accounts only make sense if they permit the accumulation of a large volume of time (for example, 3,000 hours as the equivalent of three years of work), their purpose inevitably ends up clashing with the aims of optional long-term accounts. Exacerbating the point, one could speak of a conflict between optional organisation of the career biography and retirement provision in the broader sense. When we talk about long-term working time accounts in the following, we are referring both to optional and to age-related long-term accounts (known as 'lifetime accounts').

Fourth, in close interrelation with the above developments, reform strategies have been set in motion at both the national and European level that intervene directly and profoundly in both company personnel policy and the life planning of individuals (life course policy as a multilevel policy). Possibilities for early retirement and semi-retirement have been restricted in order to raise employment rates, while the retirement age has been raised to 67 years in order to recapitalise pension insurance systems. Now that semi-retirement and early retirement schemes will shortly be expiring in Germany (2009), a growing number of large enterprises are endeavouring to establish equivalent arrangements at company level in the form of lifetime working time accounts that conserve the life course model of the 'compressed work biography' (Behrens, 2004, p. 251; IQPC, 2005). This process is a good example of the interplay between policies at the national and European level, on the one hand, and at the company and individual level, on the other.

A change in two important parameters must also be taken into account when assessing the dynamics of diffusion of working time accounts. The introduction of working time accounts is fostered by the trend towards decentralisation to the company level ('Verbetrieblichung') of responsibility for the regulation of working conditions and especially of working times. Opening clauses and supplementary collective agreements allow companies to define working time 'corridors' (the range of hours that may be worked between a maximum and a minimum limit) and to implement a variety of time-accounting systems (Bispinck, 2004). The spread of working time accounts is being hindered, on the other hand, by the trend towards a longer working week, which is being pushed forward by company practices and by the revision of collective agreements (see Seifert, 2005a). The longer individual normal working hours are, the less hours are available for overtime work in excess of stipulated working time corridors, while the limits of human capacity and the reasonableness of demands become narrower. Short, collectively agreed working hours (for example, the introduction or retention of the 35-hour week) are more favourable from the point of view of the potential benefits of working time accounts and time sovereignty because the additional hours worked count as overtime that can be deposited in an account. This reflection has been taken into consideration in some works agreements that stipulate that a share of the extended working hours must obligatorily be deposited in a working time account.

9.3 ACTORS' INTERESTS AND AREAS OF ACTION

Working time accounts affect the interests of the company and the interests of the individual employee in different ways (see Figure 9.2). The stock of available knowledge on this question is very unevenly distributed in the sense that the surveys carried out to date have mainly concentrated on the complex set of interests of companies.

Company	Employees
→ Longer operating times	→ Employment security
→ Short- and medium-term capacity adjustments	→ Daily and life course time options • health/leisure • family • education • civic engagement
→ Optimisation of personnel structure through early retirement	
→ Cost reductions	
→ Employee motivation and employee loyalty (human resource management)	→ Early retirement/old-age insurance

Future social resources
- → Health
- → Family
- → Education
- → Civil society
- → Inclusion

Source: Authors' compilation.

Figure 9.2 Interests regarding working time accounts

On the company side, the following objectives are decisive for the decision to introduce working time accounts and for the type of accounting system used:

- systematic, short-term flexibilisation of working hours within a context of extended operating times (the idea of the 'around-the-clock company', especially in the area of personal services);
- medium-term flexibilisation of personnel capacity in accordance with seasonal and cyclical demand fluctuations (and an associated increase in employment stability);
- in the long term, facilitation at the company level of early retirement in an era when semi-retirement options are expiring and lifelong working time is likely to be extended;
- cost reductions through the abolition of premiums for hours worked that deviate from normal working hours within a defined range;

- increased employee motivation and employee loyalty through the provision of new options for time and income disposal (in some cases restricted to specific groups of employees, especially top achievers);
- simplification of the regulation of flexitime through the definition of working time 'corridors', within which time disposal can be organised in a rapid and uncomplicated manner.

Companies are also influenced by a range of relevant parameters, such as the costs deriving from regulations on the fiscal administration of working time accounts ('deferred taxation') and the associated social security contributions (deferment of and subjectivity to contributions in the event of company breakdowns; bankruptcy insurance), and those deriving from the administrative burden of communications, account management and bankruptcy insurance.

There is little knowledge available regarding the concrete interests of employees with respect to the introduction and implementation of working time accounts. It must also be assumed that the preferences that employees express in surveys on working time will not always necessarily coincide with the way in which they actually deal with time when they have different options at their disposal (see, for example, Bielenski et al., 2002). In very general terms, it is assumed that employees have a basic interest in some degree of time sovereignty for balancing work and life (over the course of the day, the year and the entire life cycle). At the same time, there are substantial differences between individuals depending on their age, gender, family constellation, status within their company and lifestyle (Eberling et al., 2004; Garhammer, 2005; Klenner and Pfahl, 2005; Wotschack et al., 2007). However, what is probably decisive for employees who consent to the introduction of working time accounts – which are generally justified as being necessary for the good of the company – is the expectation of improved employment security as a consequence of the fulfilment of the management's desire to increase working time flexibility.

The pressure on companies to enhance flexibility has undoubtedly grown in recent years and it is increasingly being passed directly on to employees. The compliance of employees with the demands for flexibilisation certainly derives from their recognition that these market pressures do indeed exist, but perhaps it derives even more certainly from the power asymmetry prevailing within their companies. In addition, employees are motivated by their desire to provide good-quality work and satisfy their customers. Moreover, the pressures of persisting high unemployment and largely stagnant employment growth in companies also has an effect on the working time behaviour of employees.

The regulation of working time accounts appears straightforward at first glance because of the association with cash accounts. It is based on the employment contract, according to which willingness to provide qualified work is exchanged for pay. But working time accounts are also the basis for another exchange relationship – one that regulates deviations from normal working hours. The viability of the instrument of working time accounts makes additional demands on the balance of interests between companies and employees, and this can be described using the term reciprocity (see, among others, Diewald et al., 2005, p. 226; Gouldner, 1984, p. 119; Struck and Köhler, 2004, p. 288 et seq.). The employees help to fulfil the company's flexibility requirements, but may not suffer repercussions in their private lives as a consequence. In return, the company gives them back working time that they can use for longer periods of time off for holidays lasting several months, childcare, further education or early retirement. In the ideal case, reciprocity in the context of working time accounts would consist of three elements representing three different areas:

1. An economic transaction based on time: time deposited is equal to time withdrawn (irrespective of pay components that may have been deposited or paid out).
2. A social transaction based on equal opportunities for recuperation: the restrictions on individual lifestyle imposed by a flexible overtime regime are compensated for through equipollent withdrawals of recuperation time.
3. Voluntary interaction in the form of employee participation in company time management and equitable bargaining processes to this end (negotiated optionality and time sovereignty).

The actual design and negotiation of this additional exchange is likely to proceed slowly, however. First, because it is difficult to predict future flexibility requirements and their inherent risks for both enterprises and employees. Up to now, balancing periods of one month have been used for the performance–compensation exchange, while in some cases a balancing period of one year has been used for performance-linked pay components. These periods are easy to keep track of for both parties and are clearly structured by planning and accounting routines. Few companies have a tradition of regulating systems that cover periods of up to 40 years, however, with the exception of those with company pension plans.

Working time accounts also entail a basic conflict of interest between different time regimes, and this poses a threat to the reciprocity model: the interest, on the one hand, of the company management in flexible adjustment of capacities by means of working time accounts that are alternately filled and depleted (in accordance with the concept of the 'breathing company'); and the interest, on the other hand, of the employees in sovereignty over their time – at least with respect to account withdrawals. Given that most companies want to also retain control over withdrawals from working time accounts (which they believe should be made 'with consideration for company interests'), employees' freedom to choose with respect to withdrawals is restricted – depending on the working time culture reigning in the company – and so, therefore, is the relationship of reciprocity.

As a consequence, the confidence of employees in the optionality of the arrangement, that is, their freedom to withdraw time when they want and for the purposes they want, is a basic obstacle to their acceptance of working time accounts (see, for example, Haipeter and Lehndorff, 2004, p. 160). This confidence can only develop on the basis of company practice – that is, the regulations governing time withdrawals and the practical administration of withdrawal requests – and the time culture prevailing in the company, which is expressed by the way in which the employees' desire for time sovereignty and their need to achieve a satisfactory work–life balance are handled. To this end, processes of discourse and learning are necessary on both sides.

9.4 DISTRIBUTION AND UTILISATION OF LONG-TERM WORKING TIME ACCOUNTS

Long-term working time accounts are a recent arrival to working time policy. They are still in the developmental phase, their procedures of use are not yet fully established and their ancillary effects are as yet difficult to foresee. There is still a high degree of uncertainty concerning their distribution and, in particular, concerning the *dynamics* of their distribution. Thus, the sfs Dortmund research centre's recent company survey on working time and hours of operation (see Groß and Schwarz, 2007) represented an ideal opportunity to pose a set of questions related to long-term working time accounts. The master sample of 9,700 establishments was drawn from the German Federal Labour Office's company data; in autumn 2005, 18 per cent of establishments responded to the survey. The survey is based on standardised questionnaires, which were compiled independently by each company's management and returned by post. The following data are extrapolated to all establishments from the net sample. In the following we will use the term 'companies' when we refer to the establishments as our reporting units. According to the results, a total of 6.8 per cent of companies was using long-term working time accounts when the survey was administered, while 0.9 per cent intended to introduce them. Extrapolated to the employment structure, this means that around 18 per cent of employees in

Germany work in companies with long-term working time accounts; 7.3 per cent of all employees actually have a long-term working time account.

The following section will present a first impression of the variations in distribution and utilisation of long-term working time accounts depending on specific company characteristics. The main questions concern the individual options and opportunities offered by long-term working time accounts and the characteristics of their distribution. With regard to the latter aspect, we first of all want to know to what extent long-term working time accounts are introduced and used to increase the firm's flexibility and efficiency and to what extent they are (also) motivated by sustainable and employee-oriented human resource management strategies (working time options over the life course). Proceeding from the current (rather meagre) state of research on the incorporation of such life course- and reconciliation-oriented goals in company personnel policy (see European Foundation, 2003 and 2005) and the characteristics of long-term accounts described above, we will examine the following (groups of) factors:

1. company size;
2. presence of works or staff councils;
3. flexibility needs of the company (economic setting);
4. personnel policy (long-term perspective);
5. workforce composition (share of male and female employees).

9.4.1 Expected Influences

We identify the following factors concerning the firm context that in our view are likely to foster or inhibit the diffusion and utilisation of long-term working time accounts:

We expect a higher distribution of long-term working time accounts among: (1) larger companies, due to a generally higher presence and use of sophisticated and flexible working time arrangements in these companies, greater availability of administrative, personnel and financial resources to introduce and manage them, and a generally higher level of long-term orientation with regard to personnel planning and risk prevention; (2) companies with works or staff councils, since we assume that works or staff councils have an interest in establishing opportunities for employees to save up and conserve overtime hours and to receive compensation in the form of extended paid leaves; (3) companies with a greater need for flexibility (considerable demand fluctuation) or for prolonged periods of long working hours (high labour demand) – both factors create a need for substantial amounts of overtime and time savings, respectively; (4) companies with a long-term personnel plan and that pay greater attention to future risks (such as ageing of the workforce, recruitment problems, lack of skills and qualifications, diversity issues) that can be reduced by long-term working time accounts; (5) companies with a high share of male employees, because they have a workforce that is more interested in (continuous) full-time employment, including overtime hours, than in alternative forms of flexibilisation, which would imply a loss of income and status.

With regard to the utilisation of long-term working time accounts (the options offered by the company) we would expect that options for early or progressive retirement or for training leave are more frequently found among: (1) larger companies, since they can more easily link these options to existing (formalised) retirement and training schemes and have more administrative and financial resources to manage the huge amounts of time savings (over long periods) that are required for early or progressive retirement options; (2) companies with works or staff councils, since works or staff councils have a strong interest in implementing 'closed' regulations given that these are highly predictable and controllable, avoid problems of individual negotiation with regard to replacement or interference with the ongoing work organisation, and meet employer and employee needs (low conflict potential); (3) companies with a high share of male employees, since male employees (due to the dominant gendered division of paid and unpaid work) have fewer care and family responsibilities than their female counterparts and are more interested than female workers in continuous full-time employment combined with options for earlier exit or vocational training. In contrast, we would expect that family-oriented leave options and sabbaticals are more frequently found among: (4) smaller companies, since the more informal character of work organisation, work culture and working time arrangements in these companies leaves more room for individual negotiation and tailor-made solutions; moreover, small companies have fewer resources for administering huge amounts of time savings, as would be required in the case of long-term-oriented working time options; (5) companies with a high share of female employees, since female employees (again due to the dominant gendered division of paid and unpaid work) face substantial care and family responsibilities and are thus more interested in options that allow a combination of work and care during their careers.

The following section investigates the impact of the outlined firm characteristics on the utilisation of long-term working time accounts by discussing the empirical distribution (descriptive overview) and analysing the details of the influence of the various company features (logistic regression analyses).

9.4.2 Distribution of Long-term Working Time Accounts

Our data indicate that differences due to *company size* are of particular importance for the distribution of long-term working time accounts. The analyses show a manifest higher incidence of long-term working time accounts in larger-sized companies. The share of companies with long-term working time accounts increases from 5 per cent among small establishments (1–9 employees) to 17 per cent among large establishments (250 or more employees),[2] see Table 9.1. Because of the importance of company size for the pattern of distribution of long-term working time accounts, as well as for the characteristic institutional settings, our analyses are differentiated for the following four categories: small companies (1–9 employees), small to medium-sized companies (10–49 employees), medium-sized companies (50–249 employees) and large companies (250 or more employees) (the categories are similar to those used by the IAB Institute for Employment Research).

The distribution of long-term working time accounts varies according to the characteristics of the *industrial relations* found in the companies we evaluated. Regarding the influence of the presence of works or staff councils in the company, we must bear in mind that small companies (1–9 employees) rarely have a works or staff council, while almost all large companies (250 or more employees) do. This typical pattern makes it difficult to extract the effect of the size and presence of a works or staff council. We thus refer to characteristic types of combinations of both characteristics. Our data indicate that long-term working time accounts are less often found in very small companies without a works or staff council, are more frequently found in the intermediate categories without a works council, and are mostly found in large companies (250 or more employees) that have a works or staff council. Additional analyses (not reported in the tables) show that companies bound by collective agreements and with a works agreement or an internal alliance on working hours use long-term working time accounts more often than do other companies. This suggests that the representation of employees' interests both inside and outside the company as well as the regulation of working hours by means of in-company agreements and alliances between the works council and management are important prerequisites for long-term working time accounts. This relationship is particularly evident in the case of large companies.

The analyses show a higher incidence of long-term working time accounts in companies with a greater need for flexibility (higher fluctuations in demand). With regard to high labour demand (good economic performance), small (1–9 employees) and large companies (250 and more employees) use long-term working time accounts more frequently when they are in a good economic situation. For the intermediate categories, we do not find a clear-cut relationship. Also with regard to sector, we find differences according to company size: small and medium-sized companies (10–49 employees) in the manufacturing sector have long-term working time accounts more often than do smaller companies in the service sector. By contrast, large companies in the service sector use long-term working time accounts more often than do large companies in the manufacturing sector.

Table 9.1 'Utilisation of long-term working time accounts': distribution of long-term working time accounts (in %) by structural characteristics of companies

	All companies	1–9 employees	10–49 employees	50–249 employees	250+ employees
All	7	5	12	13	17
Industrial relations					
with works or staff council	14	(43)	4	11	17
without works or staff council	6	4	13	15	(13)
Sector					
manufacturing sector	8	4	18	13	15
service sector	6	5	9	13	18
Demand fluctuations					
considerable demand fluctuations	9	6	17	16	20
no considerable demand fluctuations	5	4	12	8	13
Market situation					
good economic performance	10	9	13	13	23
average economic performance	7	5	12	12	15
bad economic performance	5	4	13	13	17
Personnel policy					
with long-term personnel plan	9	6	13	14	19
without long-term personnel plan	5	5	12	9	11
Workforce composition					
high share of male employees	6	4	10	12	20
high share of female employees	8	6	15	14	12

Source: Authors' analysis of sfs Dortmund company survey (2005).

With regard to differences in personnel policy, we had specified the existence of a long-term personnel plan as an important parameter. This assumption is confirmed by the results of the survey. Additional analysis (not reported in the tables) also confirmed the influence of the companies' social commitment. Companies that are socially active are much more likely to have long-term working time accounts than those that responded negatively to this item.

Finally, the distribution of long-term working time accounts changes with the workforce composition of the company. The pattern differs between smaller and larger firms. Long-term working time accounts are more often found among smaller companies (less than 250 employees) with a high share of female employees (50 per cent or more) and among larger companies (250 employees or more) with a high share of male employees (51 per cent or more).

9.4.3 Distribution of Possible Uses and Impediments

The different ways in which working time accounts can be used by employees are of central importance for our strategic question as to their optionality. We should keep in mind that the following data refer to possible uses offered by the companies (as they were reported by the company managers); they do not give us any information on the factual use by the employees. Our analysis of representative data shows that, in general, the range of possible uses is relatively limited. In the large majority of companies with long-term working time accounts, only one (50 per cent) or two (33 per cent) options are offered at the same time, although large companies generally offer three options. Specifically, the possible designated uses are distributed as follows among companies of different sizes (Table 9.2).

In large-sized companies, there is evident predominant use of working time accounts for the purposes of semi-retirement, early retirement and further education, while in small and medium-sized companies, family leave and temporary part-time work are the most frequent purposes of use. As company size increases, so does (rapidly) the possibility of using the accounts for semi-retirement, early retirement and further education. Because a substantial share of employees works in large companies, it can be assumed that working time accounts are used to a significant extent for age-related arrangements.

Moreover, long-term working time accounts play a considerable role in the compensation of market and demand fluctuations. A considerable share of companies in our sample uses time savings on working time accounts to 'bridge' phases of underemployment in times of low market demand. This form of utilisation increases the firm's flexibility and can at the same time increase (in the short run) the employment security of the employees. At the same time it runs the risk of competing with established, more regulated measures (like short-term work) and of shifting market risks and costs from the firm to the employee level.

Table 9.2 Possible uses of long-term working time accounts (in %) by company size

	All companies	1–9 employees	10–49 employees	50–249 employees	250+ employees
Further education	17	17	12	27	50
Sabbatical	6	2	9	17	27
Family leave	27	17	39	42	26
Temporary part-time work	30	17	45	47	28
Semi-retirement	7	6	1	23	69
Early retirement	6	6	1	20	54
Other	64	64	70	51	34
Underemployment[3]	40	35	50	56	46

Firms responding that they use long-term working time accounts (n = 204); multiple answers permitted

Source: Authors' analysis of sfs Dortmund company survey (2005).

Finally, we also asked about difficulties with implementation and other barriers related to long-term working time accounts. Surprisingly, only 8 per cent of the companies with long-term accounts said that they encountered difficulties with them. Large companies (15 per cent) reported difficulties more often than did medium-sized (8 per cent), small to medium-sized (10 per cent) and small (6 per cent) companies. Given the novelty and the complexity of this instrument, this share is lower than we had expected. The most frequent difficulty mentioned was managers' and employees' lack of experience in dealing with large volumes of time credits. This result confirmed our assumption that using a system of time accrual in order to maintain resources requires long-term and far-reaching learning processes.

Overall, the data indicate differentiated patterns of distribution and use of long-term working time accounts in German companies. There is a substantially higher incidence of long-term working time accounts in larger companies, while the influence of other firm characteristics also differs with company size. Moreover, there is empirical evidence of a limited choice of designated uses (particularly in small and medium-sized companies) and an evident predominance of uses for semi-retirement and early retirement purposes, especially in large companies. The following analysis will explore and clarify these heterogeneous patterns with regard to the expectations we formulated at the beginning of this section.

9.4.4 Multivariate Analysis

Building on the previous (descriptive) section, we distinguish four major (sets of) influences that are likely to affect the distribution and utilisation of long-term working time accounts. Since firm size and the presence of works or staff councils in the company are highly correlated (almost 95 per cent of the large firms – 250 employees and more – have a works or staff council) we distinguish four characteristic types of companies according to size and presence or absence of a works or staff council. The following factors are included in the analysis:

1. Firm types with regard to size and presence of works or staff councils:
   a. large firms (250 or more employees) with works or staff council;
   b. large firms (250 or more employees) without works or staff council;
   c. smaller firms (1–249 employees) with works or staff council;
   d. smaller firms (1–249 employees) without works or staff council.
2. Economic setting of the firm:
   a. sector: manufacturing or service sector;
   b. considerable demand fluctuations over the year: no or yes;
   c. economic performance during the last two years: bad, average or good.
3. Type of personnel policy:
   a. long-term personnel plan;
   b. no long-term personnel plan.
4. Workforce composition of the firm with regard to gender:
   a. high share of female employees (50 per cent or more);
   b. high share of male employees (51 per cent or more).

In order to examine the impact of the influences described here on the utilisation of long-term working time accounts, we use separate logistic regression analyses with the following two dependent variables: (1) utilisation of long-term working time accounts (Table 9.3, Column 1); and (2) utilisation of long-term working time accounts for defined purposes (Table 9.3, Column 2). We report the odd ratios for the different influences.[4]

Our multivariate analysis (Table 9.3) confirms a large number of the expected effects: the probability of having a long-term working time account is higher in (1) large companies with a works or staff council, (2) companies with higher demand fluctuations, (3) companies with a stronger economic performance, and (4) companies with a long-term-oriented personnel plan. In particular, the combination of large size and the presence of a works or staff council favour the introduction of long-term working time accounts.

We do not find effects for sector or workforce composition. The overall explained variance remains low (7 per cent), indicating that the factors included in the analysis do not account for much of the given distribution of long-term working time accounts. This might be due to the fact that the instrument is quite new and still in the developmental phase. Consequently, the definitive user group is still in the process of formation and is not yet fully established. This explanation is supported by the fact that while many companies in our sample use long-term working time accounts, there is not yet a definitive and 'closed' set of options for use offered by the companies.

Table 9.3 Logistic regression analyses with (a) utilisation of long-term working time accounts, and (b) utilisation of long-term working time accounts for defined purposes as dependent variable (odd ratios)

	Utilisation of long-term working time accounts[5]	for clearly defined purposes[6]
Type of company		
large company with works/staff council	2.137**	3.937**
large company, no works/staff council	(0.950)	(0.888)
small company with works/staff council	1.025	1.038
small company, no works/staff council	*reference*	*reference*
Flexibility demand		
service sector	1.166	1.924**
manufacturing	*reference*	*reference*
considerable demand fluctuations	1.670**	1.560*
no considerable demand fluctuations	*reference*	*reference*
good economic performance	1.238*	1.267
Workforce composition		
share of female employees: 50% and more	0.849	0.549*
share of male employees: 51% and more	*reference*	*reference*
Personnel policy		
long-term personnel plan	1.594**	1.832*
no long-term personnel plan	*reference*	*reference*
N	1,710	1,615
Nagelkerkes' R^2	0.070	0.137

Notes:
(*) significant at 10% level; * significant at 5% level; ** significant at 1% level.

We would presume that long-term working time accounts in these companies emerge more as a response to high labour demand and 'overflowing' (annual) working time accounts than on the basis of strategic considerations. When we exclude these companies from the sample (see Table 9.3, Column 2) and consider only companies that use long-term working time accounts for clearly defined purposes (n = 112), the effects of the firm context become stronger. The combination of large size and presence of a works or staff council now has a particularly strong impact. Moreover – and in line with our expectations – the firm being part of the service sector and a high share of male employees (workforce composition) increase the likelihood that a firm will make use of long-term working time accounts. At the same time, former effects related to high labour demand (considerable demand fluctuations) decrease or even vanish (good economic performance). The explained variance increases to 14 per cent. This pattern clearly supports our explanation above: Many companies with long-term working time accounts do not yet have a definite plan for their utilisation, but those that do are much more sensitive to the explanatory factors suggested by us.

Table 9.4 Small and large firms: logistic regression analysis with utilisation of long-term working time accounts as dependent variable (odd ratios)

	Small companies (1–249 employees) Utilisation of long-term working time accounts	Large companies (250+ employees) Utilisation of long-term working time accounts
Works or staff council		
with works or staff council	1.035	(2.110)
no works or staff council	*reference*	*reference*
Flexibility demand		
service sector	0.625*	2.460**
manufacturing	*reference*	*reference*
considerable demand fluctuations	2.127**	1.343
no considerable demand fluctuations	*reference*	*reference*
good economic performance	1.439*	1.061
Workforce composition		
share of female employees: 50% and more	1.579*	0.323**
share of male employees: 51% and more	*reference*	*reference*
Personnel policy		
long-term personnel plan	1.723*	1.341
no long-term personnel plan	*reference*	*reference*
N	1,200	510
Nagelkerkes' R^2	0.058	0.073

Notes:
(*) significant at 10% level; * significant at 5% level; ** significant at 1% level.

Since firm size is of major importance for the utilisation of long-term working time accounts, and is also related to heterogeneous variations based on other influences (see previous sections), we run separate logistic regression analyses for smaller (1–249 employees) and larger (250 and more employees) companies (see Table 9.4).

The analysis provides evidence of specific influences in smaller (1–249 employees) and larger (250 or more employees) companies. We assumed (see Section 9.4.1) that larger companies would use sophisticated flexible working time arrangements to a greater extent, would have more resources available to implement and administer long-term working time accounts, and would have a generally higher level of long-term-oriented personnel planning and risk prevention. Small companies, by contrast, are characterised by more informal working time arrangements and work culture, fewer resources and less long-term-oriented policies. These contextual differences are of crucial importance for the role and impact of other influences related to the firm setting on the utilisation of long-term working time accounts.

Smaller companies are influenced by a large set of factors concerning the firm setting, ranging from sector, market fluctuations and labour demand to workforce composition and personnel policy. They are more likely to use long-term working time accounts when they belong to the manufacturing sector, face high flexibility demand (considerable demand fluctuations) and labour demand (good economic performance), have a high share of female employees, and have long-term-oriented personnel planning. These effects are in line with our expectations, with the exception of the impact of the workforce composition. The fact that a high share of female employees increases the likelihood of smaller companies using long-term working time accounts might be due to a greater need for working time options in smaller firms that favour reconciliation between working and family life.

In contrast to smaller companies, large companies are prone to fewer influences. The likelihood of using long-term working time accounts is generally higher in these companies and increases only with the influence of sector (service sector) and a high share of male employees (workforce composition). Both effects are in line with our expectations: belonging to the service sector is related to a higher dependency on human resources, that is, to their optimal adjustment to customer demands. Male employees are usually more interested in full-time work with opportunities for overtime. At the same time, the time preferences and job design of male employees do not leave much room for a reduction of contractual working hours. This renders long-term working time accounts an instrument that particularly suits the typical 'male' working time arrangement across the life course: steadily working long hours and saving up these hours until the end of the career (early exit).

Finally, we now seek to explain variations in the types of options offered by the different types of company (see Table 9.5). Only companies with long-term working time accounts (n = 204) are included in this analysis. Four categories of possible uses are distinguished: (1) retirement (early or progressive retirement), (2) family (family leave or temporary part-time work), (3) training (vocational training) and (4) sabbaticals.

Table 9.5 Companies with long-term working time accounts (n = 207): separate logistic regression analyses with four different possible usages (offered by the company) as dependent variables (odd ratios)

	Retirement	Family	Training	Sabbatical
Type of company[7]				
large company with works/staff council	55.326**	0.401**	3.967**	6.497**
small company with works/staff council	12.523**	0.506	0.637	2.381
small company, no works/staff council	*reference*	*reference*	*reference*	*reference*
Flexibility demand				
service sector	1.505	1.975*	2.881**	2.179(*)
manufacturing	*reference*	*reference*	*reference*	*reference*
considerable demand fluctuations	2.529*	0.713	1.623	1.199
no considerable demand fluctuations	*reference*	*reference*	*reference*	*reference*
good economic performance	1.138	1.056	1.140	2.193*
Workforce composition				
share of female employees: 50% and more	0.341*	0.761	.806	0.571
share of male employees: 51% and more	*reference*	*reference*	*reference*	*reference*
Personnel policy				
long-term personnel plan	0.816	1.470	1.791	1.052
no long-term personnel plan	*reference*	*reference*	*reference*	*reference*
N	204	204	204	204
Nagelkerkes' R^2	0.590	0.070	0.259	0.236

Notes:
(*) significant at 10% level; * significant at 5% level; ** significant at 1% level.

The analysis indicates that the distribution of retirement options (early or progressive retirement) strongly depends on company size and the presence or absence of a works or staff council. It is first and foremost large companies with a works or staff council and, in second place, smaller companies with a works or staff council that offer these options. Moreover, the likelihood of retirement options is higher in companies with a high share of male employees (51 per cent or more) and in companies with considerable flexibility demand. These effects are in line with our expectations and explain almost 60 per cent of the observed variance. They confirm our assumption that large firms and firms with a works or staff council have a stronger interest in and the necessary resources to implement options for early or progressive retirement. And at the same time, early or progressive retirement options suit the working time preferences of male-dominated workforces.

The likelihood of family-oriented leave options (family leave or temporary part-time work) is significantly lower in large firms with works or staff councils; it is stronger in smaller companies without works or staff councils and in companies in the service sector. It appears that issues concerning the reconciliation of work and care have a stronger impact on the more informal working time arrangements and work cultures of smaller firms without works or staff councils. The difference between larger and smaller companies might also be caused by the availability or absence of alternative work–life balance policies. Large companies generally have more scope for introducing such policies. The need to use the long-term working time account for family-oriented options will thus be less pronounced in larger companies.

In line with our expectations, options for training leaves are found to a greater extent among large companies with works or staff councils. Moreover, they are more likely to be found in companies in the service sector. In contrast to our expectations, sabbaticals are more frequently offered by large companies with a works or staff council, by companies in the service sector (though this is only significant at the 10 per cent level) and by companies in a good economic situation.

Summing up, the analysis of the representative company survey confirms the influence of most of the firm characteristics in the ways that we expected. Particularly, the combination of large size and presence of a works or staff council is an important factor in the distribution and utilisation of long-term working time accounts.

9.5 CONCLUSIONS

Working time accounts are steadily gaining in importance as a means of regulating the redistribution of working time over the life course. As their range of uses is extended, however, the accounts are also changing their character. Earlier forms such as flexitime accounts emerged from the mutual need for daily adjustment of working hours and were designed according to the principle of short-term compensatory time off. Accumulation of credits through hours worked in advance or through overtime work was a consequence of acute market or project needs on the part of companies, while withdrawals were determined by personal employee needs that necessitated deviations from the normal rhythms of daily life (Seifert, 2005b). Now the expansion of the accounts in terms of both time and volume is extending the range of designated uses. Optional long-term working time accounts, for example, can be used for extended parental leave, for lifelong learning, for interim health measures, for sabbaticals or for periods of increased voluntary work.

Our analysis of a preliminary representative company survey carried out by sfs Dortmund (2005) gives us a first impression of the current distribution and utilisation of long-term working time accounts depending on principal company characteristics. It provides some initial information on the influence of organisational characteristics, the flexibility needs of the firm, industrial relations, differences in human resource management and workforce composition. So far, we can draw the following conclusions.

First, a clear user group has not yet become established. The instrument is rather new – it was first introduced in the mid-1990s – and so experience with and knowledge of the utilisation, potentials and difficulties posed by these accounts are still limited. A considerable share of companies still lacks a definitive set of possible usages. It is likely that long-term working time accounts have emerged in these companies more as a response to longer phases of high labour demand and 'overflowing' (annual) working time accounts than on the basis of strategic considerations. Consequently, basic firm characteristics (such as size, sector, or presence of works or staff councils) do not account for much of the given variation in the distribution of long-term working time accounts.

The wider distribution of long-term working time accounts among large firms (250 and more employees) indicates at the same time that the instrument is becoming a typical new element within the broad set of highly sophisticated, formalised working time systems in large-sized firms. Variations in flexibility demands or differences in human resource management or workforce composition are of additional but minor importance. The existence of works or staff councils in large companies is an important factor of influence. Works or staff councils are usually interested in measures that regulate and compensate hours of overtime; moreover, their active involvement facilitates the introduction and acceptance of long-term working time accounts in the company.

Second, there is evidence for a strong tendency to use long-term working time accounts for early or progressive retirement. At the same time a large share of companies reports to use working time accounts as a measure to 'bridge' phases of underemployment due to weak market demand. Large companies predominantly use long-term working time accounts for early or progressive retirement, followed by options for vocational training; they can easily combine these options with existing retirement and training schemes and also have the necessary financial and personnel resources to handle large amounts of time savings over prolonged periods. This policy is at least supported (when not actually actively promoted) by works or staff councils, which are present in almost all large companies and usually have a strong interest in establishing 'closed' regulations that meet employer and employee interests and avoid problems of individual negotiation or replacement.

From a long-term and life course perspective the utilisation of long-term working time accounts for early retirement or flexibility demands runs the risk to counteract political goals aiming at working time adjustments *over* the life course, the reconciliation of work and family life, lifelong learning, active aging, and higher labor market participation of women and older workers (European Commission, 2005; see for Germany Rürup and Gruescu, 2005; BMFSFJ, 2006). It contradicts the idea of extended employment with working hours appropriate to the employee's life phase, supports an individualised form of financing early retirement and implies a shift of risks and costs from the state and firm level to the employee level.

Third, we find characteristic differences based on company size. In contrast to large companies, the distribution of long-term working time accounts among smaller companies is prone to a large set of factors that range from the economic setting through the type of human resource management to the workforce composition. The possible uses for working time accounts offered by the company also differ strongly in relation to company size. While large companies predominantly use long-term working time accounts for early or progressive retirement, small- and medium-sized companies (10–249 employees) more often offer family-oriented working time options, particularly when they do not have a works or staff council. This might be due to the higher interdependency and more informal nature of working time arrangements and time negotiations found in smaller firms, the fact that the latter offer less alternative work–life balance measures than larger companies, and the fact that they also have fewer resources for administering the huge amounts of time savings that are required for early retirement options.

Fourth, the usage of the accounts in companies is influenced by gender differences in the workforce composition. Long-term working time accounts are more often found in large companies with a high share of male employees. In this respect, there is a fair degree of evidence that long-term working time accounts are an instrument that particularly suits the typical 'male' working time arrangement over the life course in terms of full income, continuous full-time employment (with overtime hours) and early exit. By using long-term working time accounts large firms can increase the scope of flexibility of their (mostly) full-time employed male workforce without changing the remuneration or the type of employment relationship. Large companies with works or staff councils use their long-term working time accounts more frequently for early or progressive retirement when the company has a high share of male employees. A high share of female employees in large-size companies does not lead to usages that would accommodate the interests of female employees (like family leave). Interestingly enough, such options are more often found among small and medium-sized firms, particularly when these do not have a works or staff council. Moreover, and in contrast to large-sized firms, the likelihood to have a long-term working time account increases in small and medium-sized companies when the share of female employees is high. These patterns make small- and medium-sized companies a particularly interesting subject of future research in the field of working time options and life course policies.

The data we have presented only provide information on the distribution of long-term working time accounts among companies and the possible usages offered by them. They neither inform us about the factual use of these options, nor do they provide details of the proportions, groups, motives or objections of employees. These information will be provided by a number of detailed firm-level case studies and employee surveys, which are conducted in our project. The broader range of possible uses brings with it the risk of creating excessive expectations in relation to working time accounts, however. Because of the necessarily limited volume of the accounts, employees must decide between the different designated uses, which in some sense stand in competition with each other. The extension of the range of options so as to now also include company early-retirement and semi-retirement schemes and old-age insurance (through 'lifetime' working time accounts) further exacerbates the competition between different uses. For if an employee wishes to accumulate enough credit to reduce the duration of working life by any substantial amount – three years, for example – he/she will be required to work overtime on a regular basis for a minimum of 20 years. These accumulation needs have led to the tendency to also allow the possibility of depositing income components (in so-called time-value accounts) and to make saving mandatory (for example, within the framework of shift regulations and company insurance agreements). The introduction of monetary savings processes reduces the importance of the mechanism of compensatory time off and the possibilities for reciprocity, while at the same time strengthening the orientation towards financial old-age insurance, savings models and interest terms.

Long-term working time accounts can function as a framework for stabilising and further developing both long-term company personnel policy and employees' individual life planning under conditions of growing discontinuity and increasingly rapid change (Hildebrandt, 2007). The market-oriented strategies of company managements towards increased flexibility are also leading, however, to a tendency to administer withdrawal processes from long-term accounts in accordance with company needs, which is undermining employee confidence in the optionality of the accounts. However, this confidence is an essential prerequisite for the acceptance and the successful functioning of the long-term exchange relationships represented by long-term working time accounts. In order to create reciprocity in the building up and depletion of accounts – not only in a quantitative sense but also as regards the quality of the designated uses – the time requirements of employees must be made explicit in the interpretation and daily use of long-term accounts. In this way a culture of time could develop in which long-term accounts become the backbone of new, flexible life courses (Groot and Breedveld, 2004; Klammer, 2004).

The current increase in social risks and the reduction of welfare-state guarantees and company responsibilities are at odds with the idea of a redistribution of time over the life course and a reorganisation of work–life patterns. A candid discourse about long-term working time accounts – alongside other resource-based measures – could initiate important learning processes on both sides, which could become a building block for a new, concerted life course policy.

NOTES

1. The project is funded by the Hans-Böckler Foundation.
2. Although 90 per cent of all German companies are small companies (less than 20 employees), only 28 per cent of German employees work in companies of this size. The majority of Germany's employees are employed in medium- and large-sized companies.
3. Firms responding that they use time savings on working time accounts (not necessarily long-term working accounts) to 'bridge' phases of underemployment.
4. A value above 1.0 means that the probability of having long-term working time accounts is higher (compared to the reference category); a value below 1.0 indicates a lower probability of having long-term working time accounts (compared to the reference category).
5. Of the 1,710 companies in the sample, 204 reported that they used long-term working time accounts.
6. Companies that reported utilisation of long-term working time accounts for the unspecified category 'other' are excluded from this analysis. This leaves 112 companies that reported utilisation of long-term working time accounts for clearly defined purposes.
7. The number of large companies without a works or staff council was minimal (n = 3) so these were excluded from the analysis.

REFERENCES

Behrens, J. (2004), 'Betriebliche Strategien und demographische Folgen' (Company Strategies and Demographic Consequences), *Arbeit*, **13** 3, 248–63.

Bielenski, H., Bosch, G. and Wagner, A. (2002), *Working Time Preferences in Sixteen European Countries*, Dublin: European Foundation.

Bispinck, R. (2004), 'Kontrollierte Dezentralisierung der Tarifpolitik – Eine schwierige Balance' (Controlled Decentralisation – A Difficult Balance), *WSI-Mitteilungen*, **57** (5), 237–45.

Bundesministerium für Familie, Senioren, Frauen und Jugend (German Ministry for Family Affairs, Senior, Citizens, Women and Youth, BMFSFJ) (2006), *Siebter Familienbericht: Familie zwischen Flexibilität und Verlässlichkeit*, Berlin.

Siebter Familienbericht: Familie zwischen Flexibilität und Verlässlichkeit (7th Family Report: Familiy Between Flexibility And Reliability), Berlin.

Diewald, M., Brose, H.-G. and Goedicke, A. (2005), 'Flexicurity im Lebenslauf. Wechselwirkungen zwischen pluralen Lebensformen und betrieblichen Beschäftigungspolitiken'(Flexicurity over the Life Course. Heterogeneous Life Patterns and Emplyoment Policies of Companies), in Kronauer, M. and Linne, G. (eds), *Flexicurity*, Berlin: edition sigma, pp. 223–48.

Eberling, M., Hielscher, V., Hildebrandt, E. and Jürgens, K. (2004), *Prekäre Balancen. Flexible Arbeitszeiten zwischen betrieblicher Regulierung und individuellen Ansprüchen* (Precarious Balances. Flexible Working Hours Between Company Strategies and Individual Needs), Berlin: edition sigma.

European Commission (2005), *Confronting Demographic Change: A New Solidarity Between the Generations*, 16/03/2005 Com(2005) 94 final, Brussels.

European Foundation for the Improvement of Living and Working Conditions (2003), *A new Organisation of Time over the Life Course*, Luxembourg: Publications Office.

European Foundation for the Improvement of Living and Working Conditions (2005), *Working Time Options over the Life Course: Changing Social Security Structures*, Luxembourg: Publications Office.

Garhammer, M. (2005), 'Neue Konzepte für lebensspezifische Arbeitszeiten' (New Approaches To Lifephasespecific Working Hours), in Seifert, H. (ed.), *Flexible Zeiten in der Arbeitswelt* (Flexible Times in Working Life), Frankfurt/New York: Campus, pp. 67–101.

Gouldner, A.W. (1984), 'Etwas gegen Nichts. Reziprozität und Asymmetrie' (Something Against Nothing. Reciprocity and Asymmetrie), in Adloff, F. and Mau, S. (eds), *Vom Geben und Nehmen. Zur Soziologie der Reziprozität* (About Giving and Taking. Towards a Sociology of Reciprocity), Frankfurt/New York: Campus, pp. 109–24.

Groot, L. and Breedveld, K. (2004), 'Time over the life course: Preferences, options and life course policy', *Tijdschrift voor Arbeidsvraagstukken*, **20** (3), 288–99.

Groß, H. and Schwarz, M. (2007), *Betriebs- und Arbeitszeiten 2005. Ergebnisse einer repräsentativen Betriebsbefragung* (Operating Hours and Working Hours 2005. Results of a Representative Company Survey), Dortmund: sfs Beiträge aus der Forschung.

Haipeter, T. and Lehndorff, S. (2004), *Atmende Betriebe, atemlose Beschäftigte*? (Breathing Companies, Breathless Employees?), Berlin: edition sigma.

Hildebrandt, E. (ed.) (2007), *Lebenslaufpolitik im Betrieb. Optionen zur Gestaltung der Lebensarbeitszeit durch Langzeitkonten* (Life-Course Policy in the Company. Shaping Working-Life Time by Long-Term Working-Time Accounts), Berlin: Edition Sigma.

IQPC (2005), *Betriebliche Zeitwertkonten* (Working-Life Time Accounts in the Company), Berlin: IQPC.

Klammer, U. (2004), 'Flexicurity in a life-course perspective', *Transfer*, **10** (2), 282–99.

Klenner, C. and Pfahl, S. (2005), 'Stabilität und Flexibilität. Ungleichmäßige Arbeitszeitmuster und familiale Arrangements'(Stability and Flexibility. Unregular Working Time Patterns and Family Arrangements), in Seifert, H. (ed.), *Flexible*

Zeiten in der Arbeitswelt (Flexible Times in Working Life), Frankfurt/New York: Campus, pp. 124–68.

Rürup, B. and Gruescu, S. (2005), *Familienorientierte Arbeitszeitmuster – Neue Wege zu Wachstum und Beschäftigung,* Gutachten im Auftrag des Bundesministeriums für Familie, Senioren, Frauen und Jugend ((Family Oriented Working Time Patterns – New Paths to Economic Growth and Employment, Expertise for the German Ministry For Family Affairs, Senior, Citizens, Women, And Youth, BMFSFJ), Berlin.

Seifert, H. (2005a), 'Vom Gleitzeit- zum Langzeitkonto'(From Flexitime to Working-Life Time Accounts), *WSI-Mitteilungen*, **58** (6), 308–13.

Seifert, H. (2005b), 'Arbeitszeitpolitischer Modellwechsel: Von der Normalarbeitszeit zu kontrollierter Flexibilität' (A new paradigm in working-time policies: from standard hours to controlled flexibility), in H. Seifert (ed.), *Flexible Zeiten in der Arbeitswelt* (Flexible Hours in Work Life)*,* Frankfurt/New York: Campus, pp. 40–66.

Struck, O. and Köhler, C. (eds) (2004), *Beschäftigungsstabilität im Wandel*? (Employment Policy in Transition?), Munich and Mering: Rainer Hampp.

Wotschack, P., Siegers, J., Pouwels, B. and Wittek, R. (2007), 'Labour supply: the effects of employer demands and household governance', in Van der Lippe, T. and Peters, P. (ed.), *Competing Claims in Work and Family Life*, Cheltenham, UK and Northampton, MA, USA: Edward Elgar.

PART III

Life Course Transitions and Careers

10. Active Ageing in Europe: Innovating the Management of Transitions from Work to Retirement

Günther Schmid

Life should begin with age and its privileges and accumulations, and end with youth and its capacity to splendidly enjoy such advantages (Mark Twain, 1901).

10.1 INTRODUCTION

The reversion of the life cycle by Mark Twain, unfortunately, is only a dream. But the slogan of 'active ageing' already contains a good deal of that dream. How can the management of transitions from work to retirement contribute towards increasing life quality in Mark Twain's direction? I argue that people's possibility to participate in working life as long as they wish and the opportunity to combine paid work with other self-determined activities are essential elements for a high quality of life. Such a policy would also make a contribution towards coping with the employment and pension crisis, but I consider this more as an important side-effect rather than as the main objective of 'active ageing'. In the tradition of transitional labour market (TLM) theory, I want to set a counter-mark against the exclusive focus on incentives to work, formulated for instance in many documents of the OECD. The TLM perspective aims at increasing the options of transitions from the second to the third life-phase of which gainful employment is only one.[1]

The argument will be developed in four steps: first, I will turn to the conditions and criteria for good 'active ageing' by referring to the concept of TLM and the principles of social risk management; in the second step the huge variation in labour market participation of mature workers in European member states will be demonstrated; followed, third, by checking push and pull factors that possibly explain these differences; and in the fourth and final step some innovative practices for managing transitions from work to retirement will be presented.

10.2 CONDITIONS AND CRITERIA FOR GOOD 'ACTIVE AGEING'

TLM theory (Schmid and Gazier, 2002; Schmid, 2008) suggests classifying social risks according to the critical events that occur during the life course: first, the risk of too small or of eroding income capacity over the life course; second, the risk of income volatility due to fluctuating demand or due to transitions between various employment relationships, especially between part-time and full-time work or between dependent employment and self-employment; third, the risk of limited income capacities due to social obligations, especially care of children and frail elderly; fourth, the risk of a total loss of income due to involuntary unemployment that is of limited but uncertain duration; fifth, the risk of permanently reduced or zero income capacity due to disability, chronic illness or old age. This is all well-known. However, the theory of TLM and social risk management insists on considering these life course risks as partly new risks that require a recalibration of existing institutional arrangements.

First, the distinct logic of these risks requires – according to the principle of 'requisite variety' – a differentiation of existing institutional arrangements. The risk of eroding income capacity due to new technologies, for example, cannot be treated by unemployment insurance in the narrow sense; prevention of risks through improved information systems on future skills, mitigation of risks through multiple or general skills, or coping of risks through continuous education and training, are the proper institutions to manage such risk. Limitations of income capacity due to family obligations, to give another example, cannot be individualised and allocated only to women if society values both children and equal opportunity on the labour market highly. The institutional differentiation of managing life course risks therefore has to grow as the diversity of the labour force and work organisation increases. One important consequence of this principle is the extension of unemployment insurance towards a system of work–life insurance that covers not only income risks due to involuntary unemployment but also volatile income risks due to risky transitions over the life course. Modern work–life insurance would be based on three pillars: an extended unemployment insurance covering also income risks due to job-to-job transitions (mobility); a proactive labour market policy including a rich set of employment services and social rights beyond employment; and various forms of privately or collectively organised supplementary insurances.

Second, social risk management requires making distinction between risks caused by external circumstances ('external risks') and risks caused by people's own choices ('internal risks'). This has important normative implications for risk management (Schmid, 2006). Only the principles of ethical risk-sharing[2] and not the principles of unconditional outcome equality (Rawls, 1990) can establish a fair balance between individual and collective responsibility. Although individuals cannot be held responsible for risks caused by external factors, society nevertheless can demand individual solidarity in preventing, mitigating and coping with these risks in the range of their capabilities. It is, however, society's responsibility to enable and empower people to perform individual solidarity. On the other hand, individuals must be made responsible for risks resulting from their own choices, such as a personal decision of working less, having certain (maybe exotic) preferences or choosing a particular occupation. However, even in such cases, unconditional social solidarity is required if individuals lack the capacity to cope with risks challenging their life or a decent living. The new egalitarian ethic, however, emphasises less the equality of material resources in favour of more equality of capabilities. Since income distribution is largely determined by chance and external circumstance, periodic redistributions of capabilities within and between generations are necessary to re-establish equal opportunities. According to the capability approach, however, redistributive inheritance and progressive income taxes or cash transfers will only be part of the solution; re-establishing earning capacities through proactive labour market policies, corresponding job services and social rights beyond employment will have to play an increasingly important role.

Third, in order to achieve growth in new competitive markets, to enhance the adjustment capacities to an extending degree of international labour division and to combine family life with labour market work, more flexibility is required – both for the demand and the supply side of labour. Thus, social risk management has to provide not only new securities but also flexibility incentives. To achieve flexibility, systems theory suggests loose linkages between (relatively autonomous) subsystems. This principle requires a partial decoupling of social security from specific jobs and its linkage with (flexible) lifetime employment. One important implication from such a life course perspective is to make social transfers after retirement not closely related to the last income but to the whole work–life income. Only such a decoupling allows and even encourages flexible work arrangements during the life course, and especially part-time work at the end of the work career. Another immediate conclusion from this principle is to care for the transportability of social security entitlements in case of job changes from one employer to another, from one sector to another, or from one region to the other.

Fourth, the increased complexity produced by institutional differentiation, risk-sharing and partial decoupling of social security from work requires greater coordination between the various subsystems. Thus checks will have to be carried out to ensure that the interfaces of the various social security subsystems fulfil the principle of institutional complementarity. The decision to work or to retire, for instance, depends much on the comparative incentives of social security institutions. These fragmented institutions act like communicating vessels if reforms are not coordinated. Reducing incentives of unemployment insurance for early retirement might show up in higher take-ups of disability or health insurance. Reducing the escape routes of these institutions altogether might lead to declining conditions of work if not compensated by policies of improving working conditions for the elderly. The coordination of these complexities requires legally authorised and established bargaining institutions like collective agreements by trade unions and employers organisations or even new forms of governance both in the horizontal as well in the vertical dimension of interacting agencies. According to the TLM approach, only negotiation will be able to overcome trade-offs between flexibility and security. Negotiation is the best institutional device solving asymmetries of information and risk perception, adverse selection effects and moral hazard. It is therefore to be expected that 'active ageing' depends heavily on social innovation in terms of organisational learning and new forms of governance.

Before going on to exemplify these conditions and criteria, the actual situation of employment for the elderly in Europe shall be briefly described.

10.3 EMPLOYMENT RATES OF ELDERLY (55–64) IN EUROPE

Looking at simple descriptive statistics, three important observations can be made immediately: first and apart from the United States, only Sweden, Finland and Denmark reached the Lisbon target of 50 per cent employment rate both for men and women in 2005. More important to note is that men have already surpassed the Lisbon benchmark in many countries. Most countries, however, fail with respect to women (Figure 10.1).

Second, great progress has already been made by most member states in increasing the employment rates for men and especially for women since the start of the European Employment Strategy. In this respect, Finland, Hungary and the Netherlands are the best performers; Poland and Greece have not yet contributed much to the Lisbon goal. As impressive as the overall development is, it is still far from meeting the challenges. The European Commission estimates that about 50 per cent of the 15 million net jobs that have to be created to reach the Lisbon goal of 70 per cent by 2010, would have to be filled by people aged 55–64 (Kok et al., 2003). Compared to this ambitious goal, the increase in employment rates of the elderly has still to be speeded up (Figure 10.2).

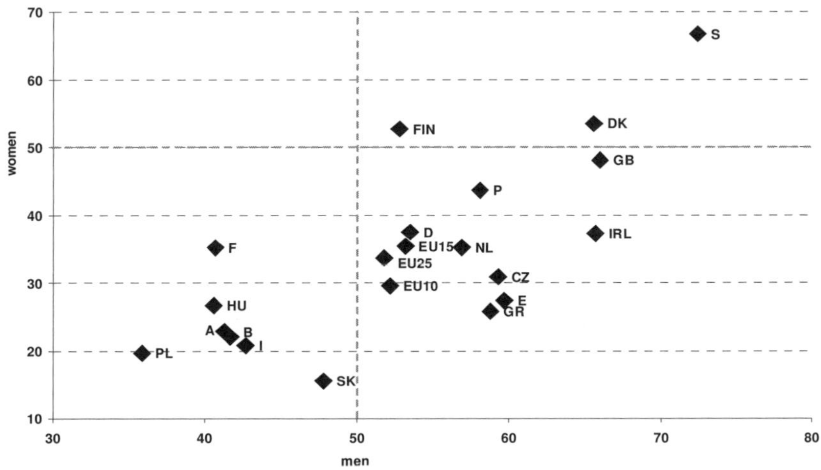

Source: Eurostat; data for EU10 (without Malta and Cyprus) and EU10 member states 1998.

Figure 10.1 Employment rates of men and women aged 55–64, 2005

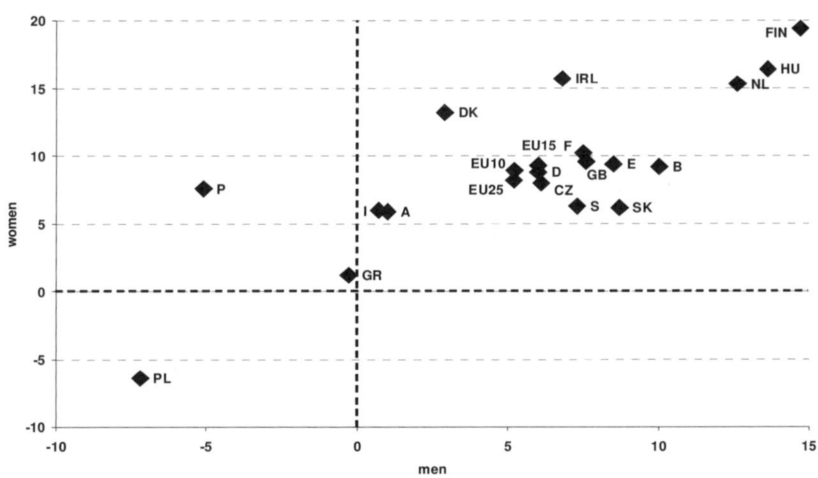

Source: Eurostat; data for EU10 (without Malta and Cyprus) and EU10 member states 1998.

Figure 10.2 Changes in employment rates of men and women aged 55–64, 1997–2005

Third, the fact that the failure of the Lisbon goal relates mainly to low-skilled people provides the first clue as to where more action is needed. All EU member states have already surpassed the Lisbon goal for high-skilled people. About 85 per cent of high-skilled elderly men and women are working in Sweden. In Germany and in the Netherlands, the figure is about 65 per cent. For the low-skilled, however, only Sweden, the United Kingdom and Portugal surpass the Lisbon goal. Even Finland, the model country for 'active ageing', will have to do some homework in order to jump over the Lisbon benchmark of 50 per cent. The education level of the workforce plays a crucial role in raising the employment rate of elderly people. It is especially the low-skilled people who have problems of reaching the envisaged retirement age of 65 (Figure 10.3).

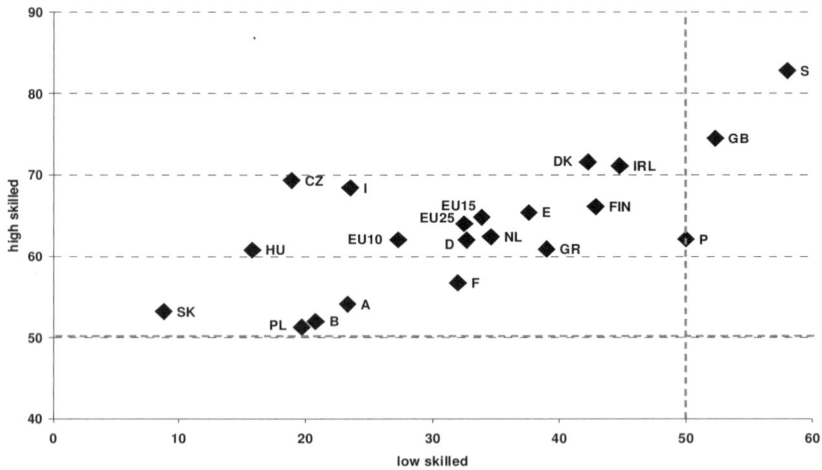

Note: Data for second quarter 2005; high skilled: ISCED 5–6, low-skilled ISCED 0–2.

Source: Eurostat.

Figure 10.3 Employment rates by level of education, workers aged 55–64, 2005

However, education alone is obviously not the solution. The factors determining employment are much more complex. Let us try to check briefly other possible determinants. What pushes mature workers out of the labour market? What pulls them in?

10.4 DETERMINANTS AND EXPLANATIONS OF EMPLOYMENT IN 'OLD AGE'

The first pull factor that comes into mind is labour demand. The higher that demand induced by economic growth, the higher the demand also for elderly people. If one takes into account that spatial mobility declines with age, then labour demand has to be qualified in regional terms. Jobs offered should be within the local reach of elderly people. Furthermore, one has to think of the kind of work that is suited most to elderly people. Hard physical work as in coal mining or manufacturing does not fit with the physical capabilities of many elderly people. Taken all together, it is to be assumed that labour demand in education, health and social work, in other community services or private households will be favourable for the employment of mature workers. This demand factor will have a double pull effect. The availability of such services on the market allows especially women to leave or to stay on the labour market since they can buy such services – by cash or indirectly via taxes – which they otherwise would provide themselves and through unpaid housework. An indicator for the availability of such marketed or publicly provided services is the employment rate of elderly people in education, health and community services, which varies tremendously among EU member states (see Figure A10.1, Appendix).

Education has already been mentioned as a pull factor attracting people to gainful labour market work. The share of people aged 55–64 with tertiary education is probably a valid indicator for the complex causal relationships behind this factor. It is probably a mix of economic incentives, skill requirements and non-pecuniary rewards of work. Economic incentives pulling high-skilled people in employment are of two kinds: first the incentive of wages rising with formal skill levels, second the late entry into the labour market which demands a longer stay in old age in order to fulfil the time requirements of pension entitlements.

Since skills are eroding or getting outmoded by age, they need to be refreshed or replaced regularly over the life course. The participation rate in continuous education and training is therefore another evident factor pulling elderly people in employment. It varies in my sample of 18 EU member states between 43 per cent in Sweden and only 2 per cent in Greece, 4 per cent in Italy, Portugal, Spain and Hungary (see Figure A10.2, Appendix).

Next, the TLM perspective requires both flexibility of work organisation as well as flexibility of social security arrangements to provide options of combining work with retirement. Although a very crude measure, the proportion of elderly people working part-time is probably a good indicator reflecting both sides of the flexibility coin. Currently, the variation of this measure is tremendous in Europe: it ranges from 49 per cent of the elderly working part-time in the Netherlands to only 5 per cent in Greece. As is well-known, the differences between men and women are even greater – 83 per cent of elderly women work part-time in the Netherlands (in contrast to only 12 per cent in Greece) compared to 29 per cent of elderly men (in contrast to only 2.5 per cent in Greece) (see Figure A10.3, Appendix).

Employability is another factor keeping elderly people in employment. The TLM perspective insists here especially on the availability of options for gainful employment outside the regular labour market. Such options have to be provided by proactive labour market policies, either in the form of in-work benefits, or in the form of jobs adjusted to the capabilities of workers or in the form of protected workplaces. A good indicator for such options is the expenditure on active labour market policies other than training or placement measures. This indicator varies in our sample between 2 per cent of GDP in Denmark and 0.02 per cent in the United Kingdom.

The decision for or against retirement depends also on job satisfaction: the more people like their job, the more likely they are to stay on as long as possible. In 2003, the European Foundation for the Improvement of Living and Working Conditions provided for the first time such information for all 25 EU member states according to age groups and gender. On a scale from 1 (not at all satisfied) to 10 (very satisfied), the elderly Danes are with 8.6 the most satisfied compared to the Greeks who at 6.3 were the least satisfied.

In economics, relative wage costs are the central determinant that might push people out of employment: the higher the wages of mature workers compared to younger workers, the higher the probability that they are dismissed or not hired if employers have to downsize their workforce. Of course, implicit contract theory (Lazear, 1990) has found good reasons for the efficiency of seniority wages, which means wages rising from below to above the income capacity (or productivity) of workers. However, there are also good arguments that the preconditions of seniority wage schedules are weakening, since internal labour markets reflecting stable product markets are eroding. Thus, high wages of elderly people in relation to young people have to be considered as a negative push factor.

Finally, taxes can also play a role, pushing mature workers out of the labour market. Romain Duval (2004) calculated the implicit tax rate with which workers are confronted when deciding between work and retirement. The higher the taxes on work income related to transfers in retirement, the lower the probability of remaining in work. Five years prior to regular retirement, a Belgian worker would earn 7 per cent more than expected transfers in retirement, whereas a Swedish colleague has 80 per cent more in the pocket. The impact of this tax wedge between expected work income and transfers is very strong. It functions like an early retirement trap as Duval demonstrated in an econometric study. The size of and changes to this tax wedge explain about one-third of the declining employment rate of the elderly in OECD countries in the 1980s and 1990s.

On the basis of these push and pull factors, I have constructed a summary index by simply aggregating the z-values for each country in our sample, whereby the demand factor and the tax-wedge factor got a double weight. This methodology is of course at a crude stage. However, it can be defended with two arguments: first, the elements of the summary index are chosen on a sound theoretical basis and carefully selected to avoid the problem of multicollinearity; data required for more sophisticated econometric models are not available. The summary index explains about two-thirds of the variation in employment rates (Figure 10.4). Subdivided by gender – not shown here – the model explains even more for women.

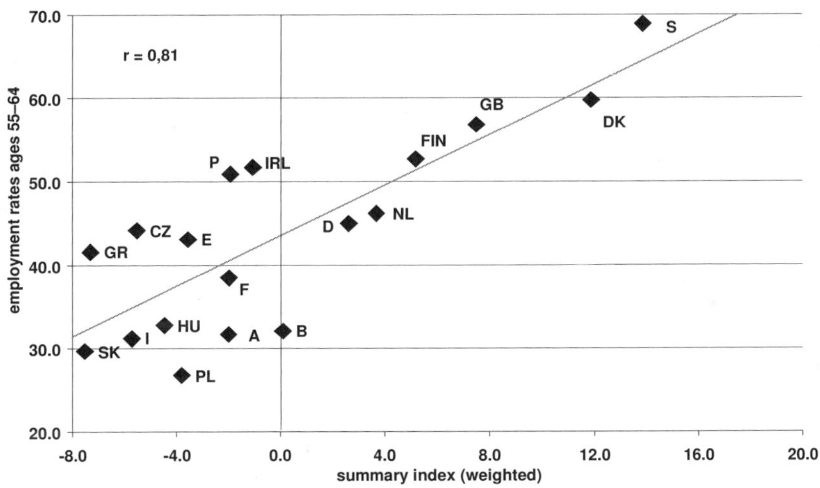

Source: Eurostat, OECD, own calculations.

Figure 10.4 Summary index of push and pull factors and employment rates of workers aged 55 to 64 in Europe, 2005

10.5 INNOVATIVE MANAGEMENT OF TRANSITIONS FROM WORK TO RETIREMENT

The determinants explaining much of the differences in elderly employment rates can now be reversed in policy strategies. These strategies can be grouped according to the four principles formulated at the beginning: first, the necessity to differentiate institutions according to the principle of requisite variety, especially the transformation of unemployment insurance into a work–life insurance; second, the normative principle of risk-sharing through a responsibility and capability based egalitarianism; third the principle of decoupling social security from discontinuities over the life course; and fourth the principle of negotiation to overcome trade-offs between flexibility and security.

10.5.1 Moving towards a Work–Life Insurance System

Given the level of technology, employment opportunities are first of all a function of demand through economic growth. We have seen that regionally located public or private services are especially favourable to the employment security of elderly people. Although of high importance, I address demand management for age-relevant services in only one aspect.[3] Social insurance theories allocate to the state the role as an insurer of the last resort (Atkinson, 1991; Sinn, 1995). As far as this role is concerned, the state either has to support the proper institutional framework for marketed services that render these services affordable, not only to the rich but also to the poor households, and/or – depending on citizens' preferences – to create itself corresponding jobs as an employer of the last resort. It is widely known that the Scandinavian countries incorporate this function to a large extent in terms of publicly financed and publicly provided jobs in social services. It is, however, less well-known that the most recent 'job miracle' of the liberal welfare regime in the UK has been largely founded on the expansion of public service jobs.[4]

We have further seen that wage costs can be a serious impediment to sustainable employment for mature workers. In principle, the gap between productivity and wages can be narrowed in two ways: first by increasing the productivity, second by decreasing the wages or by a combination of both. An extended unemployment insurance that also covered income risks related to job-to-job transitions would contribute to increased acceptance of mobility, even if this leads to lower wages, and would thereby contribute to the employment security of elderly people. The question is: why should we only insure total wage loss due to involuntary unemployment and not also partial wage loss due to mobility required, either for lack of income capacity or for structural change? Before we turn to more general principles of such insurance, we should briefly refer to one clearly successful example: the wage insurance scheme in Switzerland.

The Swiss 'Zwischenverdienst' is an intermediary in-work benefit which works as follows: if a job is accepted that pays less than a person's unemployment compensation, the unemployment insurance fund pays an intermediary benefit to compensate for the loss of income. Let us assume, for example, that the wage before unemployment was €4,000. The Swiss – in fact generous – unemployment benefit would amount to €3,200, 80 per cent of the former wage. Let us further assume that the market offers a suitable job for €2,400, €800 less than the unemployment benefit. The Swiss unemployment insurance system would compensate 80 per cent of the €1,600 difference between the former wage and the new wage. The worker would have an intermediary wage of €2,400 plus €1,280, together €3,680.

The entitlement to this intermediary benefit is limited to the first 12 months of the new job. For insured persons supporting children and insured persons over 45 years old, the maximum entitlement period is two years. Security is further enhanced by the fact that employment with intermediary benefit is counted as the qualifying period to renew unemployment benefit entitlement. A rigorous evaluation study gave this scheme the highest efficiency score of Swiss labour market policies (Lechner et al., 2004).

In 2003, Germany introduced a comparable scheme. However, it was less successful for various reasons which we will leave aside for the moment. If we take a closer look at the development of unemployment insurance in various countries, we find some functional equivalents to the principle of wage insurance. Sweden, Finland and the Netherlands pay partial unemployment benefits if the unemployed take up involuntary part-time jobs. Working tax credits, as applied for instance in the British 'New Deal 50 plus', or in-work benefits ('Eingliederungszuschüsse'), as applied in Germany, also endorse the decision of the elderly to take up new jobs.

Denmark and Austria practice lay-off schemes in which many unemployed return to the same employer. This allows employers to adjust to fluctuating demand by maintaining the trained workforce. Although we need empirical confirmation, we can assume that especially mature workers of small and medium-sized employers profit from this implicit mobility insurance. Transition agencies, for instance the Austrian work foundations, would be another example: they provide intermediary employment for displaced workers until they have found a new job through extensive counselling and placement services. We find in Germany too, and probably in almost all other EU member states, more and more good practices of such transition or transfer agencies.[5]

Austria has gone further by establishing a true mobility insurance in 2003. According to the changed severance pay law ('Abfertigungsrecht'), in case of dismissal, each employee receives a severance pay. He or she can also put the severance pay entitlement into a savings account, even if he or she has only a brief employment record or leaves the position of his/her own free will. The former system required a minimum contribution period of three years, excluding thereby the majority of flexibility enhancing workers with low average employment spells. It also trapped (especially small-scale) employers who accumulated substantial liabilities in the form of severance entitlements of their employees with long service periods. The size of severance pay rises continuously and reaches the maximum value of 12 monthly wages after 37 years.[6] The new 'separation account' model achieves the underlying goal of income maintenance (or rather 'net wealth' maintenance) by making sure that employees can make claims on their account when facing separation. In particular, the working poor (making less than €12,000 a year), who are typically employed for less than three years by one employer, are now included in the separation account system. Even if they work just a few hours a week or a few days a month, they accumulate entitlements. Financing comes from employers' contributions of 1.53 per cent of the gross salary. Payment of severance is excluded as long as contributions do not exceed three years, in case of quitting or dismissal for personal failure. However, even in these cases, the entitlement remains on the account until it comes to a legitimate claim of payment. The employees can then decide whether they want to receive a cash payment or to authorise an additional premium to their pension fund. Upon retirement, employees can claim a cash payment (taxable at 6 per cent) or convert their entitlements into a tax free annuity (Hofer, 2006; Synthesis, 2006).

In generalising the principle of mobility insurance, it is quite obvious that adverse selection and moral hazard problems loom here as large as in any insurance. The entitlement to such insurance, therefore, probably has to be restricted to external risks. One example would be structural change due to globalisation, for instance trade adjustment. The United States are a prime example having introduced wage insurance related to this risk. Another example would be loss of earnings capacity, for instance due to the attrition of work-ability. It is obvious that in particular mature adult workers need such insurance, since they face large income losses in case of unemployment and subsequent re-employment. This need is also nourished by the fact that internal labour markets that previously provided implicit wage insurance are eroding. Mature workers might also have difficulties in coping with demanding jobs in terms of responsibility and overly long working hours. Furthermore, the escape to early retirement as an income insurance device is no longer an option.

Mobility insurance would thus increase the willingness to accept lower paid jobs. Apart from social networking, many employers – even for low paid jobs – provide training on the job. As we know from many evaluation studies, on-the-job training is often more effective than training off the job, where reemployment prospects are uncertain. Depending on the situation and on individual need, mobility insurance could – or even should – be complemented with training vouchers to make the new jobs sustainable or to improve the chances of climbing up the career ladder again. So, as with unemployment insurance, mobility insurance works best combined with active labour market policy.

Mobility insurance would also reduce workers' opposition to trade liberalisation which is, according to surveys, high in cases of no assistance. The highly contested freedom of services in Europe might become more accepted, if such insurance could be institutionalised or at least coordinated and supported at the European level. The likely costs are probably a tiny fraction of the benefits from freer trade within the EU member states as well as with the rest of the world. Mobility insurance could be a new equitable and efficient redistribution device to balance the lot between the winners and losers of innovation and globalisation. Mobility insurance might therefore have a big potential in the future European Employment Strategy for balancing flexibility and security. It could even become one of the first transnational instruments of an active European labour market policy.

10.5.2 Enhancing Individual Responsibility and Capabilities

Enhancing individual responsibility and capabilities first of all requires the establishment of new social rights that go beyond employment. As forcefully presented by Alain Supiot and others, these social rights are new in content, scope and nature (Supiot, 2001). They are new in content insofar as they cover subjects unfamiliar to industrial wage-earners: rights to education and training, rights to appropriate working hours, rights to a family life and to care for dependent family members if they get ill, and rights to further training and retraining or vocational rehabilitation, if the old occupation can no longer be fulfilled. Their scope is also new, since they would not just cover 'regular' wage-earners but also the self-employed, the semi-self-employed and people on fixed-term and temporary contracts. They are new in nature because they often take the form of vouchers or social drawing rights, which allow workers to rely on solidarity within defined and perhaps collectively bargained limits when exercising their new freedoms.

These new securities can no longer be seen as being given in exchange for subordination (as in the old employment contract), but as the foundations of a new freedom to act. They can be considered as active social securities that go hand-in-hand with worker's initiatives to shoulder the risks of flexible employment relationships instead of restricting them. In the following, some examples of these new rights relevant especially for mature workers shall be given.

First, transforming entitlements to passive benefits into social drawing rights with a wider spectrum: in most EU member states, the concept of active labour market policy has already extended the insurance principle to those unemployed who need education or training in order to find a new job.

Proactive labour market policy would go further. It would generalise the right to use entitlements to unemployment benefits under certain conditions as training vouchers or in-work benefits. The right to in-work benefits would enhance the capabilities especially for low-skilled elderly workers. Evaluation research has repeatedly shown that learning on a matched job in a firm is much more efficient than formal training outside the firm for this target group. From a TLM perspective, it would therefore make more sense to endow elderly employees with vouchers to be used for various employability measures, instead of extending the duration of unemployment benefits for this group as currently being debated in Germany. In practice, active labour market policy in Denmark and Sweden has evolved in this direction.

Second, the entitlement to financially compensated care leave: this right is increasingly important for the so-called sandwich generation, which has not only to care for its children, but to an increasing extent also for frail parents or even grandparents. The right to care leave is particularly well developed in Sweden. Here, workers have the right to take paid care leave of up to 60 days per year.

Third, the entitlement to career breaks: Belgium is the pioneer in enhancing individual responsibility and capabilities by offering the option of a career break. According to a recent national agreement, the Belgian state subsidises not only savings accounts for a career break, but furthermore entitles employees to have career interviews. Having reached the age of 40 years, employees automatically qualify for biennial career interviews within their companies, and the right to an interview with an external consultant every five years about the direction of their career. From the age of 55, employees also have the right to reduce their working time to four-fifths of their previous working hours and to receive unemployment benefits to cover the time they do not work.[7]

Fourth, periodic redistribution of life cycle chances: the active welfare state should use its redistributive capacity of taxation to ensure a second or third chance for those who were unlucky in the education and training market as young people. Such intergenerational risk-sharing could take the form of financing periodically targeted programmes for lifting the overall level of competence of the disadvantaged. An instructive example is the Swedish 'Knowledge Lift' (kunshaftsliftet) programme. From 1997 to 2002, it spent an annual sum of about €350 million on upgrading the competence of the low-skilled, independent of their status as employed or unemployed. The programme in part explans why Sweden has the highest participation rate of elderly people in continuous education and training. Applied to Germany, this would amount to a yearly investment of about €3.5 billion and 900,000 additional participants in continuing education and training.

Fifth, and this might sound provocative, the entitlement to non-work: as we know from many surveys on work attitudes, the transition from work to retirement is not only determined by push and pull factors but also by jump factors. Jump factors relate to preferences of active leisure, which means self-determined activities that focus on self-realisation in an active 'third age' outside – but not necessarily unrelated to – gainful labour market work. The consequence of taking this factor seriously into any active ageing strategy is to endorse the freedom of choice between work and leisure especially for mature workers. Activation strategies forcing elderly people into the labour market by workfare measures are not compatible with the TLM concept. It is often deplored that especially in Denmark, Sweden and the Netherlands the activation strategies for the elderly are not really enforced. This is, for instance, reflected in the fact that the more inactive elderly in these countries are living on transfers without being counted as unemployed, as is the case in Germany. The recent German labour market reforms have pushed elderly people back into the labour market without sufficient employment opportunities, resulting in excessive unemployment figures compared to most other European countries.[8] Keeping a balance between overly costly early retirement options and workfare-kind activation measures is of course a delicate task. Our impression is, however, that Germany has gone too far in the workfare direction, whereas the 'flexicurity'[9] model countries do more justice to the jump-option, but might still have to do some homework in terms of widening employment opportunities.

10.5.3 Decoupling Social Security Entitlements from Contingencies of the Life Course

The implicit tax rate related to transitions between work and retirement gives us a clue on how gradual – instead of abrupt – retirement could be fostered. Apart from flexible work organisation, which would allow flexible working hours according to individual preferences or capabilities, social security arrangements play an important role in deciding for a combination of gainful employment with unpaid activities. Four strategies contribute to such an 'active ageing': first of all, diminishing or mitigating the causes of the discontinuity of work–life careers (risk prevention); second, reversing the incentive structure of the present tax wedge in favour of employment; third, providing options to combine transfer income with labour market income; fourth, rewarding instead of punishing wanted or unavoidable discontinuities in the work–life career.

With regards to the first strategy, the most plausible option – especially aimed at the low labour force participation of women aged 50 and over – is to 'de-familialise' care obligations for the elderly and frail, as the Scandinavian model suggests. Survey research shows that in Scandinavia, virtually no women need to curtail their career in order to care for kin, whereas for example in the Netherlands, the burden of care approaches the equivalent of a part-time job, and a full-time commitment in Spain. Denmark spends about 3 per cent of its GDP on full financial coverage of caring for the elderly and frail via home help or nursing homes. The Danish model prioritises home help and seeks to minimise the use of residential care because the elderly prefer the former, and because it is far more cost-effective. Even with daily visits, per client cost of home help is less than a third of a place in a residential home. The model seems to be largely self-financing, since exiting the labour force implies major foregone lifetime income and probably inferior pension entitlements, and to society it implies foregone tax revenue (Esping-Andersen, 2006). With increasing educational levels, especially among women, the opportunity costs of exiting the labour market will drastically increase.

The second strategy is to reverse the incentive structure of the present tax wedge in favour of employment suitable for mature workers. Such employment might imply lower wages or reduced working time. Pension entitlements, however, are disproportionately reduced if the method of calculation is heavily biased towards the final wage or salary. This disincentive can be easily removed by changing the basis of calculation, for instance by taking average earnings over the life course or by partially offsetting losses of income incurred during spells of part-time work. Most countries have moved already in this direction.

Some countries have turned this idea into a positive incentive measure, stimulating employment beyond the statutory retirement age. To give some examples: in Estonia, one year of employment beyond the qualifying age increases the pension by 11 per cent, in Hungary and in the Czech Republic by 6 per cent. Spain, France and Greece now provide financial incentives for remaining in employment over the age of 60. Finland applies experience-rating to both disability and unemployment pensions in companies with more than 50 employees. This implies that the employer pays the cost of the benefit stream that is received by those employees who retire from that company. Such an adaptation of social security contributions provides incentives for employers to invest in the work environment, for example measures to improve health and safety at work. It also renders lay-offs of older workers more costly through raising social security costs for remaining employees.

The third strategy is to provide options for combining transfers with labour market income. Such options can take various forms. First priority, here, is to avoid transfer traps by providing incentives to come back to work if work-ability has recovered, for instance through rehabilitation or improved health conditions. The willingness to return to work, however, will diminish if people are in danger of losing their transfer entitlements, should the new job turn out not to be suitable. In the UK and Sweden, new work incentive schemes ensure the option of returning quickly to disability pensions; these schemes also enhance part-time employment by ensuring independent partial benefit rights. The Netherlands and Sweden, as well as Denmark, also provide a good deal of employment opportunities in the form of protected jobs.

A further example of good practice is the so-called 'flexjobs' in Denmark. The target group consists of persons with a permanently reduced work-ability and who are not entitled to pre-pensions. The employer receives a wage subsidy amounting to one-third, one-half or two-thirds of the minimum wage depending on the extent to which the work-ability of the person is reduced. The person in a 'flexjob' receives a wage according to the collective agreement. The number of people in such jobs rocketed recently to a level of 40,000, which would correspond in Germany to a level of 600,000 or 1.5 per cent of the active labour force. There is, however, rising critical concern regarding the substitution of regular jobs and the lack of some general labour market rights for 'flex-jobbers', for instance the exclusion of 'flex-jobbers' from regular unemployment insurance. Such critics hint at a general problem of trading off flexibility and security – something we will come back to in the last section (Rosdahl, 2002).

The fourth strategy of decoupling social security entitlements from contingencies of the life cycle is to make transitions pay. Most European pension schemes make little – if any – provision for the risks associated with discontinuous work histories. Positive incentives to encourage people to assume greater responsibility for such risks, thereby enhancing overall labour market flexibility, are rare. One important impediment to flexible retirement, however, is the lack of coordination between old age insurance and flexible work histories.

One innovative way of building flexibility into the social protection system for the elderly would be to institutionalise flexible entitlements as a self-regulatory device. The basic idea is to link each entitlement based on real contributions from gross earnings with a virtual entitlement that reflects the risk of fluctuating income streams (usually) associated with career breaks. These flexible entitlements would be activated in the event of a risk actually occurring. If a person has a reduced income – for example by taking parental leave, an unpaid sabbatical or an enforced change of occupation with a lower starting salary – the flexible entitlement account could be used to top up the gap between former contributions and reduced contributions. If no such risk occurs during an individual's lifetime – in other words: if he or she remains in a standard employment relationship throughout the life course – then that person will have redistributed some of the gains from such an untroubled career to those less fortunate, who have had to face such risks, whether deliberately or involuntarily.[10] Accumulated flexible entitlements could also be used to compensate for loss of earnings during gradual retirement.

A similar provision aiming at partially offsetting losses of income exists in Belgium. After a qualifying period (15 years), pension entitlements for people with low earnings and/or in part-time work are inflated up to a level of around 45 per cent of average earnings. Another example is Spain where – under certain conditions – a multiplier coefficient of 1.5 for social security contributions of part-timers has been introduced to balance the minimum duration requirements. Extending such arrangements from part-time work to other periods of limited earning capacities, such as caring periods, would be a further innovation to manage old-age risks. A radical application of making transitions pay would even include the transition to unpaid care, if society acknowledges such care as real work. In other words: unpaid care could be treated as virtual employment that carries a social security entitlement, as if the work had been provided on the 'regular' labour market. The German care insurance has recently introduced such an option.[11]

Finally, the Dutch life course scheme introduced in 2006 is – at least in principle – a good practice example for making transitions pay. This regulation goes beyond a precursory collective agreement that existed from 2001 to 2005 and allowed workers to save up to 12 per cent of their earnings tax-free. The workers could then use these accounts to finance unpaid leave, parental leave or further education, but not early retirement. The maximum amount of time off permitted was 2.1 years at 70 per cent of the last drawn wage. Under the new regulation, 12 per cent of gross wages can be saved and the maximum time off has been increased to three years, still at 70 per cent wage replacement. The lifetime working hours account can now also be used to supplement income in the event of early retirement (Wotschack, 2006).

However, from a normative point of view, some criticism regarding the present conception of the Dutch life course scheme must be expressed. First, such purely income-based tax incentives favour high incomes. Second, workers will now presumably use these accounts less often to lighten their workload or to pursue further education during compressed phases of working life. They will rather tend to use the saved-up time simply as a means of early retirement. This incentive structure works against the goals of 'active ageing'. A solution might be to apply special tax regulations to periods of long-term further education or unpaid child-rearing or care-giving, even going so far as to apply the concept of 'negative income tax' to such flexibility accounts. This would mean that in life phases, in which income is low and often no tax is paid, the savings efforts could be supported by tax credits.

Apart from these critics, the Dutch life course scheme is also attractive in another respect. It is a good example of multilevel governance that can be generalised as an innovative strategy for managing transitions. It is basically a two-phase approach starting with universal rules for labour market exit, whose implementation is negotiated by legally binding collective agreements. The details of implementation, however, are then negotiated at sectoral or company level to ensure that prevailing local conditions are met and that compromises between conflicting interests are found. This leads us to the fourth strategy.

10.5.4 Managing Transitions through Negotiated Flexibility and Security

Ideally, flexibility and security are complementary, leading to a virtuous circle. As in the Danish flexicurity model, external flexibility complemented by active labour market policy and buffered by generous unemployment benefits can lead to more job opportunities and thereby higher employment security (Madsen, 2006). In the Dutch flexicurity model, high job security, complemented by high internal flexibility and buffered by basic income security, can lead to higher employment through work and income sharing. However, there is also a worst case scenario where flexibility and security are complementary, thus leading to a vicious circle. For instance, a chronic lack of skilled workers lowers external flexibility as well as employment security due to a lack of competitiveness.

In practice, however, the flexibility–security nexus is probably dominated by trade-offs. Flexibility is often at the expense of security, and vice versa, security is often at the expense of flexibility. In both cases, the conflicting interests can be solved through negotiation, in which information asymmetries are reduced and potential win–win solutions tapped by compromises. It is our contention that the Dutch and Danish models of flexicurity cannot be understood without acknowledging their endowment with successful institutions of negotiated flexibility or negotiated security. Good examples of negotiated flexibility and security, however, can also be found in other countries. Among good practices, three general strategies can be distinguished: first, national compacts focusing on information gathering and coordinating activities; second, public–private partnerships; and third, local or regional task forces. For each of these strategies, the general logic will be developed and good practice illustrated by one or two examples.

National compacts are a kind of negotiated public deliberation based on three steps: first, agenda setting understood as normative and cognitive reframing; second, hammering out a programme by including all relevant actors and stimulating corresponding focused research; and third, coordinating disparate activities at various levels according to a compact eventually agreed upon by all relevant actors. The outstanding example for this strategy is the Finnish 'National Programme for Ageing Workers' (FINPAW). Under this five-year plan, Finland has impressively moved from a laggard to one of the leaders in implementing successful policies managing transitions from work to retirement. The plan followed the principle of moving away from standard patterns of retirement age and taking a life course approach based on three pillars: lifelong learning, occupational health and safety and incentives for flexible retirement. The reform introduced a flexible retirement age between 62 and 68, with a sharp rise in the accrual rate after 62. Entitlements are based on lifetime earnings instead of formerly basing them on the last ten years of employment. A follow-up compact, the 'VETO Programme 2003–2007', especially promotes the earning capacities of the elderly through training and workplace adjustment based on monitoring the results of earlier activities.

Public–private partnerships – other terms are alliances or covenants – are especially well developed in the Netherlands.[12] Partnerships are written agreements between two or more parties or partners and signed by each of them with the understanding that they are committed to cooperation for an overarching common goal. In many cases, the state is involved as an initiating and co-signing partner. Unlike private or public contracts, public–private partnerships are voluntary and require no legal framework. Partners thus retain an exit option if the risk-taking appears excessive. On the other hand, the agreements also contain voice options regulating procedures to solve problems step by step as they arise. Because the balance of costs and benefits for the partners involved might change at each step, there must be trust that corrective measures are taken in pursuit of the common goal. Such 'induced decision-making' through learning-by-doing, muddling through step by step, and learning-by-monitoring are the essence of compacts to establish such trust relationships.[13] Partnerships can be characterised as a combination of framework agreements plus ongoing negotiation about the terms of agreement as concrete problems in implementation arise. They are a kind of soft law, overcoming state failure in regulating flexibly complex issues, and they close the gaps of inadequate laws that are either not followed properly or even circumvented.

There are reportedly several hundred partnerships in the Netherlands. They pertain to environmental issues, energy-saving, educational matters, health care, traffic and transport, housing, and especially to working conditions for the elderly. There can be chains of partnerships: for instance, the Dutch Foundation of Labour came to an agreement recommending to the collective bargaining parties and the firms the implementation of activating arrangements for older workers. In 2003, bargaining on 'age aware personnel policies' was an issue in 30–40 per cent of the negotiations in the sectors and firms. According to a survey, 40–65 per cent of the companies implemented flexible pre-pensions, additional periods of leave and holidays and flexible working hours in human resource policies. The government stepped in by a policy of sticks and carrots: the obligation of workers over the age of 57 receiving unemployment benefits to look for work was reintroduced and the incentives of early retirement were more quickly abolished than in most other EU member states; in exchange, the government introduced tax subsidised life course saving arrangements and occasionally co-finances active ageing measures at local or company level (Tros, 2005, p. 304).

Local or regional task forces composed of various actors determined to proceed with a common goal are a third form of negotiated flexibility and security. Such task forces can be a result or element of the two former strategies – national compacts or public–private partnerships. The Danes again deliver good examples for such task forces.[14] They are the outcome of a national campaign on social responsibility of enterprises begun in 1994 and including a huge corresponding research programme some years later. The so-called 'Enterprise Pools' are networks of public or private enterprises which can apply for financial support for projects promoting social responsibility of enterprises; elderly people are prominent target groups of such projects. Another institution is the 'Local Coordinating Committees' established in 1999. All Danish municipalities are obliged to set up such committees alone or together with other municipalities. The aim of the committees is to negotiate agreements between various actors at local level to promote employment possibilities for citizens in danger of exclusion from the labour market and citizens having special difficulties in obtaining employment under normal conditions. A national 'Council Responsible for Social Initiatives on the Inclusive Labour Market' coordinates and monitors these activities. The government steps in by 'social clauses' which favour suppliers with good social records in their tender policy.[15]

10.6 CONCLUSIONS

The possibility of working in the later phase of the life course is a central determinant to the quality of life. However, this only holds true as long as individual freedom in employment decision, good working conditions and possibilities for combining paid with unpaid work are ensured. Considering active ageing only under the viewpoint of restoring the pension funds and international competitiveness is not sufficient. We thus developed normative criteria for active ageing from the TLM perspective and examined innovative practices in this light. Four generalised conclusions can be drawn.

The first conclusion is that innovative management of transitions from work to retirement must not be sought mainly in the characteristics of the older workers, for example in their alleged or possible declining productivity. The most important condition of employment opportunities for elderly people is the pace of employment growth in the service sector. A policy that begins here contributes to resolving several inter-related problems: it does justice to the increasingly limited mobility associated with ageing, it creates the kind of economic and social infrastructure that allows young adults with children to reconcile their family life with their work, and in particular it allows mature women to participate more extensively and for longer periods in working life than to date.

The second conclusion is that 'active ageing' must not only start with elderly people but much earlier on in the life cycle. New life cycle risks require new social rights beyond employment – such as care leave and career breaks, and even the right not to work in the transition from the second to the third life phase. The new right beyond employment concerns in particular sustainable employability. This means that qualifications and skills required for gainful work have to be enhanced over the entire life course. Elderly workers must be motivated to participate in further education more than ever before. However, it has also become clear that the level of continuous education and training is related more closely to the base level of education than to age. Active ageing, therefore, starts with education in the 'Kindergarten'. Choosing the right timing in lifelong learning is also important. Further education opportunities have to be offered already in the middle phase of the life cycle, when the horizon of expectation of the fruits of investment is still long enough to motivate both the enterprise and the employee. There is also a lack of practicable financing instruments that guarantee fairly distributed risk-sharing. In particular, the problem of the time incongruence has to be solved. Low-income people need credits for investment, and innovative management tools have to be found to bridge the gap between the moment when education costs have to be paid out and the period where the benefits are finally reaped.

The third conclusion is that early intervention is also necessary in view of long-term interruptions of employment. Such discontinuities still affect mainly women and translate into long-term wage penalties, higher probabilities of sustained precarious employment careers and in low labour force participation in advanced adulthood. Labour market policy for active ageing is therefore also to be understood as a policy that reinforces ties to the labour market in critical phases of the life course. On the other hand, every necessary or desired deviation from standard employment still implies an insufficiently insured risk with respect to continuous income flows, occupational careers and social security in old age. This acts as a massive deterrent to established employees, who contemplate making risky transitions, for instance the transition from full-time to part-time work, from dependent to self-employment, from higher to lower paid jobs or from one occupation to another. In order to be considered worth the risk, such transitions must pay off (Gazier, 2002). This contribution therefore suggested supplementing unemployment insurance by work–life insurance, and demonstrated elements of such an insurance, for example wage insurance, mobility insurance, lifetime working time accounts or in-work benefits.

The fourth conclusion states that it is not enough to manipulate single parameters, for example, by reducing labour costs for older workers through wage–cost subsidies. It is also not enough to turn only the regulatory steering wheel in what is considered to be the right direction, for instance, by relaxing dismissal protection or increasing statutory retirement age. The review of good practices in Europe indicates clearly that those countries which have been most successful to date, have followed integrated approaches, coordinating different areas as well as different levels of policy. Integrated approaches allow package deals in reform policies to arrive at workable compromises, reliable compensation of losers and finally a win–win situation for all. In hammering out such compromises, we detected new and soft forms of negotiated flexibility and security. Especially national compacts, public–private partnerships and task forces at the company, regional or sectoral level are innovative forms of governance to manage transitions from work to retirement.

As an overall conclusion, the application of these four strategies would debunk two myths: the myth that mature workers take jobs away from younger workers and the myth that productivity declines rapidly with age. A sustainable policy reform must, on the contrary, proceed strategically on the basis of the opposite assumption: the productivity of young and mature adults is mutually complementary. Where the employment of older people has increased, the employment of young people has risen as well;[16] and the edge enjoyed by one group with respect to modern knowledge is complemented by the other group's advantage in the sphere of experience knowledge.

NOTES

1. This contribution is partly based on Hartlapp and Schmid (2007). I am grateful to Miriam Hartlapp for commenting on this version. Many thanks for excellent research assistance go to Jutta Höhne and Simone Modrack, and I am especially grateful for the editorial assistance of Angelika Zierer-Kuhnle and Thomas Crowe. See, among others, OECD (2005a, p. 18).
2. Formulated, for instance, by Ronald Dworkin (2000) and Amartya Sen (2001).
3. For other aspects, see the relevant literature, for example Fagan et al. (2005), OECD (2005b).

4. Using data from the Office of National Statistics, Hicks (2005) demonstrates that between 1998 and 2005, public sector employment rose by 13.2 per cent, while private sector employment increased by 7.2 per cent only.
5. For a helpful discussion of the criteria for good transition agencies and the provision of some examples for Germany (Vivendi, Schering Bergkamen) and Sweden (Trygghetsradet, TRR), see Kirsch and Mühge (2006).
6. In the former system, severance pay entitlements 'jumped' at specific points of employment duration, already reaching the maximum after 25 years.
7. Cf. European Industrial Relations Review, March 2006, pp. 28–9.
8. See Konle-Seidel and Lamg (2006).
9. See Wilthagen and Tros (2004) for an overview of the concept of flexicurity.
10. Such a model has been proposed in Germany by Langelüddeke et al. (1999), and calculated by Thiede (2000).
11. The law now treats unpaid care like formal employment. Depending on the unpaid working time, a person can accumulate pension entitlements between €6.83 and €20.49 per month (West Germany) or €6.00 and €17.99 (East Germany), corresponding to the regular contributions of a wage between €644 and €1,932 (Western Germany) or €541 and €1,624 (Eastern Germany). Example: A daughter who provides care for parents for 15 hours a week, would accumulate pension entitlements that correspond to a wage of €858.67 per month. This example also demonstrates that looking only at the 'marketed' level of employment – that is the employment rate – might underestimate 'non-marketed' but nevertheless prosperity-creating activities.
12. On this point and in the following passages, I rely heavily on the excellent and stimulating paper by Korver and Oeij (2005) who use the term covenant.
13. On the concepts of induced decision-making, learning-by-monitoring and policy learning, see also Hirschman (1967), Sabel (1995), Hemerijck and Visser (2003).
14. The following is based on Bredgaard and Larsen (2005) and Rosdahl (2002).
15. Comparable to the Danish local coordinating committees was the Swedish institution of 'Adjustment Groups'. Swedish enterprises with more than 50 employees had to establish such groups composed by representatives of the management, the workers, medical experts, the municipality, the local public employment agency and the regional agency for rehabilitation. The task of these groups was to find out and to negotiate an agreement on the future employment possibilities for people faced with serious work-ability problems. This institution, unfortunately, has recently been abolished (personal communication by Eskil Wadensjö).
16. The OECD (2006, p. 140) reports a correlation coefficient of 0.62 for the period 1992–2002. In the most recent period, however, the correlation declined to 0.40 (see Figure A10.4 in Appendix). It is not clear why. On the one hand, it may be due to erratic developments in some of the acceding countries or extended schooling of the young adults; on the other hand, it might be that in some countries, the recruitment of young workers has been substituted indeed by keeping or hiring elderly workers.

REFERENCES

Atkinson, A.B. (1991), 'Social Insurance: The Fifteenth Annual Lecture of the Geneva Association', in *The Geneva Papers on Risk and Insurance Theory*, **16** (2), 113–31.

Bredgaard, T. and Larsen, F. (eds) (2005), 'Flexicurity and Older Workers on the Danish Labour Market', in Bredgaard, T. and Larsen, F. (eds), *Employment Policies from Different Angles*, Copenhagen: DJOF Publishing Copenhagen, pp. 311–30.

Duval, R. (2004), *The Retirement Effects of Old-age Pensions and Early Retirement Schemes in OECD Countries*, OECD Economics Department Working Papers No. 370, Paris: OECD.

Dworkin, R. (2000), *Sovereign Virtue. The Theory and Practice of Equality*, Cambridge, MA. and London: Harvard University Press.

Esping-Andersen, G. (2006), 'Putting the Horse in Front of the Cart: Towards a Social Model for Mid-century Europe', in WRR (ed.), *WRR lecture 2005: Towards a New Welfare State*, The Hague: WRR/Scientific Council For Government Policy, pp. 31–69.

Fagan, C., O'Reilly, J. and Halpin, B. (2005), *Job Opportunities for Whom? Labour Market Dynamics and Service Sector Employment Growth in Germany and Britain*, Berlin: WZB-Discussion Paper SP I 2005–111.

Gazier, B. (2002), 'Transitional Labour Markets: From Positive Analysis to Policy Proposals', in Schmid, G. and Gazier, B. (eds), *The Dynamics of Full Employment. Social Integration Through Transitional Labour Markets*, Cheltenham, UK and Northampton, MA, USA: Edward Elgar, pp. 196–232.

Hartlapp, M. und Schmid, G. (2007), 'Arbeitsmarktpolitik für aktives Altern: Zur Zukunftsfähigkeit Deutschlands im Lichte europäischer Erfahrungen', in Kocka, J. (ed.), *Zukunftsfähigkeit Deutschlands. Sozialwissenschaftliche Perspektiven*, WZB-Jahrbuch 2006, Berlin, edition sigma, pp. 157–77.

Hemerijck, A. and Visser, J. (2003), *Policy Learning in European Welfare States*, Amsterdam, Den Haag: mimeo.

Hicks, S. (2005), 'Trends in public sector employment. a summary of trends in public sector employment between 1991 and 2005, in National Statistics feature', *Labour Market Trends*, **113** (12), 477–88.

Hirschman, A.O. (1967), *Development Projects Observed*, Washington, DC: The Brookings Institutions.

Hofer, H. (2006), *Reform of Severance Pay Law in Austria*, Wien: Institute for Advanced Studies (IHS), Discussion Paper 30 Nov/1 Dec.

Kirsch, J. and Mühge, G. (2006), 'Das Prinzip „Einzelfall"', *Mitbestimmung*, **12**, 18–21.

Konle-Seidel, B. and Lang. K. (2006) 'Erwerbsfähige Transferbezieher im internationalen Vergleich: Von der Ausgliederung zur Integration in den Arbeitsmarkt', *Bundesarbeitsblatt*, **10**, 14–22.

Kok, W. et al. (2003), *Jobs, Jobs, Jobs. Creating More Employment in Europe*, Report of the Employment Taskforce Chaired by Wim Kok, Luxembourg: Office for Official Publications of the European Communities, www.europa.eu.int/comm /employment_social/employment_ strategy/task_en.htm.

Korver, T. and Oeij, P.R.A. (2005), 'The soft law of the covenant: making governance instrumental', *European Journal of Industrial Relations*, **11** (3), 367–84.

Langelüddeke, A., Rabe, B. and Thiede, R. (1999), 'Flexible Anwartschaften und Anwartschaftszeiten. Ein Vorschlag zum Ausbau der eigenständigen Frauenaltersicherung und zur Anpassung der Rentenversicherung an den Wandel der Arbeit', *Die Angestelltenversicherung*, **46** (1), 7–13.

Lazear, E. (1990), 'Job Security Provisions and Employment', *Quarterly Journal of Economics*, **105** (3), 699–726.

Lechner, M., Frölich, M. and Steiger, H. (2004), *Mikroökonometrische Evaluation aktiver Arbeitsmarktpolitik*, Abschlussbericht für NFP 43, Projekt-Nr. 4043-058311, Sankt Gallen: Universität St. Gallen.

Madsen, P.K. (2006), 'How Can It Possibly Fly? The Paradox of a Dynamic Labour Market', in Campbell, J.L., Hall, J.A. and Pedersen, O.K. (eds), *National Identity and the Varieties of Capitalism. The Danish Experience*, Montreal and Kingston/London/Ithaca: McGill-Queen's University Press, pp. 321–55.
OECD (2005a), *Education at a Glance*, Paris: OECD.
OECD (2005b), *Enhancing the Performance of the Service Sector*, Paris: OECD.
OECD (2006), *Live Longer, Work Longer*, Paris: OECD Publications.
Rawls, J. (1990), A *Theory of Justice*, Oxford: Oxford University Press.
Rosdahl, A. (2002), *The Policy to Promote Social Responsibility of Enterprises in Denmark*, Working Paper 10: 2002, Socialforskingsinstituttet (The Danish National Institute of Social Research).
Sabel, C.F. (1995), 'Bootstrapping reform: rebuilding firms, the welfare state, and unions', *Politics and Society*, **23** (1), 5–48.
Schmid, G. (2006), 'Social risk management through transitional labour markets', *Socio-Economic Review*, **4** (1), 1–33.
Schmid, G. (2008), *Full Employment in Europe. Managing Transitions and Risks*, Cheltenham, UK and Northampton, MA, USA: Edward Elgar.
Schmid, G. and Gazier, B. (eds) (2002), *The Dynamics of Full Employment. Social Integration Through Transitional Labour Markets*, Cheltenham, UK and Northampton, MA, USA: Edward Elgar.
Sen, A. (2001), *Development as Freedom*, New York: Alfred A. Knopf.
Sinn, H.-W. (1995), 'A theory of the welfare state', *Scandinavian Journal of Economics*, **97** (4), 495–26.
Supiot, A. (2001), *Beyond Employment: Changes in Work and the Future of Labour Law in Europe*, Oxford: Oxford University Press.
Synthesis Forschung (2006), *Frome Severance Pay to the Separation Account. A Labour Economics Point of View on the Austrian Reform Process*, Wien: Synthesis Forschung Gesellschaft.
Thiede, R. (2000), 'Alterssicherung – Modell zur Modernisierung des Rentensystems', *Soziale Sicherheit*, **49** (2), 48–52.
Tros, F. (2005), 'Flexicurity in the Policies for the Older Workers', in Bredgaard, T. and Larsen, F. (eds), *Employment Policies from Different Angles*, Copenhagen: DJOF Publishing Copenhagen, pp. 291–310.
Twain, M. (1901), 'Letter to Edward Dimmitt', 19 July.
Wilthagen, T. and Tros, F. (2004), 'The concept of "flexicurity": a new approach to regulating employment and labour markets', *Transfer*, **10** (2), 166–86.
Wotschack, Philip (2006), *Lebenslaufpolitik in den Niederlanden. Gesetzliche Optionen zum Ansparen längerer Freistellungen*, Discussion Paper, SP I 2006–115, Berlin: Wissenschaftszentrum Berlin für Sozialforschung.

APPENDIX

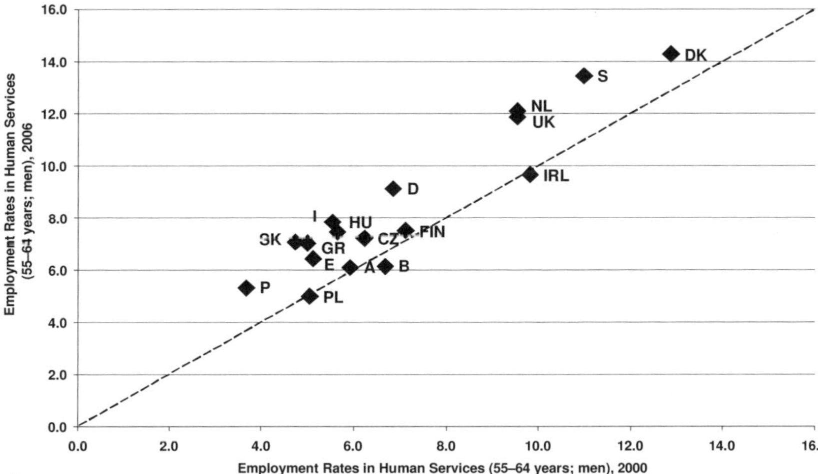

a) men

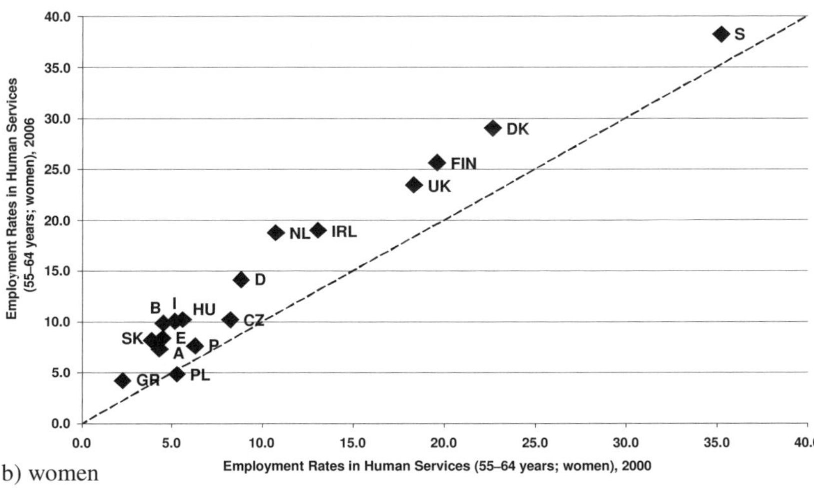

b) women

Notes:
* 'Human Services' include Education; Health and Social Work; Other Community Services; due to lack of data, household-oriented personal services are not included.
Data: Second quarter 2000 and 2006

Source: Eurostat.

Figure A10.1 Employment rates of men and women in Human Services (workers aged 55 to 64), 2000 and 2006*

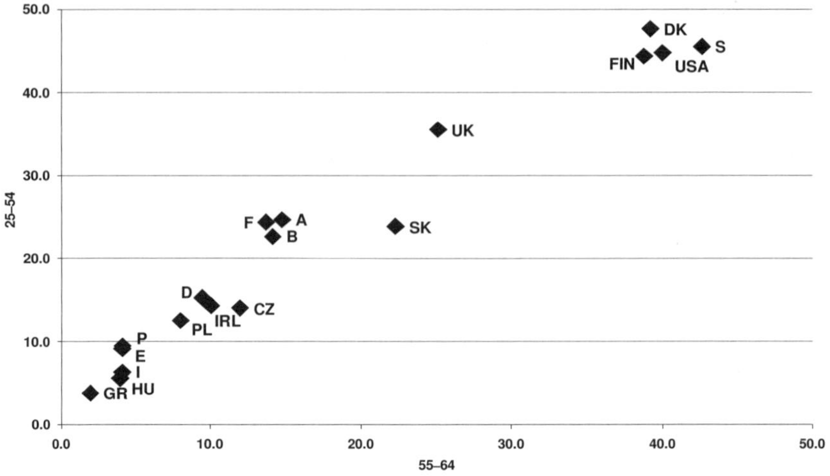

Source: OECD (2005a, Table C6.4).

Figure A10.2 Participation in non-formal job-related continuing education and training for the labour force, by age, 2003

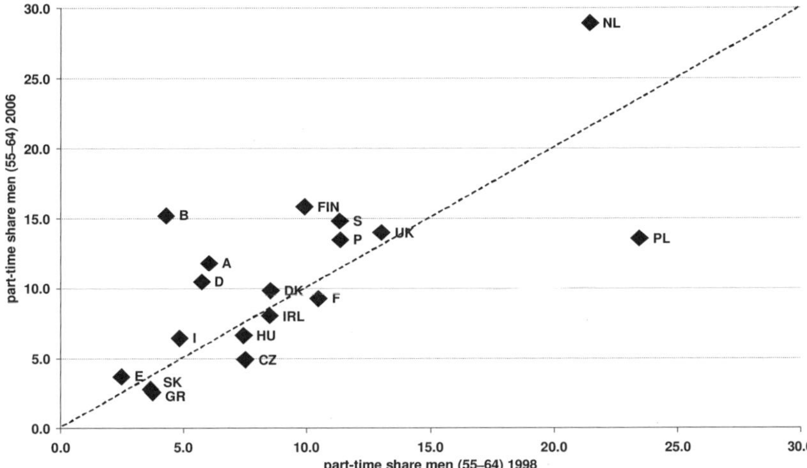

a) men

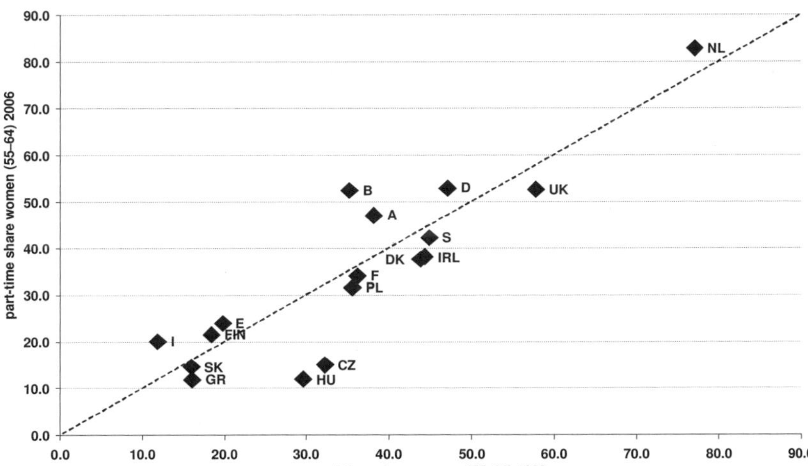

b) women

Notes:
Data: Second quarter 1998, France and Austria first quarter 1998; second quarter 2006, Ireland first quarter 2005.

Source: Eurostat.

Figure A10.3 Share of part-time working men and women aged 55 to 64 in Europe, 2000 and 2006

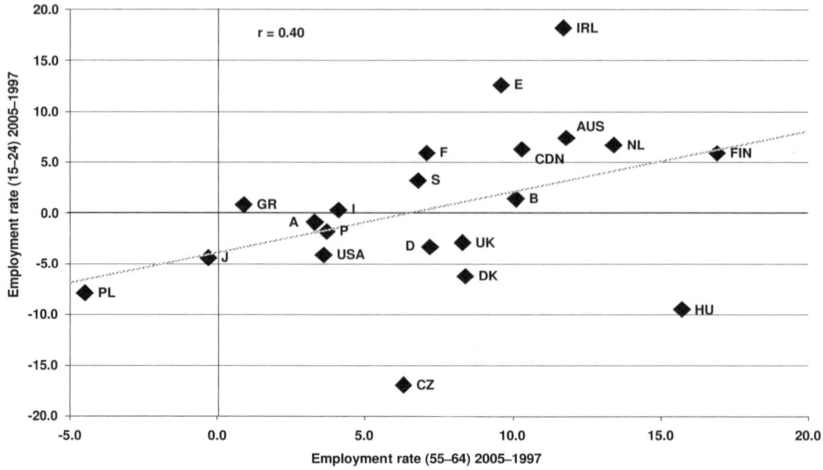

Notes:
Data: 2005 and 1997, for Sweden and Netherlands 2004.

Source: OECD Employment Outlook 2006, 2001, Table C, Employment/population ratios.

Figure A10.4 Change of employment rates for elderly (55–64) and young (15–24) adults, 2005–1997, percentage points

11. Get the Balance Right: Risk and Flexibility in School-to-Work Transition Sequences

Christian Brzinsky-Fay

11.1 INTRODUCTION

Many European countries have active labour market policies that aim either to integrate school leavers into the labour market or to keep young people at work. In most cases, these policies are targeted at certain problem groups that face higher risks of labour market exclusion – migrants and early school leavers are typical examples. These groups need help in particular situations, such as when they are looking for an apprenticeship or a job. But any focus on labour market transitions must look not only at single situations or status changes, but also at changes over the longer period, that is, at sequences of transitions. For example, a single change from unemployment to employment does not really provide much information about the integrative or risk character of the whole process of labour market entry. To assess this process properly, it is essential to extend the observation window and consider more than just one transition at a time.

The objective of this chapter is to identify different types of school-to-work transition sequences in ten European countries by using the methods of optimal matching and cluster analysis. Such an approach requires access to comparative longitudinal data, which in this case is provided by the monthly labour market status information contained in the European Community Household Panel (ECHP). As regards the risks inherent in the process of labour market entry, the school-to-work transition should provide an adequate amount of security (in terms of future employment prospects or income) and at the same time should allow for sufficient flexibility (in terms of training opportunities and adjustment to individual desires and market requirements). In order to assess the observed transition types in terms of how they balance flexibility and security, indicators of volatility and integrative potential are constructed. We then examine how the attributes of gender, education, migration background and country determine the probability of passing through a certain type of transition sequence. For this purpose, a multinomial logit model is estimated. The following questions will be addressed in this chapter: Which types of labour market status sequences have low or high integrative potential? Are volatile transitions associated with a high risk of labour market exclusion? How are certain labour market entry sequences distributed across countries or transition regimes? Which groups of young people are associated with certain sequence types on the labour market?

Sociological research is still interested in the form and the process of school-to-work transitions and in labour market integration. Because the school-to-work transition is a critical period that has a major influence on the opportunities that will be available during the further course of the employment career, it deserves further attention. The interesting question here is whether there are distinct chains of statuses that reflect deterministic pathways on the way from school to work. There are a number of determinants at the individual level that influence the transitions of school leavers into the labour market. In fact, identifying the target groups that could be helped by policies is not difficult, but formulating policies that respond to the transition problems these people have to face appears to be more complicated.

One reason is that by far most of the risk analyses dealing with problem groups of young people only refer either to static status distributions, for which cross-sectional data are used, or to single transitions such as unemployment risks, using event history models. Both methods have disadvantages. In the first case, the causal effect is not given, because when two or more pieces of cross-sectional information are used, then the data concerns different individuals and so only the aggregate information is usable. In the second case, we can indeed estimate comprehensive causal models, but these become inaccurate as the number of events increases (Halpin, 2003). Overall, then, there is a lack of research examining the school-to-work transition as a *period* that involves more than one single transition between education and employment or between education and unemployment (Hillmert, 2002, p. 676).

The link between the macro and the micro levels is an enduring and substantial problem in the social sciences in general, and this is particularly true for the life course approach. Here, the difficulty is reflected by the gap between the two empirical concepts of 'transition' and 'trajectory'. It is not really possible to identify a causal relationship between a trajectory offered by institutions or policies, on the one hand, and an individual decision to undertake a certain transition, on the other. With the sequence concept, however, it is possible to look at periods containing a large number of transitions and to categorise these periods in groups that can be taken as ideal types, which in turn can be associated with individual and/or institutional factors. From the policy perspective, the linking of transition types to individual socioeconomic factors enables policymakers to improve their policies, focus better on target groups and develop more process-oriented rather than situation-fixed measures (McVicar and Anyadike-Danes, 2002).

This chapter describes an explorative analysis of labour market entry sequences consisting of 60 consecutive monthly labour market statuses (Brzinsky-Fay, 2007). The resulting classification of labour market entry sequences is then subjected to a causal analysis that attributes the fact that an individual experiences a certain type of transition sequence to variables such as gender, education, migration background and country. After outlining the theoretical framework (Section 11.2) and describing the methodology in more detail (Section 11.3), the explorative part of the work is carried out by applying optimal matching together with cluster analysis, while the causal analysis is based on the estimation of a multinomial logit model (Section 11.4). Finally, conclusions are drawn and policy implications are discussed (Section 11.5).

11.2 THEORETICAL FRAMEWORK

11.2.1 Research Review

The most important individual factor with respect to the process of labour market integration is level of education. Though young women and those with a migration background can be particularly disadvantaged, it is still the educational careers and qualifications of young people that have the strongest impact on their employment prospects and occupational status (Gangl et al., 2003). Otherwise, family background also seems to play a role in determining the course of the school-to-work transition (McVicar and Anyadike-Danes, 2002).

Country differences and the impact of institutions on the school-to-work transition have been the object of investigation in a number of research studies. The dual system of apprenticeship was the first focus of those efforts (see Blossfeld, 1992; Korpi et al., 2003; Tremblay and le Bot, 2003; Wagner, 1998). Institutional factors have also been considered in research studies, though to a lesser extent. These factors are, first, the structure of the education system; second, the structure of the labour market; third, the regulation of the labour market, including employment protection and collective bargaining; and, fourth, active labour market policies, which are said to be becoming increasingly institutionalised and to constitute an important aspect of school-to-work transitions (Müller and Gangl, 2003).

From the institutional perspective, Gangl et al. (2003) found that there are three configurations of education systems in Europe: countries with extensive vocational training at secondary level; countries with predominantly general education at secondary level; and countries with a low level of educational attainment.

The theoretical foundations of the empirical analysis of labour market sequences have been developed through sociological life course research (see Sackmann and Wingens, 2003). The sequence concept connects the macro level, represented by the concept of trajectories, and the micro level, represented by single transitions. A trajectory can be seen as a pathway offered by the institutional configuration in a particular country. Of course, there is more than one possible trajectory in every country, because (vocational) education systems are designed for different professions and different skill levels. A transition is simply a change in an individual's labour market status. This can be the transition from employment to unemployment or from education to employment after finishing school. A sequence is defined as 'any life course movement that includes at least two transitions between states (in a given state space)' (Sackmann and Wingens, 2003). Within the framework of this concept, and in an effort to capture policy-relevant forms of sequences, we now construct a group of different theoretical sequence types. These theoretical types are to a certain extent derived from empirical data, namely the European Community Household Panel (ECHP). More precisely, eight distinct transition types were isolated from data relating to more than 3,000 school leavers, where the data included the monthly labour market status of each individual over a five-year period (Brzinsky-Fay, 2007).

The more normative aspect of favourable school-to-work transitions was investigated by concentrating on particular properties of transition sequences: volatility and integrative capability. The volatility of a transition sequence can have positive or negative effects per se, depending on the respective statuses of individuals who are undergoing change. In this respect, it is argued that the major problem regarding the labour market integration of young people is their lack of work experience and the lack of information about their vocational qualifications. This circumstance inhibits potential employers from hiring inexperienced young people. The amount of information generally increases for both employers and employees when young people participate in further education, an apprenticeship or a combination of the two. Hence, these statuses reflect a comparatively positive volatility, whereas episodes of unemployment and inactivity can be regarded as negative volatility. Transition types that have several transitions between education, employment and apprenticeship were found in countries with a well-developed system of further training, such as Denmark, or with an established apprenticeship system, such as Germany. On the other hand, transition types with negative volatility were predominant in countries with a low degree of institutional coordination between the education system and the labour market, such as the southern European countries (Brzinsky-Fay, 2007). The integrative capability of a transition type is a measure of how quickly and to what extent young people are integrated into the labour market. Because of the standardised length of the sequences examined here, this property can be assessed only by looking at the share of people who become employed during the observation period. Because integration means that employment should be the final goal of the process, a stronger weight is given to later employment spells. Transition types with low integrative capability were mainly found in the southern European countries, whereas transition types with a high level of integrative capability predominate in the United Kingdom. Germany shows a medium level of integrative capability (Brzinsky-Fay, 2007).

From a policy perspective, the concept of transitional labour markets (TLMs) serves as the theoretical background for the analysis of labour market sequences (Schmid, 1998, 2002; Schmid and Schömann, 2004). Proceeding on the basis of the consideration that globalisation, technological progress and individualisation create an increasing demand for flexibility, and that at the same time social security must be ensured, this concept encourages the take-up of labour market transitions through institutional regulations and policies that safeguard and motivate both employers and employees. These institutions are called 'transitional labour markets' and are located at crucial points on the labour market, such as the transition between the education system and employment. To ascertain in what way TLMs need to be configured, it is essential to know the empirical shape that transition sequences take. When applying the TLM concept, one differentiates between integrative, maintenance and exclusionary transitions (O'Reilly et al., 2000), and risk management becomes an important concern (Schmid, 2006). This refers to changing risk types with respect to the life course. Traditionally, the main risk in the transition from school to work was to gain access to a particular job in a more or less straightforward manner. In modern societies, the variety of possible pathways to work is increasing together with the possibility of wrong decisions leading into dead-end streets. At the same time, the whole process of school-to-work transitions is becoming destandardised and more than just a single choice may account for failure. Hence, the aim of this chapter is to look at the school-to-work transition as a whole in order to identify regularities and assess their quality regarding flexibility and security, which are measured by indicators derived from the TLM concept, namely volatility and integrative capability.

11.2.2 Hypotheses

As mentioned above, it is clear that the institutions of individual countries offer more than just one trajectory because a (vocational) education system has to achieve coordination between the heterogeneous skills of young people and the demands of different professions. This is also reflected in the transition sequence types of each country. But the broad variation of institutional configurations between countries leads to each sequence type exhibiting different weights in each country. And not only country characteristics determine individuals' transition probabilities, but also individual characteristics such as gender, education and migration background.

Regarding the effect of education on sequence type, it can be expected that a higher level of education will have a positive effect on the type of transition made by an individual. This means that school leavers with a higher ISCED level have a higher probability of entering the labour market via a transition type with high integrative capability and high volatility and vice versa.

> *Hypothesis 1*
> Young people with a high educational level will have higher probabilities of passing through a sequence type with high integrative capability and/or high volatility.

The opposite relation can be assumed for migration background. School leavers with a migration background will have a higher probability of passing through a sequence type with low integrative potential and/or low volatility.

> *Hypothesis 2*
> Young people with a migration background will have lower probabilities of passing through a sequence type with high integrative capability and/or high volatility.

Regarding gender, there is no clear-cut theoretical reason why women should have different probabilities of entering the labour market via a certain transition type, apart from the fact that women are usually more frequently inactive because of family responsibilities.

> *Hypothesis 3*
> Apart from more frequent incidences of inactivity among women, no gender differences are assumed regarding types of school-to-work transitions.

Because of the differences found in institutions, policies and economic situations, country differences are expected to be significant, at least to the extent that particular transition types appear in particular countries (Brzinsky-Fay, 2007). The southern European countries are characterised by a lower level of both educational attainment and vocational education. School leavers in these countries are expected to have high probabilities of passing through 'bad' transition types and, at the same time, they will show lower probabilities for 'good' transition types. The opposite will be true for countries with mainly general qualifications or extensive vocational training systems.

> *Hypothesis 4*
> School leavers from countries with lower levels of educational attainment have a higher probability of bad transition types than those from countries with general education or extensive vocation education.

11.3 DATA AND METHODS

The European Community Household Panel (ECHP) is the only comparative panel data set available on socioeconomic issues. It is a longitudinal data set that was built up by Eurostat and the national statistics offices of the member states of the European Union from 1994 to 2001. It contains a large variety of variables covering a number of socioeconomic issues at both the individual and household levels.[1] According to previous research (see Franz et al., 2000; Gangl, 2003; Russell and O'Connell, 2001), the most important individual factors with respect to the labour market integration of young people are gender, educational attainment and migration background, which are all included in the survey.

For this study, five countries could not be analysed on technical grounds. Only cross-sectional data are available for Sweden, while it was not possible to examine transition types for the Netherlands because there are only missing values in the calendar variables. Luxembourg, Austria and Finland also had to be excluded on the grounds of too few valid cases.

Brzinsky-Fay (2007) defines the beginning of school-to-work transitions as the point at which young people leave full-time general education. Hence, apprenticeships are included in the observation window and are not considered part of the initial education. One reason is that an apprenticeship is a form of qualification that is specifically related to a particular vocation, so that it should be viewed as belonging to the domain of employment, even if participants in apprenticeships spend a large amount of their time at school.[2] Another reason to distinguish apprenticeships from initial education is the crucial role that work experience plays in obtaining a job. Work experience is provided by a job as well as by vocational training such as an apprenticeship, but not by a general education. Furthermore, in order to identify the relevance of apprenticeships for school-to-work transitions, it is necessary to examine the weight that they have within the transition period. In the interests of having a comparable framework, the observation window is defined equally for all countries, namely 60 months (5 years).

The calendar data used to extract transition types are retrospective and contain information from January 1993 to December 2000, which amounts to 96 months.[3] The categories of the monthly calendar variables for 'labour market status' are 'employed', 'unemployed', 'apprenticeship', 'inactive/household' and 'education'. Employed persons are those who are either self-employed or in dependent employment, while inactivity includes housework, family care and military service. The status of 'education' includes both university education and further education.

The two indicators constructed from the sequence data that capture the integrative potential and the volatility of the labour market entry sequences can be taken as quality measures of school-to-work transitions. The integration indicator was created after the types of sequences had been derived and simply gives the total months of employment, which are weighted by their position in the sequence. The later the employment episodes are located, the stronger is their weight. Thus, later employment episodes are regarded as more important because of the sequential character of the data. Earlier employment episodes only maintain their relative value if they are related in some way to later employment episodes. The volatility indicator gives the mathematical share of the number of episodes in employment, education and apprenticeship, as well as the overall number of episodes. The higher the value of this indicator, the more favourable are sequences with respect to flexibility in the particular country. One advantage of this indicator is that it is independent of the overall level of episode changes because it only reflects the relationship between two kinds of episodes. Both indicators are calculated at the individual level and summarised at the cluster level. The integration indicator can be seen as a measure of transition risk because it depends to a great extent on employment opportunities following the end of the observation period. The volatility indicator reflects some kind of favourable flexibility with regard to labour market changes.

The analysis is carried out in two parts. First, a description is given of the different transition types, which were found by calculating the differences between monthly labour market status sequences and then grouping similar sequences together.[4] Then the clusters of sequence types are associated with the individual characteristics listed above as independent variables in a multinomial logit model.

11.4 TRANSITIONS SEQUENCES FROM SCHOOL TO WORK

11.4.1 Clusters of Labour Market Entry Sequences

The cluster analysis was carried out using only the second of two steps, with the first step (the calculation of a dissimilarity measure) being replaced by the optimal matching algorithm. For the second step (the fusion of groups), the classic Ward linkage algorithm was used. When operating with a hierarchical fusion algorithm, a decision has to be made on the crucial question of the appropriate number of clusters. For contextual and practical reasons, in this case an eight-cluster solution was chosen.[5]

To get a general picture of the clusters, the monthly proportion of statuses is shown in Figure 11.1.

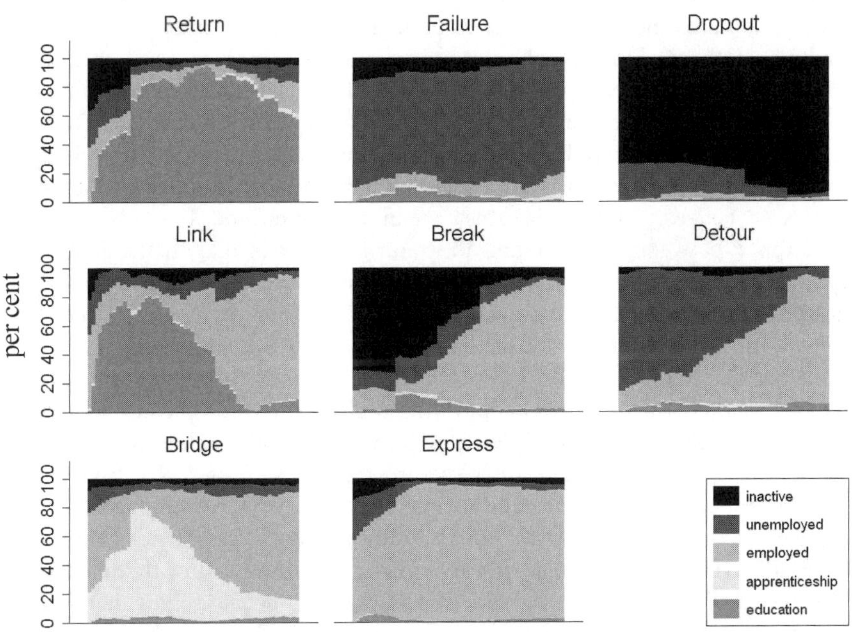

Source: ECHP, own calculations.

Figure 11.1 Monthly proportion of statuses by cluster

It must be pointed out that this figure does not show individuals' sequences, rather only the share of monthly statuses. In the first cluster, at the beginning of the observation period around 40 per cent of school leavers are employed, 40 per cent are inactive and 20 per cent are unemployed. These numbers decrease sharply in the first year and the share of education remains at a very high level throughout the entire five-year period. According to the sequence typology developed by Sackmann and Wingens (2003), this cluster is primarily built on return-type sequences and therefore can be called the return cluster. Reasons for returning to education can be escape from unemployment (Scherer, 2001, p. 135) or so-called waiting loops, whereby young people take up work only as an interlude between general and higher education. Unemployment is the primary labour market status in the second cluster, and it is spread more or less evenly across all five years. That is why this cluster can rightly be called the failure cluster. The only difference between the failure cluster and the third cluster is that in the latter, inactivity is the most important status. There is a 25 per cent share of unemployment at the beginning of this cluster, but this disappears over the course of the observation period. Because inactive people are by definition outside the labour market, the third cluster can be labelled the dropout cluster. The failure and the dropout clusters correspond to rupture and change in Sackmann and Wingens' typology. The fourth cluster includes a good share of education, as well as a considerable share of employment. Because education is concentrated at the beginning and employment at the end of the observation period, it can be assumed that education has a linking function in these sequences. Thus, this cluster can be called the link cluster. The difference between the link and the return cluster is that in the latter, the education episodes are spread across the whole observation period, whereas in the former most of them come to an end after three years. The fifth cluster shows much inactivity at the beginning and a lot of employment at the end. Most of the sequences lead to employment and thus to integration into the labour market. Because the people in this cluster are completely outside of the workforce in the initial years following school-leaving for whatever reason, this sequence type will be named the break cluster. We find a very similar structure in the sixth cluster, where we only have employment at the beginning instead of inactivity. In this cluster, moreover, 90 per cent of the school leavers are employed after five years. Because most of the unemployment episodes are located at the beginning and because the unemployed belong to the workforce, this sequence type is labelled detour. A good portion of the school-to-work transitions that include apprenticeships are grouped in the seventh cluster, which also contains a lot of employment and, therefore, reflects perfectly what Sackmann and Wingens describe as the bridge type. In other words, the aspired status of employment is reached from the starting point of education via a hybrid status, and this type of sequence is therefore called the bridge cluster. Sequences with a major share of employment are pooled in the last cluster. Employment episodes are found from the very beginning in this cluster, which can therefore be called the express cluster because it contains all the individuals who are integrated into the labour market very rapidly.

In order to construct indicators for a quantitative distinction between the clusters, the durations of statuses, the average number of episodes and the two indicators for integrative potential and volatility are extracted for the respective clusters, as shown in Table 11.1.

Table 11.1 Characteristics of clusters

		Cluster							
		Return	Failure	Dropout	Link	Break	Detour	Bridge	Express
Average duration in:	education	42.5	2.4	0.5	23.9	2.4	2.2	1.7	1.1
	apprenticeship	0.8	0.8	0.1	0.4	0.5	0.6	22.9	0.1
	employment	6.2	5.5	1.5	26.6	28.0	26.8	28.6	52.0
	unemployment	5.5	46.1	8.7	5.9	7.2	28.3	4.2	4.0
	inactivity	4.9	5.2	49.2	3.2	21.8	2.0	2.5	2.8
Average number of episodes in:	education	1.7	0.3	0.1	1.6	0.3	0.3	0.2	0.2
	apprenticeship	0.1	0.1	0.0	0.1	0.1	0.1	1.1	0.0
	employment	1.3	0.9	0.2	2.3	1.6	2.0	1.9	1.5
	unemployment	0.7	2.0	0.5	1.0	1.0	2.1	0.7	0.7
	inactivity	0.6	0.5	1.3	0.7	1.4	0.3	0.3	0.4
Integration indicator		9.4	9.6	2.4	59.2	63.8	59.2	55.8	90.6
Volatility indicator		65.4	24.2	6.1	72.0	45.4	50.2	79.8	70.9
N		347	625	586	164	314	465	299	1,217

Source: ECHP, own calculations.

The transition sequences of the 347 individuals found in the return cluster are characterised by the status of education, which on average accounts for 42.5 months of the 60 months following the end of school education. The volatility of this cluster is at an average level, whereas the integration indicator shows a low level of integrative potential. This is due to the fact that this cluster contains university students, who naturally need a longer time to integrate into the labour market. Unemployment and inactivity constitute the most important statuses in the failure and the dropout clusters. The former contains slightly more months spent in education, apprenticeship and employment than the latter. Both clusters have low volatility and integration values, but the dropout cluster is both less integrative and less volatile than the failure cluster. The link cluster created by the algorithm consists mainly of education and employment months. The level of volatility is the second highest of all the clusters and the integrative potential is at a medium level. With only 164 cases, this is the smallest of all the clusters.

The break cluster is composed of 28 months of employment and 21.8 months of inactivity and has a medium integrative potential as well as a medium level of volatility. Employment and unemployment are the most important statuses in the detour cluster, by contrast. As in the break cluster, the integration and volatility indicators show medium values here. The bridge cluster is the only cluster that mainly contains apprenticeship statuses, while employment also has a high weight in this cluster. The level of volatility is the highest of all the clusters here, whereas the integrative potential is at a medium level. In the express cluster, employment is by far the most important status: the school leavers in this cluster are employed on average for 52 out of 60 months. Thus, here we find the highest value for the integration indicator and the third-highest value for volatility. The express cluster is the largest among the eight clusters, accounting for 1,217 individuals.

To examine the sequential character of the transition process, it is necessary to look at the graphical display of individual sequences by cluster (Figure 11.2). This step verifies the conclusions drawn from the monthly proportions and gives an impression of the complexity of transition sequences. Individuals in the return cluster frequently start with an episode of employment, unemployment or inactivity lasting roughly one year, and after that they return to education for the rest of the observation period. There are some sporadic interruptions, which in some cases can be interpreted as student summer employment, but a major change of status rarely occurs.

The sequence index plot of the failure cluster shows a predominance of unemployment, which is conspicuously spread across the entire period. Only a very small share of the people in this cluster are employed at the end of the transition period. The same is true for the dropout cluster, but instead of unemployment, this cluster is characterised by inactivity. The linking function of education statuses in the link cluster is obvious: the education periods are clearly short, so that the majority of school leavers enter employment after two or three years. The break and the detour cluster, together with the link cluster, represent long-term successful integration processes, each of them with a different entrance status. It is noteworthy that the values of their integration indicators are at similar levels, while they differ in volatility. The bridge cluster shows the bridging function of apprenticeships, but also reveals that it is not always the case that young people immediately find employment after finishing an apprenticeship. The bridge cluster is also the second-smallest cluster. Sequences from the express cluster rarely start with unemployment and are seldom interrupted by any other status, so that they nearly always terminate in employment.

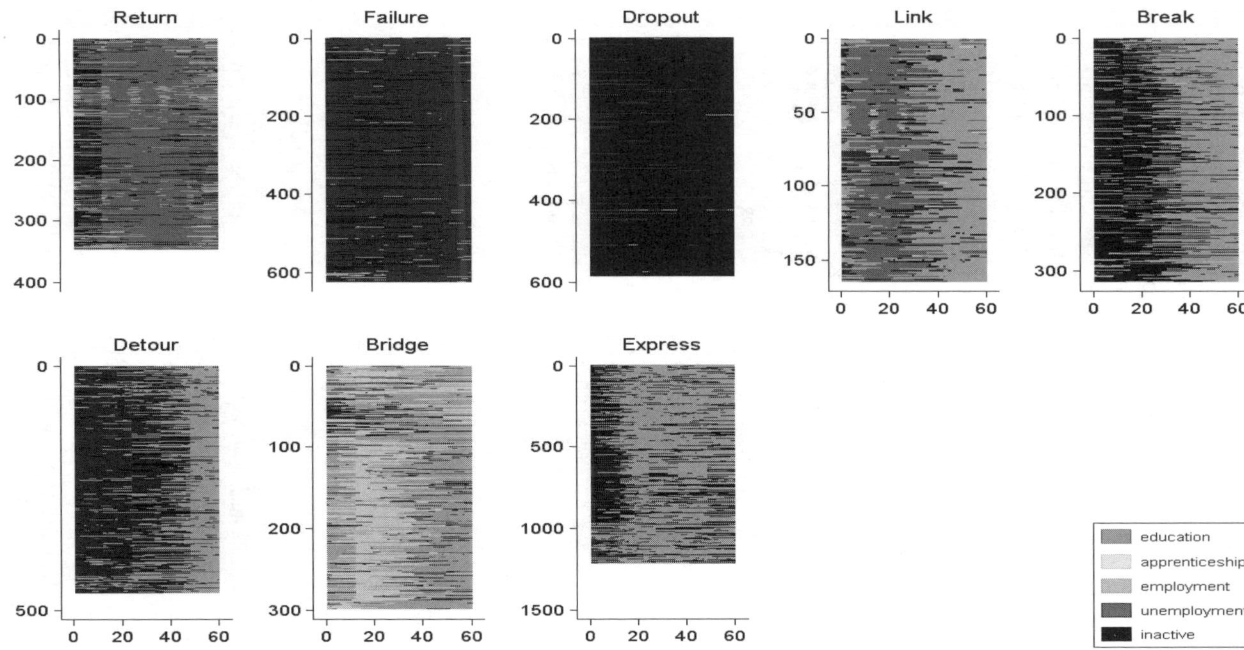

Source: ECHP, own calculations; ww.wzb.eu/~brzinsky-fay/get_the_balance_right.en.htm.

Figure 11.2 Sequence index plots by cluster

To summarise, there are distinct types of transition sequences that show explicit differences in the proportion and order of labour market statuses as well as in their integrative potential and volatility. What is important for institutional comparison is the question as to whether or not these clusters are country specific, and this question will be examined in the following subsection.

As Figure 11.3 shows, the incidence of the different clusters varies substantially across countries. With the exception of the bridge cluster, for which no cases could be found in France, all remaining clusters appear in all countries.

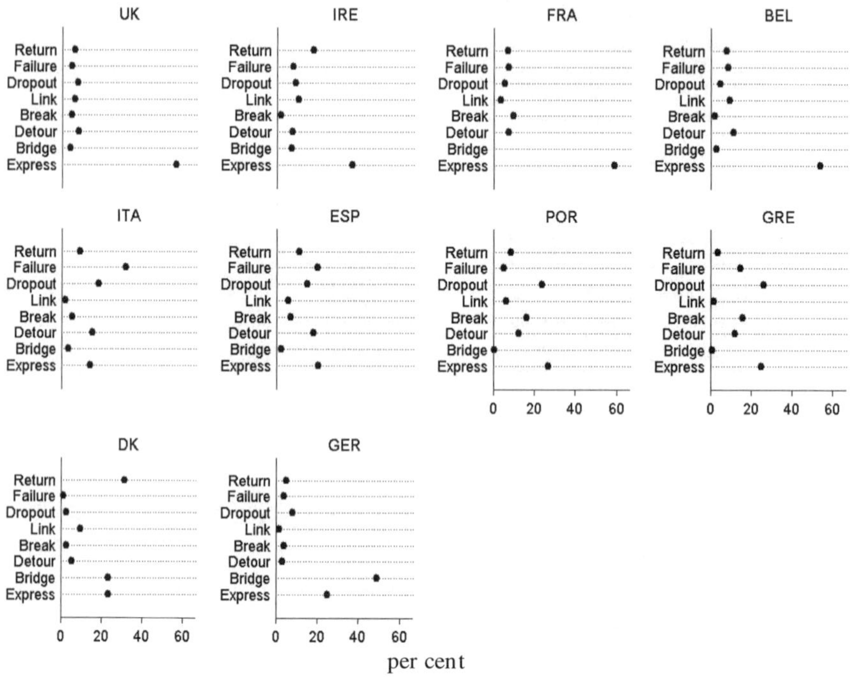

Source: ECHP, own calculations; www.wzb.eu/~brzinsky-fay/get_ the_balance_right.en.htm.

Figure 11.3 Incidence of sequence types in countries

Transition sequences from the return cluster are found by far most frequently in Denmark, but transition sequences of this type also play an important role in Ireland and Spain. The link cluster appears, in particular, in Ireland, Denmark and Belgium. The bridge cluster is very common in Germany and Denmark, where apprenticeship systems exist. In Germany, nearly 50 per cent of all school leavers enter transition sequences of this type, compared to almost 25 per cent in Denmark. An outstanding share of express sequences is found in France, the United Kingdom and Belgium, where between 50 per cent and 60 per cent of school leavers belong to this cluster. The highest share of detour sequences can be found in the southern European countries and in Belgium. Portugal and Greece show the highest shares of break sequences. The failure and the dropout clusters show up most often in the southern European countries of Spain, Italy and Greece and – to a lesser extent – in Portugal. In Italy, more than 50 per cent of all transition sequences belong to these two clusters, while the share is 40.7 per cent in Greece and 35 per cent in Spain. The lowest proportion of failure and dropout sequences can be found in Denmark.

To sum up, the distribution of sequence types across countries shows that the most country-specific transition sequences are the bridge type for Germany and – to a lesser extent – for Denmark, the failure and dropout type for the southern European countries, and the link type for Denmark and Ireland. The express cluster is spread across all countries, although its size varies considerably. The sequences of the link, the detour and the break type are distributed most evenly across the countries under observation and at the same time they to some extent reflect the general trend of destandardisation of life courses.

11.4.2 Individual Characteristics and Transition Sequences

One of the most interesting questions remaining now is how socioeconomic characteristics determine the probability of belonging to a certain transition sequence type? To assess this probability, we estimate a multinomial logit model that includes the independent variables of gender, educational level (at the beginning of the transition period) and migration background.[6] Country dummies are added to control for national influences. The results are shown in Table 11.2.

Surprisingly, the pseudo-R^2 for the overall fit of the model is quite low, which means that apart from the three predictor variables used here, there must be other important, unobserved influencing factors that determine the labour market entry sequence. However, most of the coefficients are significant. The coefficients are expressed as relative risk ratios, whereas values between 0 and 1 are calculated as negative reciprocals in the interests of interpretative clarity. In addition, the coefficients must be interpreted relative to the express cluster, which is defined as the base outcome because it represents the most favourable labour market entry sequence type. Thus, women are six times more likely than men to be in the dropout cluster than in the express cluster. At the same time, women are 1.3 times less likely to be in the break cluster.

Table 11.2 Multinomial logit model (relative risk ratios)

Cluster	Educational level				Country								
	Medium	High	Non-nationals	Wo-men	BEL	FRA	IRE	ITA	GRE	ESP	POR	GER	UK
Return	4.20***	2.74***	n.s.	n.s.	–21.55***	–20.51***	–6.71***	–5.62***	–25.14***	–4.97***	–8.27***	–13.45***	–28.78***
Failure	–2.69***	–4.77***	n.s.	1.44***	–2.75***	–5.18***	–2.55***	4.03***	n.s.	1.68***	–4.15***	–4.30***	–5.12***
Dropout	–7.99***	–22.60***	3.56***	6.32***	–9.51***	–15.36***	–4.23***	1.56***	n.s.	–1.56**	–2.42***	–11.16***	–5.82***
Link	1.54*	2.16***	n.s.	n.s.	–10.00***	–25.93***	–5.23***	–11.09***	–20.85***	–5.40***	–5.45***	–18.40***	–15.34***
Break	–2.10***	–2.43***	n.s.	–1.36**	–11.72***	–3.50***	–9.04***	n.s.	n.s.	–1.51*	n.s.	–2.93***	–4.99***
Detour	–1.55***	–2.19***	2.11*	n.s.	–3.17***	–6.14***	–3.54***	1.45**	–1.55**	n.s.	–1.89***	–9.23***	–4.39***
Bridge	1.40*	–2.45***	–2.22***	1.04	–16.70***	n.s.	–5.38***	–5.02***	–28.75***	–7.21***	–45.20***	2.06***	–10.41***
N	4,005												
Pseudo R^2	0.24												

Notes:
The coefficients are relative risk ratios. For values between 0 and 1 the reciprocal is calculated, because of interpretative clearness.
Express is the base outcome, reference categories: Denmark and low level of education.Significance levels: *** p = < 0.01; **p = < 0.05; * p = < 0.1.

Source: ECHP, own calculations.

If we bear in mind that both clusters include spells of inactivity, and that these are longer in the dropout cluster, then we must conclude that starting the transition period with inactivity is much riskier for female than for male school leavers. This can be explained by the childcare periods young women go through in this age group. In addition, young women have a higher probability of starting with a labour market entry sequence of the failure type than men. For people with a migration background, the probability of belonging to a sequence of the dropout type is 3.5 times higher than for natives. Migrants also have a higher probability of entering detour sequences and a 2.2-times lower likelihood of starting their labour market career with a bridge sequence type, which means that apprenticeships fail to integrate immigrants.

The factor of educational level clearly shows the correlation between qualification and labour market outcome: the higher the level of education, the higher the probability of entering the labour market in a favourable way. This is in line with human capital theory, which implies that a high educational level increases the chances of obtaining a favourable position in the labour market. The effect is most obvious in the dropout cluster: the chance of school leavers with a medium level of education belonging to this cluster is 8 times lower than for those with a low educational level, while for those with high level of education, the chance is a hefty 22.6 times lower. Looking at the link and the return clusters, we find that education is a cumulative property, which means that those who are already educated are more likely to receive additional education than those who are not educated to begin with. In the return and the link clusters, the probabilities of undergoing further education are higher for those with medium- and high-level educations than for less educated school leavers. The lower educated also have higher probabilities of being found in the failure, break and detour clusters. The situation is different with respect to the bridge cluster because school leavers with a medium level of education have higher probabilities of belonging here than those with a high level of education. This reflects the fact that apprenticeships – the main component of this cluster – are created for people with a medium level of education.

The coefficients of the country dummies are highly significant in most of the cases and their values are higher than those of the other covariates. Thus, it can be stated that institutional factors are more important for the labour market entry sequences than socioeconomic characteristics. On the basis of these coefficients, we can also identify country-specific sequence types. The reference category here is Denmark and the coefficients again indicate the probability of having a certain sequence type relative to the express cluster. The return cluster, for example, seems to be very typical for Denmark, given that the coefficients for all the other countries are clearly smaller. This can be seen as a consequence of Denmark's well-established systems of higher and further education. The failure cluster is typical for Italy, Greece and Spain: the coefficients in these three countries are positive, which means that their residents have a probability ranging from 1 (Greece) to 4 times (Italy) higher of having a labour market entry sequence from the failure type. These three countries are characterised by an absence of institutional regulations and policies regarding the integration of school leavers into the labour market. The lowest probabilities for the failure cluster can be found in the United Kingdom and in France. It can be assumed that young people in the United Kingdom find work quickly because of this country's liberal labour market and the high income differences found there, which indicate the possibility of low entry wages. In France, where young people are also more likely to enter the labour market according to the express sequence type than to the failure sequence type, the existence of mainly internal labour markets explains the low probability of failure. But it can be assumed that the stigmatising effect on those who once experienced this transition type is high, which is reflected by the low probabilities of belonging to the break, detour and return clusters. A quite similar picture emerges for the dropout cluster, with the values for France and Germany being more extreme, while again the southern European countries – and particularly the women living in southern Europe – have the highest probabilities of belonging to the dropout cluster. Sequences of the link type also seem to be typical in Denmark, again indicated by the fact that all the other countries have smaller values. And once again this is evidence of the institutional effect of Denmark's well-established education and training systems. As mentioned above, the probability of having a link-type labour market entry sequence is very low in France because of its internal labour markets. The break and the detour cluster seem to be the most unspecific types, given that the coefficients are small in every country. The probability of having a labour market entry sequence of the bridge type is highest in Germany because of this country's dual system of apprenticeship. Germany remains the only country where this probability is higher than the probability of belonging to the express cluster, so the bridge cluster is very typical for Germany.

11.5 CONCLUSIONS

The sequence concept has a number of advantages. First, it enables a link to be made between the macro and the micro levels. Second, it is able to reduce the complexity of information generated by the huge number of theoretically possible sequences, while neglecting short and unimportant episodes and emphasising crucial transitions. And, third, it allows us to incorporate the sequential information into causal models. These advantages mean that the method lends itself to studies of transition processes. Additionally, active labour market policies that aim to support the integration of young people into the labour market and that are targeted at specific problem groups can be improved by using sequence information. Taking into account both institutional peculiarities and individual characteristics, the probability of belonging to a certain labour market entry sequence can be used to better fit policies to the expected needs of school leavers.

The explorative analysis – that is, optimal matching in conjunction with cluster analyses – reveals eight distinct types of school-to-work transitions that differ in terms of volatility and integrative potential. The transition types are distributed very unevenly across countries but, with the exception of the bridge type, all of them appear in every country. The clear differences in the distribution of all transition types across countries indicate that national institutional configurations have a strong influence. This is particularly true for the southern European countries, which show a high degree of similarity. The most country-specific transition types are the bridge cluster for Germany, the return and link clusters for Denmark, and the failure and dropout clusters for the southern European countries. Germany has a very well-established initial vocational training system, while Denmark boasts a well-established further training system (OECD, 2005).

The regression of gender, educational level, migration background and country on the transition types confirms that the impact of individual factors on the transition types is weaker than that of the country dummies, which also leads to the conclusion that institutional differences are more relevant. Among the individual variables, education seems to be the most important one and to have a positive effect on the probability of belonging to the link, return or express cluster. The education effect on the bridge cluster is only positive for the medium level of education; however, these school leavers are by definition the target group of apprenticeships. At the same time, the probability of having a labour market entry sequence of the dropout or failure type decreases with increasing level of education. Thus, Hypothesis 1 is confirmed. The effect of a migration background is only significant for the dropout cluster (which has the lowest value for volatility and integrative capability), for the bridge cluster and for the detour cluster. In all of these three cases, the coefficients show the expected effect, so that Hypothesis 2 is also confirmed. The gender effect is only significant in three cases, one of which is the dropout cluster. This confirms Hypothesis 3, because this cluster contains most of the inactivity spells. However, to get a full picture of what determines the labour market entry sequence of school leavers, other variables – apart from gender, educational level and migration background – need to be included. Other factors might be family background or regional labour market conditions, but up to now there is no comparative panel data set that includes all of these variables.

Denmark and Germany appear to have favourable institutional configurations. In both countries, the share of transition types with the highest volatility – return, link, bridge and express clusters – is higher than 80 per cent. The share of transition types with a high integrative capability – first and foremost, the express cluster, but also the break, detour, link and bridge clusters – is lowest in those countries that have a lower level of educational attainment, so that Hypothesis 4 is confirmed. These countries are the southern European countries, which constitute a more or less homogeneous group with respect to school-to-work transition sequences. Their transition systems urgently need to be upgraded and/or advanced by policies. This is particularly important because the trend towards individualisation is diminishing the reparative function of the family. Denmark in some way constitutes a best practice example thanks to its established initial and further training system, which helps even bad starts to turn out positively.

From these findings two lessons can be drawn for the design of flexicurity policies. First, we found that there are clear effects of socioeconomic characteristics on the probability of passing through a certain labour market entry sequence. If these findings can be refined – for example by including more variables – targeted active labour market policies can be applied to particular groups of school leavers (see McVicar and Anyadike-Danes, 2002, p. 332) in order to establish a proactive early detection system of labour market risks. Second, it shows up that those systems exhibit the highest shares of favourable entry sequences, which distribute labour market entry risks between many levels – that is individual, enterprise, state – as well as having a strong emphasis on (further or vocational) education. This refers to Denmark, Ireland and Germany, whereas in the United Kingdom, which also performs well, the very fast labour market integration is reached at the expense of low quality jobs. Hence, flexicurity policies are of great value for early detection, if they consider educational matters and distribute risks on many shoulders.

NOTES

1. For a description and critique of the ECHP, see Peracchi (2002).
2. Apprenticeship spells are defined as 'paid apprenticeships', which excludes them from being counted as measures under active labour market policy.
3. For more information on the generation of the transition types, see Brzinsky-Fay (2007).
4. This was done using optimal matching (OM). Together with Ulrich Kohler and Magdalena Luniak, the author of this paper has created a bundle of commands for optimal matching analysis for the Stata software package. It is available from the SSC archive at

http://ideas.repec.org/s/boc/bocode.html. An article on this tool is published in the Stata Journal (Brzinsky-Fay et al., 2006).

5. A number of coefficients can be applied in order to indicate the optimal cluster solution, but none of these test statistics can be used for sequence analysis because they do not take into account the sequential character of the data. After checking for all solutions from three to ten clusters, the decision was driven by the existence of analytically meaningful groups. Another argument for the eight-cluster solution is that it enables the research to obtain groups with a sufficient number of cases.
6. The quality of the migration variables in the ECHP is very heterogeneous across countries. Therefore, migration background is measured here using a dummy variable that indicates whether an individual was born within the country of residence (national) or not (non-national).

REFERENCES

Blossfeld, H.-P. (1992), 'Is the German Dual System a Model for a Modern Vocational Training System?', *International Journal of Comparative Sociology*, **33** (3–4), 168–81.

Brzinsky-Fay, C. (2007), 'Lost in Transition? Labour Market Entry Sequences of School Leavers in Europe', *European Sociological Review*, **23** (4), 409–22.

Brzinsky-Fay, C., Kohler, U. and Luniak, M. (2006), 'Sequence Analysis Using Stata', *Stata Journal*, **6** (4), 435–60.

Franz, W., Inkmann, J., Pohlmeier, W. and Zimmermann, V. (2000), 'Young and Out in Germany: On the Youths' Chances of Labor Market Entrance in Germany', in Blanchflower, D.G. and Freeman, R.B. (eds), *Youth Employment and Joblessness in Advanced Countries*, Chicago: The University of Chicago Press, pp. 381–425.

Gangl, M. (2003), 'The Structure of Labour Market Entry in Europe: A Typological Analysis', in Müller, W. and Gangl, M. (eds), *Transitions from Education to Work in Europe*, Oxford: Oxford University Press, pp. 95–116.

Gangl, M., Müller, W. and Raffe, D. (2003), 'Conclusions: Explaining Cross-National Differences in School-to-Work Transitions', in Müller, W. and Gangl, M. (eds), *Transitions from Education to Work in Europe. The Integration of Youth into EU Labour Markets*, Oxford: Oxford University Press, pp. 277–305.

Halpin, B. (2003), *Tracks Through Time and Continuous Processes: Transitions, Sequences and Social Structure*, Paper presented at the Frontiers in Social and Economic Mobility, Cornell University, March 27–29.

Hillmert, S. (2002), 'Labour Market Integration and Institutions: An Anglo-German Comparison', *Work, Employment and Society*, **16** (4), 675–701.

Korpi, T., De Graaf, P., Hendrickx, J. and Layte, R. (2003), 'Vocational Training and Career Employment Precariousness in Great Britain, the Netherlands and Sweden', *Acta Sociologica*, **46** (1), 17–30.

McVicar, D. and Anyadike-Danes, M. (2002), 'Predicting Sucessful and Unsuccessful Transitions from School to Work by Using Sequence Methods', *Journal of the Royal Statistical Society*, **165** (2), 317–34.

Müller, W. and Gangl, M. (2003), 'The Transition from School to Work: A European Perspective', in Müller, W. and Gangl, M. (eds), *Transitions from Education to Work in Europe. The Integration of Youth into EU Labour Markets*, Oxford: Oxford University Press, pp. 1–19.

O'Reilly, J., Cebrián, I. and Lallement, M. (eds) (2000), *Working-Time Changes. Social Integration Through Transitional Labour Markets*, Cheltenham, UK and Northampton, MA, USA: Edward Elgar.

OECD (2005), *Education at a Glance. OECD Indicators 2005*, Paris: OECD.

Peracchi, F. (2002), 'The European Community Household Panel: A Review', *Empirical Economics*, **27**, 63–90.

Russell, H. and O'Connell, P. (2001), 'Getting a Job in Europe: The Transition from Unemployment to Work among Young People in Nine European Countries', *Work, Employment & Society*, **15** (1), 1–24.

Sackmann, R. and Wingens, M. (2003), 'From Transitions to Trajectories. Sequence Types', in Heinz, W.R. (ed.), *Social Dynamics of the Life Course. Transitions, Institutions, and Interrelations*, New York: Aldine de Gruyter, pp. 93–115.

Scherer, S. (2001), 'Early Career Patterns: A Comparison of Great Britain and West Germany', *European Sociological Review*, **17** (2), 119–44.

Schmid, G. (1998), *Transitional Labour Markets: A New European Employment Strategy* (Vol. FS I 98–206), Berlin: Wissenschaftszentrum Berlin für Sozialforschung (WZB).

Schmid, G. (2002), 'Towards a Theory of Transitional Labour Markets', in Schmid, G. and Gazier, B. (eds), *The Dynamics of Full Employment. Social Integration Through Transitional Labour Markets*, Cheltenham, UK and Northampton, MA, USA: Edward Elgar, pp. 151–95.

Schmid, G. (2006), 'Social Risk Management Through Transitional Labour Markets', *Socio-Economic Review*, **4** (1), 1–33.

Schmid, G. and Schömann, K. (2004), *Managing Social Risks Through Transitional Labour Markets. Towards a European Social Model* (Vol. 2004–01), Amsterdam: SISWO/Institute for the Social Sciences.

Tremblay, D.-G. and Le Bot, I. (2003), *The German Dual Apprenticeship System. Analysis of its Evolution and Present Challenges* (Vol. 2003–4A), Québec: Université du Québec.

Wagner, K. (1998), *The German Apprenticeship System after Unification* (Vol. FS I 98–301), Berlin: Wissenschaftszentrum Berlin (WZB).

12. Diverging Career Paths: Mind Your Step!

Amelia Román, Joop Schippers and Leen Heylen

12.1 INTRODUCTION

The unremitting process of individualisation – where personal choice prevails in the organisation of life course biographies – creates a diversification of life course patterns in European societies (Du Bois-Reymond, 1998; Giddens, 1991). Paid labour takes a central but no longer automatically predominant position within these life course patterns. The more traditional breadwinner's career and the partner's role of housewife of previous generations, is losing ground as an increasing number of women enter and remain active participants in the labour market. This creates new challenges for combining work with other important life domains such as care, training and leisure. This is particularly true during the period in the life course when work (through career building) and home (in raising a family) are experienced as conflicting demands in households resulting in a time squeeze (Groot and Breedveld, 2004). Facilities for combining work and care are increasingly being provided in many countries and we know from research that these play an important role in keeping women active in the labour market. Studies providing insight regarding the long-term consequences of the use of such facilities are however, rather scarce (see among others Vlasblom and Schippers, 2005).

Enhancing the labour participation throughout the life course is one of the central building blocks of the European Employment Strategy.[1] If Europe can achieve this goal, the negative consequences of dejuvenation (lower birth rates) and the aging baby boom cohort can, for the most part, be compensated. An increase in labour participation requires, for example, that women work more hours than they currently do, even when there are young children to be cared for. Growth in the labour participation throughout the life course also necessitates a reverse in the current trend of early labour market exit by older workers. One important instrument to initiate the behavioural change, both by employees and employers, is to incorporate an adequate life course policy. The need for some kind of a life course arrangement is evident and policymakers in various EU countries are constructing life course facilities to accommodate households in the rush hour of working life while optimising the labour participation of all possible contributors, particularly women and older workers (Bovenberg, 2003). These frameworks are created for implementing flexible labour forms while accommodating labour markets with employees who are capable of managing their own employability in terms of know-how, productivity and longer-term availability. Manoeuvring through such life course models demands new competences from individuals, not the least of which is the ability to plan well ahead (Ester et al., 2003). The choices that individuals make early in their careers can be vital for their spectrum of alternatives in the future (Román, 2006). This indicates that it is not simply a case of providing adequate instruments, but that it is imperative that individuals are guided and supported throughout their careers. This implies an all-encompassing life course policy, not just the introduction of ad-hoc instruments. Or, to be more concrete: life course policies should already start at school, where children can learn that choices made in childhood may not be without repercussions in later life. In this manner, life course policy takes form through instruments that promote lifelong learning, not only for those who are in employment and can benefit from educational and training facilities provided by their employer, but also and especially for those who have (temporarily) dropped out of the labour market. Another dimension of the life course policy system is the support it lends to people who want to combine work and private life during the rush hour of life. Finally, adequate life course policies ascribe the issue of active ageing: gradually leaving the labour market, while still promoting the use of senior potential and the inclusion of the elderly in society.

As classic patterns make way for new, deviating from a standard career path is increasingly becoming an option for individuals to combine paid labour with other important life domains. These career detours emerge in diverse labour forms such as part-time jobs, temporary working hour reductions and labour force time-outs, and are used by individuals to alleviate conflicting time demands throughout careers, especially during the rush hour of working life. Are standard full-time working careers becoming less the norm? Is there evidence of an increase in transitions from, to, and within the labour market? This chapter investigates the existence of new and diverse patterns of labour participation on the labour market. To do this, we have opted for the Belgian labour market as a case study and this is for two reasons. The first reason is because the Belgian government has a relatively highly-developed life course policy, certainly concerning labour market participation. The second reason is because of the availability of a dataset containing a retrospective career module in the 2002 survey among Belgian households including extensive career history information for more than 4,400 individuals.

The transitional labour market approach provides a useful framework for our research. After all, a career path is in essence a sequence of transitions and periods between consecutive transitions. The traditional life courses of women, and more specifically of men are characterised by a limited number of transitions during the life course, and relatively long stays in a particular state. The more modern life course would then be distinguished by shorter stays and more frequent transitions. Because the modernisation of the life course occurs gradually by cohort, it would be reasonable to assume that the modern life course will chiefly be an issue for younger generations. Life course with (again using the terminology of Schmid (2006)) 'bad transitions' are life courses that can be recognised by their intermittent periods of illness, disability and unemployment. Life courses that are chiefly discernible by part-time work are life courses that, again in TLM terms, involve partial transitions, namely combinations of activities in different domains. Because of the existence of a rather large group of elderly men who once chose a traditional pattern, we assume that this pattern will be the most considerable in number. We also expect to observe a clearly recognisable pattern of those individuals (namely women) who during the larger part of their life course combined work and care. Regarding the 'modern' pattern, we anticipate a less consistent picture. It is because of the great number of possible transitions that the variance will be much larger here and it may be the case that no one type stands out.

The organisation of this chapter is as follows. In Section 12.2 the Belgian career break system, a highly innovative life course policy instrument, is described. In Section 12.3 the data are introduced along with both methods of analyses. In Section 12.4 labour patterns are analysed and typologies are established. In Section 12.5 these typologies are used for a cohort analysis. In Section 12.6 the use of the career break by each career type is discussed. The last section (12.7) summarises the main findings and draws conclusions.

12.2 THE BELGIAN CAREER BREAK SYSTEM

This account begins in the mid 1980s, when most Western countries were faced with economic setbacks characterised by sluggish or even shrinking economies, soaring inflationary rates and alarming levels of unemployment. It was especially the disproportionally high youth unemployment that called for drastic measures.

At this time, the Belgian Federal government introduced a system of career breaks to deal with these problems which would allow individuals to exit the labour market while still retaining their binding labour contract with their employer. Employers were then obligated to replace the worker on leave for a discrete period of time with someone who was currently unemployed and receiving unemployment compensation. This was essentially designed to be a self-financing employment oriented policy measure. The system was innovative in that, up to that time, individuals wishing to take any kind of extended leave from work were forced to quit their jobs, be it for health reasons, to care for young children, care of spouse or extended family member, or educational training. Although the Belgian career break system was originally intended as an employment measure, it has, through its many amendments, evolved into a life-course-oriented employment policy, one of the most fully developed in Europe. Initially the design of the Belgian career break system was quite rigid, requiring immediate hiring of an unemployed person in the temporarily vacated position. Over the years, several amendments have allowed for a more flexible implementation both for employers and employees.

In the Belgian career break system, during the period of leave-taking, the worker receives no salary, does not accrue vacation time, but does continue to build pension entitlements. Although the government provides subsidy for the worker taking leave, it is a small, lump sum of a few hundred euros per month with some minor adjustments for full-time/part-time, lone parents and lower income groups. It does not compensate for the missed earnings, nor is it intended to. What it does create is a buffer of security for the employee to temporarily exit the labour market knowing that his or her place will be there upon return. This type of security is especially important when labour markets are more dynamic and non-institutionalised exits can translate to longer than intended absence from working life with all of the social and financial repercussions that ensue (see Román and Schippers, 2005).

The Belgian career break system is quite flexible. The exit or hours reduction is not restricted by the reason for taking leave. The individual is not obliged to justify the motivation to take a career break. On the other hand, the employer is required to permit the career break as long as the maximum number of employees on leave is not exceeded or, if work continuity without the employee is not possible, the employer is obligated to well-motivate the denial. The current maximum period of time for the (time credit) break is one year although extensions are possible through many of the collective labour agreements.

In the second half of the nineties, a new amendment to the Belgian system introduced three thematic leaves: parental, medical care and palliative care of the terminally ill.[2] Thematic leaves have priority over regular career breaks and are not subtracted from the amount of time allowed for regular career breaks. Thus, thematic leaves are *in addition to* career breaks. Individuals taking a thematic break are also entitled to a higher compensation than individuals taking regular career breaks. The same logistic restrictions still apply, however. Leave-taking is not necessarily full-time. It can also be a reduction of working hours by one-fourth, one-third or one-half, which is essentially an official introduction of part-time work to the Belgian labour market albeit for temporary periods.

12.3 DATA AND METHODOLOGY

12.3.1 The PSBH Career Module Data

The data used for this research is from the Panel Study on Belgian Households (PSBH), a survey originating in 1992 with annual waves following the original 4,439 random selected household counting 11,000 individual members. The survey is conducted using face-to-face interviews. Respondents are adults in private households (aged 16 years and older). All of Belgium is covered with an achieved sample size of 4,439 households and a response rate between 85 and 93 per cent. The fieldwork is expedited during the period from May to November. The sampling frame is the Postcode Address File of the National Registration Office.

In the 2002 wave of the panel, a special module on careers was included. It was completed by 4,453 respondents answering questions on the entire career path starting with the moment that their initial schooling was completed or terminated through to their retirement from active labour participation. Of the 4,453 individuals completing the career module, a total of 99 persons registered having made use of a full-time career break (between 1985 and 2002) at some time during their working career (just over 2 per cent). Unfortunately, the part-time career breaks are not identifiable in our data set, as only one labour market state per year could be registered, and in this case two – namely part-time employment and part-time career break – are occurring simultaneously. There are obvious drawbacks to using retrospective data, especially when the survey questions are covering such lengthy periods of time. However, the career module is designed using questions that carefully guide respondents to register their periods of labour participation, inactivity, unemployment, schooling, and so on, using major life course events as their historical markers (that is marriage, birth of children, and so on).

12.3.2 Capturing Career Patterns

As stated in the introduction, the purpose of this chapter is to gain insight into the existence and the development of careers and career patterns. Such a pattern can be characterised by a sequence of the possible periods and positions or labour market states. For instance: as a student (in preparation of entering the labour market), being employed, being self-employed, being unemployed, being sick or disabled, as care-giver (of children or the elderly), as a pensioner, and so on. Theoretically, numerous labour market states and periods can also be repeated during the life course such as re-entering the labour market after a period of caring for a first baby, and again a few years later for the second. During the greater part of the twentieth century, the dominant male pattern after a period of initial education was to enter the labour market in full-time continuous employment – usually remaining with one employer – until retirement some 40 years later. This period was only interrupted in cases of unemployment, illness or disability. After reaching the eligible pension age, men entered a phase of rest. For women, the standard pattern was one of initial education – caring – and then rest although their caring tasks remained even after reaching the official pensioner's age. Paid employment was not more than something that occurred at the beginning of the mature life cycle, for instance in the period before marriage or during the period in which there were no children to care for. An exception to this rule were the women in the country who worked with their husbands and took an active part in the work on the farm. During the second half of the twentieth century paid labour also became part of the life course pattern of urban women. It can be expected that the diversity in life course patterns have successively increased and that women will exhibit a leading role in this diversity of patterns.

12.3.3 Using OMA to Capture Career Patterns

The first method for analysing career patterns is Optimal Matching Analysis which has its roots in molecular biology and more specifically DNA research. Optimal Matching Algorithms were used to recognise patterns in the DNA and protein sequences. The technique calculates for each pair of sequences how much the second sequence differs from the first. A predefined maximum number of mutations are established whereby those sequences requiring more than that maximum number fall into a new category. The adaptation for the social sciences was pioneered by Abbott and Hrycak (1990).

In terms of our analysis, the series of employment states of a respondent measured at each consecutive point in time forms one sequence that is analysed as a career path. This is a logical approach to the data because we would like to determine whether there is observable evidence of changing career patterns. A transition is a move from one labour market state to another. Persons who are studying and have not yet entered the labour market are not included. Only one labour market status is possible per year assessed by registering the labour market status for which the most time during that year is spent.

The dependent variable employment status is a nominal variable with nine categories: unemployment, unpaid activity, inactivity due to sickness or handicap, study/training, new part time job, part-time job, new full-time job, full-time job and pension.

The OMA technique is based on a number of assumptions that are inherent in the structure of the data. A timeline is assumed with multiple points of measurement t_1, t_2, …, t_n. The variable X is measured at every point in time, which results in a range of observations. In this manner a sequence of observations of variable X at time t is made. This range represents the course or career path for that respondent over the points of measurement of the variable, see Table 12.1.

Table 12.1 Sequence measurement

Respondent	X at t_1	X at t_2	X at t_n	Sequence
1	9	7	25	Sequence 1
2	3	6	18	Sequence 2
3	1	4	19	Sequence 3

The distance between sequence one (the first respondent) and sequence two (the second respondent) is calculated using a transformation measure. This shows the 'cost' of transforming sequence 1 into sequence 2. The transformation is made by inserting, deleting, or substituting elements. Each step entails transformation costs with a deletion or an insertion equalling 1 and a substitution equalling 2. The lower the transformation costs, the more similar the sequences are. This results in a distance or dissimilarity matrix. A dissimilarity matrix is used to establish when the maximum distance has been reached.[3] Once the distance matrix is calculated, the sequences are organised into career typologies using hierarchical agglomerative cluster analysis, first defining every case as unique and gradually grouping similar cases (Chan, 1995). The actual decision on the final number of clusters is made based on the content of the clusters.

12.3.4 Latent Class Regression Analysis for Identifying Career Patterns

Unlike the previous method, Latent Class regression analysis is from the family of latent structure models (Vermunt, 2004; Vermunt and Magidson, 2004). Latent means that the analysis is directed to look for similarities that are not obvious or immediately discernible. For instance, in much the same way that a factor analysis can establish underlying dimensions that group similar survey questions, latent class establishes underlying similarities in scores, with the aid of covariates to identify like groups.

There are no assumptions concerning the measurement level; both indicator and latent variables can be nominal which permits us to use multivariate regression analysis with a nominal dependent variable. This is important when establishing career patterns as no hierarchy is entered in the model concerning career paths. Determining the correct number of classes in the model is essential because using too many classes makes for an unstable model, while too few classes does injustice to the variety in the data.[4] Latent Class analysis allows for two types of control variables to be added to the model: predictors or explanatory variables and covariates for descriptive distributions. The dependent variable is the nominal variable; labour market status, this time with five categories: unemployment, nonparticipation (including students, voluntary nonparticipants and involuntary nonparticipants as in the case of persons ill or disabled), pension, full-time work and part-time work.

A number of assumptions are now introduced, in particular how labour patterns are influenced during particular life course stages. For this we include in the model an explanatory variable (predictor), the variable age, entered with three categories to reflect major life course stages: younger than 30 years of age, 30–49 years of age (time squeeze) and 50 and older. Further, three variables are added as inactive (non-explanatory) covariates to distinguish how personal characteristics are distributed over the classes: gender, cohort (using the same six categories as the OMA) and the variable – past career break – ever having taken an institutionalised career break in the past.

12.4 DEFINING TYPOLOGIES FROM THE ESTABLISHED PATTERNS

12.4.1 OMA Typologies

The career module includes respondents who began their career as far back as 1931 making a maximum number of 72 measurements possible (1931–2002).

There are also respondents who have only just begun their careers with no more than one or two employment status measurements. A total of 4,268 respondents have been included in the analysis. The clustering of the distance matrix resulted in a total of 17 identifiable patterns. A brief explanation of each of the 17 types will now be given.

1. Student
   Students are still involved with their initial education and do not actively participate in the labour market.
2. Stable entrant
   This group has only recently joined the labour market actively. This initial entrance has been without any noticeable problems. The number of transitions is limited to a maximum of one; this is often a transition from one job to the next.
3. Short limited transitional career
   Although this group has participated a bit longer and working in full-time jobs has a central position, many of these respondents have changed jobs already a few times.
4. Job hopper
   These respondents regularly change both their jobs and their employment status. Job-hopping is the central theme here. By the very tendency to change so often, the image is one of an unstable career pattern.
5. Stable full-time
   These respondents fulfil the transitional career image in which full-time work is the common denominator. Full-time employment is carried out for longer periods and in the same job.
6. Transitional full-time
   Just as the previous type, here too, working full-time is dominant with the main difference being that these respondents have a less stable career path. In this group, job transitions are more common.
7. Stable part-time
   These are the real part-time employees displaying a very stable pattern of part-time employment and only a few transitions.
8. Unstable part-time
   This group is quite similar to the previous groups but has a much less stable career path.
9. Stable nonparticipation
   The career path for this group is predominantly unpaid labour revealing quite a stable pattern.
10. Unstable nonparticipation
   This group also demonstrates a predominant pattern of unpaid activity but their pattern is much less stable.

11. Unemployed
    These respondents have been unemployed for the major part of their career.
12. Sickness or handicap
    These careers are characterised by long periods of illness and disablement.
13. Atypical career
    An atypical career path is characterised by periods of unemployment, unpaid activity, schooling and illness, and is as diverse as can be imagined.
14. Insecure career
    The insecure career path shows periods of employment that are often interrupted for shorter and longer periods of unemployment and unpaid activity.
15. Standard career
    These respondents have followed the traditional career path. After a stable full-time career with few or even no transitions, they retire from the labour market.
16. Transitional full-time – retirement
    These respondents have also worked almost their entire career in full-time positions, ending their careers with retirement.
17. Atypical career – retirement
    This last group has had a less traditional career considering that periods of full-time employment are not necessarily the main ingredient.

Table 12.2 provides a descriptive presentation of the career patterns found in the career module data using the OMA method.

The largest group is the longer labour careers with most of the respondents showing stable full-time employment throughout their careers. This group also has the second largest subgroup showing a predominance of transitional full-time employment. This is very much the norm and represents the standard career type. Of the six career types the students are yet to begin, leaving actually five discernible groups.

As can be observed in the table, either men or women dominate in a number of the typologies. Although at the start of the career path, women and men are evenly represented as labour market entrants, women are clearly over-represented among the job-hoppers at the start of their careers. Why this is so is not apparent. It would indicate a more transitional nature in terms of career styles. It certainly is worth looking into more deeply. Women have more diversity in their career paths. This is well-known and was one of the decisive factors in Mincer and Polachek's (1974) developing alternative models for analysing women's earnings. The fact that this diversity is so evident at the beginning of career paths is not so well-known.

Further, it can be noted that women dominate just about every typology where the word unstable or atypical is used: unstable part-time, unstable career of unpaid work, atypical career path and even the atypical longer career and retirement. Diversity and transitional are terms with less of a negative connotation to describe the highly varied career paths of women.

Table 12.2 OMA career typologies, distribution by gender and in population (percentages) and frequencies

Nr.	Type	Total %	% Women	*n*
1	Students	8	53	329
2	Stable entrant	8	51	329
3	Less stable entrant	7	52	317
4	Job hopper	4	71	176
5	Stable full-time	20	40	853
6	Transitional full-time	12	32	506
7	Stable part-time	2	95	93
8	Unstable part-time	2	99	91
9	Stable nonparticipation	9	99	403
10	Unstable nonparticipation	1	98	60
11	Unemployment	1	58	51
12	Sickness or handicap	2	51	73
13	Atypical career	4	79	188
14	Insecure career (unemployment)	2	56	87
15	Standard career	10	35	431
16	Transitional full-time career – retirement	6	25	241
17	Atypical longer career – retirement	1	92	40
	Total	100	54	4,268

Source: PSBH career module, 2002 wave.

12.4.2 The Typologies Established with Latent Class Analysis

The first task at hand is distinguishing the relevant career types resulting from the analysis. This is done using the 11-class model results which are presented in Table 12.3. The programme establishes classes in the analysis in a particular order, and class size gets progressively smaller as the class number rises. The numbers assigned by the programme will not be changed. For the presentation of the analysis results, the arrangement of classes in the tables is not consecutive by number of class but grouped by type. In the table each of the 11 classes is shown with the most common labour market status per age category. By entering an age category as an explanatory variable into the analysis, it is possible to capture life course patterns during the career path that give a more dynamic view of how labour market patterns evolve during careers and throughout life course stages. Each of the 11 typologies is displayed as a percentage of the population as well with the percentage of women observed for each of the career types.

Table 12.3 Career types resulting from latent class nominal regression analysis, classes 1–11

Nr	Type	Age < 30	Age 30–50	Age 50+	Class %	% Women
1	Early retirement	full-time	full-time	pension	28.5	33.2
2	Standard career	full-time	full-time	full-time	27.7	34.1
8	There is more to life	full-time	full-time	non-participation	4.3	59.3
4	Redundancy	full-time	full-time	un-employment	6.4	51.9
6	Bridge group	full-time	full-time	part-time	5.3	78.8
3	Home-maker	non-participation	non-participation	non-participation	7.3	96.2
7	The merry widow	non-participation	non-participation	pension	4.4	88.2
5	Part-time career	part-time/ full-time	part-time	part-time	5.5	92.3
9	Midlife career	non-participation	full-time	pension	4	56.4
11	Midlife part-time career	non-participation	part-time	non-participation	3.1	95.8
10	Career of unemployment	un-employment	un-employment	un-employment	3.7	75.2

Source: PSBH career module 2002 wave.

Early retirement

Regarding the first of the 11 career types distinguished, class one is the largest and consists of 29 per cent of the population. These are full-time employees who, for the most part, exit the labour market somewhere around age 50 for early retirement. There is no part-time work observed, no unemployment, and only a small (2 per cent) likelihood of not participating in the labour market during the early years of the labour career (younger than 30 years of age), probably due to a longer initial educational period. This is one of the two male-dominated classes showing only a third of this class to be female.

Standard career

Class two is the second largest, with 28 per cent of the population. Persons belonging to this class are full-time workers throughout their career. They retire later than the persons from class one. This group also exhibits a small chance of having a late entrance onto the labour market most likely due to greater investments in initial education. This is the second male-dominated class with slightly less than two-thirds being men.

There is more to life

This class is 60 per cent women who work full-time during the first two life course stages and then exit the labour market not as pensioners but as nonparticipants. Possibly these women have not worked enough to receive pension benefits, but leave the labour market at the same time that their partners do.

Redundancy

This group is equally distributed among men and women. They are full-time workers throughout the first two life course stages. At age 50, they encounter some bad luck along the way and are for the most part unemployed. For this group, there are no early retirement packages, or at least none that they can afford to take.

The bridge group

This class is female dominated. They work full-time throughout the first two life course stages and opt for working part-time during their last working phase as a bridge to ease into retirement, possibly because their partner has already gone into retirement.

The homemaker

This group includes 7 per cent of the population and is a highly female-dominated class. They are the traditional housewives who do not participate in any form of paid labour during their potential working lives.

The merry widow

The first stage of this classes' working career is either working full-time or characterised by nonparticipation. It represents more than 4 per cent of the population, and is made up of almost 90 per cent women. The second life course stage is one of unpaid work. These women have exited the labour market to take up the more traditional role of housewife. For the last phase of their labour career they opt for early retirement which is more than likely possible due to a spouse's pension or a widower's pension.

The part-time career
This class is made up of more than 90 per cent women. They work either full-time or part-time until they are 30 years of age. Then they all work part-time, but do so consistently until reaching retirement age.

The midlife career
This group is more or less equally distributed by gender, exhibiting a period of non-participation in their early years followed by full-time work from the age of 30 to 50 years before entering early retirement.

The midlife part-time career
This too is a female-dominated class (96 per cent) exhibiting diversity throughout the career. The first phase is either nonparticipation or full-time work. At age 30, they make the transition to part-time work, most likely to accommodate their responsibilities at home. At age 50, they either continue working part-time or exit the labour market as nonparticipants. They have not built up enough rights to exit in early retirement.

Career of unemployment
This class is almost 4 per cent of the population, three-quarters of whom are women. This group is unemployed from the start to the finish of their career. It is a relatively large group that never effectively enters and participates in the labour market.

Only two of the classes are predominantly male (1 and 2). Six classes are predominantly female (3, 5, 6, 7, 10 and 11). Three classes are more or less evenly distributed by gender (4, 8 and 9). The resulting career types have been possible to characterise by their size in the total population and their gender distribution. But what can be observed regarding whether these are up and coming patterns in the labour market or whether they are more or less dying out? For this, information on the distribution by cohort is essential.

12.5 LABOUR TYPES SEEN FROM A COHORT PERSPECTIVE

The typologies are presented once again, but now by birth cohort in Table 12.4. This gives an impression of which career types are most likely to diminish or increase. Leaving the starters and the retirees out of the picture, we focus on the longer labour career types, the career breakers and the atypical career paths.

Table 12.4 OMA career typology by birth cohort (percentages)

Nr	Type	<1930	1930–39	1940–49	1950–59	1960–69	>1970	Total
2	Stable entrant	0.00	0.00	0.00	0.82	4.39	94.79	100
3	Less stable entrant	0.00	0.00	0.00	5.63	55.85	38.52	100
4	Job hopper	0.00	0.00	0.96	9.81	66.12	23.11	100
5	Stable full-time	4.28	3.73	23.08	41.00	25.93	1.98	100
6	Transitional full-time	0.82	4.67	21.98	43.62	28.56	0.35	100
7	Stable part-time	3.92	12.18	13.41	24.39	43.97	2.13	100
8	Unstable part-time	1.62	14.89	27.36	37.55	18.57	0.00	100
9	Stable nonparticipation	34.39	28.44	19.88	11.59	5.54	0.16	100
10	Unstable nonparticipation	14.73	19.48	30.43	21.88	12.96	0.52	100
11	Unemployment	2.75	1.61	3.98	11.26	26.41	54.00	100
12	Sickness or handicap	6.09	28.49	41.17	17.33	4.67	2.24	100
13	Atypical career path	0.00	0.97	4.38	15.37	47.05	32.22	100
14	Insecure career (unemployment)	0.90	7.37	33.39	28.83	17.73	11.78	100
15	Standard career	47.24	39.36	12.97	0.43	0.00	0.00	100
16	Transitional full-time – pension	42.17	43.57	13.82	0.44	0.00	0.00	100
17	Atypical longer career – pension	84.83	15.17	0.00	0.00	0.00	0.00	100
	Total	13.68	13.13	15.33	20.31	22.40	15.15	100

Source: PSBH career module, 2002 wave.

A higher level of transitional careers can be found for the younger cohorts. This is a first indication of a shift to more transitional careers. The new trend of part-time work is also apparent with a high percentage of stable part-time employment in the 1960–69 cohort. These are certainly women combining paid labour and caring tasks. Among the career breaker types, we observe that the stable career of unpaid work is definitely a downward trend. This is rapidly disappearing on the Belgian labour market, as is the unstable career of unpaid activity, although it still has a rather equal distribution over the cohorts. High percentages of unemployment are most visible among the very young, reflecting high youth unemployment. The atypical career path has a high representation under the youngest cohorts.

Table 12.5 is the proportion of career types per cohort relative to the overall average where 1 is the equilibrium. Any number higher demonstrates a disproportionately higher representation of the class type in the cohort, and lower than 1 is then a disproportionally lower representation of the class in the cohort. This provides an indication of whether certain career patterns are more prevalent by younger or older cohorts, which in turn is a sign of advancing or diminishing career types.

The two more standard, male-dominated careers of working full-time (class one opting for early retirement) and class two (working through to retirement age) are still very strong although, as can be observed, it is the older cohorts that are over-represented in this career type.

Table 12.5 Proportion of class type per cohort relative to overall average

Nr	Type	<1930	1930–39	1940–49	1950–59	1960–69	>1970
1	Early retirement	1.54	1.43	0.39	0.91	1.01	1.02
2	Standard career	0.29	0.35	1.70	1.23	1.03	0.95
8	More to life	0.96	1.59	1.15	0.95	0.75	0.90
4	Redundancy	0.38	0.68	1.17	1.16	1.03	1.21
6	The bridge group	0.12	0.29	0.96	1.09	1.4	1.38
9	Midlife career	2.71	2.21	0.60	0.63	0.63	0.46
5	Part-time career	0.20	0.31	0.49	0.91	1.66	1.60
11	Midlife part-time career	0.63	0.92	1.39	1.29	0.84	0.82
10	Career of unemployment	0.03	0.10	0.36	0.91	1.54	2.14
7	Merry widow	1.95	1.36	0.86	0.91	0.89	0.56
3	Homemaker	2.53	2.37	1.39	0.54	0.28	0.35

Source: PSBH career module, 2002 wave.

The two more traditional female-dominated careers of homemaker (class 3 and class 7) are on their way out. This type of career characterised by nonparticipation for the greater part seems no longer an option for younger cohorts of women. Classes 6, 5 and 10 are up and coming career patterns, all three of which are female-dominated. Class 6 and 5 are highly participative, either full-time or part-time throughout the working life. Class 10 shows a high over-representation by the two youngest cohorts and this class is one long state of unemployment. These women have missed their ticket onto the labour market. This may be because they have left school without qualifications or with qualifications for which there simply was no work.

12.6 HOW THE DIFFERENT CAREER TYPES ARE IMPLEMENTING CAREER BREAKS

The last question to be answered is how the 99 career break users are distributed among the career types that have been established. We start with the 17 types resulting from the OMA. This is presented in Figure 12.1.

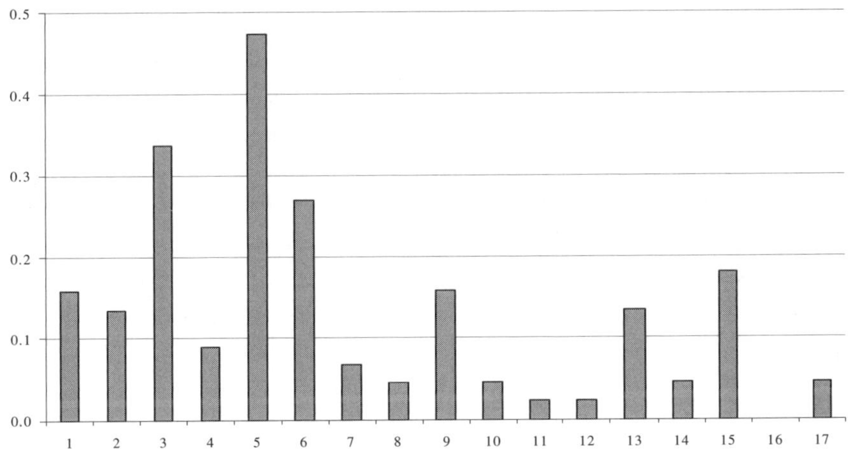

Source: PSBH career module, 2002 wave.

Figure 12.1 Distribution of career break users relative to the average over the 17 types (career break user as percentage within type)

Career break users can be found in almost all of the 17 career types. The total average in the sample is just over 2 per cent. The variation in distribution among the 17 types is presented in Figure 12.1 which demonstrates that the career type showing the greatest percentage of career break users is type 5 (with almost 5 per cent). These are stable full-time employees with longer working careers, which indicates that these workers are using career breaks to facilitate a greater participation and extended careers. Type 3 consists of the less stable labour market entrants that are from younger cohorts. The respondents in type 6 are the traditional full-time workers. What we observe up to now, is certainly not a picture of career break users as labour market drop-outs. The three types in which career break users are most frequently observed are active labour market participants. Those individuals using the career break to exit the labour market can be found in type 9 (the nonparticipants) and 15 (the completed careers). In the last case, they use the career break as an exit for early retirement.

Another way of looking at the career breakers is to show their distribution over the 11 classes found in the latent class analysis. This figure is different from the presentation for OMA in Figure 12.1 where that was in relation to the total average. In Figure 12.2 the distribution of the 99 career breakers is presented. With a total of 99 respondents in this data set who have taken a full-time career break during some period in their working life, we observe that most of the career breakers fall into three distinguishable classes: 7, 8 and 11. Knowing that class 7 is decreasing in size per cohort, combined with the fact that the career break system is increasing in popularity, we can assume that types 8 and 11 will either increase or that we will see a growth coming from other class types. Class 2 also merits attention, as this is a typical male class, yet still almost 10 per cent of the career break users are from this group. It is also the class that works full-time right on through to the pension age which indicates that individuals are indeed using career breaks to enable longer working careers.

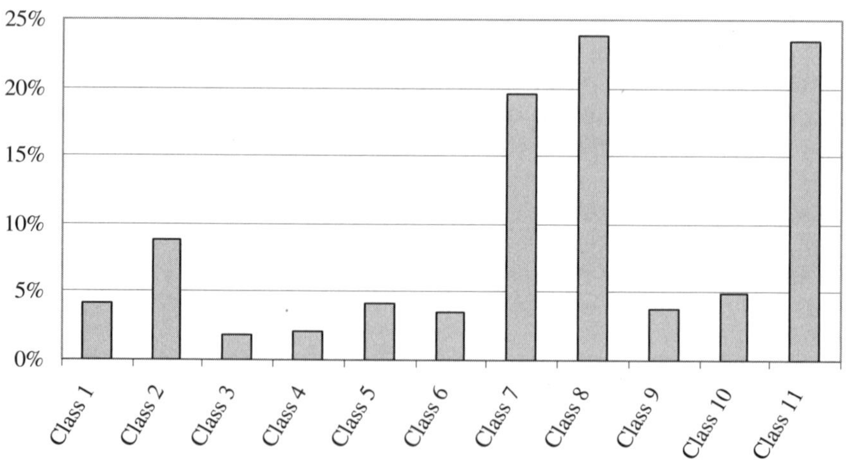

Source: PSBH career module, 2002 wave.

Figure 12.2 Distribution of total number of career break users over the 11 classes (percentages)

12.7 SUMMARY OF THE RESULTS

In this chapter, we use two methods to capture career patterns. The results show that both techniques are useful for analysing such sequence trajectories. The OMA methodology is clearly appropriate when the analysis is focused on the actual labor market states, and due to the relative stability in career paths, OMA is quite useful for making clear and interpretable differentiations. However, if careers do become less stable as we assume, OMA will become a less useful methodological tool. The Latent Class method uses a different approach to sequences. It has the strength of adopting covariates in the clustering allowing for more historical (or in our case life course) anchors than OMA. The clustering is denser and the technique allows for more detailed model fitting controls than OMA. Unfortunately this strength can also be a weakness. When incorporating covariates in a typology, the possibilities of using the typology in later, causal, analyses is somewhat reduced. All interaction effects need to be tested within the LC framework which lessens the opportunities to use the typology in a different context.

What have the two methods of analysis told us about how careers are developing and what can be expected in the future? And what is the role of career breaks among the wide variety of labour market instruments and the great number of transitions made by individuals during their working lives? What have we learned about the career detours from this exploration of the information on life courses and careers of a large group of Belgian citizens? Both the OMA and the Latent Class established a growth in part-time work among younger, female-dominated cohorts, which means that part-time work is also a growing phenomenon in the Belgian labour market as it is in the labour market in the Netherlands. Nonparticipation is decreasing as a labour market option in Belgium similar to the situation in the Netherlands. Career break users show a distribution across cohorts and labour market states, but predominate in three of the typologies. One of these types is diminishing with each new cohort entering the labour market. This is the more 'traditional' use of the career break system as a labour market exit rather than a labour market detour.

The career break is also evident in one of the male-dominated classes, a standard career type of full-time work where the career path extends through to the age of retirement. This is quite interesting as it indicates that men and women are indeed using the career break system to continue their working careers over a longer period, and this is precisely one of the goals of the Belgian career break system. The Latent Class analysis also established an increase in the career type of perpetual unemployment, particularly among younger females. This type of career deviation will no doubt continue to be a part of a dynamic market economy. The persistence of the unemployment period within this career type was rather alarming. It would seem that young individuals (three-quarters of this class was female) who do not make a successful entry onto the labour market are in danger of remaining unemployed for the duration of their potential working life.

The latent class approach is more compact leading to 11 classes (compared to the 17 from OMA), two of which are dominated by men and six of which are dominated by women, making even more evident the fact that women have more diverse career types than men do. The rise in part-time work in Belgium is almost exclusively a female phenomenon. However, the career break is being used by an increasing number of men. These men are using the break for the most part to ease into retirement. It appears that this is an option for an increasing number of men instead of premature exits. Still, 20 per cent of the population was in the transitional full-time employment, two-thirds of which are men. Although women still have more varied careers than men do, this new type of male career, a transitional one, indicates the new style of working, one where job security is exchanged for individual responsibility for employability. Women have probably always worked under these conditions and we have not found any indications that this is likely to change in the near future.

Throughout the years, a major focus of TLM theorists has been the development of policy measures aimed at facilitating so-called 'good' transitions and preventing 'bad' transitions. To develop the 'proper' policy instruments it is useful and necessary to know the major life course patterns among a country's population. Traditional life course patterns were adequately accommodated by the whole system of rules and regulations we have come to know as the breadwinner model. The analyses presented in this chapter show that traditional life course patterns are fading away and so have much of the institutional arrangements belonging to the breadwinner model. The question concerning the alternative(s) is not as easy to answer, although it is clear that there is a considerable need for institutional arrangements that fit into a life course that is characterised by part-time work and the combination of paid labour and (unpaid) care. What is needed policy-wise is, based on the analyses in this chapter, not unambiguously determinable. Within the 'other patterns' (other than the standard career or standard homemaker), there is no one single pattern that can as yet be labelled as representing 'the modern pattern'. Whether this is only temporary or whether modern patterns as such can only be characterised by their variety, is not clear at this time. The growing diversity in life courses is still too much of a recent phenomenon. The best answer that policy can offer is actually already given at the beginning of this chapter: namely an integral life course policy that provides people with the tools while at the same time empowering them during their life course to make the right choices and to choose transitions and a combination that allows them to lead a high quality balanced life.

NOTES

1. The European Council sets targets for employment population ratios (number of active labour market participants as a percentage of the total working age population) at the Lisbon top in 2000. The EU target for 2010 is 70 per cent, or 7 out of 10 persons of working age (15–64) should indeed be actively participating in the labour market. The current EU average is 51 per cent (OECD, 2003).
2. Palliative leave is restricted to terminal care for one month, which can be extended by one month per patient.
3. Ward's Minimum Variance Method.
4. This is achieved with the help of the log-likelihood values, the BIC (Basic Information Criterion) values and the number of parameters in the estimated models.

REFERENCES

Abbot, A. and Hrycak, A. (1990), 'Measuring resemblance in sequence data: an optimal matching analysis of musicians' careers', *American Journal of Sociology*, **96** (1), 144–85.

Bovenberg, A.L. (2003), *Nieuwe levensloopbenadering*, Discussion paper DISP 2003-1, Tilburg: OSA.

Chan, T.W. (1995), 'Optimal matching analysis: a methodological note on studying career mobility', *Work and Occupations*, **22** (4), 467–90.

Du Bois-Reymond, M. (1998), 'I don't want to commit myself yet: young people's life concepts', *Journal of Youth Studies*, **1** (1), 63–79.

Ester, P., Román, A. and Vinken, H. (2003), 'A challenging but uncertain future. Beliefs of the Dutch population about the future of work, work relations, and ICT in the 21st century', *Journal of Future Studies*, (August), 3–19.

Giddens, A. (1991), *Modernity and Self Identity: Self and society in the Late Modern Age*, Cambridge: Polity.

Groot, L.F.M. and Breedveld, K. (2004), 'Time over the life course: preferences, options and the life course policy', *Tijdschrift voor arbeidsvraagstukken*, **20** (3), 288–302.

Mincer, J. and Polachek, S. (1974), 'Family investments in human capital: earnings of women', *The Journal of Political Economy*, **82** (2), Part 2, 76–108.

OECD (2003), *Employment outlook. Towards more and better jobs*, Paris: OECD.

Román, A. (2006), *Deviating from the Standard: Effects on Labour Continuity and Career Patterns*, Amsterdam: Dutch University Press.

Román, A. and Schippers, J.J. (2005), *To Work or not to Work: A Vital Life Course Decision and How it Affects Labour Careers*, Tilburg: OSA.

Schmid, G. (2006), 'Social risk management through transitional labour markets', *Socio-Economic Review*, **4**, 1–33.

Vermunt, J.K. (2004), 'Toepassingen van latent klasse analyse in sociaal wetenschappelijk onderzoek', *Sociale Wetenschappen*, **47**, 2–14.

Vermunt, J.K. and Magidson, J. (2004), 'Latent class analysis', in Lewis-Beck, M., Bryman, A. and Liao, T.F. (eds), *The Sage Encyclopedia of Social Sciences Research Methods*, Thousand Oaks: Sage, pp. 549–53.

Vlasblom, J.D. and Schippers, J. (2005), *Arbeidsmarktconsequenties van Kinderen Krijgen: Een Verkenning van de Langetermijngevolgen*,Tilburg: OSA.

13. Conclusions on Innovating European Labour Markets: Dynamics and Perspectives

Ruud Muffels, Joop Schippers, Ton Wilthagen and Peter Ester

13.1 MAIN QUESTIONS

13.1.1 Transitional Labour Markets, Flexicurity and the Life Course

The questions raised in Chapter 1 of this volume dealt with the way welfare states cope with the ongoing challenges labour markets face with a view to the diversification of employment forms and contracts, resulting in the rise of non-standard labour contracts and part-time work, and the changing needs with respect to the work–life balance associated with the diversification and individualisation of life courses. The increased volatility on the labour market together with the rising shares of non-standard work forms such as part-time work, fixed-term employment contracts and new forms of self-employment such as freelance and telework signal, according to some scholars, a shift from 'lifetime employment' to the 'boundaryless career' (Stone, 2001, 2005). The backdrop of these changes was formed by a number of economic and social-cultural changes such as the increased international competition, the wake and rise of the 'knowledge economy' and demographic changes in the form of rising immigration flows, reduced fertility rates, increased family instability and population ageing. These changes stood also at the basis of the Lisbon strategy formulated in 2000 aimed at making the European Union (EU) the most competitive economy in the world. Since 2001 the Lisbon strategy consists of an economic pillar to boost productivity and employment growth, a social pillar to modernise social protection and to tackle social exclusion and an environmental pillar to decouple economic growth from the use of natural resources. With a view to the growing dynamics on the labour market the book raises the issue to what extent these impact on the labour market transition patterns of males and females over the life course. Do the careers of workers in the different stages of the life course change as a consequence of the ongoing trends and, if so, how do they change and which categories of workers are particularly confronted with these changes? The second main question raised in this volume is to what extent the theoretical perspectives of TLM and flexicurity have resulted into 'best practices' within the European context. This not only concerns labour market policies at the national and the EU level but especially also at the firm level. Innovating firms' policies with respect to creating flexible working time options and to elaborating life-course-oriented human resource policies seems critical to respond successfully to the ongoing fundamental changes.

In Chapter 1, we referred already to the success of the two basic perspectives used in this volume: the TLM and the flexicurity approach to which we added the life course perspective that we see as a constituent element of and as the link between the two main approaches. Within the TLM approach the basic idea is to 'make transitions pay' for which reason policies should facilitate 'good transitions' on the labour market during the entire life course. The flexicurity approach stresses the dimensions of flexibility and security and the need to define policies aimed at reinforcing both. Both approaches acknowledge the importance of improving the work–life balance. The latter concept refers to opportunities people have to combine work, care and education as they wish to do so with a view to their responsibilities and duties in the various stages of the life course (Klammer et al., 2008; Muffels et al., 2008b). In the TLM approach the life course is viewed as a sequence of decisions and transitions related to the occurrence of important life events such as childbirth, single parenthood or job loss. Also the flexicurity approach pays heed to the life course approach by seeing firms and employees as the managers of risks which arise over the life course of the firm as well as of the individual employee.

The work–life balance was already part of the debate on the European Social Model and the subsequent 'flexibility' and 'security' debate in European policy circles, but a genuine life-course-oriented approach has still not been developed. However, it might be inspired by policy perspectives and innovative arrangements which are elaborated in the TLM and flexicurity approaches.

13.1.2 The Various Contributions

In the various contributions to the volume, both comparative empirical research as well as national policy case studies have been performed to provide answers to the two main research questions posed in this book. Part I of the volume deals with transitional labour markets in Europe and the problems various countries face with a view to how current policies operate and how institutions are shaped in coping with the challenges put on them.

Part II of the volume discusses the responses of labour markets and firms' policies to the shifts in the employee relationship as a consequence of the wake and rise of the 'knowledge-based economy' and the changes in working time preferences especially among women due to changes in the work–life balance needs. Finally, in Part III of the volume we look into the life course issue more thoroughly.

Outline

In Section 13.2 we discuss the subsequent findings in the three parts of the book whereas in 13.3 we formulate some conclusions with a view to the lessons to be drawn for future research and policies.

13.2 CONCLUSIONS WITH RESPECT TO THE VARIOUS PARTS OF THE BOOK

13.2.1 Part I: Transitional Labour Markets in Europe

In the decades to come labour markets in Europe confront increased competition, a rising imbalance between the supply and demand of skills, a rapid ageing of the workforce leading to a shortage of labour and rapidly rising migration flows. If this is coupled to trends of the diversification and individualisation of the life course and accompanying changing needs with a view to the work–life balance, it is not difficult to understand the assessment of the Flemish Minister for Employment and Education, Frank Vandenbroucke, that European labour markets undergo fundamental changes to which they need to respond. We then can also comprehend his view that this assessment is not a matter of doom-mongering, but of facing up to the 'inconvenient truth', based on real facts. Countries and regions that do not take measures or take them too slowly will fall behind. In presenting the Flemish and Belgian country case study using macro-level data and figures about the level of flexibility and employment performance of the Flemish and Belgian labour market compared with the labour markets in the Netherlands, the Nordic countries and Europe as a whole, he showed the urgency of the need for innovating labour market policies. The Flemish labour market – but the same seems to hold for many other continental or southern countries – can be characterised by the so-called 'compressed career' model, indicating that people are employed in paid work between the age of 25 and 55 years but much less so before, due to prolonged education, and after, due to early retirement exit. If this feature is coupled to its poor employment performance with respect to the immigrants and the low-skilled, the Flemish labour market is characterised by the so-called insider–outsider cleavage. In trying to explain this, Frank Vandenbroucke points to the impact of the strong labour market regulation and the generosity of benefits for the elderly and the unemployed causing disincentives to employment and to investing in human capital formation.

Pathways to flexicurity in Europe

This supports the conclusions by Ruud Muffels who compared the dissimilar performance of various pathways in Europe to balancing flexibility and security for males and females distinctly by elaborating and applying gender-based dynamic outcome indicators for mobility and employment and income security. The main hypothesis was derived from institutional theories dealing with how institutions might affect labour market behaviour and hence the transition decisions and mobility patterns of males and females differently in the various countries under scrutiny. The chapter looked into the effect of regime type as well as into the effect of specific institutions such as the strictness of the employment regulations in a country, the generosity of unemployment benefits, active labour market policies and the availability of working time options at the company level on the individual mobility patterns of males and females. Whereas Vandenbroucke used macro-level data and static measures to look into the relationship between mobility indicated by average tenure (or seniority as he called it) and employment performance, Muffels adds to his approach by using dynamic micro-level data and dynamic measures for mobility and security. However, the results being rather robust across the different sets of indicators used show markedly different outcomes between especially the Nordic and Anglo-Saxon countries on the one hand, with high levels of labour market mobility and employment security (though with low income security especially for females in the Anglo-Saxon regimes), and the Southern countries on the other hand, with moderate levels of mobility but rather poor levels of employment and income security.The contrasting evidence for these regime types are even more pronounced for females than for males. The results also indicate that rather different pathways seem equally successful or equally unsuccessful in balancing mobility and security goals showing that there is no one-size-fits-all approach.

Also Sandrine Cazes and Alena Nesporova in their chapter provide rather strong evidence on the dissimilar way the post-socialist or transition countries perform in combining flexibility or mobility and employment security. They show that the transition countries are not particularly successful in raising employment in the 2000–2004 period; on the contrary, in a number of the Eastern welfare states employment has even declined, which tempted the authors to suggest that these Eastern regimes represent rather typical cases of jobless growth in Europe. Their results confirm largely what Philips and Eamets (2007) also found for these countries showing moderate levels of flexibility, low levels of benefit generosity, high (long-term) unemployment and poor employment records which are even worse than the poor records of the Southern countries. The Eastern countries due to their typical past seem to set themselves clearly apart also from the Southern regimes in Europe. Compared with the Southern countries they share a poor employment record though coupled to a higher level of flexibility with a view to their employment protection regulations. A second remarkable finding is that even though these transition countries experienced rather satisfactory levels of economic growth labour turnover indicated by the so-called accession (movements into employment) and separation rates (movements out of employment) remained rather stable or even declined over the period 1999–2003 in most countries. The evidence showed that the accession and separation rates have fallen over these years in these countries. The counter-cyclical patterns found here are rather remarkable from an economic point of view while for the Western countries and mainly for supply-side reasons a pro-cyclical behaviour of these rates can be observed, especially induced by the pro-cyclical behaviour of voluntary moves. The only exceptions to this counter-cyclical development are Hungary and Bulgaria. The authors explain this unexpected trend with the term 'defensive restructuring', indicating that since most firms in these transition countries have left their restructuring stage behind, as a result of which they do not need to dismiss workers in large numbers any more, their economies still do not perform well enough to open new job positions. The weak growth in part-time employment that the authors observed and the strongly increasing share of temporary contracts in these countries also signal their poor employment record in the years 2000.

The impact of institutions

The TLM approach assigns a large role to institutions in shaping the outcomes of particular policy configurations. Some contributions in this part looked into the role of specific institutions. The findings confirm what Vandenbroucke claims in his chapter, that strict employment protection rules in a country seem to jeopardise the level of labour market mobility or turnover on the labour market and therewith to increase the insider–outsider cleavage acting as a barrier to attain high levels of employment stability and security. Also Muffels in his chapter found rather strong and adverse effects of the level of employment protection regulation on the individual mobility, patterns especially for males but also for females. He also observed that the availability of working time options in firms tend to lower mobility suggesting that if workers have more opportunities to reconcile work and private life there is less need for them to change jobs for meeting their working time needs. The finding that the Nordic countries perform best in balancing flexibility and security might be attributed to the particular design of their policies, in particular in the case of Denmark, that is commonly praised and judged as being the 'flexicurity' model for Europe (see also Muffels and Luijkx, 2008). The combination of rather lean employment protection regulations, generous benefits and a strong commitment of all parties to improve worker's employability seem key to the success of the Danish case for which reason Madsen (Jørgensen and Madsen, 2007) has called it the 'golden triangle'. The Flemish approach to resolve the weak flexibility–employment record of its labour market as Vandenbroucke illustrated seems very much in accordance with the Danish flexicurity approach but also follows the principles and recipy of the TLM approach. His idea of the need for policies to resolve so-called 'vicious circles' caused by persistent false beliefs geared to a very strict institutional set-up seems to be in the heart of the current debate on employment and social policy in Europe.

Vicious circles and policies to resolve them

Vandenbroucke stresses the impact of the institutional context in conjunction with what he calls 'persistent false beliefs' leading to vicious circles which explain why progress has been so slow, with regard to both regulatory reform and practical change on the shop floor. He mentions two vicious circles with respect to older workers and immigrants. The vicious circle for older workers is that they are considered less productive and that they wish to retire earlier, while employers do not invest in their human capital and create high incentives for early exit, reinforcing therewith the belief that older workers are less productive and eager to exit and that there are no jobs available to them. Vandenbroucke argues that workers due to the 'rat race' in the economy and the combination of work and family duties had to work so hard that they feel 'squeezed out like a lemon', and aspire to leave the labour market early, or are forced to do so. But if the work pressure is lowered by, for example, more flexible working time schedules allowing workers to better meet their worklife balance needs or by investments in the human capital of the older workers and the creation of incentives to stay in work, there is no reason to assume that older workers want to retire early and that there are no jobs available to them. Also immigrants confront a vicious circle: due to being less easily hired, they tend to invest less in their own human capital formation, thus reinforcing the tendency of employers not to hire them and therewith providing new ammunition for the belief that they are less productive. If the barriers for potential employers as well as employees to invest in human capital are removed the vicious circle might be resolved. This seems to be the way chosen by the Danes to avoid the insider–

outsider dilemma through the upgrading of skills and therewith to improve the employability of workers. This seems to imply that workers do not end up in unemployment or bad jobs, and because they are better equipped with the necessary skills they are able to safeguard their 'employment security' over their entire career. The particular features of the Flemish policy measures as mentioned by Vandenbroucke seem attractive while they are explicitly geared to the life course approach:

- The *time credit* system, being a very attractive leave scheme to be used for various purposes, is an example of an innovative policy approach to relax work or career pressures during active life. Vandenbroucke adds a proviso, though, saying that it should be geared to safeguarding prolonged working life because otherwise it could even increase the workload of those who do not take up the time credit.
- The *competence management* agenda, that concerns the detection, recognition and development of formal (education, training) as well as the informal qualifications people have obtained at work but also in other social contexts. Other elements pertain to creating options for broader access to career counselling, development of personal portfolios and access to lifelong learning practices. In the end, the fundamental idea is that the right to personal development is settled as a guaranteed right and duty, since competence development should be viewed as a shared responsibility.
- The *diversity plans* and the special *training scheme* for unprivileged groups among the unemployed, the former providing a wage–cost subsidy to employers to hire immigrants and the latter to provide a subsidy to cover the costs of in-firm training during a time limited contract after which the employer is committed to render the candidate a standard permanent contract.

Also the last idea to create incentives to employers to invest in training for workers on temporary contracts in exchange for the employer's commitment to hire the worker after the training on a permanent contract seems innovative especially with a view to the insider–outsider issue. It seems a way to reduce the gap between temporary and open–ended contracts in terms of employment security as well as in terms of income security also in the longer run for the entire career.

Migration and employability policies: challenges to the Eastern countries

These training policies might also be a way forward for the Eastern countries to progress, given the poor employment growth in their economies. The authors of Chapter 4 therefore call for more active labour market policies in the transition countries to create more equal labour market opportunities for the various population groups and to invest in education and training policies much more than was the case hitherto. These recommendations suggest that the low skill level of the Eastern labour force needs to be upgraded to become more competitive for the countries concerned also in terms of providing a better quality of products and services. On the other hand if in these transition countries there is not sufficient employment as the findings clearly indicate, the best workers might be inclined to look for better opportunities in another country causing a 'brain drain' in these countries and a rapidly rising migration flow from the East to the West. This is another 'vicious circle' these countries confront and that they need to resolve to be able to sustain economic growth geared to rising employment levels with jobs of better quality.

Research on the issue of migration as reported in Chapter 5 by Didier Fouarge and Peter Ester suggests that the accession of the Eastern countries in the EU has boosted mobility intentions in these countries. The consequences of the rise in migration flows are huge not only for the countries from which they move (the donor countries) but also for the countries these migrants move to (the host countries) for which reason it has drawn a lot of attention at the national and the EU policy level in the last couple of years with the enlargement of the EU. One in twenty Europeans has such a migration intention but the differences across countries are huge. In the Baltic states and in Poland the migration intention is especially large but not so much in the other former socialist countries. Across the population it is the younger people (in particular students), the higher educated and singles who express an intention to migrate to another country in the near future and not so much the lower educated as initially many commentators feared. The findings from the Eurobarometer surveys which the authors used, convincingly show that the fear of a 'brain drain' is not without reason in the Eastern countries since the fraction of people among the higher educated intending to move are larger in these countries than in the other countries. Apart from a brain drain it also seems that a youth drain is occurring. The authors, trying to explain the migration intention by performing multivariate analyses, confirm the descriptive findings reported earlier. They also show that the loss of social networks acts as a barrier to migrate and especially so for people in the Eastern countries, although unexpectedly not so for people in Poland or the Baltic states. Migration for many of the migrants is seen as an investment in their human capital they need to make for a temporary period in order to improve their future labour market and economic prospects, which investment would otherwise not have been realised in their home countries. To break this vicious circle by strong investments in the human capital formation seems to be the major challenge these countries face. To the extent that they are successful in achieving this, it means for the Western countries that they have to search for other solutions to relieve the pressure on their labour markets due to ageing, either through inducing migration flows from other countries or by reducing the labour intensity of their economies. Another way forward would certainly be for the transition countries to facilitate the creation of part-time jobs to improve the opportunities for women to reconcile work and life and to better meet their working time needs. This, however, is discussed in the second part of the book.

13.2.2 Part II: Flexicurity and Working Time Arrangements

The discussion on flexicurity is primarily a discussion on balancing rights and duties, balancing employers' interests and workers' concern for the institutional arrangements that can help to bring about this balance and to avoid the scale tipping towards one particular group or one particular interest. This discussion concerns legal rules as developed by the European Union, by national governments, collective agreements between social partners and the labour contract of individual workers. In this part of the book the focus is on the meso level, the relation between employers or organisations and their employees. One major dimension of the flexibility discussion that is relevant to every individual employee from day to day concerns working time arrangements, including the opportunities for part-time work. Legal clauses or clauses in individual contracts on dismissal rules and dismissal compensation may become relevant once or twice during an individual's life course. Working time arrangements relate to everyday life and are essential for employees' opportunities to reconcile work and family life, for their opportunities to participate in civil society and of course for basic conditions such as health. That is why working time arrangements are essential to the flexicurity discussion.

Organising employer–worker cooperation

In this part of the book Marsden first compares the 'standard', traditional employment relationship with contracts that govern different forms of project-based employment as a relatively new and modern way of organising employment relations. He concludes that compared with the 'standard' employment relationship, one might consider project-based employment as being open-ended in terms of collaborators' task obligations, but not so in relation to its temporal duration. People may well collaborate on successive projects, but the implicit promise of open-ended duration employment is absent, and renewed collaboration is contingent on getting new commissions.

Economic theory as well as insights from psychology predict different behaviour of the individual working on different types of contract. Economists have pointed to the so-called hold-up problem concerning human capital investments: without a continuous relation between an employer and his employee both parties may be reluctant to invest in the acquirement of new human capital, because of the uncertainty that there will be enough revenues from these investments (Teulings and Hartog, 1998). This does not imply that one should reject project-based employment. It does, however, call for additional institutional arrangements to safeguard an adequate level of human capital investments. Marsden looks at employment relationships in sectors using project-based models of organisation, in order to understand how workers and firms have solved problems of cooperation. These models have developed a number of mechanisms that help to control opportunism and foster a zone of shared interests in order to strengthen cooperation. Nevertheless, these functional equivalents to the mechanisms governing the established employment relationship were often less well developed, and tensions between them undermined their influence. This should not come as a surprise given the long history of thinking in terms of long-term stable employment relations. In the minds of many employers and most employees this still is the standard that drives expectations and conditions behaviour. Finally, Marsden concludes that there is some evidence also that compared with occupations which have more structured entry and careers, those in which project-based employment is more developed are characterised by a more unequal distribution of earnings and of economic security.

Europe shows a variety of working time flexibility arrangements

Several authors have previously pointed to the fact that employers and workers may differ with respect to their appreciation of different working time arrangements (see for example Den Dulk et al., 1999). For instance parents generally do appreciate some kind of working time flexibility, but more often than not this is not the kind of working time flexibility preferred by employers. Employers want to respond quickly to unexpected and unpredictable peaks in the demand for their goods and services. Consequently, they like to have a pool of flexible workers who can be called up more or less immediately to lend a hand. Parents, on the contrary, despise this kind of unpredictability because it disrupts their usually carefully designed system of care for the children. The chapter by Kerkhofs, Chung and Ester fits with this discourse perfectly. They present their study of working time arrangements and related flexibility strategies, based on a recent establishment survey in 21 European countries. On the basis of a range of indicators they develop a typology of organisation strategies regarding working time flexibility and the work–life balance. The resulting typology discerns six flexibility profiles – two very flexible, three moderately flexible and one relatively inflexible – and is seen to distinguish organisations and organisation strategies by the degree of flexibility as well as the focus of the flexibility profile. The two most flexible profiles have a relatively high take-up of most of the arrangements involved, but one puts more weight on the aim of supporting the workers' work–life balance and the other on accommodating workload variations and preferences of customers and business relations. This clearly shows that working time flexibility should not be treated as a one-dimensional concept ranging from low to high flexibility. The most widespread profile – having a high level of working time flexibility, mainly focused on the organisation's operational needs – applies to 22 per cent of the European organisations. Their findings imply that in terms of working time flexibility there is no single dominant profile, or in other words European firms do not tend to favour one form of flexibility in particular. A multivariate analysis, relating the flexibility profiles to other characteristics of the organisation – such as its line of business and the size and composition of the workforce – shows that the country in which it is located and the size of the establishment are the strongest determinants of the flexibility profile of the organisation. This supports the conclusion drawn earlier by Wilthagen et al. (2006) that flexicurity arrangements cannot be seen apart from the welfare state regime of the country. Kerkhofs et al. furthermore report that there is some evidence that social and economic problems particularly arise in the highly flexible organisations that prioritise operational needs and in the intermediately flexible organisations that adopt overtime and irregular working hours; the fewest problems are observed in worker-oriented high-flexibility organisations and in low flexibility organisations.

Flexibility, security and trust

To analyse what has been realised in terms of flexicurity arrangements at the organisational level Vermeylen takes the discussion back to the original flexibility debate of the 1980s and 1990s of the twentieth century. If you want an answer to 'the question of balance' you need to go back to the 'original' dimensions of flexibility as put forward by someone like Atkinson (1984) and study the achievements on each of these dimensions. Even though it would require additional study to meet this challenge a first attempt to answer the questions put forward by Vermeylen would result in making a distinction between time and money. Looking at the development of European labour markets over the last decade one is inclined to conclude that flexibility has made much more progress when it comes to time than in the field of pay. Even though this very broad and general conclusion calls for all kinds of qualifications immediately it has a certain degree of plausibility, especially if one relates it to another point brought up by Vermeylen and that is the issue of trust. Looking from this point of view one might argue that employees might be more confident to guard some kind of balance when it comes to working time arrangements than in the case of flexibility of pay. In the latter case they seem much more dependent on the employer and may show little trust in their own opportunities to restore the balance in case of any disturbance.

Working time arrangements in a life course perspective

Another issue related to innovative working time arrangements deals with so-called working time accounts which are developed with a view to the life course perspective. They discuss the findings of a research project on the preconditions and practices of long-term working time accounts in Germany and their effects on the distribution of working time over the life course. Leading is the question how long-term working time accounts change the dynamics of company working time policy, and whether or not these accounts help to stabilise discontinuous life courses. A working time account introduces a kind of flexibility with respect to time such as a bank account offers with respect to money: it helps individuals to redistribute resources over the life course. From an employer's point of view it is the dynamic form of quantitative flexibility. Hildebrandt and Wotschack examine the evolution of long-term and lifetime working time accounts in addition to flexitime accounts and annual working time accounts, which are both already widespread. Mechanisms for transferring credits between the different types of accounts are being created, which is leading to the dissolution of the boundaries between day-to-day flexibility and life cycle flexibility. However, the configuration of the new boundaries is dealt with in a variety of different ways. Flexible benefit plans may even connect or integrate working time and financial saving accounts (Hillebrink, 2006). Employees' choices will depend on rules and regulations governing the accounts (for example taxation of savings, the possibilities to use time saved for early retirement and so on). Extending the term of a working time account brings up the question of the continuity of the labour relation between an employer and the employee as well as the issue of trust. If it concerns a pension savings account with a company it is (relatively) easy to organise some form of compensation for the employee in case of bankruptcy of a company. But how can you 'repay' a loss of hours on a working time account in case of bankruptcy? This question relates immediately to the issue of transferability. Some countries – like the Netherlands – have successfully resolved the question of the transferability of (company) pension savings between industries and companies. But with working time accounts some new questions emerge. The authors discuss a series of problems to be solved and the direction where possible solutions can be found. However, it is clear that a lot of research and development still has to be done before companies all over Europe will be able to introduce working time accounts successfully.

Even though the four chapters from this second part of the book could cover only few of the items under discussion at the meso level it is clear, however, that:

- the discussion on flexicurity and life course arrangements at the meso level is still in its infancy. European countries appear to differ markedly with respect to such arrangements;
- companies are struggling with the need to balance their own needs with those of their employees and sometimes come up with very creative and innovative arrangements;
- trust is a major issue when solving the problem of conflicting interests between employers and employees and developing arrangements promoting a balance between flexibility and security;
- there is a close relation between meso-level flexicurity and life course arrangements and national arrangements.

13.2.3 Part III: Life Course Transitions and Careers

Active ageing starts in the 'Kindergarten'

Part III of the book explicitly focuses on life course transitions and careers. All three chapters discuss different life course events and transitions that can be considered sources of 'insecurity', either in terms of employment or in terms of income later in life. All three chapters also discuss forms of life course policy and life course arrangements that can be considered as an instrument to reduce insecurity. Günther Schmid points to the fact that the opportunities for 'active ageing' differ between individuals, not only depending on their past experiences throughout the life course, but also on the institutional framework governing old age and retirement. He concludes that 'active ageing' must not only start with elderly people but much earlier in the life cycle. New life cycle risks require new social rights beyond employment – such as care leave and career breaks. Schmid even proposes the right not to work in the transition from the second to the third life-phase. The new right beyond employment is referred to by him as the concept of 'sustainable employability', meaning that qualifications and skills required for gainful work have to be enhanced over the entire life course. It also concerns the elderly workers who must be motivated to participate in further education more than ever before. However, it has also become clear that the level of continuous education and training is related more closely to the base level of education than to age. Therefore, active ageing starts with education in the 'Kindergarten'.

Another conclusion of Schmid is that early intervention is also necessary in view of long-term interruptions of employment. Such discontinuities still affect mainly women and translate into long-term wage penalties, higher probabilities of sustained precarious employment careers and in low labour force participation in advanced adulthood. Labour market policy for active ageing is therefore also to be understood as a policy that reinforces ties to the labour market in critical phases of the life course. On the other hand, every necessary or desired deviation from standard employment still implies an insufficiently insured risk with respect to continuous income flows, occupational careers and social security in old age. This acts as a massive deterrent to established employees, who contemplate making risky transitions, for instance the transition from full-time to part-time work, from dependent to self-employment, from higher to lower paid jobs or from one occupation to another. In order to be considered worth the risk, such transitions must pay off. Schmid therefore suggests supplementing unemployment insurance by work–life insurance.

Finally, based on comparative studies, Schmid argues in favour of integrated policy approaches, allowing package deals in reform policies to arrive at workable compromises, reliable compensation of losers and finally a win–win situation for all. In particular national compacts, public–private partnerships and task forces at company, regional or sectoral level are innovative forms of governance to manage transitions from work to retirement.

Looking for new typologies

One of the outcomes of empirical life course studies is the increasing variety among individuals compared to the situation half a century ago. Then we had two major life course patterns: the male and the female one. For males it was a sequence of learning – working – resting, while for women it was learning (though often less than for men) – caring – resting (though once more less for men, because the caring in fact never stopped until the end of life). Both from a scientific and from a policy point of view there is need for new typologies. Both the chapter by Christian Brzinsky-Fay and the chapter by Amelia Román, Joop Schippers and Leen Heylen are looking for such typologies. Both chapters use new and innovating analytical techniques to establish such typologies. Brzinsky-Fay finds eight distinct types of school-to-work transitions that differ in terms of volatility and integrative potential. The transition types are distributed very unevenly across countries but, with the exception of the bridge type, all of them appear in every country. The clear differences in the distribution of all transition types across countries indicate that national institutional configurations have a strong influence. This is particularly true for the southern European countries, which show a high degree of similarity. Analysing the effects of gender, educational level, migration background and country on the transition types reveals that the impact of individual factors on the transition types is weaker than that of the country dummies, which also leads to the conclusion that institutional differences are more relevant. Denmark and Germany appear to have favourable institutional configurations. In both countries, the share of transition types with the highest volatility – return, link, bridge and express clusters – is higher than 80 per cent. The share of transition types with a high integrative capability – first and foremost the express cluster, but also the break, detour, link and bridge clusters – is lowest in those countries that have a lower level of educational attainment. These countries are the southern European countries, which constitute a more or less homogeneous group with respect to school-to-work transition sequences. Their transition systems urgently need to be upgraded and/or advanced by policies. This is particularly important because the trend towards individualisation is diminishing the reparative function of the family. Denmark in some way constitutes a best practice example thanks to its established initial and further training system, which helps even bad starts to turn out positively.

These analyses show that those systems exhibit the highest shares of favourable entry sequences, which distribute labour market entry risks between many levels – that is individual, enterprise, state – as well as having a strong emphasis on (further or vocational) education. This refers to Denmark, Ireland and Germany, whereas in the United Kingdom, which also performs well, the very fast labour market integration is reached at the expense of low-quality jobs. Hence, flexicurity policies are of great value for early detection, if they consider educational matters and distribute risks on many shoulders.

Román, Schippers and Heylen investigate the existence of new and diverse patterns of labour participation on the Belgian labour market. The Belgian government has a relatively highly-developed life course policy, certainly concerning career breaks in labour market participation. The authors analysed a quite unique dataset containing a retrospective career module in the 2002 survey among Belgian households including extensive career history information for more than 4,400 individuals. The analyses established a growth in part-time work among younger, female-dominated cohorts, which means that part-time work is also a growing phenomenon on the Belgian labour market. Nonparticipation is decreasing as a labour market option in Belgium. Career break users show a distribution across cohorts and labour market states, but predominate in three of the typologies. One of these types is diminishing with each new cohort entering the labour market. This is the more 'traditional' use of the career break system as a labour market exit rather than a labour market detour.

The career break is also evident in one of the male-dominated classes, a standard career type of full-time work where the career path extends through to the age of retirement. This is quite interesting as it indicates that men and women are indeed using the career break system to continue their working careers over a longer period, and this is precisely one of the goals of the Belgian career break system. The analysis also established an increase in the career type of perpetual unemployment, particularly among younger females. The persistence of the unemployment period within this career type was rather alarming. It would seem that young individuals (three-quarters of this class was female) who do not make a successful entry onto the labour market are in danger of remaining unemployed for the duration of their potential working life.

Throughout the years, a major focus of TLM theorists has been the development of policy measures aimed at facilitating so-called 'good' transitions and preventing 'bad' transitions. To develop the 'proper' policy instruments it is useful and necessary to know the major life course patterns among a country's population. Traditional life course patterns were adequately accommodated by the whole system of rules and regulations we have come to know as the breadwinner model. The analyses presented by Román et al. show that traditional life course patterns are fading away and so have many of the institutional arrangements belonging to the breadwinner model. The question concerning the alternative(s) is not as easy to answer, although it is clear that there is a considerable need for institutional arrangements that fit into a life course that is characterised by part-time work and the combination of paid labour and (unpaid) care. What is needed policy-wise is, based on the analyses in this chapter, not unambiguously determinable. Within the 'other patterns' (other than the standard career or standard homemaker), there is no one single pattern that can as yet be labelled as representing 'the modern pattern'. Whether this is only temporary or whether modern patterns as such can only be characterised by their variety, is not clear at this time. The growing diversity in life courses is still too much of a recent phenomenon. The best answer that policy can offer is actually already given by Schmid in his chapter: namely an integral life course policy that provides people with the tools while at the same time empowering them during their life course to make the right choices and to choose transitions and combinations that allow them to lead a high quality balanced life.

13.3 FUTURE RESEARCH AND POLICY

13.3.1 Research Agenda

The book examines how the trend of individualisation and diversification of the life course affects the careers and lives of different categories of workers and population groups in different countries differently and how regional, national and EU policies might or actually respond to these ongoing changes in the life course with a view to maintaining high levels of flexibility and income and employment security simultaneously. However, the data analyses performed mainly used comparative but cross-sectional firm-level data with respect to mapping countries on the working time flexibility dimension or comparative but rather short-running panel data as the ECHP to map countries on the numerical flexibility and income and employment security dimension. Only for Belgium was use made of real life course data in which questions were asked to the members of a running panel to recall their entire work history. It is beyond doubt that life course data potentially provide a rich source for research in the way in which the individualisation and diversification of life courses affect people's behaviour and hence the outcomes of policy interventions.

For future research we need real life course data which are becoming increasingly available now. Apart from Belgium also the UK, the Netherlands, Germany, Italy and Sweden have established real life course data which are already or might become available for research. They are of course not really comparative in the sense that they are set up in the same way and harmonised in advance, though in quite a few attempts it appeared possible to perform comparative analyses by ex post harmonisation of definitions and concepts (Fouarge et al., 2006; Muffels et al., 2008a).

But even if we were to have real comparative life course data they deal with the supply side of the labour market and not with the company or demand side. Hence, the availability of life course data of firms seems something that is still far ahead of us viewing the current situation. However, panel data at the firm level might provide a good substitute for life course data of firms to obtain information on at least substantial parts of the firms' life courses. But also these company-level panel data are not yet widely available in Europe, especially not if one wants to link the employee information to the company level information as in matched employer–employee surveys. However, there is still a lot to do in exploiting the existing life course datasets and firm-level panel data to examine changes in life courses and their effects in a much more detailed and thorough way. In order to avoid missing out the company's perspective and therewith neglecting the aspect of internal functional flexibility and employability, in several chapters we used company-level data either at the national (see Chapter 9) or the comparative level (see Chapter 7) to deal with these issues, though it is fairly clear that in future research comparative company-level panel studies are needed to fill in the gap on firms' dynamics and therefore also on the way firms cope with the changing work–life balance needs of particular groups of workers.

The results of our analyses on the impact of institutions on mobility and on the performance of countries in balancing flexibility and security in different stages of the life course could have been more robust if we had had more countries than the ECHP (European Community Household Panel) contained. For the near future the data of SILC (Statistics on Income and Living Conditions) covering nearly all EU countries from 2005 on, though with a shorter time horizon, might allow us to test the impact of a larger variety of regimes, pathways and policy measures on the socio-economic outcomes in Europe. Another way to progress would be to examine the existing longer-running panel data for a limited number of countries (the UK, Germany, the Netherlands, Belgium and Luxembourg) and to look at the country level into the impact of specific policy measures on the flexibility and security outcomes in the various stages of the life courses of people and to the occurrence and causation of policy and regime shifts over time.

For the important agenda of migration we only had data on the migration intentions of people living in different countries but not on real migration decisions and mobility flows. That would require comparative panel data in which people are followed when they move to another country. Another way would be to ask people retrospectively about their migration behaviour in surveys. The availability of prospective and retrospective migration data would open new roads for migration research, especially with a view to explaining why people move at which stage in the life course for which reasons and how policies might influence or respond in a different way with different levels of success to changes in migration behaviour.

In quite a few chapters mention is made of the important role assigned to values, beliefs and social norms in society to attain the goals social actors in society strive for in their respective communities. However, there is a lack of attitudinal data which are linked to information on actual cultural or socio-economic behaviour. The question as to whether individual values, beliefs and attitudes in conjunction with social norms in society might explain why people behave as they do and why policies in one country are more or less successful in country A than in country B cannot therefore be answered. Adding subjective attitudinal information to socio-economic panel surveys or structural questions to values surveys seems indispensable for progressing on research into this intriguing question.

13.3.2 Policy Agenda

In the introductory chapter we used Talcott Parson's well-known AGIL scheme (adaptation, goal attainment, integration and latency) to illustrate which functions are critical in the process of collective decison making, not just for survival of the system but to create successful examples of 'social engineering' to cope with the pressures society faces due to the ongoing changes. The AGIL model might teach us about the ingredients of the recipe for innovative policies: improving the *adaptability* to change for warranting high levels of productivity and welfare; improving *goal attainment* by raising the commitment to clearly set targets; recognising the need to improve social *integration* by way of fostering security and solidarity in society; and maintaining *latency*, pertaining to values vested in shared social norms, attitudes and beliefs. The 'flexicurity' strategy of the European Commission to which all stakeholders have committed themselves in the course of time, might be seen as an example of such a 'social engineering' endeavour aiming at attaining the initial and revised Lisbon targets as they are defined in 2000 and 2003 respectively. For that reason, from a macro-level perspective, flexicurity policies seem excellently suited to being studied them using the AGIL framework.

Adaptation and integration

With respect to adaptation and integration we found that both the adaptability of countries to respond to changes in the labour market and the capability to safeguard security through integration in the labour market and to avoid social exclusion, differ markedly due to differences in the institutional design of their labour market and social security policies. In this volume we translated adaptability into the various forms of flexibility: numerical flexibility to adapt the workforce and working times to changes in demand; functional flexibility to adapt the workplace and the function and worktasks of workers to changes in product demand, technology or knowledge requirements (employability); and working time flexibility to adapt working times to changes in the needs of employers to manage production time and the workers with respect to their work–life balance. Security is translated into income and employment security. In a few contributions the countries were mapped on the attained level of numerical and working time flexibility and income and employment security, and the results were very dissimilar across Europe showing that there are different pathways in Europe each with different levels of success in attaining high levels of flexibility and security simultaneously. Europe is therefore featured by 'unity in diversity' while the findings show that equal levels of success might be attained by quite dissimilar pathways, also showing that there is no one-size-fits-all policy approach that should be set as the 'golden standard' to strive for.

Another conclusion is that to avoid the insider–outsider effects of segmented labour markets, the gap between workers in permanent contracts and on time-limited contracts should be narrowed down. This might be achieved through policies such as in Flanders to make temporary jobs more similar to permanent jobs by creating incentives to employers to invest in training of temporary workers and to create permanent jobs for them after the training period.

Another option that is very similar to a French proposal is to define a new contract form ('contrat unique') – a form that is less secure than the standard contract but more secure than the non-standard contract (see also Blanchard and Tirole, 2003; Cahuc and Kramarz, 2004; Chéron, 2007). This option would entail the establishment of a 'new uniform tenured employment relationship' replacing all more or less open-ended and temporary contract forms for all employees, and which is less focused on job security but more on safeguarding employment security over the entire career. The job will be less secure in terms of its open-ended character and hence more flexible, but the employment career will be more secure by improving the 'employability' dimension through safeguarding investments in training and employment career development and the creation of working time options to meet the changing work–life balance needs. This option fits in the 'make transitions pay' notion of the Transitional Labour Market approach through creating more transition security through employability investments resembling in a way the 'golden triangle' approach in Denmark.

Another way to increase the employment security of the worker which fits very well in the 'flexicurity' approach is to focus on preventing unemployment through shifting the responsibility for employment and re-employment after lay-offs or quits more from the government to the employer, or to make it a shared responsibility, providing that the individual worker fully keeps his own responsibility to acquire a new job. The employer and employee might agree to split but the employer retains the responsibility to find new employment for the employee during a certain period in which the employee is paid his normal salary and after which he gets a benefit. In economic upturns the re-employment of the worker will be less of a problem than in downturns, for which reason it will take longer for the worker to be re-employed and therefore be more costly to the employer. In downturns the costs might therefore be more equally shared between the employer and the government also with a view to the need to upgrade workers' skills for improving a person's transition security once the economy has recovered.

Life course policies

Much of what has been written in this volume deals with the life course approach to policies and in quite a few contributions a call is made for the creation of a so-called integrated life course approach to policy that empowers and allows workers to better meet their changing work–life balance needs in different stages of the life course. One of the proposals referred to is related to the creation of *work–life insurances* for covering the needs during particular stages in the life course. This boils down, according to Günther Schmid, to creating innovative arrangements such as wage insurances, mobility insurances, lifetime working time accounts and in-work benefits. Another important ingredient is the enhancement of what Günter Schmid has called '*sustainable employability*' meaning that investments in skills have to start at childhood and need to be continued over the entire life course. There is no country that yet has fully integrated life course arrangements made available to their workers, but in a number of countries there are so-called 'best practices' in particular domains that need to be recognised. We mentioned the innovative time-credit system in Belgium that serves two goals: to improve the security of outsiders who replace the worker who leaves and to allow workers to temporarily leave the labour market for caring duties, upgrading of skills or reorientation. We also referred to the unique life course saving arrangement in the Netherlands being a savings scheme to save for care or education leave or even early retirement. At the company level we also referred to what happens in German companies with respect to the creation of long-term or life-course-oriented working time accounts. Another option is to create so-called flexible benefit plans which may even connect or integrate working time and financial savings accounts. We also discussed some of the problems involved such as the difficulty in tuning the working time needs of the employers and the employees as well as to resolve the transferability issue in the case of changing jobs or bankruptcy of the employer. Key to success seems to what extent the negotiated terms under which arrangements are created reflect the needs of all stakeholders, employers as well as employees. The evidence certainly suggests that whatever form the arrangements might have or get, their salient effects for better meeting the workers' working time preferences and for improving the productivity and the motivation of the workers and therewith their job satisfaction seems uncontested. That the EU has set work–life balance issues more prominently on the social policy agenda in recent years will certainly provide an impetus to create more and innovative measures at the company and the national level which better serve the needs of employers and employees simultaneously and resolve much of the issues discussed earlier.

Goal attainment and latency

The commitment to the attainment of shared goals is in particular relevant with respect to the relationship between the various levels of authority, between the regional and national level and between the national and supranational level. In one of the contributions the relationship between the regional and national level is discussed and in quite a few contributions the role of the OMC (open method of coordination) process at the EU level has been brought up. It is concluded that flexicurity as well as life course policies at the EU level but also at the national, regional and company level are still in their infancy and the range of 'best practices' at these levels is still rather limited. The commitment to the flexicurity principles is warranted by the agreement between the member states on the flexicurity principles, but how these principles will be or can be translated into concrete practices still needs to be elaborated at all levels of authority. The contributions in this volume have illustrated that an integrated life course approach is indispensable for its success but the first signs are that countries are tempted to engage in 'cherry picking' rather than on an encompassing approach induced by practical considerations of receiving more easily wide support on some of the cherries rather than on all. 'Cherry picking' is often the result of budgetary considerations. Even though policymakers might agree on the desirability or even necessity of a package of policy measures, only those measures that can be fitted into the (often very tight) national and EU-budgetary restrictions are being implemented. The remainder of the package is being shelved until later. One striking example is the introduction of the Dutch life course savings scheme. As unique as it still might be it was meant originally as part of a whole package not only granting individuals the fiscal-friendly opportunity to save for a period of leave, but also granting them the right to take up this leave and using it for a period of renewed investment in human capital, linked to a kind of personal development scheme. In fact only a minimal version of the life course scheme has been introduced. And because the adjacent measures are lacking, the scheme has not been much of a success up until now, thereby damaging the potential succes of further life-course-oriented policy measures. Another reason for 'cherry picking' can be the lack of agreement on the package as a whole. This might be the case if part of the package is dependent on the cooperation of the social partners. If there is no agreement (yet) the government might decide to implement just those measures for which it has sole responsibility. Such a step can either seduce social partners into participating, or can also result in social partners making a joint stand against the government. And finally there is sometimes a lack of imagination among policymakers that stands in the way of developing the parts of the package that are necessary to a successful life course approach. An example is the social security reforms that have taken place all over

Europe, which call for adjacent measures in the field of lifelong learning and investment in human capital. But more often than not social security reforms have been completed, while lifelong learning measures are still on the drawing board.

The commitment to shared goals however can only be achieved if it is vested in shared values, attitudes and beliefs in society. In some of the contributions the important role of consensus and trust is mentioned as a prerequisite for getting the support of all the social actors to reform labour market and social security policies according to the ideas embedded in the TLM and flexicurity approach, especially with a view to life-course-oriented policies. The powers of consensus building and of creating a high social trust are critical to TLM and flexicurity approaches of becoming a success. The lessons to be drawn from the Danish 'flexicurity model' confirm this assessment (Jørgensen and Madsen, 2007; Madsen, 2008).

We sincerily hope that some of the ideas set out in this book on flexicurity, transitional labour market and the life course might inspire social actors involved in the policymaking process to create 'innovative' but 'practical' arrangements which can generate the necessary social support for their implementation and their success in achieving a better balance between flexibility and security over the life course.

REFERENCES

Atkinson, J. (1984), 'Manpower strategies for flexible organisations', *Personnel Management*, 16.

Blanchard, O. and Tirole, J. (2003), 'Protection de l'emploi et procédures de licenciement', Paris, Paper.

Cahuc, P. and Kramarz, F. (2004), *De la précarité à la mobilité: vers un Sécurité sociale professionnelle*, Report to the Ministries of Economic, Financial and Employment Affairs.

Chéron, A. (2007), *Would a New Form of Employment Contract Provide Greater Security for French Workers?*, Nice: EDHEC Business School.

Den Dulk, L., Van Doorne-Huiskes, A. and Schippers, J. (eds) (1999), *Work-Family Arrangements in Europe*, Amsterdam: Thela Thesis.

Hillebrink, C. (2006), *Flexible Benefit Plans in Dutch Organisations*, Utrecht.

Fouarge, D., Luijkx, R., Manzoni, A. and Muffels, R. (2006), *Careers of Working Mothers after First Childbirth*, Dublin, Tilburg: European Foundation, OSA-Tilburg University.

Jørgensen, H. and Madsen, P.K. (2007), *Flexicurity and Beyond. Finding a New Agenda for the European Social Model*, Copenhagen: DJØF Publishing Copenhagen.

Klammer, U., Muffels, R. and Wilthagen, T. (2008), *Flexibility and Security over the Life Course. Key Findings and Policy Messages from the Foundation Research*, Dublin: European Foundation for the Improvement of Working and Living Conditions.

Madsen, P.K. (2008), 'The Danish Road to "Flexicurity": Where are we Compared to Others? And How did we Get There?', in Muffels, R. (ed.), *Flexibility and Employment Security in Europe: Labour Markets in Transition*, Cheltenham, UK and Northampton, MA, USA: Edward Elgar.

Muffels, R. and Luijkx, R. (2008), 'Labour market mobility and employment security of male employees in europe: "trade-off" or "flexicurity?"', *Work, Employment and Society*, **122** (2), 221–42.

Muffels, R., Chung, H., Fouarge, D., Klammer, U., Luijkx, R., Manzoni, A., Thiel, A. and Wilthagen, T. (2008a), *Flexibility and Security over the Life Course*, Luxembourg: Office for Official Publications of the European Communities.

Muffels, R., Klammer, U. and Wilthagen, T. (2008b), *Diversing Patterns of Employment and Working Time in Europe*, Report prepared for the Directorate-General for Employment, Social Affairs and Equal Opportunities of the European Commission, Brussels: European Commission.

Philips, K. and Eamets, R. (2007), *Approaches to Flexicurity: EU Models*, Luxembourg: Office for Official Publications of the European Communities, European Foundation.

Stone, K.V.W. (2001), 'The new psychological contract: implications of the changing workplace for labor and employment law', *UCLA Law Review*, **48** (3), 519–661.

Stone, K.V.W. (2005), 'Procedural justice in the boundaryless workplace: the tension between due process and public policy', *Notre Dame Law Review*, **80** (2), 501–21.

Teulings, C. and Hartog, J. (1998), *Corporatism or Competition? Labour Contracts, Institutions and Wage Structures in International Comparison*, Cambridge: Cambridge University Press.

Wilthagen, T., Bekker, S and Schippers, J. (2006), 'Werk maken van de transitionele arbeidsmarkt' (Working on a transitional labour market), in Ester, P., Muffels, R. and Schippers, J. (eds), *Dynamiek en levensloop. De arbeidsmarkt in transitie* (Dynamic and Life Course: The Labour Market in Transition), Assen: Van Gorcum, pp. 241–68.

Author Index

Subject Index